Corporate Governance

Corporate Governance

SECOND EDITION

Christine A. Mallin

OXFORD
UNIVERSITY PRESS

OXFORD

UNIVERSITY PRESS

Great Clarendon Street, Oxford OX2 6DP

Oxford University Press is a department of the University of Oxford.
It furthers the University's objective of excellence in research, scholarship,
and education by publishing worldwide in

Oxford New York

Auckland Cape Town Dar es Salaam Hong Kong Karachi
Kuala Lumpur Madrid Melbourne Mexico City Nairobi
New Delhi Shanghai Taipei Toronto

With offices in

Argentina Austria Brazil Chile Czech Republic France Greece
Guatemala Hungary Italy Japan Poland Portugal Singapore
South Korea Switzerland Thailand Turkey Ukraine Vietnam

Oxford is a registered trade mark of Oxford University Press
in the UK and in certain other countries

Published in the United States
by Oxford University Press Inc., New York

British Library Cataloguing in Publication Data
Data available

Library of Congress Cataloging in Publication Data
Data available

Typeset by Laserwords Private Limited, Chennai, India
Printed in Great Britain
on acid-free paper by
Ashford Colour Press Limited, Gosport, Hampshire

ISBN 978–0–19–928900–4

5 7 9 10 8 6 4

■ DEDICATION

To: Mum and Dad

■ PREFACE

Corporate governance is an area that has grown rapidly in the last few years. There has been an explosion of interest in the corporate and investment sectors and more and more universities, both in the UK and internationally, are offering corporate governance as a module, either on undergraduate or postgraduate degree programmes. Some universities have dedicated taught masters in corporate governance and/or PhD students specializing in this as their area of research.

Corporate governance is now an integral part of everyday business life and this book provides insights into its importance not just in the UK, but also globally including the USA, Europe, Asia, South Africa, Latin America, India, and Australia. This book is designed to provide an understanding of the development of corporate governance over the last decade and to illustrate the importance of corporate governance to the company itself, to directors, shareholders and other stakeholders, and to the wider business community.

CAM
December 2006

■ ACKNOWLEDGEMENTS

I would like to thank everyone who has encouraged and supported me in writing this book.

First, thanks go to those who have encouraged me to research and write about corporate governance. In the early 1990s, Sir Adrian Cadbury inspired me to undertake research in the field of corporate governance and has continued to do so. Other leading figures who have influenced me with their contributions to the development of corporate governance include Robert (Bob) A.G. Monks, Nell Minow, Jonathan Charkham, Steve Davis, and Professor Bob Tricker, to name but a few.

Thank you to everyone at Oxford University Press who has contributed to the publication of this book. Thanks also go to two anonymous reviewers who constructively reviewed earlier drafts of the book and gave many helpful comments.

A heartfelt thanks to family and friends who have encouraged me to write this book, and have always been there for me, especially to: Rita, Bernard and Christopher; Pam and Tom; Liz and Tony; Alice, Yu-Loon and Thorsten; Ioana, Costin and Mara; Jane, and Paul. Also a special thank you to Ben. Finally, to Merlin and Harry for their patience, devotion and sense of fun at all times.

■ SOURCE ACKNOWLEDGEMENTS

The author and publisher wish to thank the following for kind permission to use copyright material: the Australian Stock Exchange for extracts from the Principles of Good Corporate Governance and Best Practice Recommendations, ASX Corporate Governance Council, (2003); the Basel Committee on Banking Supervision for extracts from Enhancing Corporate Governance for Banking Organisations (2006) [please note: in this book the English spelling 'Basle' has been used]; the Budapest Stock Exchange for extracts from the Corporate Governance Recommendations 2004; the China Securities Regulatory Commission for extracts from the Code of Corporate Governance For Listed Companies in China (2001); the Conference Board for extracts from the Commission on Public Trust and Private Enterprise Findings and Recommendations Parts 1, 2, and 3 (2002, 2003); the Copenhagen Stock Exchange for extracts from the Nørby Commission's Recommendations for Good Corporate Governance in Denmark (2001); the Czech Securities Commission for extracts from the Revised Corporate Governance Code (2001); Ethical Investment Research Service for details of socially responsible investment strategies; the Internal Market Directorate General of the European Communities 2002, for Gregory, H.J. and Simmelkjaer, R.T. (2002) *Comparative Study of Corporate Governance Codes Relevant to the European Union and its Member States*; the Financial Reporting Council for extracts from the Combined Code on Corporate Governance (2006) as well as inclusion of the full text of the Code as an appendix; Gee Publishing Ltd. for extracts from the Report of the Committee on the Financial Aspects of Corporate Governance (1992); the German Commission for extracts from the German Corporate Governance Code (2002); ICI for extracts from its Remuneration Report 2002; Hermes Pensions Management Limited for extracts from The Hermes Principles (2002) and the Hermes Corporate Governance Principles (2006); the UK Institute of Directors for extracts from Standards for the Board (2006); the South African Institute of Directors for extracts from the King Report on Corporate Governance (2002); the Investment Management Association for extracts from the Responsibilities of Institutional Shareholders and Agents – A Statement of Principles (2002 and 2005); the Japan Corporate Governance Forum for extracts from the Revised Corporate Governance Principles; Maciej Dzierzanowski and Piotr Tamowicz of the Gdansk Institute for Market Economics for extracts from the Corporate Governance Code for Polish Listed Companies (2002); Ruth Aguilera and George Yip for 'Global strategy faces local constraints', *Financial Times*, 27 May 2005; John Ward for 'Keeping business within the family', *Financial Times*, 3 June 2005. Crown copyright material is reproduced under Class Licence Number C01P0000148 with the permission of the Controller of HMSO and the Queen's printer for Scotland. The author and publisher also wish to thank the *Financial Times* for: Authers, J. and Wighton, D. (2005) 'Unhappy investors force change', 7 November; Harvey, F. (2006) 'Investors shine a green light on risk assessment', 27 February; Palma, M. (2005) 'Misys separates chairman and chief roles', 4 November; Daroudi, S. (2006) 'Compass faces criticism over executive pay', 4 February; Limbach, I.

and Michaels, A. (2006) 'Scandals prompt Italy to toughen governance code', 15 March; Song, J. (2006) 'Korea sees rise of domestic activists', 6 March; Burgess, K., Chung, J., Ostrovsky, A. and Thomas, H. (2005) 'Dicey Russian flotations challenge London investors' appetite for risk', 6 December; Maitland, A. (2005) 'A responsible balancing act', 1 June.

Every effort has been made to trace all copyright-holders, but if any have been inadvertently overlooked the publishers will be pleased to make the necessary arrangements at the first opportunity.

■ CONTENTS

PREFACE   vii
ACKNOWLEDGEMENTS   viii
SOURCE ACKNOWLEDGEMENTS   ix
LIST OF FIGURES   xv
LIST OF TABLES   xvi
LIST OF ABBREVIATIONS   xvii
GLOSSARY   xviii

1   Introduction   1

PART ONE **Developments in Corporate Governance**

---

2   Theoretical Aspects of Corporate Governance   11
Introduction   11
Theories associated with the development of corporate governance   12
Agency theory   12
Separation of ownership and control   13
Transaction cost economics   14
Stakeholder theory   16
Stewardship theory   16
The theories in context   17
Convergence   18
Conclusions   18

3   Development of Corporate Governance Codes   21
The growth in corporate governance codes   21
Corporate governance in the UK   22
Cadbury Report (1992)   29
OECD Principles of Corporate Governance (1999) as revised (2004)   31
World Bank   33
Global Corporate Governance Forum   33
International Corporate Governance Network   34
Commonwealth Association for Corporate Governance   34
EU Company Law Experts   35
Basle Committee   35
US corporate governance   36

Delaware corporate law 37

Employee Retirement Income Security Act 1974 37

Sarbanes–Oxley Act 2002 37

Commission on Public Trust and Private Enterprise 2003 39

Conclusions 42

PART TWO **Owners and Stakeholders**

---

4   **Shareholders and Stakeholders**   **49**

Shareholders and stakeholders 49

Stakeholder groups 50

Guidance on shareholders' and stakeholders' interests 53

Roles of shareholders and stakeholders 57

Conclusions 58

5   **Family-owned Firms**   **65**

Introduction 65

Ownership structures around the world 65

Family-owned firms and governance 67

Smaller quoted companies 69

Conclusions 71

6   **The Role of Institutional Investors in Corporate Governance**   **80**

Introduction 80

Growth of institutional share ownership 81

Influence of institutional investors 82

Institutional investors' relationship with investee companies 86

Tools of corporate governance 86

Corporate governance and corporate performance 92

Conclusions 94

7   **Socially Responsible Investment**   **101**

Introduction 101

SRI and corporate governance 102

Strategies for SRI 103

Institutional investors' policies 104

International guidance 106

CSR indices 107

Corporate social responsibility 108

The impact on shareholder value 109

Conclusions 110

PART THREE **Directors and Board Structure**

8	**Directors and Board Structure**	**121**
	Introduction	121
	Unitary board versus dual board	121
	Combined Code	123
	The board of directors	124
	Role of the board	124
	Role, duties, and responsibilities	125
	Board sub-committees	128
	Audit committee	128
	Remuneration committee	129
	Nomination committee	129
	Risk committee	131
	Non-executive directors	132
	Independence of non-executive directors	132
	Contribution of non-executive directors	134
	Higgs Review	134
	Director evaluation	134
	Conclusions	136
9	**Directors' Performance and Remuneration**	**142**
	The directors' remuneration debate	142
	Key elements of directors' remuneration	143
	Role of the remuneration committee	144
	Performance measures	145
	Remuneration of non-executive directors	147
	Disclosure of directors' remuneration	147
	International guidance on executive remuneration	148
	Conclusions	149

PART FOUR **International Corporate Governance**

10	**Corporate Governance in Continental Europe**	**159**
	Background	159
	Germany	162
	Denmark	167
	France	172
	Italy	176

Convergence or divergence | 181
Conclusions | 181

11 Corporate Governance in Central and Eastern Europe | **188**
Introduction | 188
Privatization process and its implications | 189
The Czech Republic | 190
Poland | 198
Russia | 202
Hungary | 207
Conclusions | 212

12 Corporate Governance in the Asia-Pacific | **219**
Introduction | 219
Japan | 220
South Korea | 225
Malaysia | 228
China | 231
Australia | 236
Conclusions | 241

13 Corporate Governance in South Africa, India, and Brazil | **247**
Introduction | 247
South Africa | 248
India | 251
Brazil | 254
Conclusions | 259

14 Conclusions | **266**

FRC: THE COMBINED CODE ON CORPORATE GOVERNANCE (2006) | 271
INDEX | 311

◼ LIST OF FIGURES

2.1   Main theories influencing the development of corporate governance   17

3.1   Development of corporate governance in the UK   23

4.1   The corporation and its stakeholders   50

5.1   Possible stages in a family firm's governance   68

6.1   Beneficial ownership of UK shares at end 2004   82

■ LIST OF TABLES

2.1   Summary of theories affecting corporate governance development   12

5.1   Areas of the Combined Code that may prove difficult for smaller companies   70

6.1   Summary of main categories of share ownership in the UK 1963–2004   81

10.1   Predominant board and leadership structure   161
10.2   Summary of key differences between supervisory and management boards   162
10.3   Key characteristics influencing German corporate governance   164
10.4   Key characteristics influencing Danish corporate governance   168
10.5   Key characteristics influencing French corporate governance   172
10.6   Key characteristics influencing Italian corporate governance   177

11.1   Ownership structures of companies in selected transition countries   190
11.2   Key characteristics influencing corporate governance in the Czech Republic   192
11.3   Key characteristics influencing Polish corporate governance   199
11.4   Ownership change in Russia   203
11.5   Key characteristics influencing Russian corporate governance   203
11.6   Key characteristics influencing Hungarian corporate governance   208

12.1   Key characteristics influencing Japanese corporate governance   222
12.2   Key characteristics influencing South Korean corporate governance   225
12.3   Key characteristics influencing Malaysian corporate governance   228
12.4   Key characteristics influencing Chinese corporate governance   232
12.5   Key characteristics influencing Australian corporate governance   237

13.1   Key characteristics influencing South African corporate governance   249
13.2   Key characteristics influencing Indian corporate governance   252
13.3   Key characteristics influencing Brazilian corporate governance   255

■ LIST OF ABBREVIATIONS

ABI	Association of British Insurers
AITC	Association of Investment Trust Companies
APEC	Asia-Pacific Economic Co-operation
ASX	Australian Stock Exchange
ASIC	Australian Securities and Investments Commission
CACG	Commonwealth Association for Corporate Governance
CalPERS	California Public Employees' Retirement System
CEO	Chief executive officer
CEPS	Centre for European Policy Studies
CFO	Chief financial officer
CLERP	Corporate Law Economic Reform Program
CLR	Company Law Review
CR	Corporate responsibility
CSR	Corporate social responsibility
CSRC	China Securities Regulatory Commission
Defra	Department for Environment, Food, and Rural Affairs
EIRIS	Ethical Investment Research Service
FRC	Financial Reporting Council
FTSE	Financial Times Stock Exchange (Index, UK)
ICGN	International Corporate Governance Network
IMA	Investment Management Association
IMF	International Monetary Fund
ISC	Institutional Shareholders' Committee
KPI	Key performance indicator
MOF	Ministry of Finance
NAPF	National Association of Pension Funds
OECD	Organization for Economic Co-operation and Development
PBOC	People's Bank of China
PIRC	Pensions Investment Research Consultants
PSPD	People's Solidarity for Participatory Democracy
RREV	Research recommendations electronic voting
SETC	State Economic and Trade Commission
SID	Senior independent director
SRI	Socially responsible investment
SVWG	Shareholder Voting Working Group

■ GLOSSARY

Agency theory One party, the principal, delegates work to another party, the agent. In a corporate scenario, the principal is the shareholder and the agent the directors/managers. Agency theory relates to the costs involved in this principal–agent relationship, including the costs of aligning the two sets of interests.

Audit The examination by an independent external auditor to determine whether the annual report and accounts have been appropriately prepared and give a true and fair view.

Audit committee The audit committee is a sub-committee of the board and is generally comprised of independent non-executive directors. It is the role of the audit committee to review the scope and outcome of the audit, and to try to ensure that the objectivity of the auditors is maintained.

Auditor rotation The audit firm is changed after a number of years in order to help ensure that the independence of the external auditor is retained. There are disparate views on the effectiveness of auditor rotation.

Bank-oriented system Banks play a key role in the funding of some companies and so may be able to exercise some control via the board structure, depending on the governance system.

Board evaluation Boards should be evaluated annually to determine whether they have met the objectives set. The board as a whole, the board sub-committees, and individual directors should each be assessed.

Board sub-committees The board of directors may delegate various duties in specific areas to specialised committees such as the audit committee, remuneration committee, and nomination committee.

Chairman The chairman is responsible for the running of the board and chairing board meetings.

Chief Executive Officer The chief executive officer is responsible for the running of the company.

Civil law Tends to be prescriptive and based on specific rules. Generally gives less protection to minority shareholders.

Co-determination The right of employees to be kept informed about the company's activities and to participate in decisions that may affect the workers.

Common law Based on legal principles supplemented by case law. Generally gives better protection to minority shareholders.

Comply or explain A company should comply with the appropriate corporate governance code but if it cannot comply with any particular aspect of it, then it should explain why it is unable to do so.

Controlling shareholders Those who have control of the company, although this may be indirectly through their holdings in other entities, and not directly.

Corporate social responsibility Voluntary actions that a company may take in relation to the management of social, environmental and ethical issues.

Directors' remuneration Directors' remuneration can encompass various elements including base salary, bonus, stock options, stock grants, pension, and other benefits.

Directors' share options Directors may be given the right to purchase shares at a specified price over a specified time period.

Dual board A dual board system consists of a supervisory board and an executive board of management.

Fiduciary duty This is an obligation to act in the best interests of another party, for example, directors have a fiduciary duty to act in the best interests of the shareholders.

Inclusive approach The company considers the interests of all of its stakeholders.

Independent directors Directors who have no relationships with the business, or its directors and management, or other circumstances, which could affect their judgement.

Information asymmetries Different parties may have access to different levels of information, which may mean that some have a more complete, or more accurate, picture than others.

Insider system Ownership of shares is concentrated in individuals, or a group of individuals, such as families or holding companies.

Institutional investors Generally large investors such as pension funds, insurance companies, mutual funds.

Internal controls Policies, procedures, and other measures in an organization, which are designed to ensure that the assets are safeguarded, that systems operate as intended, that information can be produced in a timely and accurate manner, and that the business operates effectively and efficiently.

Market-oriented system The influence of banks does not tend to be prevalent and does not impact on the company's board structure.

Minority rights The rights of shareholders who own smaller stakes in a company. They should have the same rights as larger shareholders but often this is not the case.

Minority shareholders Shareholders who have smaller holdings of shares.

Nomination committee The nomination committee is a sub-committee of the board and should generally comprise independent non-executive directors. Its role is to make recommendations to the board on all new board appointments.

Non-executive director Non-executive directors are not full-time employees of the company (unlike most executive directors). As far as possible they should be independent and capable of exercising independent judgement in board decision-making.

Outsider system There is dispersed ownership of shares and hence individuals, or groups of individuals, do not tend to have direct control.

Proxy vote The casting of shareholders' votes by shareholders, often by mail, fax, or electronic means.

Remuneration committee The remuneration committee is a sub-committee of the board and should

generally comprise independent non-executive directors. Its role is to make recommendations to the board on executive directors' remuneration.

Risk assessment An assessment of the overall risk that a company may be exposed to. Overall risk can include many different types of risk including financial risk, operating risk, and reputation risk.

Shareholder value The value of the firm after deducting current and future claims.

Socially responsible investment Involves considering the ethical, social, and environmental performance of companies selected for investment as well as their financial performance.

Stakeholder theory This theory takes into account the views of a wider stakeholder group and not just the shareholders.

Stakeholders Any individual or group on which the activities of the company have an impact, including the employees, customers, local community.

Supervisory board In a dual board system, the supervisory board oversees the direction of the business whilst the management board is responsible for the running of the business.

Transaction cost economics Views the firm itself as a governance structure, which in turn can help align the interests of directors and shareholders.

Unitary board A unitary board of directors is characterized by one single board comprising of both executive and non-executive directors.

1 Introduction

Businesses around the world need to be able to attract funding from investors in order to expand and grow. Before investors decide to invest their funds in a particular business, they will want to be as sure as they can be that the business is financially sound and will continue to be so in the foreseeable future. Investors therefore need to have confidence that the business is being well managed and will continue to be profitable.

In order to have this assurance, investors look to the published annual report and accounts of the business and to other information releases that the company might make. They expect that the annual report and accounts will represent a true picture of the company's present position – after all, the annual report and accounts are subject to an annual audit whereby an independent external auditor examines the business' records and transactions, and certifies that the annual report and accounts have been prepared in accordance with accepted accounting standards and give a 'true and fair view' of the business' activities. However, although the annual report may give a reasonably accurate picture of the business' activities and financial position at that point in time, there are many facets of the business that are not effectively reflected in the annual report and accounts.

There have been a number of high-profile corporate collapses that have arisen despite the fact that the annual report and accounts seemed fine. These corporate collapses have had an adverse effect on many people: shareholders who have seen their financial investment reduced to nothing; employees who have lost their jobs and, in many cases, the security of their company pension, which has also evaporated overnight; suppliers of goods or services to the failed companies; and the economic impact on the local and international communities in which the failed companies operated. In essence, corporate collapses affect us all. Why have such collapses occurred? What might be done to prevent such collapses happening again? How can investor confidence be restored?

The answers to these questions are all linked to corporate governance: a lack of effective corporate governance meant that such collapses could occur; good corporate governance can help prevent such collapses happening again and restore investor confidence.

To illustrate why corporate failures might occur, despite the companies seeming healthy, it is helpful to review a few examples from recent years, each of which has sent shock waves through stock markets around the world.

Barings Bank

The downfall in 1995 of one of England's oldest established banks was brought about by the actions of one man, Nick Leeson, which actions have been immortalized in the film

Rogue Trader. Nick Leeson was a clever, if unconventional, trader with a gift for sensing the way that stock market prices would move in the Far Eastern markets. In 1993, he was based in Singapore and made more than £10 million, about 10 per cent of Barings' total profit that year. He was highly thought of at that time.

However, his run of good luck was not to last and, when a severe earthquake in Japan affected the stock market adversely, he incurred huge losses of Barings' money. He requested more funds from Barings' head office in London, which were sent to him, but unfortunately he suffered further losses. The losses were so great, £850 million, that Barings Bank collapsed and was eventually bought for £1 by ING, the Dutch banking and insurance group.

Barings Bank has been criticized for its lack of effective internal controls at that time, which left Nick Leeson able to cover up the losses that he was making for quite a number of months. The case also illustrates the importance of having effective supervision, by experienced staff with a good understanding of the processes and procedures, of staff who are able to expose the company to such financial disaster. The collapse of Barings Bank sent ripples through financial markets across the world as the importance of effective internal controls and appropriate monitoring was reinforced.

Enron

Enron was ranked in the USA's Fortune top ten list of companies, based on its turnover in 2000. Its published accounts for the year ended 31 December 2000 showed a seemingly healthy profit of $979 million and there was nothing obvious to alert shareholders to the impending disaster that was going to unfold over the next year or so, making Enron the largest bankruptcy in US history.

Enron's difficulties related to its activities in the energy market and the setting up of a series of 'special purpose entities' (SPEs). Enron used the SPEs to conceal large losses from the market by giving the appearance that key exposures were hedged (covered) by third parties. However, the SPEs were really nothing more than an extension of Enron itself and so Enron's risks were not covered. Some of the SPEs were used to transfer funds to some of Enron's directors. In October 2001, Enron declared a non-recurring loss of $1 billion and also had to disclose a $1.2 billion write-off against shareholders' funds. Later in October, Enron disclosed another accounting problem, which reduced its value by over $0.5 millon. It looked as though a takeover might be on the cards from a rival, Dynegy, but in November, announcements by Enron of further debts led to the takeover bid falling through, and in December 2001, Enron filed for bankruptcy.

In retrospect, it seems that the directors were not questioned closely enough about the use of the SPEs and their accounting treatment. What has become clear is that there was some concern among Enron's auditors – Andersen – about the SPEs, and Enron's activities. Unfortunately, Andersen failed to question the directors hard enough and Andersen's own fate was sealed when some of its employees shredded paperwork relating to Enron, thus obliterating vital evidence and contributing to the demise of Andersen, which has itself been taken over by various rivals.

The Enron case highlights the overriding need for integrity in business: for the directors to act with integrity and honesty, and for the external audit firm to be able to ask searching questions of the directors without holding back for fear of offending a lucrative client. This latter situation is exacerbated when auditors receive large fees for non-audit services that may well exceed the audit fee itself, thus endangering the independence of the auditors. Enron also highlights the need for independent non-executive directors who are experienced enough to be able to ask searching questions in board and committee meetings to try to ensure that the business is operated appropriately.

Royal Ahold

Royal Ahold is a Dutch retail group with international interests, and is the third largest food retailer in the world. The financial scandal surrounding it unfolded during 2003 and was referred to as 'Europe's Enron'. In February 2003, Royal Ahold announced that it had overstated the earnings of its US subsidiary by $500 million. Royal Ahold's chief executive officer and chief financial officer resigned immediately.

There were a few warning signs at Royal Ahold before the further problems became apparent in 2003: the chief executive officer was dominant and had a long service agreement; directors' remuneration was spiralling upwards; its management had a poor reputation for their relations with investors; in 2001, Royal Ahold had introduced a voting system for voting on board members which meant that it was effectively impossible for shareholders to oppose the board's nominations. These were all signs of a company in which the directors may have been acting in a way that was detrimental to the shareholders. Royal Ahold is now trying to rebuild its reputation and restore the trust of its investors. To that end, it has made sweeping changes to its corporate governance including the appointment of new independent board members and a whistle-blower's programme.

Parmalat

Parmalat, an Italian company specializing in long-life milk, was founded by Calisto Tanzi. It seemed to be a marvellous success story although, as it expanded by acquiring more companies, its debt increased and, in late 2003, Parmalat had difficulty making a bond payment despite the fact that it was supposed to have a large cash reserve. After various investigations had been carried out, it transpired that the large cash reserves were non-existent and Parmalat went into administration. With debts estimated at £10bn, Parmalat has also earned itself the name of 'Europe's Enron'.

Calisto Tanzi was a central figure in one of Europe's largest fraud trials started during 2005. He was accused of providing false accounting information and misleading the Italian stock-market regulator.

HIH

HIH was one of Australia's largest insurers and became one of its biggest corporate collapses with debts of over $A5bn. It went into liquidation early in 2001 as a result of having sold insurance too cheaply, combined with not having put enough aside to meet its future commitments. The situation was made worse by the fact that, during the 1990s, it had expanded by acquiring other insurance businesses for which it overpaid. The Australian government has had to underwrite many of the failed policies, an expensive exercise.

HIH highlights the complexities of the insurance business and what can happen when there is a lack of due diligence. Various board members have been brought to court on charges including giving misleading information with the intention of deceiving other board members and the company's auditor.

China Aviation Oil

China Aviation Oil (Singapore) is the subsidiary of a Chinese state-owned holding company, China Aviation Oil Holding Company. In late 2004, it suffered near-collapse after losing some $US550 million on speculative oil derivatives trading. In Singapore, this seemed to echo the case of almost a decade earlier when Nick Leeson's trading had similarly caused tremendous losses to Barings Bank. This time, it was the CEO, Chen Jiulin, who was criticized for carrying on with these trades even though losses had crystallized on some of them. Chen Jiulin was arrested and investigations into suspected violations of securities laws are under way.

The six examples above of high-profile corporate collapses and scandals in the UK, USA, Europe, Australia, and Singapore have had, and continue to have, international implications, and would seem to illustrate a number of shortcomings in the way that the companies were run and managed.

- Barings appears to highlight the lack of effective internal controls and the folly of trusting one employee without adequate supervision and understanding of his activities.
- Enron appears to highlight: a basic need to ensure, as far as possible, that directors are people of integrity and act honestly; that external auditors must be able to ask searching questions unfettered by the need to consider the potential loss of large audit/accounting fees; and the contribution that might be made by independent directors on boards and committees who question intelligently and insightfully.
- Royal Ahold appears to highlight what may happen if the involvement of investors is suppressed: a corporate structure that had empowered a dominant chief executive officer, that had enabled the directors to have overgenerous remuneration packages, and that ultimately led to Ahold's demise when income was found to be overstated.
- Parmalat appears to highlight some of the weaknesses that may exist in family-owned firms where members of the family take a dominant role across the board structure as a whole. In Parmalat's case, the board lacked independence as, of the thirteen directors, only three were independent. This had a knock-on effect on the composition of the various board committees where independent directors were a minority rather than a majority. There was also a lack of timely disclosure of information.
- HIH appears to highlight some of the dangers inherent in the insurance business and the complexities of the risks involved. A risk management system appropriate to the organization, together with relevant disclosure of the risks involved and how they are managed, is clearly of fundamental importance. Directors have a key role to play in ensuring that such a system is in place and that the board as a whole is kept

informed of the process, as should be the shareholders via the annual report disclosures.

- China Aviation Oil appears to highlight that some Chinese state-owned subsidiaries, including those operating outside China, may have a poor level of corporate governance. CEOs may be all-powerful and able to take decisions that are not in the best interests of the company and its shareholders. Limited disclosure may exacerbate the situation.

This brings us back to our original questions about corporate failures such as those mentioned above. Why have such collapses occurred? What might be done to prevent such collapses happening again? How can investor confidence be restored? The answers to these questions are all linked to corporate governance.

Corporate governance is an area that has grown very rapidly in the last decade, particularly since the collapse of Enron in 2001 and the subsequent financial problems of other companies in various countries. As mentioned above, emerging financial scandals will continue to ensure that there is a sharp focus on corporate governance issues, especially relating to transparency and disclosure, control and accountability, and to the most appropriate form of board structure that may be capable of preventing such scandals occurring in future. Not surprisingly, there has been a significant interest shown by governments in trying to ensure that such collapses do not happen again because these lead to a lack of confidence in financial markets. In order to realize why corporate governance has become so important, it is essential to have an understanding of what corporate governance actually is and how it may improve corporate accountability.

A fairly narrow definition of corporate governance is given by Shleifer and Vishny (1997): 'Corporate governance deals with the ways in which suppliers of finance to corporations assure themselves of getting a return on their investment.' A broader definition is provided by the Organisation for Economic Co-operation and Development OECD (1999), which describes corporate governance as: '...a set of relationships between a company's board, its shareholders and other stakeholders. It also provides the structure through which the objectives of the company are set, and the means of attaining those objectives, and monitoring performance, are determined.' Similarly Sir Adrian Cadbury (1999) said: 'Corporate governance is concerned with holding the balance between economic and social goals and between individual and communal goals...the aim is to align as nearly as possible the interests of individuals, corporations and society.' These definitions serve to illustrate that corporate governance is concerned with both the shareholders and the internal aspects of the company, such as internal control, and the external aspects, such as an organization's relationship with its shareholders and other stakeholders. Corporate governance is also seen as an essential mechanism helping the company to attain its corporate objectives and monitoring performance is a key element in achieving these objectives.

It can be seen that corporate governance is important for a number of reasons, and is fundamental to well-managed companies and to ensuring that they operate at optimum efficiency. Some of the important features of corporate governance are as follows:

- it helps to ensure that an adequate and appropriate system of controls operates within a company and hence assets may be safeguarded;

- it prevents any single individual having too powerful an influence;
- it is concerned with the relationship between a company's management, the board of directors, shareholders, and other stakeholders;
- it aims to ensure that the company is managed in the best interests of the shareholders and the other stakeholders;
- it tries to encourage both transparency and accountability, which investors are increasingly looking for in both corporate management and corporate performance.

The first point above refers to the internal control system of a company whereby there are appropriate and adequate controls to ensure that transactions are properly recorded and that assets cannot be misappropriated. Each year, a company has an annual audit and a key part of the auditor's job is to assess whether the internal controls in a business are operating properly. Of course, the auditor has to exercise a certain degree of judgement regarding the assurances given by the directors, the directors being ultimately responsible for the implementation of an appropriate internal control system in the company. The directors are also responsible for ensuring that there are risk assessment procedures in place to identify the risks that companies face in today's business environment, including, for example, exposures to movements in foreign exchange and risks associated with business competition.

As well as being fundamental to investor confidence, good corporate governance is essential to attracting new investment, particularly for developing countries where good corporate governance is often seen as a means of attracting foreign direct investment at more favourable rates. As the emphasis on corporate governance has grown during the last decade, we have seen a sea change in many countries around the world. Developed and developing countries alike have introduced corporate governance codes by which companies are expected to abide. The codes emphasize the importance of transparency, accountability, internal controls, board composition and structure, independent directors, and performance-related executive pay. There is much emphasis on the rights of shareholders and an expectation that shareholders, especially institutional investors, will take a more proactive role in the companies in which they own shares and actually start to act more as owners rather than playing a passive shareholder role. Corporate governance is an exciting area, fast developing to accommodate the needs of a changing business environment where investor expectations are higher than ever before; the cost to companies that ignore the benefits of good corporate governance can be high and, ultimately, can mean the collapse of the company.

This text seeks to chart the development of corporate governance over the last decade and to illustrate the importance of corporate governance to the company itself, to directors, shareholders and other stakeholders, and to the wider business community. The text is structured in four major parts. Part One contains two chapters that chart the development of corporate governance and look at the various theoretical aspects, including the frameworks within which corporate governance might be developed, and the development of corporate governance codes in various countries. Part Two contains four chapters, the first of which, Chapter 4, looks at the role of shareholders and stakeholders, identifies the various stakeholder groups, and discusses their role in companies and in corporate governance. The text recognizes that corporate ownership across the world varies and that the family-owned firm is the dominant form of business in many countries: Chapter 5 is devoted solely to family-owned firms and their governance. Chapter 6 looks at the role of institutional investors in corporate governance; institutional investors are the predominant type of owner in the UK and the USA. Chapter 7 is devoted to socially responsible investment, or ethical investment, because it is an area that is attracting increasing interest in many countries and in which institutional investors in particular are taking much more of an interest. Part Three concentrates on various aspects of directors and board structure: Chapter 8 examines the role of directors, their duties, their responsibilities, and looks at the important areas of boards and board sub-committees. Non-executive directors (outside), emphasized in many of the corporate governance codes as being a key element of good corporate governance, are discussed in detail. Chapter 9 looks at directors' performance and remuneration. It reviews the background to the debate on directors' remuneration and looks at the ways in which directors' performance and remuneration may be effectively linked. The text is designed to appeal to a global audience and Part Four is devoted to corporate governance development in various continents around the world: Chapter 10 looks at corporate governance in Continental Europe; Chapter 11, corporate governance in the Central and Eastern European countries; Chapter 12, corporate governance in South East Asia; Chapter 13, corporate governance in a number of other countries including South Africa, India, and Brazil. Chapter 14 provides some concluding comments on these developments in corporate governance, the evolution of the various shareholder and stakeholder groups, and the potential future developments in corporate governance.

At the start of each chapter, there are learning objectives that identify the key objectives of the chapter, and at the end of each chapter, there is a useful summary of the key points raised. There are short discussion questions and mini case studies to illustrate the key issues raised in various chapters, and references to appropriate publications and websites for each chapter.

An important new feature of the book is the accompanying Online Resource Centre (ORC), which contains additional useful material such as student learning tools incorporating questions and web links, and lecturers' material including PowerPoint slides and updates (on an annual basis) of significant new material. Throughout each chapter, links to the Online Resource Centre are indicated by an icon in the margin.

■ **REFERENCES**

Cadbury, Sir Adrian (1999), Corporate Governance Overview, World Bank Report.

OECD (1999), *Principles of Corporate Governance*, OECD, Paris.

Shleifer, A. and Vishny, R. (1997), 'A Survey of Corporate Governance', *Journal of Finance*, Vol. LII, No. 2.

PART ONE

Developments in Corporate Governance

2 Theoretical Aspects of Corporate Governance

LEARNING OBJECTIVES

- To understand the various main theories that underlie the development of corporate governance
- To be aware of the impact of the form of legal system, capital market, and ownership structure on the development of corporate governance

---

Introduction

Corporate governance has only relatively recently come to prominence in the business world; the term 'corporate governance' and its everyday usage in the financial press is a new phenomenon of the last fifteen years or so. However, the theories underlying the development of corporate governance, and the areas it encompasses, date from much earlier and are drawn from a variety of disciplines including finance, economics, accounting, law, management, and organizational behaviour.

It must be remembered that the development of corporate governance is a global occurrence and, as such, is a complex area including legal, cultural, ownership, and other structural differences. Therefore some theories may be more appropriate and relevant to some countries than others, or more relevant at different times depending on what stage an individual country, or group of countries, is at. The stage of development may refer to the evolution of the economy, corporate structure, or ownership groups, all of which affect how corporate governance will develop and be accommodated within its own country setting. An aspect of particular importance is whether the company itself operates within a shareholder framework, focusing primarily on the maintenance or enhancement of shareholder value as its main objective, or whether it takes a broader stakeholder approach, emphasizing the interests of diverse groups such as employees, providers of credit, suppliers, customers, and the local community.

Table 2.1 Summary of theories affecting corporate governance development

Theory name	Summary
Agency	Agency theory identifies the agency relationship where one party, the principal, delegates work to another party, the agent. In the context of a corporation, the owners are the principal and the directors are the agent.
Transaction cost economics	Transaction cost economics views the firm itself as a governance structure. The choice of an appropriate governance structure can help align the interests of directors and shareholders.
Stakeholder	Stakeholder theory takes account of a wider group of constituents rather than focusing on shareholders. Where there is an emphasis on stakeholders, then the governance structure of the company may provide for some direct representation of the stakeholder groups.
Stewardship	Directors are regarded as the stewards of the company's assets and will be predisposed to act in the best interest of the shareholders.
Class hegemony	Directors view themselves as an elite at the top of the company and will recruit/promote to new director appointments taking into account how well new appointments might fit into that elite.
Managerial hegemony	Management of a company, with its knowledge of day-to-day operations, may effectively dominate the directors and hence weaken the influence of the directors.

Theories associated with the development of corporate governance

Given that many disciplines have influenced the development of corporate governance, the theories that have fed into it are quite varied. Table 2.1 gives a summary of some of the theories that may be associated with the development of corporate governance.

The main theories that have affected the development of corporate governance – agency theory, transaction cost economics, stakeholder theory, and stewardship theory – are discussed in more detail below. For a comprehensive exposition of theories underlying the development of corporate governance, Clarke (2004) is well worth reading.

Agency theory

A significant body of work has built up in this area within the context of the principal–agent framework. The work of Jensen and Meckling (1976) in particular, and of Fama and Jensen (1983), are important. Agency theory identifies the agency relationship where one party, the principal, delegates work to another party, the agent. The agency relationship can have a number of disadvantages relating to the opportunism or self-interest of the agent: for example, the agent may not act in the best interests of the principal, or the agent may act only partially in the best interests of the principal. There can be a number of dimensions to this including, for example, the agent misusing his power for pecuniary or other advantage, and the agent not taking appropriate risks in pursuance of the principal's interests because he (the agent) views those risks as not being appropriate (he and the principal may have different attitudes to risk). There is also the problem of information asymmetry whereby the principal and the agent have access to different levels of information; in practice, this means that the principal is at a disadvantage because the agent will have more information.

In the context of corporations and issues of corporate control, agency theory views corporate governance mechanisms, especially the board of directors, as being an essential monitoring device to try to ensure that any problems that may be brought about by the principal–agent relationship, are minimized. Blair (1996) states:

Managers are supposed to be the 'agents' of a corporation's 'owners', but managers must be monitored and institutional arrangements must provide some checks and balances to make sure they do not abuse their power. The costs resulting from managers misusing their position, as well as the costs of monitoring and disciplining them to try to prevent abuse, have been called 'agency costs'.

Much of agency theory as related to corporations is set in the context of the separation of ownership and control as described in the work of Berle and Means (1932). In this context, the agents are the managers and the principals are the shareholders, and this is the most commonly cited agency relationship in the corporate governance context. However, it is useful to be aware that the agency relationship can also cover various other relationships including those of company and creditor, and of employer and employee.

Separation of ownership and control

The potential problems of the separation of ownership and control were identified in the eighteenth century by Smith (1838): '…the directors of such companies [joint stock companies] however being the managers rather of other people's money than of their own, it cannot well be expected that they should watch over it with the same anxious vigilance [as if it were their own].' Almost a century later, the work of Berle and Means (1932) is often cited as providing one of the fundamental explanations of investor and corporate relationships. Berle and Means' work highlighted that, as countries industrialized and developed their markets, the ownership and control of corporations became separated. This was particularly the case in the USA and the UK where the legal systems have fostered good protection of minority shareholders and hence there has been encouragement for more diversified shareholder bases.

However, in many countries, especially where there is a code of civil law as opposed to common law, the protection of minority shareholders is not effective and so there has been less impetus for a broad shareholder base. The common law system builds on England's medieval laws whilst the civil law system is based on Roman law. A succinct comparison of the two legal systems is provided by Wessel (2001), who states that 'common-law countries – including the US and other former British colonies – rely on independent judges and juries and legal principles supplemented by precedent-setting case law, which results in greater flexibility', whilst 'in civil-law countries – which include much of Latin America – judges often are life-long civil servants who administer legal codes packed with specific rules, which hobbles them in their ability to cope with change'. In countries with a civil law system, there is therefore more codification but weaker protection of rights, hence there is less encouragement to invest.

In other words, the relationship between ownership and control outlined by Berle and Means is largely applicable to the USA and the UK but not to many other countries. This was highlighted by La Porta et al. (1999) who found that the most common form of ownership around the globe is the family firm or controlling shareholders, rather than a broad shareholder base (family firms and their corporate governance implications are discussed in more detail in Chapter 5).

However, the influence of Berle and Means' work cannot be underestimated: it has coloured thinking about the way companies are owned, managed, and controlled for over seventy years, and represents the reality in many US and UK companies. Monks (2001) states: 'The tendency during this period [the twentieth century] has been the dilution of the controlling blocks of shares to the present situation of institutional and widely dispersed ownership – ownership without power.'

In the last few years, there has been increasing pressure on shareholders, and particularly on institutional shareholders who own shares on behalf of the 'man in the street', to act more as owners and not just as holders of shares. The drive for more effective shareholders, who act as owners, has come about because there have been numerous instances of corporate excesses and abuses, such as perceived overpayment of directors for poor performance, corporate collapses, and scandals, which have resulted in corporate pension funds being wiped out, and shareholders losing their investment. The call for improved transparency and disclosure, embodied in corporate governance codes and in International Accounting Standards (IASs), should improve the information asymmetry situation so that investors are better informed about the company's activities and strategies.

Once shareholders do begin to act like owners again, then they will be able to exercise a more direct influence on companies and their boards, so that boards will be more accountable for their actions and, in that sense, the power of ownership will be returned to the owners (the shareholders). Useem (1996) highlights, however, though that institutional investors will ultimately become accountable to 'the millions of ultimate owners . . . who may come to question the policies of the new powers that be. Then the questions may expand from whether the professional money managers are achieving maximum private return to whether they are fostering maximum public good. Their demands for downsizing and single-minded focus on shareholder benefits – whatever the costs – may come to constitute a new target of ownership challenge'.

Transaction cost economics

Transaction cost economics (TCE), as expounded by the work of Williamson (1975, 1984), is often viewed as closely related to agency theory. TCE views the firm as a governance structure whereas agency theory views the firm as a nexus of contracts. Essentially, the latter means that there is a connected group or series of contracts amongst the various players, arising because it is seemingly impossible to have a contract that perfectly aligns the interests of principal and agent in a corporate control situation.

In the discussion of agency theory above, the importance of the separation of owner-ship and control of a firm was emphasized. As firms have grown in size, whether caused by the desire to achieve economies of scale, by technological advances, or by the fact that natural monopolies have evolved, they have increasingly required more capital, which has needed to be raised from the capital markets and a wider shareholder base has been established. The problems of the separation of ownership and control and the resultant corporate governance issues have thus arisen. Coase (1937) examines the rationale for firms' existence in the context of a framework of the efficiencies of internal, as opposed to external, contracting. He states:

the operation of a market costs something and by forming an organisation and allowing some authority (an 'entrepreneur') to direct the resources, certain marketing costs are saved. The entrepreneur has to carry out his function at less cost, taking into account the fact that he may get factors of production at a lower price than the market transactions which he supersedes.

In other words, there are certain economic benefits to the firm itself to undertake transactions internally rather than externally. In its turn, a firm becomes larger the more transactions it undertakes and will expand up to the point where it becomes cheaper or more efficient for the transaction to be undertaken externally. Coase therefore posits that firms may become less efficient the larger they become; equally, he states that 'all changes which improve managerial technique will tend to increase the size of the firm'.

Williamson (1984) builds on the earlier work of Coase, and provides a justification for the growth of large firms and conglomerates, which essentially provide their own internal capital market. He states that the costs of any misaligned actions may be reduced by 'judicious choice of governance structure rather than merely realigning incentives and pricing them out'.

Hart (1995) states that there are a number of costs to writing a contract between principal and agent, which include the cost of thinking about and providing for all the different eventualities that may occur during the course of the contract, the cost of negotiating with others, and the costs of writing the contract in an appropriate way so that it is, for example, legally enforceable. These costs tend to mean that contracts are apt to be incomplete in some way and so contracts will tend to be revisited as and when any omissions or required changes come to light. Hart indicates that, 'in a world of incomplete contracts (where agency problems are also present), governance structure does have a role. Governance structure can be seen as a mechanism for making decisions that have not been specified in the initial contract'.

Stiles and Taylor (2001) point out that 'both theories [TCE and agency] are concerned with managerial discretion, and both assume that managers are given to opportunism (self-interest seeking) and moral hazard, and that managers operate under bounded rationality... [and] both agency theory and TCE regard the board of directors as an instrument of control'. In this context, 'bounded rationality' means that managers will tend to satisfice rather than maximize profit (this, of course, not being in the best interests of shareholders).

Stakeholder theory

In juxtaposition to agency theory is stakeholder theory. Stakeholder theory takes account of a wider group of constituents rather than focusing on shareholders. A consequence of focusing on shareholders is that the maintenance or enhancement of shareholder value is paramount, whereas when a wider stakeholder group, such as employees, providers of credit, customers, suppliers, government, and the local community, is taken into account, the overriding focus on shareholder value becomes less self-evident. Nonetheless, many companies do strive to maximize shareholder value whilst at the same time trying to take into account the interests of the wider stakeholder group. One rationale for effectively privileging shareholders over other stakeholders is that they are the recipients of the residual free cash flow (being the profits remaining once other stakeholders, such as loan creditors, have been paid). This means that the shareholders have a vested interest in trying to ensure that resources are used to maximum effect, which in turn should be to the benefit of society as a whole.

Shareholders and stakeholders may favour different corporate governance structures and also monitoring mechanisms. We can, for example, see differences in the corporate governance structures and monitoring mechanisms of the so-called Anglo-American model, with its emphasis on shareholder value and a board comprised totally of executive and non-executive directors elected by shareholders, compared to the German model, whereby certain stakeholder groups such as employees, have a right enshrined in law for their representatives to sit on the supervisory board alongside the directors. Chapter 4 is devoted to shareholders and stakeholders, and discusses various aspects in more detail.

An interesting development is that put forward by Jensen (2001), who states that traditional stakeholder theory argues that the managers of a firm should take account of the interests of all stakeholders in a firm but, because the theorists refuse to say how the trade-offs against the interests of each of these stakeholder groups might be made, there are no defined measurable objectives and this leaves managers unaccountable for their actions. Jensen therefore advocates enlightened value maximization, which he says is identical to enlightened stakeholder theory: 'Enlightened value maximization utilizes much of the structure of stakeholder theory but accepts maximization of the long-run value of the firm as the criterion for making the requisite trade-offs among its stakeholders . . . and therefore solves the problems that arise from multiple objectives that accompany traditional stakeholder theory.'

Stewardship theory

Stewardship theory draws on the assumptions underlying agency theory and TCE. The work of Donaldson and Davis (1991) cautioned against accepting agency theory as a given and introduced an alternative approach to corporate governance – stewardship theory.

The thrust of Donaldson and Davis' paper was that agency theory

emphasises the control of managerial 'opportunism' by having a board chair independent of the CEO and using incentives to bind CEO interests to those of shareholders. Stewardship theory stresses the beneficial consequences on shareholder returns of facilitative authority structures which unify command by having roles of CEO and chair held by the same person...The safeguarding of returns to shareholders may be along the track, not of placing management under greater control by owners, but of empowering managers to take autonomous executive action.

Whilst Table 2.1 gives a summary of the theories that may be associated with the development of corporate governance, Figure 2.1 illustrates the main theories that have influenced the development of corporate governance: agency theory, transaction cost economics, stakeholder theory and stewardship theory.

The theories in context

The approach taken in this book is to assume a public corporation business form (that is, a publicly quoted company), unless specifically stated otherwise. Therefore the theories discussed above should be viewed in the light of this type of business form. In the UK, this type of business form generally has a dispersed shareholder base, although there is concentration of shareholdings amongst the institutional investors such as the pension funds and insurance companies. Agency theory, together with the work of Berle and Means, seems particularly relevant in this context.

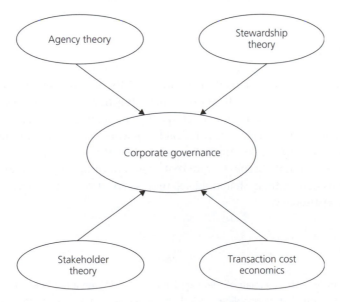

Figure 2.1 Main theories influencing the development of corporate governance

The theories that have affected the development of corporate governance should also be viewed in conjunction with the legal system and capital market development, as well as the ownership structure. For example, countries like the UK and the USA have a common law system that tends to give good protection of shareholder rights, whilst civil law countries, such as France, tend to have less effective legal protection for shareholder rights, and more emphasis may be given to the rights of certain stakeholder groups.

However, it is clear that companies cannot operate in isolation without having regard to the effect of their actions on the various stakeholder groups. To this end, companies need to be able to attract and retain equity investment, and be accountable to their shareholders, whilst at the same time giving real consideration to the interests of their wider stakeholder constituencies.

Convergence

There are a number of views as to where corporate governance systems are converging or are likely to converge. Branson (2004) and Guillén (2004) argue against convergence occurring on economic, legal, and cultural grounds. For example, the family-owned firm is the dominant form of business around the globe and not the publicly owned corporation on which US and UK corporate governance is premised, hence we can see that one size is unlikely to fit all and that there will likely continue to be some divergence. There does, however, seem to be convergence on the core aspects of corporate governance, such as transparency, disclosure, and the important contribution that independent non-executive directors can make.

Conclusions

Corporate governance is a relatively new area and its development has been affected by theories from a number of disciplines, including finance, economics, accounting, law, management, and organizational behaviour. The main theory that has affected its development, and that provides a theoretical framework within which it most naturally seems to rest, is agency theory. However, stakeholder theory is coming more into play as companies increasingly become aware that they cannot operate in isolation and that, as well as considering their shareholders, they need also to have regard to a wider stakeholder constituency.

■ SUMMARY

- Corporate governance is a relatively new area and its development has been affected by theories from a number of disciplines, including finance, economics, accounting, law, management, and organizational behaviour.

- Agency theory has probably affected the development of the corporate governance framework the most. Agency theory identifies the agency relationship where one party, the principal, delegates work to another party, the agent. In the context of a corporation, the owners are the principal and the directors are the agent.

- Stakeholder theory takes account of a wider group of constituents rather than focusing on shareholders. Where there is an emphasis on stakeholders, then the governance structure of the company may provide for some direct representation of the stakeholder groups.

- The development of corporate governance is a global occurrence and, as such, is a complex area including legal, cultural, ownership, and other structural differences. Therefore some theories may be more appropriate and relevant to some countries than others.

■ QUESTIONS

The discussion questions below cover the key learning points of this chapter. Reading of some of the additional reference material will enhance the depth of the students' knowledge and understanding of these areas.

1. Critically discuss the main theories that have influenced the development of corporate governance.

2. Do you think that different theories are more appropriate to different types of ownership structure?

3. What are the main problems that may arise in a principal–agent relationship and how might these be dealt with?

4. What links might there be between a country's legal system and capital market developments, and the impact of the theories underlying corporate governance?

5. 'Shareholders are more likely to lose money because the relevant people in the firm are not up to the mark than merely because they are ``agents'' bent on pursuing their own interests at the expense of others.' (Charkham and Simpson, 1999) Critically discuss this statement.

6. 'Stakeholders can, and should, be principals enabling them to further their interests in the same way as shareholders.' Critically discuss this statement.

■ REFERENCES

Berle, A.A. and Means, G.C. (1932), *The Modern Corporation and Private Property*, Macmillan, New York.

Blair, M. (1996), *Ownership and Control: Rethinking Corporate Governance for the Twenty-first Century*, Brookings Institution, Washington.

Branson, D.M. (2004), 'The Very Uncertain Prospects of "Global" Convergence in Corporate Governance' in *Theories of Corporate Governance*, T. Clarke (ed.), Routledge, London.

Charkham, J. and Simpson, A. (1999), *Fair Shares: The Future of Shareholder Power and Responsibility*, Oxford University Press, Oxford.

Clarke, T. (2004), *Theories of Corporate Governance*, Routledge, London.

Coase, R.H. (1937), 'The Nature of the Firm', *Economica* IV, 13–16.

Donaldson, L. and Davis, J.H. (1991), 'Stewardship Theory or Agency Theory: CEO Governance and Shareholder Returns', *Australian Journal of Management*, Vol. 16(1).

Fama, E.F. and Jensen, M. (1983), 'Separation of Ownership and Control', *Journal of Law and Economics* 26.

Guillén, M.F. (2004), 'Corporate Governance and Globalization: Is There Convergence Across Countries' in *Theories of Corporate Governance*, T. Clarke (ed.), Routledge, London.

Hart, O. (1995), 'Corporate Governance: Some Theory and Implications', *The Economic Journal* 105.

Jensen, M. (2001), 'Value Maximization, Stakeholder Theory, and the Corporate Objective Function', *Journal of Applied Corporate Finance*, Vol. 14, No. 3.

—— and Meckling, W. (1976), 'Theory of the Firm: Managerial Behaviour, Agency Costs and Ownership Structure', *Journal of Financial Economics* 3.

La Porta, R., Lopez-de-Silanes, F., Shleifer, A. and Vishny, R. (1999), 'Corporate Ownership Around the World', *Journal of Finance* 54.

Monks, R.A.G. (2001), *The New Global Investors*, Capstone Publishing, Oxford.

Smith, A. (1838), *The Wealth of Nations*, Ward Lock, London.

Stiles, P. and Taylor, B. (2001), *Boards at Work: How Directors View Their Roles and Responsibilities*, Oxford University Press, Oxford.

Useem, M. (1996), *Investor Capitalism: How Money Managers Are Changing the Face of Corporate America*, Basic Books, New York.

Wessel, D. (2001), 'Capital: The Legal DNA of Good Economies', *Wall Street Journal*, 6 September 2001.

Williamson, O.E. (1975), *Markets and Hierarchies*, Free Press, New York.

—— (1984), 'Corporate Governance', *Yale Law Journal* 93.

■ USEFUL WEBSITES

http://asp.thecorporatelibrary.net Contains many useful and topical articles/references for the study of corporate governance.

http://leadership.wharton.upenn.edu/governance Contains references to key academic articles in a number of corporate governance areas.

3

Development of Corporate Governance Codes

LEARNING OBJECTIVES

- To understand the key factors affecting the development of corporate governance codes
- To be aware of the main developments in corporate governance codes
- To have an awareness of the corporate governance codes that have been most influential globally
- To assess critically the characteristics of corporate governance codes and the mode of operation

---

The growth in corporate governance codes

During the last decade, each year has seen the introduction, or revision, of a corporate governance code in a number of countries. These countries have encompassed a variety of legal backgrounds (for example, common law in the UK, civil law in France), cultural and political contexts (for example, democracy in Australia, communist in China), business forms (for example, public corporations compared to family-owned firms), and share ownership (institutional investor-dominated in the UK and USA, state ownership in China). However, in each of the countries, the introduction of corporate governance codes has generally been motivated by a desire for more transparency and accountability, and a desire to increase investor confidence (of both potential and existing investors) in the stock market as a whole. The development of the codes has often been driven by a financial scandal, corporate collapse, or similar crisis.

The corporate governance codes and guidelines have been issued by a variety of bodies ranging from committees, appointed by government departments and usually including prominent respected figures from business and industry, representatives from the investment community, representatives from professional bodies, and academics, through to stock exchange bodies, various investor representative groups, and professional bodies, such as those representing directors or company secretaries.

As regards compliance with the various codes, compliance is generally on a voluntary disclosure basis, whilst some codes, such as the UK's Combined Code (2003), are on a 'comply or explain basis', that is, either a company has to comply fully with the code and state that it has done so, or it explains why it has not.

In this chapter, the development of corporate governance in the UK is covered in some detail, particularly in relation to the Cadbury Report (1992), which has influenced the development of many corporate governance codes globally. Similarly, the OECD Principles are reviewed in detail as these have also formed the cornerstone of many corporate governance codes. The impact of various other international organizations on corporate governance developments, including the World Bank, Global Corporate Governance Forum, International Corporate Governance Network, and Commonwealth Association for Corporate Governance, are discussed. Recent developments in the EU, which have implications both for existing, and potential, member countries' corporate governance, are covered. There is also a brief overview of the Basle Committee recommendations for corporate governance in banking organizations.

Finally, recent corporate collapses in the USA have had a significant impact on confidence in financial markets across the world and corporate governance developments in the USA are discussed in some detail.

Corporate governance in the UK

The UK has a well-developed market with a diverse shareholder base including institutional investors, financial institutions, and individuals. The UK illustrates well the problems that may be associated with the separation of the ownership and control of corporations and hence has many of the associated agency problems discussed in Chapter 2. These agency problems, including misuse of corporate assets by directors and a lack of effective control over, and accountability of, directors' actions, contributed to a number of financial scandals in the UK.

As in other countries, the development of corporate governance in the UK was initially driven by corporate collapses and financial scandals. The UK's Combined Code (1998) embodied the findings of a trilogy of codes: the Cadbury Report (1992), the Greenbury Report (1995), and the Hampel Report (1998). Brief mention is made of each of these three at this point to set the context, whilst a detailed review of the Cadbury Report (1992) is given subsequently in this chapter because it has influenced the development of many codes across the world. Reference is made to relevant sections of various codes in appropriate subsequent chapters.

 Figure 3.1 illustrates the development of corporate governance in the UK. The centre oval represents the Combined Code published in 2006 by the Financial Reporting Council. Around the centre oval, we can see the various influences since 1998 (the original Combined Code, published in 1998, encompassed the Cadbury, Greenbury, and Hampel report recommendations). These influences can be split into four broad areas. First, there are reports that have looked at specific areas of corporate governance: the Turnbull report on internal controls, the Myners review of institutional investment, the

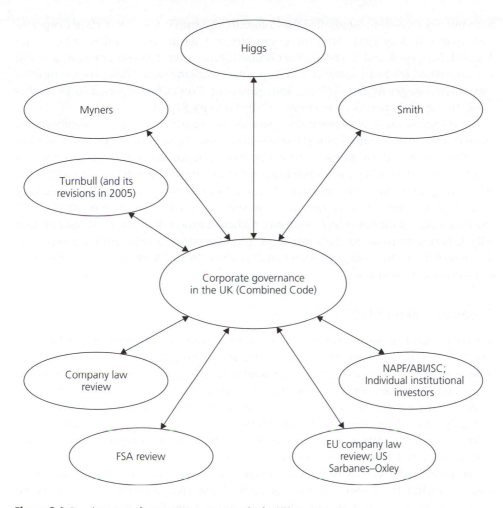

Figure 3.1 Development of corporate governance in the UK

Higgs review of the role and effectiveness of non-executive directors, and the Smith review of audit committees. Secondly, there has been the influence of institutional investors and their representative groups. Thirdly, influences affecting the regulatory framework within which corporate governance in the UK operates have included the UK company law review and the Financial Services Authority review. Fourthly, there have been what might be termed 'external influences' such as the EU review of company law and the US Sarbanes–Oxley Act. Each of these is now discussed in turn.

Cadbury Report (1992)

Following various financial scandals and collapses (Coloroll and Polly Peck, to name but two) and a perceived general lack of confidence in the financial reporting of many UK companies, the Financial Reporting Council, the London Stock Exchange, and the accountancy profession established the Committee on the Financial Aspects of Corporate Governance in May 1991. After the Committee was set up, the scandals at BCCI and Maxwell happened, and as a result, the Committee interpreted its remit more widely and looked beyond the financial aspects to corporate governance as a whole. The Committee was chaired by Sir Adrian Cadbury and, when the Committee reported in December 1992, the report became widely known as 'the Cadbury Report'.

The recommendations covered: the operation of the main board; the establishment, composition, and operation of key board committees; the importance of, and contribution that can be made by, non-executive directors; the reporting and control mechanisms of a business. The Cadbury Report recommended a Code of Best Practice with which the boards of all listed companies registered in the UK should comply, and utilized a 'comply or explain' mechanism. This mechanism means that a company should comply with the code but, if it cannot comply with any particular aspect of it, then it should explain why it is unable to do so. This disclosure gives investors detailed information about any instances of non-compliance and enables them to decide whether the company's non-compliance is justified.

Greenbury Report (1995)

The Greenbury Committee was set up in response to concern at both the size of directors' remuneration packages and their inconsistent and incomplete disclosure in companies' annual reports. It made, in 1995, comprehensive recommendations regarding disclosure of directors' remuneration packages. There has been much discussion about how much disclosure there should be of directors' remuneration and how useful detailed disclosures might be. Whilst the work of the Greenbury Committee focused on the directors of public limited companies, it hoped that both smaller listed companies and unlisted companies would find its recommendations useful.

Central to the Greenbury Report recommendations were strengthening accountability and enhancing the performance of directors. These two aims were to be achieved by (i) the presence of a remuneration committee comprised of independent non-executive directors who would report fully to the shareholders each year about the company's executive remuneration policy, including full disclosure of the elements in the remuneration of individual directors, and (ii) the adoption of performance measures linking rewards to the performance of both the company and individual directors, so that the interests of directors and shareholders were more closely aligned.

Since that time (1995), disclosure of directors' remuneration has become quite prolific in UK company accounts. The main elements of directors' remuneration are considered further in Chapter 9.

Hampel Report (1998)

The Hampel Committee was set up in 1995 to review the implementation of the Cadbury and Greenbury Committee recommendations. The Hampel Committee reported in 1998. The Hampel Report said: 'We endorse the overwhelming majority of the findings of the two earlier committees.' There has been much discussion about the extent to which a company should consider the interests of various stakeholders, such as employees, customers, suppliers, providers of credit, the local community, etc., as well as the interests of its shareholders. The Hampel Report stated that 'the directors as a board are responsible *for relations with* stakeholders; but they are accountable *to* the shareholders'. However, the report does also state that 'directors can meet their legal duties to shareholders, and can pursue the objective of long-term shareholder value successfully, only by developing and sustaining these stakeholder relationships'.

The Hampel Report, like its precursors, also emphasized the important role that institutional investors have to play in the companies in which they invest (investee companies). It is highly desirable that companies and institutional investors engage in dialogue and that institutional investors make considered use of their shares – in other words, institutional investors should consider carefully the resolutions on which they have a right to vote and reach a decision based on careful thought, rather than engage in 'box ticking'.

Combined Code (1998)

The Combined Code drew together the recommendations of the Cadbury, Greenbury, and Hampel reports. It has two sections, one aimed at companies and another aimed at institutional investors. The Combined Code operates on the 'comply or explain' basis mentioned above. In relation to the internal controls of the business, the Combined Code states that 'the board should maintain a sound system of internal control to safeguard shareholders' investment and the company's assets' and that 'the directors should, at least annually, conduct a review of the effectiveness of the group's system of internal control and should report to shareholders that they have done so. The review should cover all controls, including financial, operational, and compliance controls and risk management' (Part D.2.1). The Turnbull Report issued in 1999 gave directors guidance on carrying out this review.

Turnbull (1999)

The Turnbull Committee, chaired by Nigel Turnbull, was established by the Institute of Chartered Accountants in England and Wales (ICAEW) to provide guidance on the implementation of the internal control requirements of the Combined Code. The Turnbull Report confirms that it is the responsibility of the board of directors to ensure that the company has a sound system of internal control, and that the controls are working as they should. The board should assess the effectiveness of internal controls and report on them in the annual report. Of course, a company is subject to new risks both from the outside environment and as a result of decisions that the board makes about corporate strategy and objectives. In the managing of risk, boards will need to take into account the existing internal control system in the company and also whether any changes are required to ensure that new risks are adequately and effectively managed.

Myners (2001)

The Myners Report on institutional investment, issued in 2001 by HM Treasury, concentrated more on the trusteeship aspects of institutional investors and the legal requirements for trustees, with the aim of raising the standards and promoting greater shareholder activism. For example, the Myners Report expects that institutional investors should be more proactive, especially in the stance they take with underperforming companies. Some institutional investors have already shown more of a willingness to engage actively with companies to try to ensure that shareholder value is not lost by underperforming companies.

Higgs (2003)

The Higgs Review, chaired by Derek Higgs, reported in January 2003 on the role and effectiveness of non-executive directors. Higgs offered support for the Combined Code whilst making some additional recommendations. These recommendations included: stating the number of meetings of the board and its main committees in the annual report, together with the attendance records of individual directors; that a chief executive director should not also become chairman of the same company; non-executive directors should meet as a group at least once a year without executive directors being present, and the annual report should indicate whether such meetings have occurred; chairmen and chief executives should consider implementing executive development programmes to train and develop suitable individuals in their companies for future director roles; the board should inform shareholders as to why they believe a certain individual should be appointed to a non-executive directorship and how they may meet the requirements of the role; there should be a comprehensive induction programme for new non-executive directors, and resources should be available for ongoing development of directors; the performance of the board, its committees and its individual members, should be evaluated at least once a year, the annual report should state whether these reviews are being held and how they are conducted; a full-time executive director should not hold more than one non-executive directorship or become chairman of a major company; no one non-executive director should sit on all three principal board committees (audit, remuneration, nomination). There was substantial opposition to some of the recommendations but they nonetheless helped to inform the Combined Code. Good practice suggestions from the Higgs Report were published in 2006.

Smith (2003)

The Smith Review of audit committees, a group appointed by the Financial Reporting Council, reported in January 2003. The review made clear the important role of the audit committee: 'While all directors have a duty to act in the interests of the company, the audit committee has a particular role, acting independently from the executive, to ensure that the interests of shareholders are properly protected in relation to financial reporting and internal control' (para 1.5). The review defined the audit committee's role in terms of a high-level overview – it needs to satisfy itself that there is an appropriate system of controls in place but it does not undertake the monitoring itself.

Combined Code (2003)

The revised Combined Code, published in July 2003, incorporated the substance of the Higgs and Smith reviews. However, rather than stating that no one non-executive director should sit on all three board committees, the Combined Code stated that 'undue reliance' should not be placed on particular individuals. The Combined Code also clarified the roles of the chairman and the senior independent director (SID), emphasizing the chairman's role in providing leadership to the non-executive directors and in communicating shareholders' views to the board; it also provided for a 'formal and rigorous annual evaluation' of the board's, the committees', and the individual directors' performance. At least half the board in larger listed companies were to be independent non-executive directors.

Revised Turnbull Guidance (2005)

In 2005, revised guidance on the Turnbull Report (1999) was published. There were few substantive changes but boards were encouraged to review their application of the guidance on a continuing basis and to look on the internal control statement as an opportunity to communicate to their shareholders how they manage risk and internal control. They should notify shareholders, in the annual report, of how any 'significant failings or weaknesses' in the effectiveness of the internal control system have been dealt with.

Combined Code (2006)

An updated version of the Combined Code was issued in June 2006 and is included as an Appendix to this text. There were three main changes made:

(i) to allow the company chairman to serve on (but not to chair) the remuneration committee where he is considered independent on appointment as chairman;

(ii) to provide a 'vote withheld' option on proxy appointment forms to enable a shareholder to indicate that they wish to withhold their vote;

(iii) to recommend that companies publish on their website the details of proxies lodged at general meetings where votes were taken on a show of hands.

Institutional investors and their representative groups

Large institutional investors, mainly insurance companies and pension funds, usually belong to one of two representative bodies that act as a professional group 'voice' for their views: the Association of British Insurers (ABI) and the National Association of Pension Funds (NAPF). Both the ABI and the NAPF have best practice corporate governance guidelines that encompass the recommendations of the Combined Code. They monitor the corporate governance activities of companies and will provide advice to members.

Some large institutional investors are very active in their own right in terms of their corporate governance activities. Hermes is a case in point, and it has recently published the Hermes Principles, which detail how it perceives its relationship with the companies in which it invests (investee companies), what its expectations are of investee companies, and what investee companies can expect from Hermes.

The role and influence of institutional investors is covered in detail in Chapter 6.

Company Law Review

In the UK, the corporate law has been in need of a thorough review for some years and the Modern Company Law Review culminated in July 2002 in the publication of outline proposals for extensive modernization of company law, including various aspects of corporate governance. These proposals included: statutory codification of directors' common law duties; enhanced company reporting and audit requirements, including a requirement that economically significant companies produce an annual operating and financial review; disclosure on corporate websites of information relating to the annual report and accounts, and disclosure relating to voting.

The government published the Company Law Reform Bill in November 2005, which proposed reforms, inter alia, to encourage shareholder engagement and a long-term investment culture, and to ensure better regulation. It will impact on areas such as a company's annual general meeting and also on codifying directors' duties and responsibilities. The UK also has an important role to play in ensuring that its voice is heard in the current European Union developments relating to company law and corporate governance.

Financial Services Authority Review

In September 2002, the Financial Services Authority (FSA) launched a review of the listing regime with the main aim being to assess the existing rules and identify which should be retained, and which changed. The areas covered by the review are: corporate governance; continuing obligations (encompassing corporate communication, and shareholders' rights and obligations); financial information; the sponsor regime.

The FSA Review took place against the background of potentially significant changes in both the EU and UK regulatory environments, and although some changes were made, there was much continuity in the proposals introduced in the summer of 2005.

Financial Reporting Council

The Financial Reporting Council (FRC) has five operating bodies: the Accounting Standards Board (ASB), the Auditing Practices Board (APB), the Professional Oversight Board for Accountancy (POBA), the Financial Reporting Review Panel (FRRP), and the Accountancy Investigation and Discipline Board (AIDB).

The importance placed on corporate governance is evidenced by the fact that, in March 2004, the FRC set up a new committee to lead its work on corporate governance.

Overall, the FRC is responsible for promoting high standards of corporate governance. It aims to do so by:

- maintaining an effective Combined Code on Corporate Governance and promoting its widespread application;
- ensuring that related guidance, such as that on internal control, is current and relevant;
- influencing EU and global corporate governance developments;
- helping to promote boardroom professionalism and diversity;
- encouraging constructive interaction between company boards and institutional shareholders.

The FRC carried out an implementation review of the Combined Code (2003) between July and October 2005. The FRC consulted widely and an amended Combined Code on Corporate Governance was published in June 2006 (as discussed earlier).

'External' influences

The report of the EU High Level Group of Company Law Experts had implications for company law across Europe including the UK, and is further discussed below in the context of an international development. The impact of recent legislation in the USA, the Sarbanes–Oxley Act, has also made its influence felt in the UK, and is also discussed in detail below.

online resource centre

Influential corporate governance codes

Corporate governance codes and guidelines for various countries around the world will be looked at in more detail in some of the later chapters, whilst in this chapter codes and guidelines that have had a fundamental influence on the development of corporate governance more generally will be examined. It is always slightly contentious to try to state which corporate governance codes have had the most influence on the development of corporate governance codes in other countries, but the following codes and principles have undoubtedly had a key impact on the development of corporate governance globally.

Cadbury Report (1992)

The Cadbury Report recommended a Code of Best Practice with which the boards of all listed companies registered in the UK should comply, and utilized a 'comply or explain' mechanism. Whilst the Code of Best Practice is aimed at the directors of listed companies registered in the UK, the Committee also exhorted other companies to try to meet its requirements. The main recommendations were as follows.

THE CODE OF BEST PRACTICE

1. The Board of Directors

1.1 The board should meet regularly, retain full and effective control over the company, and monitor the executive management.

1.2 There should be a clearly accepted division of responsibilities at the head of a company, which will ensure a balance of power and authority, such that no one individual has unfettered powers of decision. Where the chairman is also the chief executive, it is essential that there should be a strong and independent element on the board, with a recognized senior member.

1.3 The board should include non-executive directors of sufficient calibre and number for their views to carry significant weight in the board's decisions.

1.4 The board should have a formal schedule of matters specifically reserved to it for decision to ensure that the direction and control of the company is firmly in its hands.

1.5 There should be an agreed procedure for directors in the furtherance of their duties to take independent professional advice if necessary, at the company's expense.

1.6 All directors should have access to the advice and services of the company secretary, who is responsible to the board for ensuring that board procedures are followed and that applicable rules and regulations are complied with. Any question of the removal of the company secretary should be a matter for the board as a whole.

2. Non-executive Directors

2.1 Non-executive directors should bring an independent judgement to bear on issues of strategy, performance, resources, including key appointments, and standards of conduct.

2.2 The majority should be independent of management and free from any business or other relationship which could materially interfere with the exercise of their independent judgement, apart from their fees and shareholding. Their fees should reflect the time which they commit to the company.

2.3 Non-executive directors should be appointed for specified terms and reappointment should not be automatic.

2.4 Non-executive directors should be selected through a formal process and both this process and their appointment should be a matter for the board as a whole.

3. Executive Directors

3.1 Directors' service contracts should not exceed three years without shareholders' approval.

3.2 There should be full and clear disclosure of directors' total emoluments and those of the chairman and highest-paid UK director, including pension contributions and stock options. Separate figures should be given for salary and performance-related elements and the basis on which performance is measured should be explained.

3.3 Executive directors' pay should be subject to the recommendations of a remuneration committee made up wholly or mainly of non-executive directors.

_____ continues

4. Reporting and Controls

4.1 It is the board's duty to present a balanced and understandable assessment of the company's position.

4.2 The board should ensure that an objective and professional relationship is maintained with the auditors.

4.3 The board should establish an audit committee of at least three non-executive directors with written terms of reference which deal clearly with its authority and duties.

4.4 The directors should explain their responsibility for preparing the accounts next to a statement by the auditors about their reporting responsibilities.

4.5 The directors should report on the effectiveness of the company's system of internal control.

4.6 The directors should report that the business is a going concern, with supporting assumptions or qualifications as necessary.

Source: Cadbury Code (1992)

The recommendations – covering the operation of the main board, the establishment, composition, and operation of key board committees, the importance of, and contribution that can be made by, non-executive directors, and the reporting and control mechanisms of a business – had a fundamental impact on the development of corporate governance not just in the UK, but on the content of codes across the world, among countries as diverse as India and Russia.

Today, the recommendations of the Cadbury Report and subsequent UK reports on corporate governance are embodied in the UK's Combined Code (2006). Various sections of the Combined Code are referred to in appropriate chapters and the full text of the Combined Code (2006) is included as an appendix.

OECD Principles of Corporate Governance (1999) as revised (2004)

The Organization for Economic Co-operation and Development (OECD) published its Principles of Corporate Governance in 1999, following a request from the OECD Council to develop corporate governance standards and guidelines. Prior to producing the Principles, the OECD consulted the national governments of member states, the private sector, and various international organizations including the World Bank. online resource centre

The OECD recognizes that 'one size does not fit all', that is, that there is no single model of corporate governance that is applicable to all countries. However, the Principles represent certain common characteristics that are fundamental to good corporate governance. The OECD Principles were reviewed and revised in 2004. The revised Principles are as follows.

Principle	Narrative
I. Ensuring the basis for an effective corporate governance framework	The corporate governance framework should promote transparent and efficient markets, be consistent with the rule of law, and clearly articulate the division of responsibilities among different supervisory, regulatory, and enforcement authorities.
II. The rights of shareholders and key ownership functions	The corporate governance framework should protect and facilitate the exercise of shareholders' rights.
III. The equitable treatment of shareholders	The corporate governance framework should ensure the equitable treatment of all shareholders, including minority and foreign shareholders. All shareholders should have the opportunity to obtain effective redress for violation of their rights.
IV. The role of stakeholders in corporate governance	The corporate governance framework should recognize the rights of stakeholders established by law or through mutual agreements and encourage active co-operation between corporations and stakeholders in creating wealth, jobs, and the sustainability of financially sound enterprises.
V. Disclosure and transparency	The corporate governance framework should ensure that timely and accurate disclosure is made on all material matters regarding the corporation, including the financial situation, performance, ownership, and governance of the company.
VI. The responsibilities of the board	The corporate governance framework should ensure the strategic guidance of the company, the effective monitoring of management by the board, and the board's accountability to the company and the shareholders.

Source: OECD Principles of Corporate Governance (2004)

The OECD Principles focus on publicly traded companies but, as in the Cadbury Report, there is an encouragement for other business forms, such as privately held or state-owned enterprises, to utilize the Principles to improve corporate governance.

The OECD Principles are non-binding but, nonetheless, their value as key elements of good corporate governance have been recognized and have been incorporated into codes in many different countries. For example, the Committee on Corporate Governance in Greece produced its Principles on Corporate Governance in Greece in 1999, which reflected the OECD Principles, whilst the China Securities Regulatory Commission published its Code of Corporate Governance for Listed Companies in China in 2001, which also draws substantially on the OECD Principles.

World Bank

The World Bank's corporate governance activities focus on: the rights of shareholders; the equitable treatment of shareholders; the treatment of stakeholders; disclosure and transparency; the duties of board members. Clearly, the OECD Principles are very much in evidence in this approach.

The World Bank utilizes the OECD Principles to prepare country corporate governance assessments that detail and assess the corporate governance institutional frameworks and practices in individual countries. These assessments may then be used to support policy dialogue, strategic work and operations, and to aid in determining the level of technical assistance needed in given countries in relation to their corporate governance development.

In addition, the International Monetary Fund (IMF) produces reports on the observance of standards and codes that summarize the extent to which countries observe internationally recognized standards and codes. Sections on corporate governance, accounting, and auditing are included in these reports.

Global Corporate Governance Forum

The Global Corporate Governance Forum (GCGF) is at the heart of corporate governance co-operation between the OECD and the World Bank. It is, as its name suggests, an international initiative aimed at bringing together leading groups in governance including banks, organizations, country groupings, the private sector, and professional standard-setting bodies. The GCGF plans to provide assistance to developing transition economies on corporate governance. It states that it has three functions: '... to broaden the dialogue on corporate governance; to exchange experience and good practices; to co-ordinate activities and identify and fill gaps in provision of technical assistance.'

The GCGF's work programme includes information dissemination events at national and regional levels, whereby interested parties are brought together to discuss the issues, identify priorities for reform, and to develop action plans and initiatives to achieve them.

International Corporate Governance Network

The International Corporate Governance Network (ICGN) was founded in 1995. Its membership encompasses major institutional investors, investor representative groups, companies, financial intermediaries, academics, and others with an interest in the development of global corporate governance practices. Its objective is to facilitate international dialogue on corporate governance issues.

In 1999, the ICGN issued its Statement on Global Corporate Governance Principles, which comprised three main areas. First is a statement on the OECD Principles, which the ICGN views as 'a remarkable convergence on corporate governance common ground among diverse interests, practices, and cultures', and which it sees as the minimum acceptable standard for companies and investors around the world. Secondly, the ICGN statement discusses its approach to the OECD Principles, a 'working kit' statement of corporate governance criteria that encompasses ten areas: the corporate objective; communications and reporting; voting rights; corporate boards; corporate remuneration policies; strategic focus; operating performance; shareholder returns; corporate citizenship; corporate governance implementation. Thirdly, the ICGN statement amplifies the OECD Principles, emphasizing or interpreting each principle as appropriate. For example, in relation to 'The Rights of Shareholders', the ICGN amplification includes the statement that 'major strategic modifications to the core business(es) of a corporation should not be made without prior shareholder approval of the proposed modification'.

Following the revision of the OECD Principles (2004), the ICGN reviewed its global corporate governance principles and published revised principles in 2005. Again building on the OECD Principles, the ICGN revised principles also identify some additional principles of particular concern to the ICGN and its members. The ICGN principles cover eight areas: corporate objective – shareholder returns; disclosure and transparency; audit; shareholders' ownership, responsibilities, and voting rights and remedies; corporate boards; corporate remuneration policies; corporate citizenship, stakeholder relations and the ethical conduct of business; corporate governance implementation.

Commonwealth Association for Corporate Governance

The Commonwealth Association for Corporate Governance (CACG) has produced some useful guidelines and principles of guidelines. The guidelines cover 15 principles detailing the board's role and responsibilities. These cover areas such as leadership, board appointments, strategy and values, company performance, compliance, communication, accountability to shareholders, relationships with stakeholders, balance of power, internal procedures, board performance assessment, management appointments and development, technology, risk management, and an annual review of future solvency.

EU Company Law Experts

The EU High Level Group of Company Law Experts, comprised of a group of lawyers, was established in late 2001 by the EU to provide independent advice for modernizing company law in Europe. The group was headed by Jaap Winter, hence the report produced by the group is sometimes referred to as the 'Winter Report' (2002). In relation to corporate governance issues, the group made the following recommendations for listed companies.

- EU law should require companies to publish an annual corporate governance statement in their accounts and on their websites. Companies would need to state their compliance with their national corporate governance code, on a 'comply or explain' basis.

- The nomination and remuneration of directors, and the audit of accounts, should be decided upon by non-executive, or supervisory, directors, the majority of whom are independent.

- Companies should disclose in their annual corporate governance statement who their independent directors are, why they are independent, what their qualifications are to serve on the board, and their other directorships.

- The remuneration of individual directors should be disclosed in detail.

- Share option schemes would require the prior approval of the shareholders.

- In relation to (annual) general meetings, companies should be required to publish all relevant material on their website, and should offer facilities for electronic voting.

- Companies should inform shareholders of the procedure for asking questions at general meetings, and also of the process for submitting shareholder resolutions (proposals).

Frits Bolkestein, the EU internal markets commissioner, promised an action plan to take forward the recommendations of the group, with the aim of providing a comprehensive, dynamic, and flexible framework for corporate governance in Europe. There are clear implications for all members of the EU. As far as the UK is concerned, the group's recommendations are generally similar to those of the UK Company Law Review and should not pose any problems.

In the spring of 2006, the EU Commission organized a public hearing on future priorities for the Action Plan on 'Modernizing Company Law and Enhancing Corporate Governance in the EU'. These priorities included: shareholders' rights and obligations; internal control; the modernization and simplification of European Company Law.

Basle Committee

The Basle Committee (1999) guidelines related to enhancing corporate governance in banking organizations. The guidelines have been influential in the development of corporate governance practices in banks across the world. Sound governance can be practised regardless of the form of a banking organization.

In 2006, the Basle Committee issued new guidance comprising eight sound corporate governance principles:

- Principle 1 – board members should be qualified for their positions, have a clear understanding of their role in corporate governance, and be able to exercise sound judgement about the affairs of the bank;

- Principle 2 – the board of directors should approve and oversee the bank's strategic objectives and corporate values that are communicated throughout the banking organization;

- Principle 3 – the board of directors should set and enforce clear lines of responsibility and accountability throughout the organization;

- Principle 4 – the board should ensure that there is appropriate oversight by senior management consistent with board policy;

- Principle 5 – the board and senior management should effectively utilize the work conducted by the internal audit function, external auditors, and internal control functions;

- Principle 6 – the board should ensure that compensation policies and practices are consistent with the bank's corporate culture, long-term objectives and strategy, and control environment;

- Principle 7 – the bank should be governed in a transparent manner;

- Principle 8 – the board and senior management should understand the bank's operational structure, including where the bank operates in jurisdictions, or through structures, that impede transparency (i.e. 'know your structure').

Source: Basle Committee on Banking Supervision (2006) *Enhancing Corporate Governance for Banking Organisations*.

US corporate governance

Like the UK, the USA has a well-developed market with a diverse shareholder base including institutional investors, financial institutions, and individuals. It also has many of the agency problems associated with the separation of corporate ownership from corporate control.

The USA is somewhat unusual in not having had a definitive corporate governance code in the same way that many other countries have and do. Rather there have been various state and federal developments over a number of years. Some idiosyncratic features include: the Delaware General Corporation Law, which essentially gives companies incorporated in Delaware certain advantages, and the Employee Retirement Income Security Act 1974 (ERISA), which mandates private pension funds to vote their shares. Each of these is dealt with in more detail below.

Delaware corporate law

Over the years, Delaware has built up a body of corporate case law that has become the norm in corporate America. The Delaware approach has been seen as 'company friendly' and indeed the majority of US companies listed on the New York Stock Exchange (NYSE) are registered in Delaware in order to be able to take advantage of the more flexible non-prescriptive approach. The emphasis is on giving boards of directors the authority to pursue corporate strategy and objectives whilst at the same time operating within the concept of fiduciary duty (usually this would mean acting in the best interests of the shareholders, who are the ultimate beneficiaries of the company). In addition, there are certain statutory requirements that need to be abided by such as protection of minority interests. However, on balance, the Delaware law is less procedural than other state law in the USA and hence Delaware is an attractive state in which to register a company.

Employee Retirement Income Security Act 1974

The Employee Retirement Income Security Act 1974 (ERISA) established federal statutory duties of loyalty and prudence for trustees and managers of private pension funds. ERISA has been interpreted as effectively mandating private pension funds to vote their shares, and this includes not just shares held in the USA (domestic shares), but shares held overseas too. It is recommended that a cost–benefit analysis be carried out before purchasing overseas shareholdings to ensure that it will be viable (cost-effective) to vote the overseas shares. Whilst public pension funds are not covered by ERISA, as private pension funds are mandated to vote, there is an expectation that public pension funds will also vote, and this has been the case in practice.

Sarbanes–Oxley Act 2002

More recently, and following directly from the financial scandals of Enron, Worldcom, and Global Crossing, in which it was perceived that the close relationship between companies and their external auditors was largely to blame, the US Congress agreed reforms together with changes to the NYSE Listing Rules that have had a significant impact not just in the USA but around the world. The changes are embodied in the Accounting Industry Reform Act 2002, widely known as the 'Sarbanes–Oxley Act'.

Initially, one of the most publicized aspects of the Sarbanes–Oxley Act was the requirement for CEOs and CFOs to certify that quarterly and annual reports filed on forms 10-Q, 10-K, and 20-F are fully compliant with applicable securities laws and present a fair picture of the financial situation of the company. The penalties for making this certification when aware that the information does not comply with the requirements are severe: up to $1m fine or imprisonment of up to ten years – or both.

The Sarbanes–Oxley Act seeks to strengthen (external) auditor independence and also to strengthen the company's audit committee. Listed companies, for example, must have an audit committee comprised only of independent members, and must also disclose whether they have at least one 'audit committee financial expert' on their audit committee. The 'audit committee financial expert' should be named and the company should state whether the expert is independent of management (for listed companies, the audit committee should comprise only independent members).

The Act establishes a new regulatory body for auditors of US listed firms – the Public Company Accounting Oversight Board (PCAOB) – with which all auditors of US listed companies have to register, including non-US audit firms. Correspondingly, the Securities Exchange Commission (SEC) has issued separate rules that encompass the prohibition of some non-audit services to audit clients, mandatory rotation of audit partners, and auditors' reports on the effectiveness of internal controls. The SEC implementation of the Sarbanes–Oxley Act prohibits nine non-audit services that might impair auditor independence. In many cases, these effectively prohibit the audit firm from either auditing accounting services provided by the audit firm's staff or providing help with systems that will then be audited by the audit firm. These nine areas cover:

- book-keeping or other services related to the accounting records or financial statements of the audited company;
- financial information systems design and implementation;
- appraisal or valuation services, fairness opinions, or contribution-in-kind reports (where the firm provides its opinion on the adequacy of consideration in a transaction);
- actuarial services;
- internal audit outsourcing services;
- management functions/human resources (an auditor should not be a director, officer, or employee of an audit client, nor perform any executive role for the audit client such as supervisory, decision-making, or monitoring);
- broker or dealer, investment adviser, or investment banking services;
- legal services or expert services unrelated to the audit;
- any other service that the PCAOB decides is not permitted.

Interestingly, taxation services may be provided by the auditor to the audit client and certain other services may also be provided with the prior approval of the audit committee (these include non-audit services that do not amount to more than 5 per cent of the total paid by the company to its auditor). Companies are required to disclose in their annual report the fees paid to the 'independent accountant' for each of audit, audit-related, tax, and other services.

There are also requirements relating to the rotation of audit partners such that the lead audit partner should rotate every five years, and is then subject to a five-year period during which he/she cannot be the audit partner for that company. Similarly, other partners involved with the audit, but not acting as the lead partner, are subject to a seven-year rotation followed by a two-year bar. Any member of the audit team is barred for one year from accepting employment in certain specified positions in a company that he/she has audited.

The auditor is required to report to the audit committee various information, which includes all critical accounting policies and practices, and alternative accounting treatments.

The Sarbanes–Oxley Act provides for far-reaching reform and has caused much disquiet outside the USA because the Act applies equally to US and non-US firms with a US listing. However, some of the provisions of the Sarbanes–Oxley Act are in direct conflict with provisions in the law/practice of other countries. In reality, this has led to some companies delisting from the NYSE and has deterred other non-US firms from applying to be listed on the NYSE.

Commission on Public Trust and Private Enterprise 2003

The Commission on Public Trust and Private Enterprise was formed by the Conference Board, an influential US-based non-profit-making organization, to look at the circumstances that gave rise to corporate scandals which resulted in a loss of confidence in the US markets. The Commission's work focused on three main areas – executive compensation, corporate governance, and auditing and accounting. The Commission issued its report on executive compensation in 2002 and this is covered in Chapter 9; the second report, being on corporate governance, and auditing and accounting, was issued in early 2003.

 online resource centre

The Commission listed nine principles relating to corporate governance, which cover the following areas:

- relationship of the board and management;
- fulfilling the board's responsibilities;
- director qualifications;
- role of the nominating/governance committee;
- board evaluation;
- ethics oversight;
- hiring special investigative counsel;
- shareowner involvement;
- long-term share ownership.

In relation to the board, the Commission recommends that careful thought should be given to separating the roles of chairman and CEO. This is an interesting development because the roles of chairman and CEO have traditionally tended to be combined in US companies. By splitting these roles, as in the UK, the US corporations would achieve the separation of the running of the board of directors (chairman) from the executive running of the business (chief executive). The Commission states that the chairman should be an independent director but, where he is not, then a lead independent director can be appointed. If companies choose not to separate the two roles, then a presiding director should be appointed. An important aspect of the lead independent director's role is to act as a liaison between the CEO and the other independent directors, whilst the presiding director would, in addition, take on some of the activities usually carried out by the chairman.

The Commission emphasizes the importance of a substantial majority of independent directors, with appropriate backgrounds, knowledge, and skills to enable them to take an active role in the company and to be satisfied with the company's management, legal, and ethical compliance. The independent directors should be nominated by the nominating/governance committee, whose role would also include stating the requirements for the training of directors. The evaluation of boards via a tiered approach, which would analyse board performance, sub-committee performance, and individual performance, is recommended.

The concept of an ethical culture is something that should be developed at board level and applied across the company. The Commission believes 'that ethical conduct, including adherence to the law's requirements, is vital to a corporation's sustainability and long-term success'.

Special investigative counsel should be appointed by the board (and not management) where it seems that an independent investigation is 'reasonably likely' to implicate company executives.

The Commission tries to encourage shareholders to be more active and behave as owners, and suggests that companies should allow shareholder nominations for board seats. Presently, if investors wish to put forward candidates to challenge the board nominations, they generally have to circulate the details to shareholders themselves at a cost of upwards of $250,000, an amount that is sufficient to deter most investors. However, given the Commission's recommendation and a growing tide of large institutional investors who wish to change the current situation, it seems likely that change may come in the next year or two.

Long-term share ownership, as opposed to a short-term focus, should be encouraged by the company executives adopting and communicating to investors 'a strategy specifically designed to attract investors known to pursue long-term holding investment strategies'. This should encourage a more committed, longer term shareholder base. The other side of the coin is that the Commission suggests that institutional investors should have remuneration policies that align portfolio managers' interests with the long term rather than the short term.

In relation to audit and accounting, the Commission states seven principles:

- the enhanced role of the audit committee;
- audit committee education;
- improving internal controls and internal auditing;
- auditor rotation;
- professional advisers for the audit committee;
- services performed by accounting firms;
- the business model of accounting firms.

The Commission views the seven principles as strengthening the reforms begun by the Sarbanes–Oxley Act and the NYSE, and hopes that they will help to restore public confidence in audit firms, audited financial statements, and hence in the market generally.

The Commission emphasizes that the audit committee should be comprised of independent members with appropriate knowledge and experience. The wider remit of the audit committee includes being responsible for the appointment, remuneration, and oversight of the work of the auditors, with the outside (external) auditors reporting directly to the audit committee. In its turn, the board should review the independence and qualifications of the audit committee members to ensure that they are appropriate. Audit committee members should have an induction to the work of the audit committee and thereafter follow a continuing education programme. It is recommended that all companies should have an internal audit function, with the internal auditor having reporting responsibility to the audit committee via a direct line of communication.

In addition to the above, the Commission recommends rotation of outside audit firms, for example, when the audit firm has been employed by the company for more than ten years, or when a former audit firm partner or manager is employed by the company, or significant non-audit services are provided by the company. Audit committees may retain independent professional advisers (for example, those with no ties to management or audit firm). Accounting firms should limit their services to audit services and closely related services that do not put the auditor 'in an advocacy position'. Finally, the Commission recommends that the 'Big Four' accounting firms should look at their business model, strategies, and focus to ensure that quality auditing is their top priority.

In November 2003, the Securities and Exchange Commission approved new rules on corporate governance proposed and adopted by the NYSE and the Nasdaq Stock Market. The new rules mean a significant strengthening of corporate governance standards for listed companies and are designed to enable the directors, officers, and employees to operate more effectively. The new rules should also enable shareholders to monitor the companies better in terms of their performance, and hopefully to reduce the incidences of corporate scandals or collapses.

The NYSE rules require that the majority of directors are independent and give detailed guidance on who would be classed as independent. Non-management directors should meet at regularly scheduled executive sessions without management being present. A nominating/corporate governance committee, a compensation committee, and an audit committee should each be established and be comprised entirely of independent directors. All committees should have charters detailing their purpose and there should be an annual evaluation of each committee. An internal audit function should be established in each company.

Companies should adopt corporate governance guidelines and disclose these on their websites together with the charters of the various board committees. Companies should also adopt a code of business conduct and ethics.

The CEO would be required to certify to the NYSE each year that he is not aware of any violation by the company of the NYSE's corporate governance listing standards. A public reprimand letter could be issued to any company that violates an NYSE listing standard.

These new rules should restore investor confidence in companies, and in the stock market generally, by significantly strengthening corporate governance structures and notions of ethical behaviour in companies.

Conclusions

Corporate governance is very much an evolving area. In recent years, its development has been driven by the need to restore investor confidence in capital markets. Investors and governments alike have been proactive in seeking reforms that will ensure that corporate boards are more accountable, that qualified independent non-executive (outside) directors can play a key role, that audit committees are able to operate effectively, and that external audit firms are able to perform their audits properly and appropriately. These measures will also help to ensure that the rights of shareholders are protected.

Many of the codes operate using a 'comply or explain' basis and, as we have seen, this means either that a company has to comply fully with the code and state that it has done so, or that it explains why it has not complied fully. Investors will therefore be able to determine to what extent a company has or has not complied, and to assess the company's stated reasons for non-compliance. Investor pressure would tend to be the most immediate response to non-compliance, and such instances may lead investors, particularly those who can exert significant influence on the company (for example, because of the size of their shareholding) to seek further information/assurance from the directors.

We have seen the influence of the Cadbury Code and the OECD Principles on the development of corporate governance codes in many countries. We have discussed the roles of several international bodies such as the World Bank, the Global Corporate Governance Forum, the International Corporate Governance Network, and the Commonwealth Association for Corporate Governance, in the development of corporate governance globally. The report of the EU High Level Group of Company Law Experts has had implications for company law across Europe. Finally, the impact of recent legislation in the USA, the Sarbanes–Oxley Act, and further developments in US corporate governance have been highlighted.

Whilst one can argue that a single model of corporate governance is not suitable for all countries – and certainly the stage of development of the country, its cultural traditions, legal structure, and ownership structure make it unlikely that one model would be appropriate for all countries at any given time – we have seen that there are common core principles that have been influential in the setting of codes across the globe. Whilst there should be flexibility in individual countries, it would seem that there is also a recognition of the key elements of good corporate governance in an international dimension.

■ **SUMMARY**

- The development of corporate governance has been driven, to a large extent, by the desire for more transparency and accountability to help restore investor confidence in the world's stock markets after the damage caused by financial scandals and corporate collapses.

- The Cadbury Code and the OECD Principles, in particular, have each played a major role in the development of corporate governance codes around the world.

- The Cadbury Code's main recommendations include the: establishment of key board committees (audit and remuneration), with a nomination committee suggested as an appropriate way to ensure a transparent appointments process; appointment of at least three independent non-executive (outside) directors; separation of roles of chair and CEO.

- The Cadbury Code utilizes a best practice 'comply or explain' approach in contrast to a mandatory or legislative approach.

- The OECD Principles encompass five main areas: the rights of shareholders, the equitable treatment of shareholders, the role of stakeholders in corporate governance, disclosure and transparency, and the responsibilities of the board.

- Following a few years after the publication of the Cadbury Report, the Greenbury Report, on disclosure of directors' remuneration, and the Hampel Report, which reviewed the implementation of the Cadbury and Greenbury recommendations, were published. In 2003, the Combined Code was revised to take into account the Higgs and Smith reviews. The Combined Code was further revised in 2006.

- A number of influential organizations have issued corporate governance guidelines/statements or have been instrumental in the implementation of better corporate governance globally. These organizations include the World Bank, the Global Corporate Governance Forum, the Commonwealth Association for Corporate Governance, and the International Corporate Governance Network.

- The EU High Level Group of Company Law Experts reported in 2002, making various corporate governance recommendations for listed companies. Amongst their recommendations were that companies should be required to publish an annual corporate governance statement in their accounts and on their websites, and that there should be detailed disclosure of individual directors' remuneration.

- The USA has a number of interesting features including the Delaware General Corporation Law, which gives companies incorporated in Delaware certain advantages, and the Employee Retirement Income Security Act (ERISA), which mandates private pension funds to vote their shares.

- The US Sarbanes–Oxley Act is far reaching, encompassing not only US firms but non-US firms with a US listing. The Act seeks to strengthen auditor independence and also establishes a new regulatory body for auditors for US-listed firms, the Public Company Accounting Oversight Board, with which all auditors of US-listed companies, including non-US audit firms, have to register.

- The Commission on Public Trust and Private Enterprise was formed by the Conference Board and its reports published 2002 and 2003 have focused on executive compensation, corporate governance, and auditing and accounting.

■ QUESTIONS

The discussion questions below cover the key learning points of this chapter. Reading of some of the additional reference material will enhance the depth of the students' knowledge and understanding of these areas.

1. What have been the main influences on the development of corporate governance codes and guidelines?

2. What might be the shortcomings in implementation of corporate governance codes and guidelines?

3. Critically discuss whether it would be desirable to have one model of corporate governance applicable to all countries.

4. What are the advantages and disadvantages of a 'comply or explain' model of corporate governance? How does this compare to a mandatory model?

5. In what ways might the OECD Principles of Corporate Governance help improve shareholders' rights?

6. In what ways might the legal and cultural context of a country impact on the development of the corporate governance model in a given country?

■ REFERENCES

Basle Committee on Banking Supervision (1999), *Enhancing Corporate Governance for Banking Organisations*, Bank for International Settlements, Basle.

___ (2006) *Enhancing Corporate Governance for Banking Organisations*, Bank for International Settlements, Basle.

Cadbury, Sir Adrian (1992), *Report of the Committee on the Financial Aspects of Corporate Governance*, Gee & Co. Ltd., London.

Combined Code (1998), *Combined Code, Principles of Corporate Governance*, Gee & Co. Ltd., London.

___ (2003), *The Combined Code on Corporate Governance*, Financial Reporting Council, London.

___ (2006) *The Combined Code on Corporate Governance*, Financial Reporting Council, London.

Conference Board (2003), *Commission on Public Trust and Private Enterprise Findings and Recommendations Part 2: Corporate Governance and Part 3: Audit and Accounting*, Conference Board, New York.

Employee Retirement Income Security Act (1974), Department of Labor, Washington DC.

Greenbury, Sir Richard (1995), *Directors' Remuneration*, Gee & Co. Ltd., London.

Hampel, Sir Ronnie (1998), *Committee on Corporate Governance: Final Report*, Gee & Co. Ltd., London.

Higgs, D. (2003), *Review of the Role and Effectiveness of Non-Executive Directors*, Department of Trade and Industry, London.

ICGN (1999), *Statement on Global Corporate Governance Principles*, International Corporate Governance Network, London.

_____ (2005), *Statement on Global Corporate Governance Principles*, International Corporate Governance Network, London.

Myners' Report (2001), *Myners Report on Institutional Investment*, HM Treasury, London.

OECD (1999), *Principles of Corporate Governance*, OECD, Paris.

_____ (2004), *Principles of Corporate Governance*, OECD, Paris.

Sarbanes–Oxley Act (2002), US Legislature.

Smith, Sir Robert (2003), *Audit Committees Combined Code Guidance*, Financial Reporting Council, London.

Turnbull, N. (1999), *Internal Control: Guidance for Directors on the Combined Code*, Institute of Chartered Accountants in England and Wales, London.

_____ (2005), *Internal Control: Revised Guidance for Directors on the Combined Code*, Financial Reporting Council, London.

Winter, J. (2002), *Report of the High Level Group of Company Law Experts on a Modern Regulatory Framework for Company Law in Europe*, EU Commission, Brussels.

■ USEFUL WEBSITES

www.acca.co.uk The website of the Association of Chartered Certified Accountants gives information about corporate governance and their related activities.

www.bis.org The website of the Bank for International Settlements contains information about central banks and other agencies and has the full text of the Basle Committee corporate governance recommendations.

www.conference-board.org/ The Conference Board website gives details of their corporate governance activities and publications.

www.ecgi.org The European Corporate Governance Institute website has details of global corporate governance developments. Corporate governance codes for countries around the world are listed and in most cases can be downloaded.

www.frc.co.uk The Financial Reporting Council's website contains details of its activities and those of its operating bodies.

www.fsa.gov.uk The Financial Services Authority website contains information about various regulatory aspects, including corporate governance, of capital markets.

www.icaew.co.uk The website of the Institute of Chartered Accountants in England and Wales provides updates on corporate governance issues.

www.icgn.org This website contains information about corporate governance developments and guidelines issued by the International Corporate Governance Network.

www.icsastudent.org/ This website of the Institute of Chartered Secretaries and Administrators contains useful information about various aspects of corporate governance.

www.oecd.org The OECD website contains useful information relating to corporate governance for both member and non-member states.

www.worldbank.org The World Bank website has information about various corporate governance developments.

PART TWO

Owners and Stakeholders

<table>
<tr><td>

4

</td><td>

Shareholders and Stakeholders

</td></tr>
</table>

LEARNING OBJECTIVES

- To understand the difference between shareholders and stakeholders
- To be aware of the various different stakeholder groups
- To have an overview of the way that shareholders and stakeholders are provided for in various corporate governance codes and guidelines
- To understand the roles that shareholders and stakeholders can play in companies and the development of corporate governance

---

Shareholders and stakeholders

The term 'stakeholder' can encompass a wide range of interests: it refers to any individual or group on which the activities of the company have an impact. Shareholders can be viewed as a stakeholder group but, for the purposes of this discussion, we will view shareholders as being distinct from other stakeholder groups. Why? Firstly, shareholders invest their money to provide risk capital for the company and, secondly, in many legal jurisdictions, shareholders' rights are enshrined in law whereas those of the wider group of stakeholders are not. Of course, this varies from jurisdiction to jurisdiction, with creditors' rights strongly protected in some countries, and employee rights' strongly protected in others.

As highlighted in Chapter 2 in the discussion of stakeholder theory, one rationale for effectively privileging shareholders over other stakeholders is that they are the recipients of the residual free cash flow (being the profits remaining once other stakeholders, such as loan creditors, have been paid). This means that the shareholders have a vested interest in trying to ensure that resources are used to maximum effect, which in turn should be to the benefit of society as a whole.

The simplest definition of a shareholder seems straightforward enough: an individual, institution, firm, or other entity that owns shares in a company. Of course, the reality of the situation can be much more complicated with beneficial owners and cross-holdings making the chain of ownership complex. Shareholders' rights are generally protected by

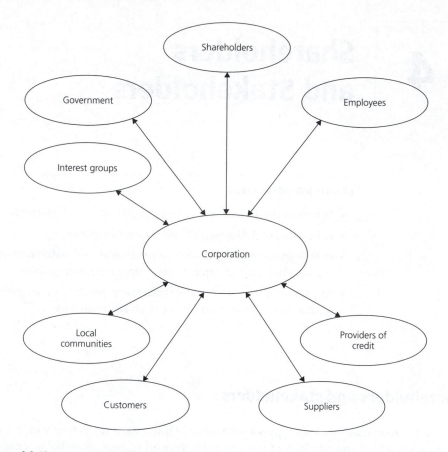

Figure 4.1 The corporation and its stakeholders

law, although the extent and effectiveness of this protection varies from country to country. However, the definition of a stakeholder is much less clear and along with this lack of clarity comes an opaqueness regarding the role of stakeholders and the protection of their rights.

There are various stakeholder groups that may have an interest in a company's performance and activities. Stakeholders include: employees, suppliers, customers, banks, and other creditors; the government; various 'interest' groups, for example, environmental groups; indeed anyone on whom the activities of the company may have an impact. Figure 4.1 illustrates the various groups whose interests the company may need to take into account.

Stakeholder groups

There are various stakeholder groups: some directly related to the company, such as employees, providers of credit, suppliers and customers; others more indirectly related to the company, such as the local communities of the towns or cities in which it operates, environmental groups, and the government. Looking at each of these in turn, we can clarify the interest that each group might have as a stakeholder.

Employees

The employees of a company have an interest in the company because it provides their livelihood in the present day and, at some future point, employees will often also be in receipt of a pension provided by the company's pension scheme. In terms of present-day employment, employees will be concerned with their pay and working conditions, and how the company's strategy will impact on these. Of course, the long-term growth and prosperity of the company is important for the longer term view of the employees, particularly as concerns pension benefits in the future.

Most companies include, in their annual report and accounts, a statement or report to the employees stating in what ways they are looking after the employees' interests. The report will usually mention training programmes, working conditions, and equal opportunities. Many companies have employee share schemes that give the employees the opportunity to own shares in the company, and feel more of a part of it; the theory being that the better the company does (through employees' efforts etc.), the more the employees themselves will benefit as their shares increase in price.

Companies need also to consider and work with the employees' trade unions, recognizing that a good relationship with the unions is desirable. The trade unions may, amongst other things, act as a conduit for company employee information dissemination, or be helpful when trying to ascertain the employees' views. Increasingly, trade unions are exerting their influence, via the pension funds, pressing for change by use of their voting rights.

Companies need also to consider and comply with employee legislation whether related to equal opportunities, health and safety at work, or any other aspect. Companies should also have in place appropriate whistle-blowing procedures for helping to ensure that if employees feel that there is inappropriate behaviour in the company, they can 'blow the whistle' on these activities whilst minimizing the risk of adverse consequences for themselves as a result of this action.

Providers of credit

Providers of credit include banks and other financial institutions. Providers of credit want to be confident that the companies to which they lend are going to be able to repay the debts. They will seek assurance from the annual report and accounts, and from various management accounts and forecasts that companies produce. It is in the company's best interest to maintain the confidence of providers of finance to ensure that no calls are made for repayment of funds, that they are willing to lend to the company in the future, and that the company is able to borrow at the best possible rate.

Suppliers

Suppliers have an interest in the companies that they supply on two grounds. First, having supplied the company with goods or services, they want to be sure that they will be paid for these and in a timely fashion. Second, they will be interested in the continuance of the company because they will wish to have a sustainable outlet for their goods and services.

Sometimes, suppliers will be supplying specialized equipment or services and if the company it supplies has financial difficulties, then this can have a severe impact on the supplier as well. Of course, on an ongoing basis, suppliers of goods and services will also like to be paid on time because otherwise they will have problems with their own cash flow and meeting their own costs, such as labour and materials, incurred in supplying the company in the first place. So, ideally, the companies supplied will treat their suppliers with understanding and ensure that they settle their debts on time. In practice, many large companies will make their suppliers wait for payment, occasionally for such a length of time that the supplier either ends up with severe financial difficulties or refuses to supply the company in future.

Customers

A company's customers will want to try to make sure that they can buy the same product time and again from the company. The company itself will presumably be building up its customer loyalty through various marketing exercises, and customers themselves will get used to a familiar product that they will want to buy in the future. Sometimes, a product bought from one company will become part of a product made by the customer, and again it will be important for the customer to be assured that they can continue to buy and incorporate that product into their own production.

Increasingly, customers are also more aware of social, environmental, and ethical aspects of corporate behaviour and will try to ensure that the company supplying them is acting in a corporately socially responsible manner.

Local communities

Local communities have a number of interests in the companies that operate in their region. First, the companies will be employing large numbers of local people and it will be in the interest of sustained employment levels that companies in the locality operate in an efficient way. Should the company's fortunes start to decline, then unemployment might rise and may lead to part of the workforce moving away from the area to seek jobs elsewhere. This, in turn, would have an effect on local schools, as the number of pupils declined, and the housing market would be hit too as demand for housing in the area declined. However, local communities will also be concerned that companies in the area act in an environmentally friendly way because the last thing they want is pollution in local rivers, in the soil, or in the atmosphere more generally. It is therefore in the local community's interest that companies in their locality continue to thrive, but do so in a way that takes account of local and national concerns.

Environmental groups

Environmental groups will seek to ensure that companies operate to both national and international environmental standards such as the CERES Principles and the Global

Reporting Initiative (GRI) Sustainability Guidelines (these are discussed in more detail in Chapter 7). Increasingly, environmental issues are viewed as part of the mainstream rather than being at the periphery as a 'wish list'. The recognition that an environmentally responsible company should also, in the longer term, be as profitable, if not more so, as one that does not act in an environmentally responsible way is in many ways self-evident. An environmentally responsible company will not subject its workers to potentially hazardous processes without adequate protection (which unfortunately does still happen despite the best endeavours of health and safety regulations), will not pollute the environment, and will, where possible, use recyclable materials or engage in a recycling process. Ultimately, all of these things will benefit society at large and the company itself.

Government

The government has an interest in companies for several diverse reasons. Firstly, as with the local and environmental groups – although not always with such commitment – it will try to make sure that companies act in a socially responsible way taking account of social, ethical, and environmental considerations. Secondly, it will analyse corporate trends for various purposes such as employment levels, monetary policy, and market supply and demand of goods and services. Lastly, but not least, it will be looking at various aspects to do with fiscal policy, such as capital allowances, incentives for investing in various industries or various parts of the country, and, of course, the taxation raised from companies.

Guidance on shareholders' and stakeholders' interests

There are a variety of codes, principles, and guidelines that include a discussion of the role of shareholders' and stakeholders' interests in a company and how the corporate governance system might accommodate these interests. This section looks at some of the most influential of these publications.

OECD

There are two main OECD publications that give some thought to this area. First, there is the OECD (1998) report on 'Corporate Governance: Improving Competitiveness and Access to Capital in Global Markets' by the Business Sector Advisory Group on Corporate Governance. This report recognizes that the company's central mission is long-term enhancement of shareholder value but that companies operate in the larger society, and that there may be different societal pressures and expectations which may impact on the financial objective to some extent so that non-financial objectives may need to be addressed as well.

The OECD Principles of Corporate Governance (1999), revised in 2004, include as one of the principles, the role of stakeholders in corporate governance. The Principles (2004) state that 'the corporate governance framework should recognize the rights of

online
resource
centre

stakeholders established by law or through mutual agreements and encourage active co-operation between corporations and stakeholders in creating wealth, jobs, and the sustainability of financially sound enterprises'. This really highlights two aspects: firstly, that the rights of stakeholders will depend to a large extent on the legal provision for stakeholders in any given country – one would expect that stakeholders would have a right of redress for any violation of their rights; secondly, that stakeholders do have a role to play in the long-term future of businesses and that the corporate governance framework should 'permit performance-enhancing mechanisms for stakeholder participation' and that stakeholders should have access to relevant information in order to participate effectively.

RSA Tomorrow's Company

The Royal Society of Arts (RSA) in the UK is a multidisciplinary independent body that has commissioned reports in various areas including one called 'Tomorrow's Company', which was led by Mark Goyder. The Tomorrow's Company Report (1995) advocated an inclusive approach for business in its relationship with various stakeholder groups. The inclusive approach recognizes that there is an interdependence between the employees, investors, customers, and suppliers, which increasingly means that the business needs to take a long-term view rather than having the short-term focus on increasing shareholder value that many businesses are perceived as having.

There was significant demand from businesses involved in the RSA Inquiry for an organization to carry forward its work and Tomorrow's Company is now well established as 'a not-for-profit research and agenda-setting organisation committed to creating a future for business which makes equal sense to staff, shareholders and society'.

The RSA itself continues to emphasize the impact of global citizenship – 'everything we do affects others everywhere' – and encourages a zero-waste society.

Hampel (1998)

The Hampel Committee was established in the UK in 1995 following the recommendations of the Cadbury (1992) and Greenbury (1995) committees that a new committee should review the implementation of their findings. Whilst recognizing that 'good governance ensures that constituencies (stakeholders) with a relevant interest in the company's business are fully taken into account', the Hampel Report (1998) stated quite clearly that the objective of all listed companies is the 'preservation and the greatest practicable enhancement over time of their shareholders' investment'.

The report took the view that whilst management should develop appropriate relationships with its various stakeholder groups, it should have regard to the overall objective of the company: to preserve and enhance shareholder value over time. The report also highlighted the practical point that 'directors as a board are responsible *for relations with* stakeholders; but they are accountable *to* shareholders'. This is a fundamental point because if it were not so, then it would be very difficult to identify exactly to which stakeholder groups directors might be responsible and the extent of their responsibilities.

Hermes Principles (2002) and Hermes Corporate Governance Principles (2006)

Hermes is one of the largest institutional investors in the UK with several million people depending on Hermes' investments to generate their retirement income. Hermes has long been one of the most active institutional investors in corporate governance and, in 2002, it published the Hermes Principles. In introducing the Principles, Hermes state:

Hermes' overriding requirement is that companies be run in the long-term interest of shareholders. Companies adhering to this principle will not only benefit their shareholders, but also we would argue, the wider economy in which the company and its shareholders participate. We believe a company run in the long-term interest of shareholders will need to manage effectively relationships with its employees, suppliers and customers, to behave ethically and have regard for the environment and society as a whole.

In 2006, Hermes introduced its Hermes Corporate Governance Principles, which form the basis of its engagement with the companies in which it, or its clients, invest. These Principles have two parts: the Global Principles and the Regional Principles. The former are based on the ICGN Global Corporate Governance Principles, whilst the latter explain which corporate governance codes or guidance, produced by local market participants or regulators, are supported by Hermes.

EU Accounts Modernization Directive

The EU Accounts Modernization Directive was intended to produce more comparability across the financial reporting of its member states. By its provisions, companies in various countries in the EU are subject to common standards of both the level of disclosure and content of disclosures. The Directive applies to all medium and large EU companies and, effective from 1 April 2005, the Directive requires additional material to be included in the Director's Report to provide an enhanced review of a company's business. The Directive states that

the review must, to the extent necessary for an understanding of the development, performance or position of the business of the company, include:

(a) analysis using financial key performance indicators, and

(b) where appropriate, analysis using other key performance indicators, including information relating to environmental matters and employee matters.

Company Law Reform

The Company Law Reform Bill was published in November 2005 after extensive consultation on the reform of existing UK companies law. There were several significant provisions in relation to shareholders and stakeholders that it is appropriate to mention in this chapter.

First, in relation to directors' duties, the Company Law Reform Bill (2005) draws on the concept of 'enlightened shareholder value'. In the DTI consultative Company Law Reform (2005) document, in relation to directors' duties, it says:

The statement of duties will be drafted in a way which reflects modern business needs and wider expectations of responsible business behaviour. The CLR [Company Law Review] proposed that the basic goal for directors should be the success of the company for the benefit of its members as a whole; but that, to reach this goal, directors would need to take a properly balanced view of the implications of decisions over time and foster effective relationships with employees, customers and suppliers, and in the community more widely. The Government strongly agrees that this approach, which the CLR called 'enlightened shareholder value', is most likely to drive long-term company performance and maximise overall competitiveness and wealth and welfare for all. It will therefore be reflected in the statement of directors' duties, and in new reporting arrangements for quoted companies under the Operating and Financial Review Regulations.

In the Company Law Reform Bill, it is made clear that a director's duty is to

act in the way he considers, in good faith, would be most likely to promote the success of the company for the benefit of its members as a whole [and] a director must (so far as reasonably practicable) have regard to:

(a) the likely consequences of any decision in the long term,

(b) the interests of the company's employees,

(c) the need to foster the company's business relationships with suppliers, customers and others,

(d) the impact of the company's operations on the community and the environment,

(e) the desirability of the company maintaining a reputation for high standards of business conduct, and

(f) the need to act fairly as between members of the company.

(Part 10, Chapter 2, section 156)

Clearly, there is a significant emphasis being given here for directors to have regard to wider stakeholder interests as well as to the shareholders. This emphasis was also apparent in the intentions of the Company Law Reform Bill, which proposed that directors of a quoted company must prepare an operating and financial review (OFR) for each financial year. The OFR would include, inter alia, information about: environmental matters including the impact of the business of the company on the environment; the company's employees; social and community issues.

However, the Chancellor announced in late November 2005 that the government had decided to remove the statutory requirement for quoted companies to prepare an OFR. Quoted companies will have to include a business review as part of the directors' report to comply with the minimum requirements of the EU Accounts Modernization Directive. The content of the business review is less prescribed although it may include much of the information that would have been contained in an OFR. However, the move to abolish a statutory OFR has caused some disquiet because it is less clear-cut as to what disclosures companies may now feel it appropriate to make on environmental, social, and related issues.

In January 2006, the Department for Environment, Food, and Rural Affairs (defra) issued voluntary guidance on environmental key performance indicators (KPIs) that companies might include in their disclosures about environmental reporting. The KPIs might also provide appropriate information for the business review.

In July 2006, the title of the Company Law Reform Bill was changed to 'Companies Bill' during its committee stage in the House of Commons.

King Report (2002)

The King Report (2002) is a comprehensive document that provides guidelines for corporate governance in South Africa. It builds on the earlier King Report published in 1994, which stated that there should be an integrated approach to corporate governance and took into account the interests of various stakeholder groups. King (2002) states that the inclusive approach is fundamental to the operation of business in South Africa. The company should define its purpose, decide on the values by which the company's day-to-day activities will be carried on, and identify its stakeholders; all of these aspects should be taken into account when the company develops its strategies for achieving corporate objectives. The King Report is covered in more detail in Chapter 13 but it is mentioned here as a good example of a code that emphasizes the inclusive approach and the importance of considering the interests of stakeholders.

Roles of shareholders and stakeholders

In reality, the involvement of shareholders and stakeholders will depend on national laws and customs and also the individual company's approach. However, even in countries whose companies traditionally have not been profit-oriented, such as state-owned enterprises, as those countries now seek to develop their capital markets and raise external finance, the shareholders' interests will rise to the top of the corporate agenda. Of course, stakeholder interests cannot, and should not, be ignored but as capital markets increasingly converge, so will the shareholders' interests become paramount in more countries.

As can be seen from the codes/principles discussed above, whilst recognizing that companies need to take into account the views of stakeholders, in the UK, the prima facie purpose of a company is the maintenance or enhancement of long-term shareholder value. In the UK, neither the legal nor the corporate governance systems make any provision for employee representation on the board, nor for representation of other stakeholder groups such as providers of finance, and there has been consistent opposition to representation of stakeholder groups on corporate boards. On the other hand, the UK has employee share schemes so employees can be involved in that way, although, of course, they do not have the same type of input as if they were represented on the board.

In the UK and the USA, the emphasis is on the relationship between the shareholders (owners) and the directors (managers). In contrast, the German and French corporate governance systems, which view companies as more of a partnership between capital and labour, provide for employee representation at board level, whilst banks (providers of finance) may also be represented on the supervisory board. However, it is interesting to note that one downside of employee representation on the board is that decisions, which may be in the best interests of the company as a whole but not of the workforce, may not get made, so leading to sub-optimal decision-making. Whilst the German and French corporate governance systems are dealt with in detail in Chapter 10, it is useful at this point to highlight the different approach to stakeholders and the impact that this may have on the company.

Another very important point is that if the directors of a company were held to be responsible to shareholders and the various stakeholders groups alike, then what would be the corporate objective? How could the board function effectively if there were a multiplicity of different objectives, no one of which took priority over the others? At present in many countries, the enhancement of shareholder wealth is the overriding criterion, but if it were not, what would be? This could actually lead to quite a dangerous situation where directors and managers were not really accountable.

Given that all companies operate within a wider society, the interests of shareholders and stakeholders are often intertwined. Also, the distinction between shareholders and stakeholders is often not clear-cut. For example, Charkham and Simpson (1999) point out that, in the UK, shareholders are often drawn from other stakeholder groups: 'Pension funds are the largest group of shareholders, yet their assets are drawn from the savings of half the workforce and invested to provide retirement income when this group becomes pensioners.' Similar statements can be made about the insurance companies, and also about individual shareholders who may also be customers of the companies in which they invest, for example, utilities.

However, what shareholders can do effectively is to bring the board to account for their actions. So we come back to the phrase in the Hampel Report (1998): 'Directors as a board are responsible *for relations with* stakeholders; but they are accountable *to* shareholders.'

Conclusions

Companies operate in a wider society not within a defined corporate vacuum. Therefore, companies should take account of the views of various stakeholders in addition to those of shareholders. Whilst the corporate objective is generally to maintain or enhance shareholder value, the impact of the company's activities on its other stakeholders must be taken into account when deciding the strategy to be developed for achieving the corporate objective.

By taking account of the views and interests of its stakeholders, the company should be able to achieve its objectives with integrity and help to achieve sustainability of its long-term operations.

■ SUMMARY

- Shareholders are the providers of capital. Often, the corporate objective is expressed in terms of maximizing shareholder value.

- Stakeholders include employees, providers of credit, customers, suppliers, local communities, government, environmental and social groups – in fact, any group on which the company's activities may have an impact.

- Most corporate governance codes and guidelines recognize that the prima facie objective of the company is the maximization of shareholder wealth. However, there is also the understanding that the achievement of this objective should have regard to the interests of various stakeholder groups.

- Stakeholders can make their views known to the company and, in some countries, may have representation on the company's decision-making bodies (such as the supervisory board in Germany). However, in the UK and many other countries, it is the shareholders who can hold the board of directors accountable for their actions.

■ QUESTIONS

The discussion questions below cover the key learning points of this chapter. Reading of some of the additional reference material will enhance the depth of the students' knowledge and understanding of these areas.

1. What stakeholder groups might directors of a company have to take into consideration, and how might the stakeholders' interests impact on the company?

2. In what ways might stakeholders' interests conflict with each other?

3. What role do you believe that stakeholders should play in corporate governance?

4. Critically contrast the roles of shareholders and stakeholders.

5. 'Directors as a board are responsible *for relations with* stakeholders; but they are accountable *to* shareholders' (Hampel 1998). Critically discuss this statement.

6. What corporate governance mechanisms might help with representing the views of stakeholders?

■ **FT ARTICLE**

Global strategy faces local constraints

RUTH AGUILERA & GEORGE YIP

Variations in national corporate governance systems and the degree to which groups of stakeholders influence strategy decisions can have a substantial impact on a company's efforts to look beyond its borders

Corporate governance systems vary across countries, and these differences directly affect both the process for developing global strategies and the kinds of strategies that can be adopted. In this article, we examine how different corporate governance systems might influence decisions about company globalisation and, in particular, decisions to take operations abroad.

Global strategy decisions pose a very tough test for the effectiveness of corporate governance systems in that they seek to maximise profits and global competitiveness, often at the expense, at least in the short term, of some corporate governance players. By definition, a global strategy means taking a global, rather than a single-country, view of strategy, and this can be hard for those players with strong ties to the company's home country. Moreover, some aspects of global strategy, particularly the overseas relocation of jobs, mean real sacrifices for some, especially employees.

Players in corporate governance

We identify five critical stakeholder players that most affect the company's decisions about global strategy:

Employees and their collective organisations, such as unions and work councils, have various legislated, statutory, contractual or negotiated rights, such as employment conditions, that must be considered.

The *board of directors* is the ultimate governing body of an organisation and, as such, it must approve all company strategies, including global ones.

The *top management team* is charged with day-to-day responsibility for strategy and operations.

Shareholders exercise their voice through their shareholder rights, such as cumulative voting or proxy voting, but they can also exit the company by selling their shares if they do not agree with globalisation strategies or other decisions.

Finally, *governments* set and enforce the overall rules of national corporate governance; they design specific norms about international business, such as trade policies; and they can selectively intervene in individual globalisation decisions, such as moving operations abroad, or subsidising a given company because of its national strategic relevance. Supranational governments, such as the European Union, also play a role in regulating corporate governance, the consultation rights of workers, bankruptcy procedures and the like. We exclude other stakeholders, such as customers, suppliers and competitors, because they tend to be less involved with corporate governance.

Cross-national differences

Corporate governance systems vary by country, as do the roles and power of the five corporate governance players. Figure 1 summarises these differences for some major countries and types of corporate governance systems: the "Anglo-American" systems of the US and UK; the "Continental" systems of Germany, France and Italy; and the "Extended" system of Japan.

In the rest of this article, we briefly describe the main characteristics of these corporate players across countries and their potential influence on global decision-making.

Employees

Two main variables differentiate employees, as a collective group, across countries. First, the country's labour market will influence the flexibility and mobility of employees. Countries such as the US that have employment at will, whereby a contract can be terminated at any time, are likely to have flexible labour markets and short-term labour commitment. Generally, the consequence is that labour training is done outside the company and employees have general and portable skills.

In more rigid labour markets, such as Germany and Japan, companies invest a great deal in bespoke, inhouse training, which tends to result in more highly skilled labour forces and company-specific skills. These, in turn, are less transferable from one company to another.

Second, the strength of labour unions and unionisation rates varies from one country to another. For instance in France, where union rights are extended to all employees regardless of union affiliation, unionisation will have a much greater influence on corporate decision-making than in the US or UK, where only union members benefit from collective bargaining agreements. Japanese companies tend to have enterprise unionism, which leads to collective bargaining at the company level and grants a strong voice to employees.

We consider that employees who are less mobile and who have a stronger voice within the company will get more involved in global strategy decisions. Generally speaking, these employees will seek to keep their jobs domestically as opposed to moving them around the globe.

In 2004 for example, employee opposition to job losses prevented the restructuring, via a merger with a foreign partner, of France's financially troubled Alstom, a major producer of ships and trains. In the same year Volkswagen, despite suffering from very high labour costs, had to promise its western German employees job security until 2011 in exchange for a wage freeze until 2007 and more flexible working hours. The company's workers wield considerable power, partly through codetermination rights, which require employees to be consulted on corporate decisions.

Top management teams

Cross-national variation in top management teams is mostly reflected in their functional background and their international experience, as well as the patterns of managerial career mobility. Managers in the US and UK tend to have professional backgrounds (often with formal business school education) and strong functional backgrounds in finance or marketing. This is not the case in Germany, where managers are more technically oriented. In France, managers often share a common *grandes écoles* background and ideology, frequently linking them back to government positions that they have previously held.

There is also variation in the international experience and background of managers, with US managers having the most foreign-born individuals in their management teams and France, Italy and Japan the least. Managerial career mobility tends to be very fluid in the US and UK due to open labour markets whereas, in Japan and France, managers tend to remain with a company for a long period of time.

The presence of foreign nationals and managers with prior international experience, combined with open labour markets, means that teams will be more likely to push global strategies. In the US, more and more companies have or had foreign-born CEOs, including Charles Bell of McDonald's, who is Australian, E. Neville Isdell of Coca Cola, who is Irish, and Carlos Gutierrez of Kellogg's, who was born in Cuba. There is also wide acceptance of leaders from across borders in the UK – consider Americans Marjorie Scardino at Pearson and Rose Marie Bravo at Burberry, Indian born Arun Sarin at Vodafone, and French born Jean-Pierre Garnier at GlaxoSmithKline.

Conversely, management teams dominated by closed labour markets and ties to government, or founding or controlling family, will be more reluctant to engage in global strategies, mostly due to their preference for keeping control domestically. For example, Germany's Bertelsmann, one of the world's largest media companies, is controlled by the Mohn family. In 2002, the company fired its chief executive, Thomas Middelhoff, for pursuing global expansion strategies too vigorously and for what was perceived as an abrasive US-style approach to management. Middelhoff was replaced by Gunter Thielen, who had long term ties to the Mohn family.

Shareholders

Countries vary in their mix of types of shareholders. At one extreme, the US and UK have mostly arms length, neutral shareholders, who are focused on shareholder value maximisation. Although many UK shareholders are large institutions, such as pension funds, these generally play passive roles, compared with the shareholder activism that arose in the US among institutional investors such as Calpers. Japan has plenty of institutional shareholders, but these tend not to be neutral and often act as part of a network, or *keiretsu*, that supports the role of the company and, hence, incumbent management. Germany's main trait is that banks play a leading role in influencing corporate policy at many companies, both as lenders and shareholders.

Employee shareholders typically use their ownership to block the global relocation of jobs. This applies even in the US where United Airlines provides a rare example of a large public company with majority ownership by its employees (55 per cent owned by an employee stock ownership plan). This employee stake and, hence, control have greatly constrained the ability of the airline to relocate jobs overseas. For example, United's flight attendants' union has been able to block plans to staff more flights from its lower-cost Taiwan base.

Boards of directors

The composition of boards of directors also shows strong contrasts across countries. For instance, Japanese companies are renowned for having very large and inefficient boards, sometimes with more than 50 members. Japanese boards also have very few outsiders to monitor managers and the strategic direction of the company.

Italian and French boards are considered medium-sized, although still quite

inefficient due to the lack of outsiders. Germany is unusual because it tends to have a wide variety of stakeholders represented in the upper (supervisory) board, such as employees, industrial banks and suppliers. In November 2004, a commission convened by BDA, the German employers association and BDI, the industry federation, concluded that the German co-determination system had become a hindrance to German companies operating internationally and a barrier to inward investment. It recommended changes to the laws, which were last revised in 1976. Under this proposal, individual companies would be free to choose a system of employee representation, taken from three options, ranging from retention of the current system to a looser consultation system separate from the supervisory board.

France Telecom provides an example of how board representation can be distorted by national interests. Although privatised in 1997, France Telecom still has significant intervention by the French government. Out of 15 members of the board of directors, only seven are elected by the shareholders meeting, while three represent employees and five members represent the French government.

The most active boards are in the UK and US, in part due to the enforcement of corporate law. In the UK, the Cadbury Report and subsequent codes of good governance have had a great deal of influence in designing efficient boards. In the US, the Sarbanes-Oxley Act of 2002 has also introduced pressure for a higher percentage of outsiders on boards.

Government

Finally, countries also differ in terms of the degree of government intervention in their economies and protectionism of their markets. Government intervention is usually in the form of market regulation. A representative measure for government intervention in the economy is regulation around takeovers. The US and, to a lesser degree, the UK have weak takeover barriers and it is mostly up to individual companies to design anti-takeover measures. Conversely, in countries such as France, Germany, Italy and Japan, government intervention often provides strong takeover barriers, such as golden shares, which bestow on the holder veto power over changes to the company's charter.

The various hindrances to hostile takeovers in many continental European countries continue to make it difficult for foreign companies to make acquisitions across borders in Europe. In 2001, plans for a European takeover code, which would guarantee the right of shareholders to be consulted during bids, were shelved following objections from the German government. The previous year Vodafone, the UK telecoms company, made a successful hostile bid for Mannesmann, a German telecoms company, and the German government was worried that other local companies might fall into foreign hands. For example, Volkswagen is protected from takeover by special law and the European code threatened to undermine this protection. Nevertheless, individual countries, including Germany, are now making gradual changes to make takeovers easier.

Sweden, which falls in the Continental governance model, is one of several countries that use multiple voting rights to help prevent its companies from becoming vulnerable to takeover. The Wallenberg family, for instance, owns only 7 per cent of Ericsson, the telecoms company, yet controls the company by owning a class of shares that carries 1,000 times the rights of ordinary shares.

France is also particularly active in preserving national ownership of major companies. In 2004, the French government brokered the takeover of Aventis, a French-German pharmaceutical company, by France's Sanofi-Synthelabo, while blocking a bid from Switzerland's Novartis. Similarly, France blocked Germany's Siemens from bidding for Alstom's railway operations, which manufacture the high-speed TGV trains.

How managers can use their corporate governance systems

Top managers need to recognise that they are not in sole charge. Global (and other) strategy is an equilibrium game among corporate governance players. Managers need to work on building coalitions and aligning interests behind a common approach.

Assuming that you want to improve your use of global strategy, then how can you do this from the various countries? If you are a manager in an Anglo-American system, then you are generally in luck. Your country's corporate governance system is a source of competitive advantage. A manager in a Continental system faces many constraints, especially from the legal involvement of employees. But, committed employees can also be a major source of global competitive advantage.

In the Continental system, managers have to align, trade off and meet other stakeholders' interests halfway. They have to craft their language and rhetoric to meet the other players' expectations. The watchwords here are consensus and social cohesion.

In the Extended (Japanese) system, companies have generally capitalised on their export-oriented model and high innovation driven by employee loyalty. But because of the rigidity of their corporate governance system, they have not exploited as much as they could the different dimensions of global strategy. We would recommend that the system becomes more open in terms of the diversity of the top management team and more flexible in their governance by introducing leaner boards as well as allowing greater levels of shareholder activism.

"Managers need to build coalitions and align interests behind a common approach"

In sum, if governments care to sustain national competitiveness and to help their companies to globalise, then they should assess the degree to which the players in their corporate governance system are aligned with each other and with their intended global strategies. For example, France might need to upgrade its compensation policies to recruit and retain world-class talent in the top management teams of its global companies.

Government policies should also become less inimical to foreign owners and use such capital to provide the much-needed global knowledge. This can only be accomplished if the right mechanisms are in place to give a voice to these foreign owners. We think that governments have the responsibility as well as the policy tools to gear the country's corporate governance system so that it enhances national competitiveness.

■ REFERENCES

Cadbury, Sir Adrian (2002), *Corporate Governance and Chairmanship: A Personal View*, Oxford University Press, Oxford.

Charkham, J. and Simpson, A. (1999), *Fair Shares: The Future of Shareholder Power and Responsibility*, Oxford University Press, Oxford.

Company Law Reform (2005), *Company Law Reform March 2005*, DTI, London.

Company Law Reform Bill (2005), *Company Law Reform Bill (HL)*, Her Majesty's Stationery Office, London.

Defra (2006), *Environmental Key Performance Indicators, Reporting Guidelines for UK Business*, Defra/Trucost, London.

Hampel, Sir Ronnie (1998), *Committee on Corporate Governance: Final Report*, Gee & Co. Ltd., London.

Hermes, (2002), *The Hermes Principles*, Hermes Pensions Management Ltd., London.

—— (2006), *Hermes Corporate Governance Principles*, Hermes Pensions Management Ltd., London.

King, M. (2002), *King Report on Corporate Governance for South Africa – 2002*, King Committee on Corporate Governance, Institute of Directors in Southern Africa, Parktown, South Africa.

OECD (1998), '*Corporate Governance: Improving Competitiveness and Access to Capital in Global Markets*', A Report to the OECD by the Business Sector Advisory Group on Corporate Governance, OECD, Paris.

—— (1999), *OECD Principles of Corporate Governance*, OECD, Paris.

—— (2004), *OECD Principles of Corporate Governance*, OECD, Paris.

Tomorrow's Company (1995), Royal Society of Arts, London.

■ USEFUL WEBSITES

http://asp.thecorporatelibrary.net The website of the Corporate Library, which has comprehensive information about various aspects of corporate governance including shareholders and stakeholders.

www.bsr.org This is the website of the Business for Social Responsibility (BSR), a global non-profit organization that promotes corporate success in ways that respect ethical values, people, communities, and the environment.

www.defra.gov.uk The website of the Department for Environment, Food and Rural Affairs, which contains various publications relating to the environment, sustainability, and related matters.

www.dti.gov.uk The website of the Department of Trade and Industry is a comprehensive source of material relating to various aspects of business success, sustainability, and globalization.

www.parliament.uk The website of the UK Parliament covers parliamentary debates in the House of Commons and House of Lords and has a wide range of publications.

www.rsa.org.uk/ The website of the Royal Society of Arts, a charity that encourages the development of a principled, prosperous society.

www.tomorrowscompany.com The website of Tomorrow's Company contains various publications produced to help achieve Tomorrow's Company's objectives.

5 | Family-owned Firms

LEARNING OBJECTIVES

- To be aware of the predominance of family-owned firms in many countries around the world
- To understand the evolution of governance structures in family-owned firms
- To realize the benefits that good corporate governance may bring to family-owned firms
- To understand the problems that may be faced by family-owned firms in implementing good corporate governance

Introduction

The dominant form of business around the world is the family-owned business. In many instances, the family-owned business takes the form of a small family business whilst in other cases, it is a large business interest employing hundreds, or even thousands, of staff. The family-owned business can encompass sole traders, partnerships, private companies, and public companies. In fact, family ownership is prevalent not only amongst privately held firms but also in publicly traded firms in many countries across the globe. However, whatever the size of the business, it can benefit from having a good governance structure. Firms with effective governance structures will tend to have a more focused view of the business, be willing to take into account, and benefit from, the views of 'outsiders' (that is, non-family members), and be in a better position to evolve and grow into the future.

Ownership structures around the world

La Porta et al. (1999) analysed the ownership structure in a number of countries and found that the family-owned firm is quite common. Analysing a sample of large firms in 27 countries, La Porta et al. used as one of their criteria, a 10 per cent chain definition of control. This means that they analysed the shareholdings to see if there were 'chains' of ownership: for example, if company B held shares in company C, who then held company B's shares. On this 10 per cent chain definition of control, only 24 per cent of the large companies are widely held, compared to 35 per cent that are family-controlled, and 20 per cent state-controlled. Overall, they show that: '1) Controlling shareholders often have control rights in excess of their cash flow rights. 2) This is true of families, who are so often the controlling shareholders. 3) Controlling families participate in the management of the firms they own. 4) Banks do not exercise much control over firms as shareholders . . . 5) Other large shareholders are usually not there to monitor the controlling shareholders. Family control of firms appears to be common, significant, and typically unchallenged by other equity holders.' La Porta et al.'s paper made an important contribution to our understanding of the prevalence of family-owned/controlled firms in many countries across the world.

A key influence on the type of ownership and control structure is the legal system. Traditionally, common law legal systems, such as in the UK and USA, have better protection of minority shareholders' rights than do civil law systems, such as those of France, Germany, and Russia. Often, if the legal environment does not have good protection of shareholders' rights, then this discourages a diverse shareholder base whilst being more conducive to family-owned firms where a relatively small group of individuals can retain ownership, power, and control. For example, in the UK and USA, where the rights of minority shareholders are well protected by the legal system, there are many more companies with diversified shareholder bases and family-controlled businesses are much less common.

However, recent research by Franks et al. (2004 and 2005) has highlighted that, in the UK in the first half of the twentieth century, there was an absence of minority investor protection as we know it today, and yet there still occurred a move from family ownership to a more dispersed share ownership. This was attributable to the issuance of shares through acquisitions and mergers, although families tried to retain control of the board by holding a majority of the seats. Franks et al. (2004) state

the rise of hostile takeovers and institutional shareholders made it increasingly difficult for families to maintain control without challenge. Potential targets attempted to protect themselves through dual class shares and strategic share blocks but these were dismantled in response to opposition by institutional shareholders and the London Stock Exchange. The result was a regulated market in corporate control and a capital market that looked very different from its European counterparts. Thus, while acquisitions facilitated the growth of family controlled firms in the first half of the century, they also diluted their ownership and ultimately their control in the second half.

On the other hand, in many countries, including European countries such as France, many Asian countries, and South American countries, the legal protection of minority shareholders is today still either non-existent or ineffective, and so families often retain control in companies because non-family investors will not find the businesses an attractive investment when their rights are not protected.

However, many countries are recognizing that, as the business grows and needs external finance to pursue its expansion, then non-family investors will only be attracted to the business if there is protection of their rights, both in the context of the country's legal framework and also in the corporate governance of the individual companies in which they invest. This is leading to increasing pressure both for legal reforms to protect shareholders' rights and for corporate governance reforms within the individual companies. However, balanced against the pressures for reform are the, often very powerful, voices of family shareholders with controlling interests who may not wish to see reform to give better protection to minority interests because this would effectively dilute their control.

Family-owned firms and governance

Whilst a family-owned business is relatively small, the family members themselves will be able to manage and direct it. One advantage of a family-owned firm is that there should be less chance of the type of agency problems discussed in Chapter 2. This is because ownership and control rather than being split are still one and the same, and so the problems of information asymmetry and opportunistic behaviour should (in theory, at least) be lessened. As a result of this overlap of ownership and control, one would hope for higher levels of trust and hence less monitoring of management activity should be necessary. However, problems may still occur and especially in terms of potential for minority shareholder oppression, which may be more acute in family-owned firms. Morck and Yeung (2003) point out some of the potential agency costs in family-owned firms:

In family business group firms, the concern is that managers may act for the controlling family, but not for shareholders in general. These agency issues are: the use of pyramidal groups to separate ownership from control, the entrenchment of controlling families, and non-arm's-length transactions (aka 'tunneling') between related companies that are detrimental to public investors.

In some countries, remedies such as formal shareholder agreements, in which the nature of each shareholder's participation in the company is recorded, may be utilized as a mechanism to help resolve the potential oppression of minorities. Furthermore, the EU Commission's proposed Shareholder Rights Directive, issued in January 2006, is designed to help strengthen the role of shareholders by ensuring that they have relevant information in a timely manner and are able to vote in an informed way. Although the proposed directive is aimed at listed companies, and so likely primarily to affect institutional investors, Member States are free to extend to non-listed companies some or all of the provisions of the proposed Directive.

Another advantage of family-owned firms may be their ability to be less driven by the short-term demands of the market. Of course, they still ultimately need to be able to make a profit but they may have more flexibility as to when and how they do so.

However, even when a family business is still relatively small, there may be tensions and divisions within the family as different members may wish to take different courses of action that will affect the day-to-day way the business operates and its longer term development. In the same way as different generations of a family will have diverse views on various aspects of life, so they will in the business context as well. Similarly, as siblings may argue about various things, so they will most probably differ in their views of who should hold power within the business and how the business should develop. Even in the early stages of a family firm, it is wise to have some sort of forum where the views of family members regarding the business and its development can be expressed. One such mechanism is the family meeting or assembly, where family members can meet, often on a formal pre-arranged basis, to express their views. As time goes by and the family expands with family by marriage and new generations, then the establishment of a family council may be advisable. Neubauer and Lank (1998) suggest that a family council may be advisable once there are more than 30–40 family members.

When a business is at the stage where family relationships are impeding its efficient operation and development, or even if family members just realize that they are no longer managing the business as effectively as they might, then it is definitely time to develop a more formal governance structure. There may be an intermediate stage where the family are advised by an advisory board, although this would not provide the same benefits to the family firm as a defined board structure with independent non-executive directors. Figure 5.1 illustrates the possible stages in a family firm's governance development.

Cadbury (2000) states that establishing a board of directors in a family firm 'is a means of progressing from an organisation based on family relationships to one that is based primarily on business relationships. The structure of a family firm in its formative years is likely to be informal and to owe more to past history than to present needs. Once the firm has moved beyond the stage where authority is vested in the founders, it becomes necessary to clarify responsibilities and the process for taking decisions'.

The advantages of a formal governance structure are several. First of all, there is a defined structure with defined channels for decision-making and clear lines of responsibility. Secondly, the board can tackle areas that may be sensitive from a family viewpoint but which nonetheless need to be dealt with – succession planning is a case in point (deciding who would be best to fill key roles in the business should the existing incumbents move on, retire, or die). Succession planning is important too in the context of raising external equity because, once a family business starts to seek external equity investment, then shareholders will usually want to know that succession planning is in place. The third advantage of a formal governance structure is also one in which external shareholders would take a keen interest: the appointment of non-executive directors. It may be that the family firm, depending on its size, appoints just one, or maybe two, non-executive directors. The key point about the non-executive director appointments is that the persons appointed should be independent; it is this trait that

Figure 5.1 Possible stages in a family firm's governance

will make their contribution to the family firm a significant one. Of course, the independent non-executive directors should be appointed on the basis of the knowledge and experience that they can bring to the family firm: their business experience, or a particular knowledge or functional specialism of relevance to the firm, which will enable them to 'add value' and contribute to the strategic development of the family firm.

Cadbury (2000) sums up the three requisites for family firms to manage successfully the impacts of growth: 'They need to be able to recruit and retain the very best people for the business, they need to be able to develop a culture of trust and transparency, and they need to define logical and efficient organisational structures.' A good governance system will help family firms to achieve these requisites.

Smaller quoted companies

In the UK, many firms with family control will be smaller quoted companies, either on the main market or on the UK's Alternative Investment Market (AIM), which can be seen as a way for smaller firms to obtain market recognition and access to external sources of finance, often before moving on to the main market.

The Combined Code 2006 forms part of the UK Listing Authority's Rules and is applicable to all UK listed companies. This means that there should be no distinction between the governance standards expected of larger and smaller companies. The Combined Code states that it encourages smaller companies to adopt the Code's approach. However, the revised Combined Code 2006 states that smaller companies (those outside the FTSE 350) should have at least two independent non-executive directors (rather than half the board being independent non-executive directors, which is the requirement for larger companies).

The Quoted Companies Alliance (QCA), formerly the City Group for Smaller Companies (CISCO), is an association representing the interests of smaller companies and their advisers. The QCA fully embraces the principles of corporate governance contained in the Combined Code and advocates that these principles should be adopted by all public quoted companies in so far as it is practicable for their size. QCA Guidance for Smaller Companies (2001), updated in 2004, urges smaller companies to comply with the Combined Code as far as they are able, but where they are unable to comply fully, then they should explain why they are unable to comply. The QCA Corporate Governance Committee (2005) published a corporate governance guide for AIM companies to help smaller companies seeking to develop their governance, or to meet the expectations of institutional investors.

online resource centre

There has been a distinct lack of research into aspects of corporate governance in small companies, with a few exceptions being Collier (1997) on audit committees in smaller listed companies, and Mallin and Ow-Yong (1998a, 1998b) on corporate governance in AIM companies and corporate governance in small companies on the main market.

Another strand of the literature concentrates on firm-level characteristics that may serve to differentiate large and small firms. Larger firms tend to be more complex, whereas smaller firms adopt simpler systems and structures; smaller firms tend to have more concentrated leadership, whilst in a larger firm control may be more diffuse, or more subject to question by a larger board (Fama and Jensen 1983; Begley and Boyd 1987). In terms of the impact on corporate governance structures, it can be expected that in general, small and medium-sized firms will have simpler corporate governance structures than large firms – this may include: combining various of the key committees (audit, remuneration, nomination); a smaller number of non-executive directors (NEDs); a combined chair/CEO; longer contractual terms for directors due to the more difficult labour market for director appointments into small and medium-sized companies.

The role and importance of NEDs was emphasised in the Cadbury Report (1992) and in the Code of Best Practice it is stated that NEDs 'should bring an independent judgement to bear on issues of strategy, performance, resources, including key appointments, and standards of conduct' (para 2.1). Similarly, the Hampel Report (1998) stated: 'Some smaller companies have claimed that they cannot find a sufficient number of independent non-executive directors of suitable calibre. This is a real difficulty, but the need for a robust independent voice on the board is as strong in smaller companies as in large ones' (para 3.10). The importance of the NED selection process is also emphasized: they 'should be selected through a formal process and both this process and their appointment should be a matter for the board as a whole' (para 2.4).

From Table 5.1, it can be seen that the areas where potential difficulties are most likely to arise tend to be those relating to the appointment of directors, particularly non-executive directors, which has implications for board structure. These differences arise partly because of the difficulties of attracting and retaining suitable non-executive directors in small companies.

Mallin and Ow-Yong (1998b) found that the most important attribute for small businesses when recruiting non-executive directors was their business skills and experience. Overall, the inference could be made that the ability to 'add value' to the business is the most important factor influencing NED appointments, which is in line with a study by Collier (1997). Similarly, the Hampel Committee (1998) stated 'particularly in smaller companies, non-executive directors may contribute valuable expertise not otherwise available to management' (para 3.8). However, many small companies do not have a nomination committee, and therefore non-executive director appointments are often made by the whole board.

In terms of the adoption of board committees, such as audit, remuneration, and nomination committees, small companies tend to have adopted audit and remuneration committees fairly widely but not nomination committees. In some smaller companies,

Table 5.1 Areas of the Combined Code that may prove difficult for smaller companies

Combined Code recommendations	Potential difficulty
Minimum two independent NEDs	Recruiting and remunerating independent NEDs
Split roles of chair/CEO	May not be enough directors to split the roles
Audit committee comprised of two NEDs	Audit committee may include executive directors
NEDs should be appointed for specific terms	NEDs often appointed for term

the committees may carry out combined roles where, for example, the remuneration and nomination committees are combined into one committee; often the board as a whole will carry out the function of the nomination committee rather than trying to establish a separate committee from a small pool of non-executive directors.

A word of caution should be sounded though in relation to quoted companies where there is still a large block of family ownership (or indeed any other form of controlling shareholder). Charkham and Simpson (1999) point out:

the controlling shareholders' role as guardians is potentially compromised by their interest as managers. Caution is needed. The boards may be superb and they may therefore be fortunate enough to participate in a wonderful success, but such businesses can decline at an alarming rate so that the option of escape through what is frequently an illiquid market anyway may be unattractive.

The points made are twofold: first, that despite a good governance structure on paper, in practice, controlling shareholders may effectively be able to disenfranchise the minority shareholders; second, that in a family-owned business, or other business with a controlling shareholder, the option to sell one's shares may not be either attractive or viable at a given point in time.

Conclusions

In many countries, family-owned firms are prevalent. Corporate governance is of relevance to family-owned firms, which can encompass a number of business forms including private and publicly quoted companies, for a number of reasons. Corporate governance structures can help the company to develop successfully – they can provide the means for defined lines of decision-making and accountability, enable the family firm to benefit from the contribution of independent non-executive directors, and help to ensure a more transparent and fair approach to the way the business is organized and managed. Family-owned firms may face difficulties in initially finding appropriate independent non-executive directors but the benefits that such directors can bring is worth the time and financial investment that the family-owned firm will need to make.

■ SUMMARY

- Family ownership of firms is the prevalent form of ownership in many countries around the globe.

- The legal system of a country tends to influence the type of ownership that develops, so that in common law countries with good protection for minority shareholders' rights, the shareholder base is more diverse, whereas in civil law countries with poor protection for minority shareholders' rights, there tends to be more family ownership and control.

- The governance structure of a family firm may develop in various stages such as starting with a family assembly, then a family council, advisory board, and finally, a defined board structure with independent non-executive directors.

- The advantages to the family firm of a sound governance structure are that it can provide a mechanism for defined lines of decision-making and accountability, enable the family firm to benefit from the contribution of independent non-executive directors, and help to ensure a more transparent and fair approach to the way the business is organized and managed.

Example: Cadbury Schweppes plc, UK

This is an example of a family firm that grew over time, developed an appropriate governance structure, and became an international business.

Today, Cadbury is a household name in homes across the world. It was founded in the first part of the nineteenth century when John Cadbury decided to establish a business based on the manufacture and marketing of cocoa. His two sons joined the firm in 1861 and, over the years, more family members joined, and subsequently the firm became a private limited liability company, Cadbury Brothers Ltd. A board of directors was formed comprising of members of the family.

Non-family directors were first appointed to the firm in 1943, and in 1962, the firm became a publicly quoted company with the family members still being the majority on the board and holding a controlling interest (50 per cent plus) in the shares. Cadbury merged with Schweppes in the late 1960s. Today, Cadbury Schweppes has a diverse shareholder base and the board of directors has been appointed from the wider business community. The direct family involvement, via either large shareholdings or board membership, has therefore declined over the years.

Example: Hutchison Whampoa, Hong Kong

This is an example of an international company where there is controlling ownership by a family via a pyramid shareholding.

Hutchison Whampoa is a multinational conglomerate with five core businesses including ports and related services, property and hotels, telecommunications, retail and manufacturing, energy and infrastructure. It ranks as one of the most valuable companies in Hong Kong and over 40 per cent of it is controlled by Cheung Kong Holdings. The Li Ka Shing family own some 35 per cent of Cheung Kong Holdings, which means that the Li Ka Shing family has significant influence over both companies, one through direct ownership, the other via an indirect, or pyramid, shareholding.

Hutchison Whampoa has, for many years, been the recipient of various awards and accolades. In 2005, it was voted the best-managed company in Hong Kong in a poll of institutional investors and equity analysts carried out for the Finance Asia annual awards. In the same poll, it was voted Asia's Best Conglomerate and its CFO received the Best CFO Award in Hong Kong. The Hong Kong Institute of Certified Public Accountants awarded its Significant Improvement Award in the Hang Seng Index Category to Hutchison Whampoa in 2005 for its 'very clear and positive approach to upgrading its corporate governance practice'. Whilst having a controlling family interest, Hutchison Whampoa is committed to good corporate governance and to its wider shareholder base.

Mini case study: Fiat, Italy

This is a good example of a firm where the founding family still have significant influence through a complex shareholding structure. However, this may change in the future as there is considerable pressure in Italy to reform this type of control derived from complex shareholding structures.

Fabbrica Italiana Automobili Torino, better known as Fiat, was founded in 1899 by a group of investors including Giovanni Agnelli. Fiat automobiles were immediately popular not just in Italy but internationally too. Fiat expanded rapidly in the 1950s and, in 1966, the founder's grandson, also Giovanni Agnelli, became the company's chairman. As well as cars, Fiat's business empire included commercial vehicles, agricultural and construction equipment, insurance, aviation, the press, electric power and natural gas distribution. In past years, it has achieved enormous financial success.

More than 90 per cent of Italian registered companies are family owned, with many companies being run by Italian families who wield great power. Traditionally, control has been achieved, often with the minimum of capital outlay, through a complex structure involving a series of holding companies. In the case of Fiat, control by the Agnelli family is via pyramids (indirect holdings) and voting trusts particularly fi in which the Agnelli family have control of all the votes.

By 2002, Fiat had significant financial problems with losses of $1.2 billion in 2002. General Motors, which had acquired a 20 per cent shareholding in Fiat at a cost of $2.4 billion, was asked to invest further in Fiat but was reluctant to do so. In 2003, the group restructured its core business area by again focusing manufacturing and service activities on the traditional motor vehicle sector.

In 2003, Umberto Agnelli died, and in 2004, Luca Cordero di Montezemolo was nominated as Chairman. Also in 2004, Sergio Marchionne was appointed as Chief Executive of Fiat and this marked a turning point in the company's fortunes. An astute and experienced businessman, Mr Marchionne oversaw changes to various areas of the Fiat business. At the beginning of 2005, Fiat announced the creation of Fiat Powertrain Technologies, a new industrial unit designed to integrate the groups' innovation capabilities and expertise in engines and transmissions. In February 2005, the boards of directors of Fiat and General Motors met to approve a contract to terminate the master agreement and related joint ventures between the two companies. The Chairman of Fiat, Luca Cordero di Montezemolo, said:

'We are delighted to have been able to conclude this agreement with General Motors. While highly beneficial to both Fiat and GM since 2000, the arrangements had become too confining for the development of Fiat Auto in today's market environment. We now have all the necessary freedom to develop strategic growth alternatives for Fiat Auto, while retaining a base on which to build a much more constructive relationship with GM in the future.'

There were also important changes to Fiat's corporate governance structure in June 2005, with Fiat extending its board of directors to 15 members, so that the board comprised a majority of independent non-executive directors. At the same time, Fiat strengthened its independence requirements for directors. In its press release, it stated:

'After a thorough review of current international practice on this issue, the Company has adopted a set of criteria which are designed to ensure that the independence qualification is held to the highest possible standard. As an example, directors who have served on the Board for more than nine years, even though not consecutively, are deemed not to be independent. Furthermore, board members who are executive directors of other companies on whose board[s] sit executive board members of Fiat are also deemed not to be independent.'

In January 2006, Fiat announced another significant strategic change with the signing of an agreement to co-operate on dealer networks with Tata Motors Ltd., which will mean that Fiat cars can be distributed via the Tata network in India. Late in January 2006, Fiat announced that it had seen its first positive quarterly trading profit after 17 successive quarters of losses.

■ QUESTIONS

The discussion questions below cover the key learning points of this chapter. Reading of some of the additional reference material will enhance the depth of the students' knowledge and understanding of these areas.

1. What are the key factors affecting the ownership structure of businesses in different countries, and how might these impact on the development of a business?

2. What are the advantages and disadvantages of a family-owned firm?

3. How might the corporate governance structure in a family firm develop?

4. Critically discuss the value of a board, including the contribution that may be made by independent non-executive directors, to the family firm.

5. 'The need for a professional business approach is arguably even greater in a family than in a non-family firm' (Sir Adrian Cadbury, 2000). Critically discuss this statement.

6. What advantages would a good governance structure bring to a family-owned firm?

Keeping the business within the family

JOHN WARD

Family owned companies have a unique set of corporate governance challenges. A relationship built on trust between owners and managers is the key to achieving success

The distinct purpose of governance for the family business, and the source of its unique competitive advantage, is to assure united and committed family ownership.

In corporate governance terms, family-controlled businesses are fundamentally different from widely-held listed companies primarily because of the discrete nature of ownership.

Family ownership concentrates control and allows for greater discretion in governance. Active and effective engagement by business families permits a governance system that empowers and trusts management to pursue long-term and unconventional strategies. Trust in management also reduces the friction of governance and the burdensome costs of board-room regulations.

The strength of family ownership is not only that it is concentrated; it is also intense and personal. Typically, most of the family's wealth is invested in the business but its connection to the company is emotional as well as economic. Thus, the family is usually highly motivated to be vigilant and to contribute.

However, there is also the temptation for families to meddle in management and in the boardroom. Also, unbridled ownership and squabbling family members will chase away good managers and the best independent directors. Therefore, proper governance of a family business requires clarity both of the roles and responsibilities of the owners, as well as family unity in determining the company vision and commitment to the business and management team.

Approximately one-third of the 1,000 largest companies in the world are controlled by families. Of these, half are traded publicly and half are privately held. The vast majority require a different model of governance than is the norm for widely held companies.

Of course, not all family businesses are alike. Some, such as News Corp, Hutchison Whampoa and BMW have only a few family owners, while others, including Henkel, Wendel and Cargill have dozens or even hundreds of family proprietors.

As a result, the wider issue for family-controlled companies is ensuring that the relationship with the business adapts over the generations. Inevitably, more family members will mean a greater chance of disunity.

Defining governance

Corporate governance refers to the structures, systems and processes that provide direction, control and accountability for an enterprise. For family businesses, I would add the responsibility to assure unity and commitment of ownership.

Most governance discussions look at the structure, roles and responsibilities of the board, and at the relationship between the board and management. For family businesses, a strong relationship between owners and managers allows the board to devote more of its attention to adding value to the company and less on monitoring management.

In addition to strong personal relationships between owners and managers, trust is enhanced by clearly defining the roles and responsibilities of each level of the governance system.

Responsibilities of owners

For family owners, there are four broad responsibilities.

Owners define the values that shape the company's culture

Many families, such as the Bonnier media company of Sweden and Cargill of the US, have regular sessions between owners and managers to discuss these issues. Hatfield Quality Meats, a meat producer based near Philadelphia, has more than 200 family shareholders. It goes further than many of its peers by putting into practice and measuring its core values, including safety, energy and waste conservation, and community support.

Owners set the vision
Family owners establish the parameters and boundaries for management's strategies. They determine if the company should be private or public, or have equity partners. They instruct management if and how they should diversify their assets. Sometimes they may define the geographic scope of the business – for example, whether to become global to expand the family's horizons – or the industries the business can pursue. For some, this could mean shunning tobacco, war materials or alcohol.

To integrate the business's strategic planning with the family's values, my colleague Randel Carlock and I have developed the parallel planning process. The idea is that the family develops its vision based on information provided by management. At the same time, it contributes to the business by putting forward its ideas on how the company should function.

In the US, the Scotts, a third-generation banking and ranching family based in Wyoming and Montana, is perfecting parallel planning. It has management propose various growth scenarios to stimulate the family's thinking about vision. Concurrently, the family offers its ideas on the purpose of their businesses. Throughout, both processes benefit from the counsel of the independent directors on the board.

Owners are responsible for the financial targets
Owners propose goals for growth, risk, liquidity and profitability. The board evaluates these aims for feasibility and consistency. The four goals force the owners to grapple with the inevitable trade-offs in expectations. In so doing, the family gets a better insight into the company which, hopefully, unifies it and leads to appropriate expectations.

Owners elect the directors and design the board
A good board should be varied in its make-up and should deal with the following issues:
• Should the board have independent non-family directors on the board? If so, how many members, and with what qualifications?
• Should the family be represented on the board? If so, by how many, and how should they be selected?

My research of companies in North America and western Europe found that no more than 25 per cent of all family-controlled businesses with more than 500 employees have at least three outside directors. In most developing economies, outside directors are even less prevalent.

Most companies without active, independent boards say they never considered establishing one, they feared losing control, or they doubted they would be able to attract high-quality, non-family directors. In fact, more family businesses need to recognise the benefits of a good board and assure themselves that they can attract directors and retain control.

Types of owners

In addition to designing the board, owners must decide what type of proprietor they want to be. There are two critical challenges: how to be watchful and contribute; and how to forge a consensus and common voice of family ownership opinion. There are several options for proprietors: they could be operating owners; governing owners; active owners; investing owners; or passive owners.

The emphasis and mix of these types is often a function of the generation of the family business. Typically, in the first and second generation, most families are operating owners, meaning they work in management full time. In later generations, as the family grows bigger or more removed from the business, the majority of owners become less involved in the day-to-day running of the company. For example, the German company Haniel has several hundred family shareholders and, by family policy, none of them is permitted in management.

Investing and passive owners are generally only interested in their economic returns. Thus, these businesses become, in effect, no different from any widely held, listed company.

Still, non-management family owners can add significant value in many ways. Some business families can be governing owners who are very involved in the business through conscientious board roles.

The Murugappa Group, an Indian conglomerate, carefully and thoughtfully defined the function of the five governing owners who sit together on the company's holding board. They are cultural ambassadors throughout their companies and spend a lot of time with their non-family CEOs and executives to provide support and to assure succession. They carry and cross-fertilise group competencies, such as technology external contacts and human resource policies across their portfolio. And they represent the family on all their company's subsidiary boards.

In a smaller, simpler form, the family can use the chairman's role to achieve most of these functions.

All family owners, even if they do not have a position on the board, can add value as active owners. These are involved and responsible contributors, who spend time to understand the business in order to provide informed opinion on management and board decisions. This strengthens the confidence and courage of management and protects against disloyalty.

Finally, involved owners deepen their emotional commitment and pride in the business. They attend to their duties in estate planning, serve as examples of the family's values and the company's wider culture, and participate in the family's continuity planning meetings.

Unity of ownership and family governance

To achieve the benefits of concentrated ownership and satisfy issues of corporate governance, families need to organise their ownership voice and work to strengthen their ownership commitment and care. To do so, business families should develop a family governance system.

Family governance often begins with informal family meetings at which the values and hopes for the business are articulated. The family educates itself on relationship skills, such as communications, conflict resolution and decision-making, to assure inter-family harmony.

Later, as the owning family grows, family governance can become more documented in the form of a family constitution. This is a comprehensive statement of the family's values, purposes and principles comprising a set of policies to address family business issues such as employment, marriage contracts, board selection and dividends. It also includes a shareholders' agreement, which defines the legal rules of ownership and redemption.

Of course, not all families need a fully fledged constitution. For example, the Mogi family of Japan, producers of Kikkoman soy sauce, has had a simple statement of 12 philosophic principles that has served it well for more than 100 years.

A higher purpose

Paradoxically, for well-established large families in business, maintaining ownership is not the ultimate end. Instead, the family's unity and commitment are most strengthened by other motivations. For example, they may rally round a social purpose for the company, like the owning family of Roche, the Swiss pharmaceutical company, which believes in the life-saving innovations of medicine.

> **"Most of the family's wealth is invested in the business but its connection to the company is emotional as well as economic"**

Or they might focus on a family foundation and harness the financial success of the company to make a difference in society. For example, the Belmont family of Peru supports economic security opportunities for women by employing thousands of them to sell their company's health and beauty products across South America. What is more, through their family foundation, they offer the women educational scholarships.

These families are more than business owning families – they are enterprising families. In other words, they work together for a collective purpose that unites them emotionally as well as economically.

The real backbone of good family business governance is the purpose and governance of the family itself. It is their commitment to family unity that motivates them to be effective owners and to support their business for the long term.

■ **REFERENCES**

Begley, T.M. and Boyd, D.P. (1987), 'Psychological Characteristics Associated with Performance in Entrepreneurial Firms and Smaller Businesses', *Journal of Business Venturing*, Vol. 2(1).

Cadbury, Sir Adrian (1992), *Report of the Committee on the Financial Aspects of Corporate Governance*, Gee & Co. Ltd., London.

_____ (2000), *Family Firms and their Governance: Creating Tomorrow's Company from Today's*, Egon Zehnder International, London.

Charkham, J. and Simpson, A. (1999), *Fair Shares: The Future of Shareholder Power and Responsibility*, Oxford University Press, Oxford.

Collier, P. (1997), 'Audit Committees in Smaller Listed Companies' in *Corporate Governance: Responsibilities, Risks and Remuneration*, K. Keasey and M. Wright (eds.), John Wiley & Sons.

Combined Code (2003), *The Combined Code on Corporate Governance*, Financial Reporting Council, London.

Fama, E.F and Jensen, M.C. (1983), 'Separation of Ownership and Control', *Journal of Law and Economics*, Vol. 26.

Franks, J.R., Mayer, C. and Rossi, S. (2004), 'Spending Less Time with the Family: The Decline of Family Ownership in the UK', *ECGI – Finance Working Paper No.35/2004*.

_____ _____ _____ (2005), 'Ownership: Evolution and Regulation', *ECGI – Finance Working Paper No.09/2003*.

Greenbury, Sir Richard (1995), *Directors' Remuneration*, Gee & Co. Ltd., London.

Hampel, Sir Ronnie (1998), *Committee on Corporate Governance: Final Report*, Gee & Co. Ltd., London.

Jensen, M.C. and Meckling, W.H. (1976), 'Theory of the Firm: Managerial Behavior, Agency Costs and Ownership Structure', *Journal of Financial Economics*, Vol. 4.

La Porta, R., Lopez-de-Silanes, F., Shleifer, A. and Vishny, R. (1999), 'Corporate Ownership Around the World', *Journal of Finance* 54.

Mallin, C.A. and Ow-Yong, K. (1998a), 'Corporate Governance in Small Companies: the Alternative Investment Market', *Corporate Governance An International Review* September 1998.

_____ _____ (1998b), *Corporate Governance in Small Companies on the Main Market*, ICAEW Research Board, ICAEW, London.

Morck R. and Yeung, B. (2003), 'Agency Problems in Large Family Business Groups', *Entrepreneurship: Theory and Practice*, Summer 2003, Vol. 27(4).

Neubauer, F. and Lank, A.G. (1998), *The Family Business: Its Governance for Sustainability*, Macmillan, Basingstoke.

Quoted Companies Alliance (2001), *Guidance for Smaller Companies*, QCA, London.

_____ (2005), *Corporate Governance Guidelines for AIM Companies*, QCA, London.

■ **USEFUL WEBSITES**

http://rru.worldbank.org The website of the Rapid Response Unit of the World Bank has matters of interest to a range of companies and countries.

www.ecgi.org The website of the European Corporate Governance Institute has details of recent research into family-owned firms and their governance.

www.fbn-i.org The Family Business Network website has items of interest to family businesses.

www.financeasia.com The website of FinanceAsia has information relating to various matters, including corporate governance, of particular interest to firms and investors in Asia.

www.ifb.org.uk The website of the Institute for Family Business, with an emphasis on the UK, has items of interest to family businesses.

www.qcanet.co.uk The website of the Quoted Companies Alliance has items of particular interest to companies outside the UK's FTSE350

6 The Role of Institutional Investors in Corporate Governance

---

LEARNING OBJECTIVES

- To appreciate who institutional investors are
- To understand the growing influence of institutional investors and why they are increasingly interested in corporate governance
- To realize the importance of institutional investors' relationships with their investee companies
- To be aware of the 'tools of governance' that institutional investors have available to them
- To be able to assess the potential impact of 'good' corporate governance on corporate performance

---

Introduction

The potential influence of large shareholders was identified back in the 1930s when Berle and Means (1932) highlighted the separation of the owners (shareholders) from the control of the business, 'control' being in the hands of the directors. This separation of ownership and control leads to the problems associated with agency theory so that the managers of the business may not act in the best interests of the owners. Throughout the twentieth century, the pattern of ownership continued to change and, in the USA and UK in particular, individual share ownership has declined and institutional share ownership has increased. Over seventy years later, institutional investors own large portions of equity in many companies across the world, and the key role played by institutional investors in corporate governance cannot be underestimated. With the internationalization of cross-border portfolios, and the financial crises that have occurred in many parts of the world, it is perhaps not surprising that institutional investors increasingly look more carefully at the corporate governance of companies. After all, corporate governance goes hand in hand with increased transparency and accountability. In this chapter, the rise of the institutional investors and their role in corporate governance is examined.

Table 6.1 Summary of main categories of share ownership in the UK 1963–2004

Type of investor	1963	2004
	%	%
Individuals	54	14
Insurance companies	10	17
Pension funds	6	16
Unit trusts	1	2
Overseas	7	32

Source: ONS Share Ownership 2005
(Other categories owning shares include banks, investment trusts, public sector, and industrial and commercial companies.)

Growth of institutional share ownership

In the UK, the level of share ownership by individuals has decreased over the last thirty years, whilst ownership by institutional investors has increased. In the UK, these institutional investors comprise mainly pension funds and insurance companies. The nature of the changing composition of the UK shareholder base is summarized in Table 6.1.

In 1963, individual investors owned 54 per cent of shares in the UK. The proportion of shares owned by this group fell steadily until, by 1989, it had dropped to just under 21 per cent. Since 1989, there have been a few factors that should have encouraged individual share ownership. First, there were the large privatization issues that occurred in the UK in the early 1990s, and in more recent years, the demutualization of some of the large building societies. However, by 2004, the percentage had dropped to 14 per cent.

In contrast to the individual investors' level of share ownership, the ownership of shares by the insurance companies and the pension funds has increased dramatically over the same period. Ownership by insurance companies has increased from 10 per cent in 1963 to 17 per cent in 2004 whilst that of pension funds has seen an increase to 16 per cent. The large increase in pension funds' investment is attributable to more people investing in pensions. There has also been a notable increase in the overseas level of ownership – this is particularly noteworthy because it has increased from 7 per cent in 1963 to 32 per cent in 2004. Many of the overseas holdings are US investors, with European Union countries being another group of overseas holdings. The US institutional investors tend to be much more proactive in corporate governance and this stance has started to influence the behaviour of both UK institutional investors and UK companies. From Figure 6.1, which shows the beneficial ownership of UK shares at the end of 2004, the extent of institutional share ownership can be seen quite clearly. Similarly, the influence of overseas investors on corporate UK is shown by their level of equity ownership.

online
resource
centre

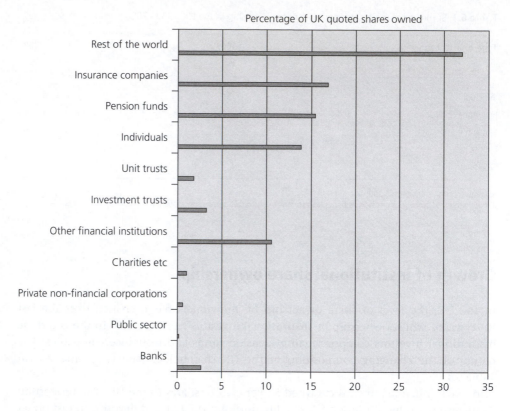

Figure 6.1 Beneficial ownership of UK shares at end 2004

Source: ONS Share Ownership 2005

Influence of institutional investors

Given the size of their shareholdings, the power of the institutional investors cannot be doubted. In his seminal work, Hirschman (1970) identified the exercise of institutional power within an 'exit and voice' framework, arguing that 'dissatisfaction [may be expressed] directly to management' (the *voice* option) or by selling the shareholding (the *exit* option). The latter choice is not viable for many institutional investors given the size of their holdings or a policy of holding a balanced portfolio.

The Cadbury Committee (1992) viewed institutional investors as having a special responsibility to try to ensure that its recommendations were adopted by companies, stating that 'we look to the institutions in particular ... to use their influence as owners to ensure that the companies in which they have invested comply with the Code'. A similar view was expressed in the Greenbury Report (1995) as one of the main action points is 'the investor institutions should use their power and influence to ensure the implementation of best practice as set out in the Code'. Similarly, in the Hampel Report (1998), it is stated 'it is clear ... that a discussion of the role of shareholders in corporate governance will mainly concern the institutions'. Therefore, three influential committees, which have reported on corporate governance in the UK, have clearly emphasized the role of institutional investors. The institutional investors' potential to exert significant influence on companies has clear implications for corporate governance, especially in terms of the standards of corporate governance and issues concerned with enforcement. In relation to institutional shareholders, the Combined Code (2006) principles of good governance are as follows:

INSTITUTIONAL SHAREHOLDERS

Dialogue with companies

1. Institutional shareholders should enter into a dialogue with companies based on the mutual understanding of objectives.

Evaluation of governance disclosures

2. When evaluating companies' governance arrangements, particularly those relating to board structure and composition, institutional shareholders should give due weight to all relevant factors drawn to their attention.

Shareholder voting

3. Institutional shareholders have a responsibility to make considered use of their votes.

Source: Combined Code 2006

In 2002, Hermes, a large and influential institutional investor based in the UK, issued its Hermes Principles. The first principle was that 'companies should seek an honest, open and ongoing dialogue with shareholders'. This clearly reflects Hermes' intention to have a dialogue with its investee companies. Similarly, in the Hermes Corporate Governance Principles (2006), global principle 3 relating to the board of directors, states that 'the board is responsible for facilitating a satisfactory dialogue with the shareholders'.

This perception of the key role to be played by institutional investors is not purely a UK phenomenon. Useem (1996) detailed the rise of 'investor capitalism' in the USA and described how the concentration of shares, and hence power, into a relatively small number of hands, has enabled institutional investors to challenge management directly on issues of concern. Monks (2001) identified 'global investors' as being:

the public and private pension funds of the US, UK, Netherlands, Canada, Australia and Japan. Through extrapolating the specific holding of a number of the largest pension schemes, we conclude that the level of ownership in virtually *all* publicly quoted companies in the world is large enough to permit the effective involvement of owners in the governance of those corporations.

Similarly, in the context of the Australian market, Bosch (1993) stated that 'institutional shareholders because of their increasing influence, by virtue of their size, should take an active interest in the governance of the Company and develop their own principles of good practice'.

This emphasis is to be expected from countries such as the USA, UK, and Australia, which all have a significant concentration of share ownership in the hands of institutional investors. However, the Centre for European Policy Studies (CEPS) reporting in 1995, stated that 'in any attempt to understand the control of corporations, the role of insurance companies, pension funds, and other institutional investors, and other actors, such as employees or banks, has to be taken into account to different extents in European countries'. The report goes on to state: 'International diversification and increasing cross-border activity of institutional investors will accelerate this process. American and British pension funds, in particular, which represent about 72 per cent of total pension fund assets in the western world, can be instrumental in changing corporate governance standards as a result of the active stance towards investment that is required by local laws and codes.' The aspect of foreign share ownership should not be underestimated as these 'new' investors in Europe will tend to be institutional investors from the USA, the UK, and other countries. The large proportion of institutional share ownership in both the USA, where around 55 per cent of US equities are owned by institutional investors and 80 per cent of all share trades are made by institutional investors, and the UK, where institutional ownership is around 65–80 per cent, mean that the voice of the institutional investor cannot go unheard. The extent of institutional ownership in the UK is now discussed in detail.

The power of institutional investors such as those cited above clearly cannot be underestimated, and the influence that they can wield is enormous. The institutional investors may be influenced in their views by the various institutional investor representative groups in the UK. Large institutional investors, mainly insurance companies and pension funds, usually belong to one of two representative bodies that act as a professional group 'voice' for their views. These two bodies are the Association of British Insurers (ABI) and the National Association of Pension Funds (NAPF). Both the ABI and the NAPF have best practice corporate governance guidelines, which encompass the recommendations of the Combined Code. They monitor the corporate governance activities of companies and will provide advice to members. Institutional investors will generally consult ABI and/or NAPF reports on whether particular companies are complying with 'good' corporate governance practice, as well as undertaking their own research and analysis. Most large institutional investors have terms of reference that incorporate corporate governance aspects, or have issued separate corporate governance guidelines. These guidelines are generally based around the Combined Code recommendations, and further guidance that may have been issued by the NAPF or ABI. Companies will try to ensure that they meet these guidelines.

The Myners Report on institutional investment, issued in 2001 by HM Treasury, concentrated more on the trusteeship aspects of institutional investors and the legal requirements for trustees, with the aim of raising the standards and promoting greater shareholder activism. For example, the Myners Report expects that institutional investors should be more proactive especially in the stance they take with underperforming companies.

The Institutional Shareholders' Committee (ISC), whose members comprise the ABI, the NAPF, the Association of Investment Trust Companies (AITC), and the Investment Management Association (IMA), issued a statement on the responsibilities of institutional investors in late 2002. The ISC states that the policies on activism that it describes 'do not constitute an obligation to micro-manage the affairs of investee companies, but rather relate to procedures designed to ensure that shareholders derive value from their investments by dealing effectively with concerns over underperformance. Nor do they preclude a decision to sell a holding, where this is the most effective response to such concerns'. In other words, the exercise of 'voice' is recommended but 'exit' is not precluded.

The ISC recommends that institutional investors should **have a clear statement of their policy on activism and on how they will discharge their responsibilities**. The policy would be a public document and would address the following areas: how investee companies will be monitored; the policy for requiring investee companies' compliance with the Combined Code; the policy for meeting with an investee company's board and senior management; how any conflicts of interest will be dealt with; the strategy on intervention; indication of when and how further action may be taken; and the policy on voting.

It also recommends that institutional investors should **monitor performance**. Monitoring performance should be a regular process, clearly communicable and checked periodically for its effectiveness. It would include reviewing annual reports and accounts, circulars and resolutions, and attending company meetings. In particular, institutional shareholders should try to satisfy themselves that the investee company's board and sub-committee structures are effective, and that independent directors provide adequate oversight, and maintain a clear audit trail of their meetings and of votes cast on company resolutions, in particular contentious issues. The ISC states that these actions should help institutional investors 'to identify problems at an early stage and minimize any loss of shareholder value'.

The ISC advocates that institutional investors **intervene when necessary** and such intervention may occur when they have concerns about a range of issues including: the company's strategy; its operational performance; its acquisition/disposal strategy; independent directors failing to hold executive management properly to account; internal controls failing; inadequate succession planning; an unjustifiable failure to comply with the Combined Code; inappropriate remuneration packages; the company's approach to corporate social responsibility. Boards should be given the chance to respond constructively but if they do not, then the institutional investors may choose to escalate their action through a range of ways, including intervening jointly with other institutions on particular issues, making a public statement in advance of the company's general meeting, or requisitioning an extraordinary general meeting possibly to change the boards. Finally, institutional investors should **evaluate and report** on the outcomes of their shareholder activism.

As might be inferred from its content, the ISC statement is aimed at significantly enhancing 'how effectively institutional shareholders discharge their responsibilities in relation to the companies in which they invest'. It is a milestone in the encouragement of institutional shareholder activism in the UK.

The ISC published a review of its 2002 Statement of Principles on the responsibilities of institutional shareholders and their agents in September 2005. The review monitored the progress of the statement for the two years since its launch in 2002 and concluded

 online resource centre

that there had been a general increase in the level of engagement of institutional investors with their investee companies. The Statement of Principles issued in 2002 has stayed the same but with two modifications: the word 'activism' has been replaced with 'engagement', with this change being 'to emphasise the importance now attached by institutional investors to developing a high-quality all-round relationship with the companies in which they invest'; given that it is a listing requirement that companies must comply with the Combined Code (2003) or explain why they do not, there is no need for institutional investors to state in their policy that they require investee companies to do this.

The International Corporate Governance Network (ICGN) has produced a new Statement of Shareholder Responsibilities (2006), a core principle of which is that institutional shareholders should exercise their rights responsibly, acting in the interests of beneficiaries, but also having regard for the well-being of the company itself. The internal governance of institutional investors is also emphasized as important.

Institutional investors' relationship with investee companies

Corporate governance may be used as a tool for extracting value for shareholders from underperforming, undervalued companies. This approach has been very successful for Lens Inc., CalPERS, Hermes, and Active Value Advisors, to name but a few. By targeting companies that are underperforming in one of the main market indices, and analysing those companies' corporate governance practices, improvements can be made that unlock the hidden value. These improvements often include replacing poorly performing directors and ensuring that the companies comply with perceived best practice in corporate governance.

Corporate governance may also be used as a key to help restore investor confidence in markets that have experienced financial crises. We have seen this happening in the last few years in Malaysia, Japan, and Russia, for example. In these countries, as in a number of other countries that have similarly been affected by a lack of investor confidence, particularly overseas investor confidence, new or improved corporate governance practices have been introduced. Key features of these changes include measures to try to improve investor confidence by improving transparency and accountability in these markets.

Tools of corporate governance

(i) One-to-one meetings

The meetings between institutional investors and companies are extremely important as a means of communication between the two parties. This is one clear example of the way in which individual investors are at a disadvantage to institutional investors: corporate management will usually only arrange such meetings with large investors who are overwhelmingly institutional investors.

A company will usually arrange to meet with its largest institutional investors on a one-to-one basis during the course of the year. The meetings tend to be at the highest level and usually involve individual key members of the board in a meeting once, or maybe twice, a week. Their 'target' institutional investor audience will include large shareholders (perhaps the top thirty) and brokers' analysts (perhaps the top ten), and any large investors who are underweight or selling their shares. In addition, they will tend to phone an institutional investor if they have not seen them in the last year to 18 months. Meetings are often followed up with phone calls by the firm to the institutional investor to ensure that everything has been discussed.

The issues that are most discussed at these meetings between firms and their large institutional investors are areas of the firm's strategy and how the firm is planning to achieve its objectives, whether objectives are being met, the quality of the management, etc. Institutional investors are seen as 'important for the way the business is managed', and their views may be fed back to the board in the planning process, and incorporated, as appropriate, in an annual strategy paper. They are seen as having a collective influence, with management paying most attention to the commonality of institutional investors' views in meetings over time. The firms want to ensure that institutional investors understand the business and its strategy so that the value of the business is fully recognized.

As a way of saying 'well done', Hermes sent letters to various companies in 2005 stating when they found their annual report particularly informative and useful in terms of various areas: for example, directors' remuneration and risk management.

(ii) Voting

The right to vote that is attached to voting shares (as opposed to non-voting shares) is a basic prerogative of share ownership, and is particularly important given the division of ownership (shareholders) and control (directors) in the modern corporation. The right to vote can be seen as fundamental for some element of control by shareholders.

The institutional investors can register their views by postal voting, or, in many companies, the facility to vote electronically is now available. Most of the large institutional investors now have a policy of trying to vote on all issues that may be raised at their investee company's AGM. Some may vote directly on all resolutions, others may appoint a proxy (which may be a board member). Generally, an institutional investor will try to sort out any contentious issues with management 'behind the scenes'; however, if this fails, then they may abstain from voting on a particular issue (rather than voting with incumbent management as they generally would) or they may actually vote against a resolution. In this case, they would generally inform the firm of their intention to vote against. It tends to be corporate governance issues that are the most contentious, particularly directors' remuneration and lengths of contract.

The high level of institutional share ownership in the UK has been discussed above. Looking back at the Cadbury Report (1992), this states: 'Given the weight of their votes, the way in which institutional investors use their power... is of fundamental importance.' It encourages institutional investors to 'make positive use of their voting rights and disclose their policies on voting'.

A number of similar statements can be found in the guidelines issued by various institutional investor representative groups. For example, the two main groups representing institutional investors in the UK, the NAPF and the ABI, both advocate voting by institutional investors. NAPF (1995) refers to 'the powerful vote' and 'encourage – as a matter of best practice – the regular exercise of proxy votes by pension funds'; ABI recommends that 'large shareholders should vote wherever possible and support boards of directors unless they have good reason for doing otherwise'. In 1999, the ABI and NAPF issued some joint guidance on responsible voting in which they emphasized the importance of voting and advocated: that voting should be done in a considered fashion rather than 'box ticking'; that it could contribute to effective corporate governance; that it could be seen as an integral part of the investment management function.

So, it would seem that the main institutional investor representative groups in the UK are in agreement that votes should be exercised on a regular basis in an informed manner.

There have been a number of efforts to try to ensure that voting levels do improve. These include the NAPF Report of the Committee of Inquiry into UK Vote Execution (1999). The report identified various impediments to voting, a major one being the cumbersome and outdated paper-based system. As a result of this, a number of projects were established to try to find a suitable electronic voting system to make voting easier and the process more efficient. The NAPF report additionally identified a number of other areas of concern including a 'lack of auditability or adequate confirmatory procedure in the voting system' and communication problems between the pension funds, fund managers, custodians, registrars, and companies. It recommended that: regular considered voting should be regarded as a fiduciary responsibility; voting policy ought to be specifically covered by agreement; the UK's voting system should be modernized; companies themselves should actively encourage voting; member associations should offer help and guidance; registrars should support electronic voting arrangements; voting in the context of stock lending should be re-examined; custodians should actively assist in the voting process.

The Shareholder Voting Working Group (SVWG) was established in 1999, under the chairmanship of Terry Pearson, as an industry-wide body to address the issue of improving the voting process in the UK. The SVWG has subsequently been chaired by Paul Myners, the current chair, and has issued several reports on the impediments to voting UK shares. Its report in November 2005 highlighted: that UK voting levels do seem to be increasing; that the voting system has become more automated with the vast majority of FTSE 100 companies now facilitating electronic voting and the expectation that all the FTSE 100 companies will in 2006; that the audit trail of the voting process has also improved; that final decisions on contentious voting issues are taken at a senior level; that various recommendations relating to a company's AGM, such as quoted companies should disclose on a website the results of polls and votes for and against at general meetings and enhancements to the rights of proxy voters, have been included in the Company Law Reform Bill. The potential problems associated with votes that are lent to other investors (stocklending), including shares not being voted at all, or being voted in a way that would be against the wishes of the original lender of the stock, are also highlighted.

Voting levels by institutional investors in the UK have gradually begun to increase in recent years, with voting levels in the FTSE 100 companies rising to around 58 per cent during 2004 and 2005 according to Manifest (2005). Institutional investors recognize that unless voting levels increase across their investee companies in the next couple of years, the government may make voting mandatory. Whilst the question of mandatory voting has been fairly widely discussed in the UK, there is no real consensus on this issue. However, there is undoubtedly a sense that institutional investors should have a more active involvement, especially in areas of corporate governance such as voting, and, in the course of time, if voting levels do not improve, then voting may well become mandatory. There is also a concern to try to ensure that individual shareholders who hold shares through nominees and not directly do not lose their right to vote – this is another dimension of institutional investor power and influence.

The situation in continental Europe is rather different because the shareholder structure in many European countries differs quite significantly from that in the UK: for example, large banks and corporations tend to dominate German and French companies, whilst Italian companies tend to be dominated by non-financial holding companies and families. However, the report of the CEPS working party set up to give policy directions on the future of corporate governance in Europe stated: 'Shareholders should be given the responsibility to exercise their voting rights in an informed and independent manner. This activity should also be adapted to the growing internationalization of shareholding and not be limited to national borders.' This seems to indicate that whatever the shareholding structure in a particular country, the vote is seen as being of importance, and once again informed voting is emphasized. It is also interesting to note the reference to the internationalization of shareholdings and the implication that cross-border holdings should be voted.

In 2002, the EU High Level Group of Company Law Experts, chaired by Jaap Winter, emphasized the importance of facilitating voting by electronic and other means, and also of enabling cross-border voting. The recommendations of this group fed into the EU Communication 'Modernizing Company Law and Enhancing Corporate Governance in the European Union – A Plan to Move Forward'. Approximately a third of the share capital of EU listed companies in any given country is held by non-residents. Non-residents may face a number of obstacles when trying to exercise their shareholder rights, such as lack of sufficient information being received in a timely manner, share blocking, and difficulties in voting cross-border shares. In the context of shareholder rights, two main objectives were identified: (i) 'to strengthen shareholder rights and third party protection, with a proper distinction between categories of companies', and (ii) 'to foster efficiency and competitiveness of business, with special attention to some specific cross-border issues'. In practice, this led to the issue in January 2006 of a Directive on Shareholders' Rights, which made the following proposals to enhance shareholders' rights:

- general meetings should be convened with at least one month's notice. All relevant information should be available on that date at the latest, and posted on the issuer's website. The meeting notice should contain all necessary information;
- share blocking should be abolished and replaced by a record date, which should be set no earlier than 30 days before the meeting;

- the right to ask questions should be accessible to non-residents. The maximum shareholding thresholds to benefit from the right to table resolutions should not exceed 5 per cent, in order to open this right to a greater number of shareholders while preserving the good order of general meetings;

- proxy voting should not be subject to excessive administrative requirements, nor should it be unduly restricted. Shareholders should have a choice of methods for distance voting;

- voting results should be available to all shareholders and posted on the issuer's website.

Like the UK, the US stock market is dominated by institutional investors. One significant difference to the UK though is that private pension funds are mandated to vote by the Department of Labor's (DOL) regulations governing proxy voting by Employee Retirement Income Security Act (ERISA) funds. ERISA was enacted in 1974 and established federal fiduciary standards for private pension funds. The fiduciary duty is deemed to encompass voting. The DOL has, especially in more recent years, been fairly proactive in monitoring compliance with ERISA, and in offering interpretive advice on it. Early in 1994, Olena Berg, Assistant Secretary for Pension and Welfare Benefits, clarified the issue of global voting by stating that 'voting foreign proxies should be treated the same way as voting domestic proxies'. However, it was recognized that voting overseas proxies can be an expensive business and it is advised that fiduciaries look at possible difficulties of voting a particular stock *before* purchasing it and also evaluate the cost of voting the shares against the potential value to the plan of voting the shares. Combined with the dramatic growth in the level of US institutional investors' holdings of overseas equities, this pronouncement can also be expected to have a significant effect on the attitude towards voting in the overseas countries in which US institutional investors hold equities.

ERISA does not apply to public pension funds but the major public pension funds tend to vote their own shares or instruct their managers how to vote. Funds such as the California Public Employees' Retirement System (CalPERS), the New York City Employees' Retirement System (NYCERS), and the State of Wisconsin Investment Board (SWIB) all have a policy of voting all their shares. CalPERS, the USA's largest pension fund and the third largest in the world, makes available its voting actions on its website.

In the Australian context, the Bosch Committee (1993) stated that institutional investors should 'take an active interest in the governance of their company' and commented that shareholders in general should make 'a sufficient analysis to vote in an informed manner on all issues raised at general meetings'. Stephen Smith, chairman of the Parliamentary Joint Committee on Corporations and Securities, argued that 'institutional investors have a clear moral, if not legal, obligation to examine each proposal and decide how they will best exercise their voting rights'. In its 1995 guidelines, the Australian Investment Managers' Association recommends that 'voting rights are a valuable asset of the investor and should be managed with the same care and diligence as any other asset', and urges that 'institutions should support boards by positive use of their voting power unless they have good reasons for doing otherwise'.

A survey of institutional investors carried out by the ICGN in 2001 found that most institutional investors state that they try to exercise their overseas proxies but that there may be problems in trying to do so. Problems that may be encountered when trying to vote cross-border include the following: timing problems whereby just a couple of weeks' notice of the agenda items to be voted on at the companies' annual general meeting may be given, making for a very tight deadline; information relating to agenda items being insufficient and/or in a foreign language, making detailed analysis of items very difficult in the available timescale; the blocking or depositing of shares, which means that shares have to be deposited with a central depository, public notary, or depositary named by the company, and so cannot be traded for a period of time before the company's annual general meeting (usually between five and eight days); finally, voting procedures or methods may be problematic in cross-border voting, for example, having physically to attend the annual general meeting to vote rather than being able to send in votes by post or other appropriate means. Recent developments in a number of countries, including various EU countries, have gone some way towards addressing a number of these issues.

However, there remain a number of barriers to the effective exercise of voice by means of voting. It is, though, a powerful and public means of exercising voice. We are likely to see increased voting levels over time as there is both increasing pressure from institutional investors on companies to try to ensure a more efficient and effective voting system, and pressure from governments on institutional investors for more institutional investors to vote regularly. If institutional investor voting levels do not increase, then the UK government may legislate so that voting becomes mandatory, but this is something that both the government and institutional investors would prefer not to happen as it is felt that this might lead to mere 'box ticking' rather than to considered voting.

(iii) Focus lists

A number of institutional investors have established 'focus lists', whereby they target underperforming companies and include them on a list of companies that have underperformed a main index, such as Standard and Poor's. Underperforming the index would be a first point of identification; other factors would include not responding appropriately to the institutional investor's enquiries regarding underperformance, and not taking account of the institutional investor's views. After being put on the focus list, the companies receive the, often unwanted, attention of the institutional investors who may seek to change various directors on the board.

(iv) Corporate governance rating systems

With the increasing emphasis on corporate governance across the globe, it is perhaps not surprising that a number of corporate governance rating systems have been developed. Examples of firms that have developed corporate governance rating systems are Deminor, Standard and Poor's, and Governance Metrics International (GMI). The rating systems cover several markets: for example, Deminor has tended to concentrate on European companies whilst Standard and Poor's has used its corporate governance rating system in quite different markets, such as Russia. GMI ratings cover a range of countries including the USA, various countries in the Asia-Pacific region and Europe. These corporate governance rating systems should be of benefit to investors, both potential and those presently invested, and to the companies themselves.

In turn, the ratings will also be useful to governments in identifying perceived levels of corporate governance in their country compared to other countries in their region, or outside it, whose companies may be competing for limited foreign investment. In emerging market countries in particular, those companies with a corporate governance infrastructure will, *ceteris paribus*, be less subject to cronyism and its attendant effects on corporate wealth. These companies will tend to be more transparent and accountable, and hence more attractive to foreign investors.

A corporate governance rating can be a powerful indicator of the extent to which a company currently is adding, or has the potential to add in the future, shareholder value. This is because a company with good corporate governance is generally perceived as more attractive to investors than one without. Good corporate governance should, for example, indicate a board that is prepared to participate actively in dialogue with its shareholders, ensuring the effective exercise of voice (Hirschman 1970) thus enabling investors to articulate their interests.

An appropriate approach for a corporate governance rating system is first to have a rating of the corporate governance in a given country: for example, how transparent are accounting and reporting practices generally in the country; are there existing corporate governance practices in place; is there a code of best practice; to what extent is that code complied with; what sanctions are there against companies which do not comply? Having set the scene in any given country, the individual company can then be given a corporate governance rating. With regard to the individual company, the ratings will generally be based on: the company's approach to the rights of shareholders; the presence of independent non-executive (outside) directors; the effectiveness of the board; the accountability and transparency of the company. Corporate governance rankings of companies in, for example, the banking sector can be assessed both within a country and also across countries, providing a valuable additional indicator/comparator benchmark for investors.

Overall, corporate governance rating systems should provide a useful indication of the corporate governance environment in specific countries, and in individual companies within those countries. Such systems will provide a useful benchmark for the majority of investors who identify good corporate governance with a well-run and well-managed company and investors will increasingly take into account companies' governance profiles in investment decisions.

Corporate governance and corporate performance

Is there a link between corporate governance and corporate performance? Whilst there have been many studies carried out to determine whether there is a link between corporate governance and corporate performance, the evidence appears to be fairly mixed.

One of the earlier and much-quoted studies is that of Nesbitt (1994). Nesbitt reported positive long-term stock price returns to firms targeted by CalPERS. Nesbitt's later studies show similar findings. Subsequently, Millstein and MacAvoy (1998) studied 154 large publicly traded US corporations over a five-year period and found that corporations with active and independent boards appear to have performed much better in the 1990s than those with passive, non-independent boards. However, the work of Dalton, Daily, Ellstrand, and Johnson (1998) showed that board composition had virtually no effect on firm performance, and that there was no relationship between leadership structure (CEO/chairman) and firm performance. Patterson (2000), of the Conference Board, produced a comprehensive review of the literature relating to the link between corporate governance and performance and stated that the survey did not present conclusive evidence of such a link.

Whilst the evidence seems to be quite mixed, there does appear to be a widely held perception that corporate governance can make a difference to the bottom line. The findings of a survey by McKinsey (2002) found that the majority of investors would be prepared to pay a premium to invest in a company with good corporate governance. The survey states that 'good' governance in relation to board practices includes a majority of outside directors who are truly independent, significant director stock ownership and stock-based compensation, formal director evaluations, and good responsiveness to shareholder requests for governance information. The findings indicate that investors would pay 11 per cent more for the shares of a well-governed Canadian company, 12 per cent more for the shares of a well-governed UK company, and 14 per cent more for the shares of a well-governed US company, compared to shares of a company with similar financial performance but poorer governance practices. The premiums rise to 16 per cent for a well-governed Italian company, 21 per cent for a Japanese company, 24 per cent for a Brazilian company, 38 per cent for a Russian company and, at the top of the scale with the highest premium for good governance, 41 per cent for a well-governed Moroccan company. It is therefore the investor's perception and belief that corporate governance is important and that belief leads to the willingness to pay a premium for good corporate governance.

Some of the significant papers in recent years that have found evidence of a positive link include Gompers et al. (2003) and Deutsche Bank (2004a and 2004b). Gompers et al. (2003) examined the ways in which shareholder rights vary across firms. They constructed a 'Governance Index' to proxy for the level of shareholder rights in approximately 1500 large firms during the 1990s. An investment strategy that bought firms in the lowest decile of the index (strongest rights) and sold firms in the highest decile of the index (weakest rights) would have earned abnormal returns of 8.5 per cent per year during the sample period. They found that firms with stronger shareholder rights had higher firm value, higher profits, higher sales growth, lower capital expenditures, and made fewer corporate acquisitions. Deutsche Bank AG (2004a and 2004b) explored the implications of corporate governance for portfolio management and concluded that corporate governance standards are an important component of equity risk. Its analysis also showed that for South Africa, Eastern Europe, and the Middle East, the performance differential favours those companies with stronger corporate governance.

Hermes (2005) provided a succinct summary of academic and practitioner research in this area, splitting it into three categories: opinion-based research, such as McKinsey (2002); focus list research and performance of shareholder engagement funds (such as

 online resource centre

'the CalPERS effect', on which there were various studies such as Nesbitt (1994)); finally, governance ranking research (such as Deutsche Bank, 2004). Hermes concludes its review of the literature by stating that it recognizes that a number of the authors of the various studies cited in the review have mentioned that there is further empirical work needed on the issue of causation but that: 'Nevertheless, we consider there to be sufficient evidence in support of our view that good corporate governance improves the long-term performance of companies.'

In sum, the evidence, both academic and practitioner, points on balance towards the view that good corporate governance helps to realize value and to create competitive advantage; this is more of an intuitive feeling because the studies are trying to single out corporate governance variables that may affect performance and this is very difficult to do. However, shareholder activism is the key to ensuring good corporate governance, and without this, there is less accountability and transparency, and hence more opportunity for management to engage in activities that may have a negative effect on the bottom line.

Conclusions

In this chapter, the extent of institutional share ownership, and hence the growth of institutions' power and influence, has been examined. The chapter highlights the emphasis that is increasingly placed on the role of institutional investors in corporate governance in a global context. The tools of governance for institutional investors, including one-to-one meetings, voting, the use of focus lists, and the use of rating systems, are discussed.

We have seen how, in the UK and the USA, institutional investors have become very important over the last thirty years as their share ownership has increased and they have become more active in their ownership role. Institutional investors tend to have a **fiduciary responsibility**, i.e. the responsibility to act in the best interests of a third party (generally the beneficial, or ultimate owners of the shares). Until recently, this responsibility has tended to concentrate on ensuring that they invest in companies that are not only profitable but which will continue to have a growing trend of profits. Whilst this remains the case, governments and pressure groups have raised the question of how these profits are achieved. We now see institutional investors being much more concerned about the internal governance of the company and also the company's relationship with other stakeholder groups. The growth of institutional investor interest in socially responsible investment is the subject of a separate chapter.

■ SUMMARY

- Institutional investors, such as large pension funds, insurance companies, and mutual funds, have become the largest shareholders in many countries, having significant shareholdings in the companies in which they invest.

- The relationship between institutional investors and their investee companies is very important. Institutional investors can have a powerful 'voice' in their investee companies.

- The 'tools' of governance include one-to-one meetings, voting, focus lists, and rating systems.

- The evidence as to whether 'good' corporate governance impacts on corporate performance is rather mixed but, looking at it another way, good governance can help to ensure that companies do not fail. Also, a company with good corporate governance is more likely to attract external capital flows than one without.

Example: Kingfisher plc

This is an example of a company that engaged in constructive dialogue with its institutional shareholders and changed certain aspects of its directors' remuneration packages after criticism from some of its institutional shareholders.

In the first half of 2002, Kingfisher plc received a number of adverse comments from some of its large institutional investors about some aspects of its directors' remuneration packages, which were seen as overly generous. Kingfisher responded by discussing the terms of the directors' remuneration packages with its institutional investors and also with two institutional investor representative bodies, the National Association of Pension Funds and the Association of British Insurers.

A compromise was reached and Kingfisher revised the terms of the packages agreeing to introduce tougher performance targets on the share options and also to reduce the amount of compensation paid in the event of loss of office, with payments limited to one year's salary.

This is a good example of both the influence of institutional investors and the usefulness of constructive dialogue between company and investors.

Kingfisher has continued to be committed to an active dialogue with its shareholders. There are regular meetings between investors and management and all non-executive directors are available for meetings with institutional shareholders.

Example: Xerox Corporation

This is an example from the USA of the use of a focus list by an institutional investor to highlight poor corporate governance in Xerox Corporation.

Xerox Corporation had shown poor performance in recent years. The Securities Exchange Commission (SEC) fined the company and forced it to restate earnings for the years 1997 to 2000. CalPERS (the Californian Public Employees' Retirement System) is one of the largest and most influential pension funds in the USA and is active in pursuing good corporate governance in its investee companies. It included Xerox on its 2003 corporate governance focus list of poorly performing companies. The main reason for Xerox's inclusion was that it retained a board that consisted of the same members as were present when Xerox was experiencing financial problems. This appeared to be affecting investor confidence in the company because the same directors remained on the board and also the company had combined the roles of chairman/CEO. CalPERS would have liked to have seen three more independent directors on the board, and believed that the audit, remuneration, and nomination committees should comprise totally independent directors. The roles of chair and CEO should be split. Xerox initially disappointed by appointing only one new independent director, although it agreed to adopt a new Charter to provide for key board committees to be comprised totally of independent directors. CalPERS' action of including Xerox on the focus list seems to have had some positive effects. Subsequently, Xerox appointed five new directors in 2004 and 2005 although it has retained a combined Chair/CEO post.

Mini case study: Premier Farnell

This is a good example of institutional investor activism in action. It illustrates the fact that institutional investors are prepared to take a public stance when they feel that their investee company is about to take an inappropriate course of action that may be damaging to shareholder value. It is particularly interesting as one of the earliest examples of corporate governance activism in the UK.

In February 1996, Farnell Electronics, a UK-based company, made a bid for fellow electronic components distributor, Premier Industrial Corporation, of the USA. The bid was for £1.1 billion and there was an immediate outcry from some of Farnell's large institutional shareholders, who feared that the company was paying too much to acquire Premier Industrial.

Some of the institutional investors took the unusual step of identifying themselves publicly as dissenting on the terms of the bid. Standard Life was an early opponent of the deal, issuing a statement that underlined the dilution to earnings per share (eps) and the risk it felt that Farnell was taking by having so much debt to pay for the deal.

However, the Farnell team managed to talk around many of the institutional investors – although not Standard Life – by making more than sixty institutional presentations to try to convince the institutional investors of the merits of the deal. Some institutional investors took more convincing than others and had to be visited twice, or even three times in some cases!

At the extraordinary general meeting (EGM), the resolution was passed in Farnell's favour with an exceptionally high level of shares being voted (77 per cent). Standard Life sold its shareholding in Farnell. In subsequent years, it seemed that Standard Life's stance had been correct as Farnell experienced problems and saw a drop in its share price of 41 per cent in 1997 alone.

In recent years, Premier Farnell has shown a fluctuating performance with earnings per share of 17p in 2001 down to 11.7p in 2005.

■ QUESTIONS

The discussion questions below cover the key learning points of this chapter. Reading of some of the additional reference material will enhance the depth of the students' knowledge and understanding of these areas.

1. Why has the influence of institutional investors grown so much in recent years?

2. What role do you think that institutional investors should play in corporate governance?

3. To what extent is the internationalization of investment portfolios responsible for institutional investors' increased interest in corporate governance?

4. What 'tools of governance' do institutional investors have at their disposal?

5. What evidence is there to show that 'good' corporate governance can improve corporate performance?

6. 'Institutional investors have a responsibility to vote the shares in their investee companies.' Critically discuss.

■ **FT ARTICLE**

Unhappy investors force change

Activism has become an investment strategy, say John Authers and David Wighton

As US boards of directors know to their discomfort, shareholder activism is back.

The past few weeks have seen a rash of companies acting to reform their corporate governance rules, or even to split up, under pressure from investors.

Shareholder activism is now regarded almost as its own separate and institutionalised asset class, with managers of mutual funds and less regulated hedge funds declaring it as a key strategy.

The latest company under attack is Sovereign Bancorp, which is facing mounting opposition to its proposed sale of a $2.4bn stake to Grupo Santander of Spain to fund the acquisition of Independence Community Bank.

On Friday, Franklin Mutual Advisers, a fund manager with a lengthy reputation for shareholder activism that has a 5 per cent stake in Sovereign, expressed "outrage" at the proposals that were among "the worst examples of management and board entrenchment and disdain for shareholder rights".

Unhappy shareholders also include Relational Advisors, a San Diego-based hedge fund that has been pressing for board changes.

Peter Langerman, Franklin's chief executive, said that although there was nothing new about shareholder activism, there seemed to have been an increasing number of examples recently.

"This may be in part related to hedge funds. But there are also investors who didn't pursue this avenue before who are becoming more active. Twenty years ago, if you were unhappy with a company you walked away. That is no longer considered acceptable."

The list of companies that have fallen foul of shareholder activists is growing. Within the past month Cendant, a conglomerate whose assets include hotel chains, has announced that it would split itself into four. Henry Silverman, chief executive, blamed pressure from hedge funds.

Last week, shares in the Knight-Ridder newspaper chain surged after Private Capital Management, a Florida-based investment manager owned by the brokerage Legg Mason, called for the company to be sold. The company has a 19 per cent stake in Knight-Ridder.

And in Europe, shareholders last week forced Deutsche Börse to take on a new chief executive, after objections to the market's hostile bid for the London Stock Exchange.

Among fund managers "shareholder activism" is now regarded as a strategy in its own right, occupying a role between traditional "value" investment – buying into under-valued companies in the expectation that they will turn round – and private equity, which involves taking controlling stakes.

A shareholder activist strategy involves taking a stake of about 20 per cent – short of control but enough to force the board to pay attention – and then hoping to improve the share price.

Interest from investors is partly because of the lacklustre returns available from conventional investment strategies in the past six years. There is also growing statistical evidence that the strategy delivers strong performance.

According to Calpers, the largest institutional money manager in the US, the 113 companies to appear on their "focus list" for bad corporate governance from 1987 to 2003 have outperformed the S&P 500 index by 8.1 per cent in the five years after coming under pressure to reform themselves. In the five years before Calpers targeted them, they underperformed the index by an average of 97 per cent.

Financial Times Monday 7 November 2005

■ REFERENCES

ABI/NAPF (1999), *Responsible Voting – A Joint ABI-NAPF Statement*, ABI/NAPF, London.

Berle, A.A. and Means, G.C. (1932), *The Modern Corporation and Private Property*, Macmillan, New York.

Bosch, H. (1993), *Corporate Practices and Conduct*, Business Council of Australia, Melbourne.

Cadbury, Sir Adrian (1992), *Report of the Committee on the Financial Aspects of Corporate Governance*, Gee & Co. Ltd., London.

Centre for European Policy Studies (1995), *Corporate Governance in Europe*, Brussels.

Combined Code (2006), *The Combined Code on Corporate Governance*, Financial Reporting Council, London.

Dalton, D.R., Daily, C.M., Ellstrand, A.E. and Johnson, J.L. (1998), 'Meta-Analytic Reviews of Board Composition, Leadership Structure, and Financial Performance', *Strategic Management Journal* 19, No. 24.

Deutsche Bank (2004a), *Global Corporate Governance Research, 'Beyond the Numbers – Corporate Governance in the UK'*, February 2004.

____ (2004b), *Global Corporate Governance Research, 'Beyond the Numbers – Corporate Governance in South Africa'*, October 2004.

Gompers P.A., Ishii, J.L., and Metrick, A. (2003), 'Corporate Governance and Equity Prices', *Quarterly Journal of Economics*, Vol. 118, No. 1 (February).

Greenbury, Sir Richard (1995), *Directors' Remuneration*, Gee & Co. Ltd., London.

Hampel, Sir Ronnie (1997), *Committee on Corporate Governance: Preliminary Report*, Gee & Co. Ltd., London.

Hermes (2002), *The Hermes Principles*, Hermes Pensions Management Ltd., London.

____ (2005), *Corporate Governance and Corporate Performance*, Hermes Investment Management Ltd., London.

____ (2006), *The Hermes Corporate Governance Principles*, Hermes Investment Management Ltd., London.

Hirschman, A.O. (1970), *Exit, Voice, and Loyalty*, Harvard University Press, Cambridge, Massachusetts.

Institutional Shareholders' Committee (1991), *Report on Investigation of Voting Rights by Institutions*, ISC, London.

____ (2002), *The Responsibilities of Institutional Shareholders and Agents – Statement of Principles*, ISC, London.

____ (2005), *Review of the Institutional Shareholders' Committee Statement of Principles on the Responsibilities of Institutional Shareholders and Agents*, ISC, London.

International Corporate Governance Network (2006), *Statement of Shareholder Responsibilities*, ICGN, London.

Manifest (2005), Manifest Information Services Ltd., Essex.

McKinsey & Co. (2002), *Global Investor Opinion Survey: Key Findings*, McKinsey & Co., London.

Millstein, I.M. and MacAvoy, P.W. (1998), 'The Active Board of Directors and Performance of the Large Publicly Traded Corporation', *Columbia Law Review* 98, No. 21.

Monks, R. (2001), *The New Global Investors*, Capstone Publishers, UK.

Myners, R. (2001), *Myners Report on Institutional Investment*, HM Treasury, London.

National Association of Pension Funds (1995), *Annual Survey of Occupational Pensions*, NAPF, London.

____ (1999), *Report of the Committee of Inquiry into UK Vote Execution*, NAPF, London.

Nesbitt, S.L. (1994), 'Long-term Rewards from Shareholder Activism: A Study of the "CalPERS Effect" ', *Journal of Applied Corporate Finance*, No. 5.

Office of National Statistics (2005), *Share Ownership, A Report on Ownership of Shares as at 31 December 2004*, HMSO, Norwich.

Patterson, D.J. (2000), *The Link Between Corporate Governance and Performance, Year 2000 Update*, Conference Board, New York.

Shareholder Voting Working Group (2005), *Review of the Impediments to Voting UK Shares*, SVWG, London.

Useem, M. (1996), *Investor Capitalism – How Money Managers Are Changing the Face of Corporate America*, BasicBooks, Harper Collins, New York.

■ USEFUL WEBSITES

www.napf.co.uk   The website of the National Association of Pension Funds offers topical articles on a range of corporate governance issues of particular relevance to UK pension funds.

www.abi.org.uk   The website of the Association of British Insurers offers topical articles on a range of corporate governance issues of particular relevance to the UK's insurance industry.

www.dti.gov.uk   The Department of Trade and Industry website offers a range of information including ministerial speeches and regulatory guidance.

http://calpers.ca.gov/   The website of the California Public Employees' Retirement System, a large pension fund active in corporate governance matters.

http://asp.thecorporatelibrary.net   The website of the Corporate Library provides a useful and topical range of corporate governance items.

http://europa.eu.int/comm/internal-market/company   The website of the European Union covering company law and corporate governance aspects.

7 Socially Responsible Investment

LEARNING OBJECTIVES

- To be aware of the origins of socially responsible investment
- To understand the different approaches that may be used for socially responsible (ethical) investment
- To appreciate the role of institutional investors in socially responsible investment
- To be aware of the different ethical indices that may be used to assess the performance of socially responsible funds
- To be aware of the evidence analysing the performance of socially responsible investment funds

Introduction

We have seen that corporate governance is concerned with many facets of a business and how that business is managed. The previous chapter highlighted how, over the last thirty years, institutional investor share ownership has increased substantially and the majority of UK equity is now owned by institutional investors. In recent years, there has been an increasing awareness of socially responsible investment (SRI) issues in the UK, and these have, in many cases, become an integral part of corporate governance policies, both of individual companies and of institutional investors.

SRI involves considering the ethical, social, and environmental performance of companies selected for investment as well as their financial performance. The term 'ethical investment' is often used interchangeably with the term 'socially responsible investment'.

The origins of socially responsible investment lie in various religious movements such as the Quakers and the Methodists. From the nineteenth century onwards, religious groups such as these have sought to invest their funds without compromising their principles. So, for example, the churches would avoid investing in companies involved in alcohol and gambling. This type of policy is common across many religions including Christianity and Islam. During the course of the twentieth century, there were various incidences with which religious groups sought to avoid investment contact, latterly one such incidence has been the avoidance of involvement with tobacco companies. It is worth mentioning that US church groups tend to be one of the most active in putting forward socially-based shareholder proposals at companies' annual general meetings. Such shareholder proposals include areas such as trying to ensure that advertising does not encourage young people to smoke.

SRI covers a wide range of areas including genetic engineering, the environment, employment conditions, and human rights. Recent cases of companies highlighted for not being socially responsible include those that have used child labour in the manufacture of their clothes overseas and retailers selling carpets that have been made by small children who are exploited by working long hours for little, if any, pay.

SRI and corporate governance

Increasingly, institutional investors have become aware of the importance of SRI on a number of fronts: client demand, corporate citizenship, and potential economic benefits. The OECD (1998) corporate governance report stated:

In the global economy, sensitivity to the many societies in which an individual corporation may operate can pose a challenge. Increasingly, however, investors in international capital markets expect corporations to forego certain activities – such as use of child or prison labour, bribery, support of oppressive regimes, and environmental disruption – even when those activities may not be expressly prohibited in a particular jurisdiction in which the corporation operates.

It is key to the development of SRI that the large institutional investors in both the UK and the USA have become more involved and willing to screen potential investments as appropriate. Increasingly, this approach is fuelled by client demand for SRI. A number of pension schemes in the UK, including British Coal and the Universities Superannuation Scheme, have asked their fund managers to take ethical and social issues into account in their investment strategy. A further motivation for SRI is highlighted by the OECD (1998): 'In accommodating the expectations of society, corporations must not lose sight of the primary corporate objective, which is to generate long-term economic profit to enhance shareholder (or investor) value. The Advisory Group recognises that, over the long term, acting as a responsible corporate citizen is consistent with this economic objective.'

The growing awareness of SRI and the involvement of the government via legislation means that institutional investors are becoming increasingly active in this field, for example, by setting up special funds or screening existing and potential investments. The value of UK ethical funds increased more than tenfold in the last decade, rising from £792 million in 1994 to £5,500 million in 2004 (EIRIS, 2005). It is expected that this trend will continue given the clear indication of the growing interest in this area.

An important development in the UK was that, from 3 July 2000, pension fund trustees have had to take account of SRI in their Statement of Investment Principles. This change means that pension fund trustees must state 'the extent (if at all) to which social, environmental or ethical considerations are taken into account in the selection, retention, and realisation of investments' (amendment to Pensions Act 1995). Therefore pension fund trustees are required to state their policy on social, environmental, and ethical issues, and if they do not have a policy in place, then this provision will also highlight that fact. A survey of pension fund trustees carried out by Gribben and Gitsham (2006), found that 'only one in ten trustees believe that companies are providing sufficient information to enable social and environmental impacts and risks to be assessed effectively'.

Strategies for SRI

Ethical Investment Research Services (EIRIS) is a leading provider of independent research into corporate social, environmental, and ethical performance; it was established in 1983 to help investors make responsible investment decisions. EIRIS has identified three basic strategies for SRI.

Three basic strategies for SRI

- **Engagement** – identify areas for improvement in the ethical, social, environmental policies of the companies invested in, and encourage them to make improvements.
- **Preference** – fund managers work to a list of guidelines that trustees prefer companies invested in to meet.
- **Screening** – trustees ask for investments to be limited to companies selected (screened) for their ethical behaviour. May be 'positive' or 'negative' screening.

EIRIS provides more detailed definitions for each of these strategies as follows.

Engagement

Engagement involves identifying areas for improvement in the ethical, social, and environmental policies of the companies invested in, and encouraging them to make those improvements. This can be done by:

- the investor telling the companies their policy and letting them know how it affects their decisions to invest in a company or respond to takeovers and share issues;
- the investor trying to persuade the company via regular meetings to improve their practices on issues such as employment practices, recycling, and pollution reduction;
- offering to help them formulate their own policy. This might be done through existing corporate governance voting policies by extending them to include ethical issues.

Preference

Fund managers work to a list of guidelines that the trustees prefer companies invested in to meet. They then select investments or portfolio weightings in them, taking into account how closely a company meets, or sets about meeting, these parameters. This approach also enables the investor to integrate ethical with financial decision-making; in cases where two companies get a similar rating against traditional financial indicators, they can be compared against the investor's ethical indicators, and the company with the better all-round performance selected.

Screening

Trustees ask the fund manager to limit their investments to a list of companies selected (screened) for their ethical behaviour. They may be companies whose conduct is viewed positively, such as those with good employment practices or those taking active steps to reduce levels of pollution. Or they may be selected for not indulging in certain 'negative' practices or proscribed industries.

Institutional investors' policies

In 1996, the National Association of Pension Funds (NAPF), in its guidance on good corporate governance, stated that:

NAPF believes it is inconceivable that, in the long run, a company can enhance shareholder value unless it takes good care to retain and develop its customer relationships; unless it provides encouragement to its employees; unless it develops effective relationships with its suppliers so that they can see the common interest in working to lower costs; unless it pays proper attention to preserving its 'licence to operate' from the community.

The sentiments embodied in this statement have become broadly accepted, and in the context of SRI, the last point is particularly pertinent: one has to have regard to the impact of a business' activities on the community at large and all that that implies, including the impact on the environment, and ethical aspects.

A number of institutional investors already have policies in place regarding SRI. The policies may be separate or incorporated as part of the institutional investors' wider corporate governance policies. Several of the largest UK institutional investors have made statements on SRI. Friends Provident stated: 'We will be using our influence as an investor to encourage companies to improve the way they (investee companies) manage environmental and ethical issues.' Friends Provident's approach is called the 'Responsible Engagement Overlay (REO)' and it is aimed at improving the behaviour of the companies in which it already invests.

Hermes Pensions Management Ltd. is a leading UK institutional investor with a portfolio of some £62bn invested in more than 3000 companies worldwide at the end of December 2005. In late January 2001, Hermes revised its corporate governance policies and called on UK companies to 'manage effectively relationships with its employees, suppliers and customers, to behave ethically and to have regard for the environment and society as a whole'. Whilst asking companies to disclose their policies on an annual basis, Hermes asked that the remuneration committee in each company, when setting incentive pay, consider the effect on the company's performance of social, environmental, and ethical matters. There should be a credible system for verifying the accuracy of social disclosures, and directors should take social issues into account when assessing risk. The statement issued by Hermes had the backing of eight investor institutions who expected to incorporate it into their policies.

In 2002, Hermes introduced the Hermes Principles. Hermes advocates that companies should be able to demonstrate that their investment decisions are sound and also demonstrate ethical behaviour. In the section on social, ethical, and environmental aspects, Hermes has two principles: principles 9 and 10. Principle 9 states: 'Companies should manage effectively relationships with their employees, suppliers and customers and with others who have a legitimate interest in the company's activities. Companies should behave ethically and have regard for the environment and society as a whole.' This principle identifies the importance of considering both stakeholder views and having regard to social responsibility aspects. Principle 10 states: 'Companies should support voluntary and statutory measures which minimise the externalisation of costs to the detriment of society at large.' This principle discourages companies from making business successful at the expense of society at large. The Hermes Corporate Governance Principles (2006) reiterate the aforesaid principle 9, but also state in principle 5 that 'we consider socially, ethically and environmentally responsible behaviour as part of the management process that companies should undertake in order to maximize shareholder value in the long term rather than as an end in itself'. Companies are encouraged to comply with internationally recognized guidelines and principles on social, ethical, and environmental matters.

Recognition of the growing importance of SRI was also evidenced by the ABI (2001) with the publication of its disclosure guidelines on SRI. The main focus of the guidelines is the identification and management of risks arising from social, environmental, and ethical issues that may affect either short-term or long-term business value. The flip side of this is that appropriate management of these risks may mean opportunities to enhance value. To this end, the guidelines recommend that the board should receive adequate information to make an assessment of the significance of social, environmental, and ethical matters that are relevant to the business and that there are appropriate systems in place for managing this type of risk, including 'performance measurement systems and appropriate remuneration incentives'. Furthermore, the guidelines state that the company's policies and procedures for managing this type of risk should be disclosed in the annual report, and not in any separate summary accounts nor on a dedicated social responsibility website. The ABI (2003) reviewed the level of compliance with its guidelines on socially responsible investment and found that

two thirds of the FTSE 100 companies made either adequate or full disclosure . . . in their annual report that their boards have assessed the business and reputational risks arising from the way they manage social, environmental and ethical issues, and that these risks are being properly managed.

The UK Social Investment Forum (UKSIF) is an active force in promoting the adoption, and propounding the virtues, of SRI in the UK. Its members encompass a wide range of interested parties including fund managers, organizations, companies, and individuals.

In the USA, there has long been an active movement for SRI. The main thrust has tended to come from church groups and ethical/environmental groups with investment interests. They have been particularly active in putting forward shareholder proposals at investee companies; it is not unusual for literally hundreds of shareholder proposals to relate to SRI. Whilst the large institutional investors have not tended to be so active in putting forward shareholder proposals (they tend to have other ways of making their 'voice' heard), they have often supported shareholder proposals put forward by these interest groups.

However, for the last few years, the Teachers' Insurance and Annuity Association – College Retirement Equities Fund (TIAA-CREF) has taken an active stand in trying to promote and ensure good workplace practice, for example. CalPERS, the USA's largest institutional investor, in its Global Proxy Voting Principles (issued 2001, revised 2005), states:

the [CalPERS] Board expects those who manage the companies whose equity securities are held in the Fund's portfolio to conduct themselves with propriety and with a view toward responsible corporate conduct that is consistent with practices and policies including, but not limited to, those articulated in the Global Sullivan Principles of Corporate Social Responsibility and the MacBride Principles.

In continental Europe too, in a number of countries including France, Germany, Belgium, and the Netherlands, there is a growing awareness of SRI. For example, in Germany, from January 2002, every pension fund provider must inform members in writing about whether, and in what form, social, ethical, and ecological aspects are taken into consideration. Similarly, there is a growing interest in SRI across the globe, for example, in Japan and also in Australia where recent changes require a description of the extent to which investment products take account of social, ethical, and environmental issues.

International guidance

There have been a large number of international guidelines and statements that are relevant to the area of SRI. These include:

- Global Sullivan Principles (1977) – principles that are directed towards increasing CSR throughout the world, based on self-help;
- the MacBride Principles (1984) – consists of nine fair employment, affirmative action principles;
- Coalition for Environmentally Responsible Economies (CERES) (1989) – a coalition of environmental, investor, and advocacy groups working together for sustainability in areas such as environmental restoration and management commitment;

- UN Global Compact (1999) – nine principles relating to the areas of human rights, labour standards, and environmental practices;

- OECD Guidelines for Multinational Enterprises (2000) – cover areas such as disclosure, environment, employment, industrial relations, bribery, and consumer interests;

- Global Reporting Initiative (GRI) Sustainability Guidelines (2002) – the United Nations Environment Programme (UNEP) and CERES formed a partnership in 1999 to encourage NGOs, business associations, corporations, and stakeholders to undertake sustainability reporting. The 2002 guidelines represent the latest consensus on a reporting framework for sustainability reporting;

- EC CSR – a Business Contribution to Sustainable Development (2002) encourages an EU framework for the development of SRI, especially promoting transparency and convergence of CSR practices and instruments.

Given that SRI and CSR are very much developing areas, further guidelines/revisions to existing guidelines are to be expected, and indeed are in process. However, it is becoming increasingly clear that companies will have to consider these as mainstream issues rather than as peripheral optional extras.

CSR indices

A number of stock market indices of companies with good corporate social responsibility (CSR) have been launched in recent years. These include the Ethibel Sustainability Index and the Domini Social Index, although perhaps the two most well-known are the FTSE4Good Indices and the Dow Jones Sustainability Indices (DJSI).

The FTSE4Good was launched in 2001 and is designed to reflect the performance of socially responsible equities. It covers four markets: the UK, US, Europe, and Global. It uses criteria for judging CSR based on three areas: human rights, stakeholder relations, and the environmental impact of a company's activities. When developing these criteria, the FTSE4Good drew on various international guidelines and statements including the United Nations Global Compact, the OECD Principles for Multinational Enterprises, the Global Sullivan Principles, the CERES Principles, the Caux Roundtable Principles, and the Amnesty International Human Rights Principles for Companies. There are four tradable and four benchmark indices that make up the FTSE4Good index series. In 2004, the FTSE4Good Japan index was launched, enabling investors to identify Japanese companies, within the FTSE Global Equity Index Series, which meet a set of internationally supported standards of corporate social responsibility. A committee of independent practitioners in SRI and CSR review the indices to ensure that they are an accurate reflection of best practice.

The DJSI are aimed at providing indices to benchmark the performance of investments in sustainability companies and funds. DJSI describes corporate sustainability as 'a business approach that creates long-term shareholder value by embracing opportunities and managing risks deriving from economic, environmental and social developments'. Components are selected by a systematic corporate sustainability assessment and include only the leading sustainability companies worldwide, thereby providing a link between companies that implement sustainability principles and investors who wish to invest in that type of company. Areas that receive higher weighting in arriving at the corporate sustainability assessment criteria include corporate governance, scorecards and measurement systems, environmental performance, and external stakeholders.

In March 2003, Business in the Community (BITC) reported on the launch of its first Corporate Responsibility Index. Companies who wished to be rated completed a substantial online survey of areas such as: their corporate strategy; the integration of CSR into the company's operations; management practice; performance and impact (social and environmental); assurance. The answers enabled BITC to score the companies. In general, the results revealed that companies seem better at creating CSR strategy than at implementing it effectively in their companies.

Corporate social responsibility

Corporate social responsibility was conceptualized by Carroll (1979) as 'the social responsibility of business encompasses the economic, legal, ethical, and discretionary expectations that society has of organizations at a given point in time'. This can be explained further as the business having a responsibility to produce goods that it sells at a profit, to abide by legal requirements, to do what is right and fair, and finally to do what might be desired of companies in terms of supporting the local community and making charitable donations. Carroll (2006) states: 'It appears that the corporate social responsibility concept has a bright future because, at its core, it addresses and captures the most important concerns of the public regarding business and society relationships.'

Gray et al. (1987) identified many of the accounting and accountability issues associated with corporate social reporting. Given the emphasis now being placed on socially responsible investment, it is not surprising that corporate social responsibility (CSR) has gained more prominence in recent years along with an emphasis on the company's board for its responsibility for relations with its stakeholders. Cadbury (2002) states that 'the broadest way of defining social responsibility is to say that the continued existence of companies is based on an implied agreement between business and society' and that 'the essence of the contract between society and business is that companies shall not pursue their immediate profit objectives at the expense of the longer term interests of the community'.

With the recognition that companies should not pursue profit without regard to the impact on wider societal interests, we can see a link with both agency theory and stakeholder theory discussed in Chapter 2. Whilst the directors manage the company on behalf of the shareholders (an agency relationship), the interests of stakeholders should also be taken into account (stakeholder theory). A Friedmanite view of the firm, whereby there is an emphasis on the purely financial aspects of the business, is no longer appropriate in a society that is increasingly taking an inclusive view of business.

Many companies have responded to this more inclusive approach by starting to report not just the traditional financial performance of the company (the bottom line) but also the 'triple bottom line', which essentially encompasses economic profit, social, and environmental performance. The triple bottom line conveys a wider information set than financial information, and helps to present the wider picture of the company's performance in relation to social and environmental matters. These aspects should now be incorporated in the operating and financial review (OFR) or the business review as part of the company's annual report to provide a deeper understanding of the impact of the company's activities on society. In Chapter 4, recent developments in EU and UK company law were highlighted. These will impact on companies' reporting in relation to CSR as companies need to disclose analysis of their performance, where appropriate, based on non-financial key performance indicators (KPIs) as well as financial KPIs.

The impact on shareholder value

An important facet of SRI is whether there is a beneficial effect on shareholder value (the value of the investment). Clearly, the OECD (1998) believes this to be so as it states that 'acting as a responsible citizen is consistent with this economic objective [of generating long-term economic profit to enhance shareholder (or investor) value]'. There have been a number of studies that have looked at the performance of SRI funds but there has been no definitive outcome one way or another as to whether SRI funds outperform non-SRI funds. In the UK, studies have included those by Luther et al. (1992), who found weak evidence of some overperformance, on a risk-adjusted basis, by 'ethical' unit trusts, although they pointed out that ethical investment seemed to be skewed toward smaller market capitalized companies, and in an extension of the paper, Luther and Matatko (1994) found that ethical funds had returns that were highly correlated with a small company index, hence abnormal returns may have been attributable more to a small company bias rather than to an ethical one. Mallin et al. (1995) analysed the performance of ethical funds and found that, on the mean excess returns, ethical funds appeared to underperform both non-ethical funds and the market in general, whereas on a risk-adjusted basis, ethical funds outperformed non-ethical funds. Research by Lewis and Mackenzie (2000), which utilized a questionnaire survey, highlighted the fact that institutional investors show general support for engaging in lobbying activity and the development of dialogue in order to improve corporate practice and influence companies to improve their ethical and environmental performance. Kreander et al. (2002) investigated the financial performance of 40 'ethical' funds from seven European countries. The results suggested that very few ethical funds significantly outperform a global benchmark after adjusting for risk; conversely, none of them significantly underperformed either. Kreander et al. (2005) studied the performance of 60 European funds from four countries and used a matched-pair approach for fund evaluation. They found no difference between ethical and non-ethical funds according to the performance measures employed.

Given that SRI is now increasingly perceived as a mainstream element of good corporate governance, the importance of SRI will continue to gain momentum.

Conclusions

SRI and CSR are of growing importance in many countries. In the UK, there has been a significant upward trend in socially responsible investment and the government has made it very much an agenda item for pension fund trustees. In the USA, it is an area that has a high profile and in which there is continuing interest. There are developments in continental Europe, Australia, and Japan, to name but a few countries, to encourage more socially responsible investment.

Institutional investors have developed policy statements on SRI either as separate statements or as an integrated part of their corporate governance policies. A number of institutional investors have developed their SRI analytical capability with new appointments or additional resources. Increasingly, SRI is seen as a mainstream corporate governance issue and, as well as the social and environmental benefits to be gained from SRI, there is the increasing perception that SRI can help to maintain or increase shareholder value. Together, these are two advantages that should mean that SRI will continue to grow apace.

■ SUMMARY

- Socially responsible investment (SRI) involves considering the ethical, social, and environmental performance of companies as well as their financial performance. The origins of SRI lie in various religious movements that, from the nineteenth century onwards, sought to invest their funds without compromising their principles.

- There are three basic strategies for SRI – engagement, preference, and screening.

- Engagement – identify areas for improvement in the ethical, social, and environmental policies of the companies invested in, and encourage them to make improvements.

- Preference – fund managers work to a list of guidelines that trustees prefer companies invested in to meet.

- Screening – trustees ask for investments to be limited to companies selected (screened) for their ethical behaviour.

- Many institutional investors have developed SRI policies/guidelines; others have incorporated their views on SRI into their mainstream corporate governance policies.

- SRI indices measure the level of corporate social responsibility (CSR) in equities. Companies are included in the indices, or score well in them, if they have a good record on CSR.

- The evidence regarding financial performance of SRI (ethical) funds is rather inconclusive but they do not underperform the market generally.

Example: Novo Nordisk

This is an example of a Scandinavian company that is committed to corporate social responsibility and has comprehensive disclosure of its policies. It utilizes the triple bottom line in its reporting. It is included in both the FTSE4Good and the Dow Jones Sustainability Indices.

Novo Nordisk is a focused healthcare company, being a world leader in diabetes care. It is the 12th largest company in Denmark, measured by turnover, and second largest in terms of its profitability. Its sustainability report states: 'In our vision of sustainability, corporate commitment is aligned with personal values.' It believes that it is possible to balance business concerns with those of stakeholders, and use the triple bottom line to frame this belief. The triple bottom line encompasses social and environmental responsibility, and economic viability. Social responsibility includes employees, people whose healthcare it serves, and local/global communities; environmental responsibility includes the environment itself, animal welfare and bioethics; financial and economic viability includes corporate growth, national growth, and investors' expectations.

The overall strategy is based on a three-tier approach: the corporate governance structure defines its commitments; a stakeholder engagement approach means it can stay attuned to stakeholder issues and concerns; target-setting with systematic follow-up procedures aids ongoing improvement and better organizational practices.

In 2005, Novo Nordisk received a number of awards, one of which was from the Dow Jones Sustainability Index in which it was ranked Super Sector Leader in Healthcare.

Example: Morley Fund Management

This is an example of a London-based institutional investor with a goal of becoming one of the world's leading global fund managers and a leader in socially responsible investment and corporate social responsibility.

Morley Fund Management has total assets under management in excess of £147bn (as at September 2005). Morley has a large, experienced team of SRI fund managers and researchers who analyse the various SRI and CSR issues that arise. Morley states that it 'believe[s] it is important to engage with companies to encourage best practice in social, environmental and corporate governance matters, in order to maximise value over the long term for our investors'.

Areas of particular emphasis in recent years include promoting international frameworks to uphold and protect human rights, improving the conditions of workers (for example, the virtual slave labour that has been used in the harvesting of cocoa beans) and trying to ensure that companies take responsibility for health problems caused by industrial processes and compensate workers accordingly.

Morley is prepared to act on its principles and vote against the annual report and accounts of companies that do not have adequate social, environmental, and ethical reporting. An example of this was when Morley voted against the Exxon annual report and accounts in 2002 because they had inadequate environmental reporting. An analysis of Morley's schedule of voting on company resolutions, shows that during 2005, it voted at 1160 shareholder meetings and at 441 of these meetings it voted against or abstained on at least one resolution. The resolutions that it voted against, or abstained on, included insufficient environmental reporting in the company's report and accounts.

Mini case study: Vodafone

This is an example of a company, the shares of which are included in many ethical investment funds because of its good record on social, environmental, and ethical issues. It is listed in the FTSE4Good and Dow Jones Sustainability Indices.

Vodafone is one of the largest companies in Europe. It made history with the first UK mobile call on 1 January 1985, and since then has gone on to become one of the largest communications companies in the world. By January 2006, Vodafone had over 179.3 million customers, and in 2005, it was rated third in the Accountability Ratings, which evaluate companies across six key areas that mirror the AA1000 framework for social, ethical, and environmental management. Out of a maximum available of 100, Vodafone scored 71 (the top-scoring company, from another sector, scored 78). Clearly then, Vodafone is high profile in terms of its corporate social responsibility (CSR) as well as its financial and sectoral performance.

In Vodafone, the executive committee, which focuses on the group's strategy, financial structure and planning, succession planning, organizational development, and group-wide policies, is the reporting line for Corporate Responsibility (CR) issues, indicative of the importance that is placed on these issues.

Vodafone's Corporate Responsibility Report for the year ended March 2005 highlights that Vodafone has six strategic goals, one of which is corporate responsibility. In his Chief Executive's letter, Arun Sarin states:

> corporate responsibility is a vehicle for achieving prosperity in society *and* in business. I believe it is about generating win-win business ideas that balance the interests of different stakeholders. In essence, when Vodafone talks about CR we mean sustainable development . . . [and] As we continue to learn from our stakeholders, my vision for corporate responsibility is that it becomes fully integrated into everything we do – it becomes instinctive.

In the CR Report, it is emphasized that CR is one of the company's top priorities and that this is substantiated with key objectives in the company's five-year plan.

The CR Report is comprehensive and provides a good picture of the depth of Vodafone's CR activities. A useful summary of various objectives and commitments that Vodafone has set itself in order to help improve its CR performance is shown at the end of the report, detailing key issues, what Vodafone has said that it will do in relation to each issue, and the deadline for the action to occur. An example is the reuse and recycling of mobile phones in relation to which Vodafone has committed to have return schemes in all of its operating companies, to support the development of programmes in at least three developing countries to repair, reuse, and recycle mobile phones, and to increase the number of phones collected for reuse and recycling by 50 per cent; all of these commitments relating to reuse/recycling of mobile phones are to be achieved by March 2007.

Vodafone meets regularly with large institutional investors to discuss a variety of topics including corporate responsibility issues.

Vodafone's commitment to CR has made it a popular choice for inclusion in ethical investment funds.

■ QUESTIONS

The discussion questions below cover the key learning points of this chapter. Reading of some of the additional reference material will enhance the depth of the students' knowledge and understanding of these areas.

1. Why might institutional investors be interested in socially responsible investment?

2. Why are more companies becoming interested in their social and environmental policies?

3. In what ways might institutional investors decide on which companies to invest in when considering their social responsibility policies?

4. Do you think that investors should be willing to sacrifice financial return, if necessary, in order to have a portfolio that is comprised of socially responsible investments?

5. 'Companies are about making money, not about social responsibility.' Critically discuss this statement.

6. Critically discuss the role of institutional investors in the area of social responsibility.

Investors shine a green light on risk assessment

Fiona Harvey talks to Joachim Faber of Allianz Global Investors and hears how the investment industry is seeing managers paying greater attention to criteria such as climate change

As if life was not hard enough for asset managers, increasingly they are coming under pressure to assess their portfolio companies on the basis of a much broader suite of criteria than the purely financial, encompassing risks such as climate change and environmental concerns that were paid scant regard in the past.

According to Joachim Faber, chief executive of Allianz Global Investors, this should be viewed as a positive development: "We are constantly pushing to get a deeper view [of companies]. If you talk about risk, it is very clear that we have undervalued climate change risk in the past."

In any case, managers had better get used to it: "We see this as an increasing trend."

Allianz Global Investors, one of the world's top five asset management groups with about €1,000bn under management, has been supporting a system of "enhanced reporting" by which companies report, alongside their financial results, on environmental issues, their exposure to risks from problems such as climate change, and aspects of their "sustainability" a buzzword much in use among non-governmental organisations and campaigning groups that broadly means growth and the use of resources in a way that does not harm the ability of future generations to meet their needs. The company was a founder member of the Carbon Disclosure Project, which asks companies to disclose production of greenhouse gases and exposure to climate change risks.

Investments that have been viewed as rather risky, such as renewable energy and environmental technologies, begin to look quite safe compared with the wider market

Customers have welcomed the initiative, Mr Faber reports: "Our clients have been responding well throughout this. We have not had a single client say, we're not interested in this, stick to your spreadsheets."

For companies and their management, reporting on these issues is complex. Mr Faber says: "For an NGO [or environmental group] it's simple but if you are an asset manager you have to balance what is right [environmentally] with the earnings for investors… on a quarterly basis."

But he believes there is growing acceptance among all sectors of the financial community that such reporting is the future: "From the investor point of view, we are all looking for additional information on softer factors. That's good for us." Such information often provides valuable insights into how well companies are being managed, he contends. And in his conversations with clients and other companies, Mr Faber says he frequently raises these issues.

In a further effort to catch the environmental wave among investors, Allianz Global Investors is planning to launch a new fund in May, to be called "Ecotrends". The new fund will focus on investing in companies with exposure to three themes: eco-energy, or renewable and low-carbon forms of energy; clean water; and pollution control. It will be investing on a global basis. Allianz Global Investors believes it will be different to other funds in this market by focusing on these three themes, where others tend to choose one of these.

Financial Times Monday 27 February 2006

In doing so, the company is showing it is in step with the times, Mr Faber thinks. Developments such as the coming into force of the Kyoto protocol on climate change, the start of the European Union's mandatory greenhouse gas emissions trading scheme just over a year ago, an increasingly vocal global debate on climate change, increasing shareholder activism and calls for greater public accountability from companies and on top of all that increasing investor interest in renewable and low-carbon forms of energy have all combined to push asset managers in this direction.

In particular, Mr Faber sees big opportunities for investors in renewable energy. At a time of low yields in products like bonds, and the market in structured products "approaching very risky levels", he sees high returns in this area.

The development of the EU's trading scheme has even encouraged Mr Faber to consider entering the carbon trading market, though he has no firm plans as yet: "We are working on some concepts."

The opportunities Mr Faber sees in renewable energy are made more attractive by the concerns he has about the broader private equity investment market. He explains: "Our private equity business is very difficult at the moment, we have trouble convincing ourselves about investment opportunities. Prices are so high, so much money is chasing very few opportunities. We are very reluctant to invest." He goes on: "What happens [to the market] depends on the supply of liquidity. The big question is can the underlying industrial activity really produce so much higher returns to support these prices?"

In these circumstances, investments that have been traditionally viewed as rather risky, such as renewable energy and environmental technologies, begin to look quite safe in comparison with the rest of the market, because they are driven by factors such as government regulation and higher oil and gas prices. These advantages, moreover, are unlikely to go away: "I can't see the oil price falling below $50 [a barrel]."

Financial Times Monday 27 February 2006

■ REFERENCES

Association of British Insurers (2003), *FTSE 100 Companies Respond Positively to the ABI SRI Guidelines*, ABI Media Centre News Release 13/02, 3 February 2003.

____ (2001), *Disclosure Guidelines on Socially Responsible Investment*, ABI, London.

Cadbury, Sir Adrian (2002), *Corporate Governance and Chairmanship, A Personal View*, Oxford University Press, Oxford.

Carroll, A.B. (1979), 'A Three-dimensional Conceptual Model of Corporate Social Performance', *Academy of Management Review*, No. 4.

____ (2006), 'Corporate Social Responsibility: A Historical Perspective' in *The Accountable Corporation*, M.J. Epstein and K.O. Hanson (eds.), Praeger Publishers, Westport, USA.

EIRIS (2005) *The Ethical Investor*, Ethical Investment Research Service, London.

Gray, R.H., Owen, D. and Maunders, K. (1987), *Corporate Social Reporting: Accounting and Accountability*, Prentice Hall International, London.

Gribben C. and Gitsham M., (2006), *Will UK Pension Funds Become More Responsible? A Survey of Trustees 2006 Edn*, Ashridge Centre for Business and Society & Just Pensions/UKSIF.

Hermes (2002), *The Hermes Principles*, Hermes Pensions Management Ltd., London.

____ (2006), *The Hermes Corporate Governance Principles*, Hermes Pensions Management Ltd., London.

Kreander, N., Gray, R.H., Power, D.M. and Sinclair, C.D. (2002), 'The Financial Performance of European Ethical Funds 1996–1998', *Journal of Accounting and Finance*, Vol. 1, 2002.

Kreander, N., Gray, R.H., Power, D.M. and Sinclair, C.D. (2005), 'Evaluating the Performance of Ethical and Non-Ethical Funds: A Matched Pair Analysis', *Journal of Business Finance and Accounting*, 32(7,8), September/October 2005.

Lewis, A. and Mackenzie, C. (2000), 'Support for Investor Activism Among UK Ethical Investors', *Journal of Business Ethics*, April 2000.

Luther, R.G. and Matatko, J. (1994), 'The Performance of Ethical Unit Trusts: Choosing an Appropriate Benchmark', *British Accounting Review*, 26.

_____ and Corner, C. (1992), 'The Investment Performance of UK "Ethical" Unit Trusts', *Accounting, Auditing and Accountability*, 5(4).

Mallin, C.A., Saadouni, B. and Briston, R.J. (1995), 'The Financial Performance of Ethical Investment Funds', *Journal of Business Finance and Accounting*, 22(4).

OECD (1998), *Corporate Governance: Improving Competitiveness and Access to Capital in Global Markets*, Report to the OECD by the Business Sector Advisory Group on Corporate Governance, OECD, Paris.

■ **USEFUL WEBSITES**

www.eiris.org The website of the Ethical Investment Research Services has information on various aspects of ethical investment.

www.sustainability-index.com/ The website of the Dow Jones Sustainability Indexes provides information about the indexes, which track the financial performance of the leading sustainability-driven companies worldwide.

www.ethibel.org The website of ETHIBEL, an independent consultancy agency for socially responsible investment.

www.ftse.com/ftse4good/index The website of the FTSE4Good index provides information about the composition of the index and related material.

www.hermes.co.uk/corporate-governance The Hermes website contains information related to various corporate governance issues.

Part Two case study: Institutional investors and socially responsible investment

This case study illustrates how, when an influential group of institutional investors work together, they can influence the operations of their investee companies where these are in a country where there are human rights abuses, political instability, and unacceptable risks. This action was part of the socially responsible investment remit of the institutional investors.

The political instability and human rights abuses make Burma a very difficult country in which to undertake business. As well as the physical dangers of such operations, companies might be subject to negative press campaigns by 'pressure' groups and corruption attempts locally. A number of the largest UK and European institutional investors including Morley Fund Management, Co-operative Insurance Services, Ethos Investment Foundation, Friends Ivory & Sime, Henderson Global Investors, PGGM and the Universities Superannuation Scheme joined forces to launch 'Business Involvement in

Myanmar (Burma) – A statement from institutional investors'. The statement called on companies to justify their involvement in Burma, given the risks that such activity may pose to shareholders, and sought assurance that company boards had considered fully these risks and had effective policies and procedures in place to manage them. Having such risk assessment and management procedures in place is in accordance with the ABI's guidelines on Socially Responsible Investment.

One of the institutional investors involved in launching the statement, Morley Fund Management, met with one of their investee companies, British American Tobacco (BAT) to discuss BAT's joint venture with the military government to manufacture cigarettes in Burma. Subsequently, in July 2003, the British Government requested BAT to reconsider its investment in Burma. BAT stated: 'We have reached what we believe is a balanced solution to meet the British government's requirement while maintaining local employment prospects and the continued orderly and responsible local marketing of our brands.' On 18 June 2004, it sold its 60 per cent shareholding in Rothmans of Pall Mall Myanmar Pte Limited (RPMM) to Distinction Investment Holdings, a Singapore-based investment company. The remaining 40 per cent of RPMM is owned by the Myanmar (Burma) Government. BAT stated: 'We have licensed brands to the new owner to manufacture and market them locally through RPMM, enabling its continued operation as a going concern and good local employer.' BAT would not necessarily have chosen to leave Burma, maybe feeling that it could influence the local situation more by maintaining a presence there, but given the British government's request, it decided to withdraw.

Directors and Board Structure

8 Directors and Board Structure

LEARNING OBJECTIVES

- To be aware of the distinction between unitary and dual boards
- To have a detailed understanding of the roles, duties, and responsibilities of directors
- To understand the rationale for key board committees and their functions
- To be able to critically assess the criteria for independence of non-executive (outside) directors
- To comprehend the role and contribution of non-executive (outside) directors

---

Introduction

This chapter covers the board structure of a company. The discussion encompasses the function of a board and its sub-committees (the most common ones being the audit, remuneration, nomination, and risk committees), the roles, duties, and responsibilities of directors, and the attributes and contribution of a non-executive (outside) director. Whilst the context is that of a UK company, much of the material is appropriate to other countries that also have a unitary (one-tier) board structure and may also be generalized to a dual (two-tier) board structure.

Unitary board versus dual board

A major corporate governance difference between countries is the board structure, which may be unitary or dual depending on the country. As in the UK, in the majority of EU Member States, the unitary board structure is predominant (in five states, the dual structure is also available). However, in Austria, Germany, the Netherlands, and

Denmark, the dual structure is predominant. In the dual structure, employees may have representation on the supervisory board (as in Germany, covered in detail in Chapter 10) but this may vary from country to country.

Unitary board

A unitary board of directors is the form of board structure in the UK and the USA, and is characterized by one single board comprising both executive and non-executive directors. The unitary board is responsible for all aspects of the company's activities, and all the directors are working to achieve the same ends. The shareholders elect the directors to the board at the company's annual general meeting.

Dual board

A dual board system consists of a supervisory board and an executive board of management. However, in a dual board system, there is a clear separation between the functions of supervision (monitoring) and that of management. The supervisory board oversees the direction of the business whilst the management board is responsible for the running of the business. Members of one board cannot be members of another, so there is a clear distinction between management and control. Shareholders appoint the members of the supervisory board (other than the employee members), whilst the supervisory board appoints the members of the management board.

Commonalities between unitary and dual board structures

There are many similarities in board practice between a unitary and a dual board system. The unitary board and the supervisory board usually appoint the members of the managerial body: the group of managers to whom the unitary board delegates authority in the unitary system and the management board in a dual system. Both bodies usually have responsibility for ensuring that financial reporting and control systems are operating properly and for ensuring compliance with the law.

Usually, both the unitary board of directors and the supervisory board (in a dual system) are elected by shareholders (in some countries, such as Germany, employees may elect some supervisory board members).

Advocates of each type of board structure, unitary or dual, identify their main advantages as respectively that, in a one-tier system, there is a closer relationship and better information flow as all directors, both executive and non-executive, are on the same single board; in a dual system, there is a more distinct and formal separation between the supervisory body and those being 'supervised', because of the separate management board and supervisory board structures. These aspects are discussed further in Chapter 10. However, whether the structure is unitary or dual, many codes seem to have a common approach to areas relating to the function of boards and key board committees, to independence, and to the consideration of shareholder and shareholder rights.

Combined Code

In Chapter 3, the Cadbury Code of Best Practice was cited as having influenced the development of corporate governance codes in many countries. The Cadbury Code clearly emphasizes, inter alia, the central role of the board, the importance of a division of responsibilities at the head of the company, and the role of non-executive directors. The Combined Code (2006) main principles in relation to 'Section A: Directors' are shown below.

online resource centre

THE COMBINED CODE

SECTION 1 COMPANIES

A. DIRECTORS

The board

1. Every company should be headed by an effective board, which is collectively responsible for the success of the company.

Chairman and chief executive

2. There should be a clear division of responsibilities at the head of the company between the running of the board and the executive responsibility for the running of the company's business. No one individual should have unfettered powers of decision.

Board balance and independence

3. The board should include a balance of executive and non-executive directors (and in particular independent non-executive directors) such that no individual or small group of individuals can dominate the board's decision taking.

Appointments to the board

4. There should be a formal, rigorous and transparent procedure for the appointment of new directors to the board.

Information and professional development

5. The board should be supplied in a timely manner with information in a form and of a quality appropriate to enable it to discharge its duties. All directors should receive induction on joining the board and should regularly update and refresh their skills and knowledge.

Performance evaluation

6. The board should undertake a formal and rigorous annual evaluation of its own performance and that of its committees and individual directors.

Re-election

7. All directors should be submitted for re-election at regular intervals, subject to continued satisfactory performance. The board should ensure planned and progressive refreshing of the board.

Source: Combined Code on Corporate Governance (2006)

The Combined Code is appended to the Listing Rules by which companies listed on the London Stock Exchange must abide. However, companies can conform with the Combined Code's provisions on a 'comply or explain' basis. 'Comply or explain' means that the company will generally be expected to comply with the provisions of the Combined Code, but if it is unable to comply with a particular provision, then it can explain why it is unable to comply. Institutional investors and their representative groups monitor carefully all matters related to the Combined Code, and will contact companies if they have not complied with a provision of the Combined Code and protest if the company does not have an appropriate reason for non-compliance.

The board of directors

The board of directors leads and controls a company and hence an effective board is fundamental to the success of the company. The board is the link between managers and investors, and is essential to good corporate governance and investor relations. As mentioned earlier, the UK has a unitary board system whilst many European countries have a dual board system (a management board and a supervisory board).

Given the UK's unitary board system, it is desirable that the roles of chairman and chief executive officer (CEO) are split because otherwise there could be too much power vested in one individual. The chairman is responsible for the running of the board whilst the CEO is responsible for the running of the business. The Combined Code (2006) states that 'the roles of chairman and chief executive should not be exercised by the same individual' (para. A.2.1). When a chief executive retires from his post, he should not then become chairman of the same company (exceptionally, a board may agree to a chief executive becoming chairman, but in this case, the board should discuss the matter with major shareholders setting out the reasons, and also declare these in the next annual report). The Higgs Review (2003) reported that only five FTSE 100 companies had a joint chairman/chief executive officer, whilst this figure rose to 11 per cent of companies outside the FTSE 350.

 online resource centre

Role of the board

The board is responsible for: determining the company's aims and the strategies, plans, and policies to achieve those aims; monitoring progress in the achievement of those aims (both from an overview company aspect and also in terms of analysis and evaluation of its own performance as a board and as individual directors); appointing a chief executive officer with appropriate leadership qualities. Sir Adrian Cadbury (2002) gives an excellent exposition of corporate governance and chairmanship, and the role and effectiveness of the board in corporate governance.

Epstein and Roy (2006) state that

high-performance boards must achieve three core objectives:

(1) provide superior strategic guidance to ensure the company's growth and prosperity;

(2) ensure accountability of the company to its stakeholders, including shareholders, employees, customers, suppliers, regulators and the community;

(3) ensure that a highly qualified executive team is managing the company.

Decisions relating to board composition and structure will be of fundamental importance in determining whether, and to what extent, the board is successful in achieving these objectives.

Role, duties, and responsibilities

It is essential that the role, duties, and responsibilities of directors are clearly defined. The Combined Code (2006) states that 'the board's role is to provide entrepreneurial leadership of the company within a framework of prudent and effective controls which enables risk to be assessed and managed' (para A.1). Directors should make decisions in an objective way and in the company's best interests.

The board should have regular meetings, with an agenda, and there should be a formal schedule of matters over which the board has the right to make decisions. There should be appropriate reporting procedures defined for the board and its sub-committees. As mentioned earlier, the roles of chair and CEO should preferably be split to help ensure that no one individual is too powerful. The board should have a balance between executive and non-executive directors. All directors should have access to the company secretary and also be able to take independent professional advice. The Combined Code (2006) recommends that directors should receive appropriate training when they are first appointed to the board of a listed company.

According to UK law, the directors should act in good faith in the interests of the company, and exercise care and skill in carrying out their duties. The Company Law Reform Bill (2005) defines, in sections 154–161, the directors' duties as follows:

- a duty to act within powers, that is, to act in accordance with the company's constitution and only exercise powers for the purposes for which they are conferred;

- a duty to promote the success of the company, so a director must act in the way he considers, in good faith, would be most likely to promote the success of the company for the benefit of its members as a whole (in fulfilling this duty, the directors should have regard to the interests of various stakeholder groups including employees, suppliers, customers, the local community, and the impact on the environment);

- a duty to exercise independent judgment;

- a duty to exercise reasonable care, skill, and diligence;

- a duty to avoid conflicts of interest;

- a duty not to accept benefits from third parties;
- a duty to declare an interest on proposed transactions or arrangements.

Given that the company is comprised of different shareholders, it may not be possible for the directors, whilst acting in the interest of the company as a whole, to please all shareholders at all times. In order to perform their role to best effect, it is vital that directors have access to reliable information on a timely basis. It is an essential feature of good corporate governance that the board will, in its turn, be accountable to shareholders and provide them with relevant information so that, for example, decision-making processes are transparent.

The roles of the Chief Executive Officer, Chairman, Senior Independent Director, and Company Secretary are discussed below.

Chief executive officer

The Chief Executive Officer (CEO) has the executive responsibility for the running of the company's business; on the other hand, the Chairman has responsibility for the running of the board. The two roles should not therefore be combined and carried out by one person, as this would give an individual too much power.

One particular problem that arises from time to time is whether a retiring CEO should become chairman of the same company. This is generally discouraged because a chairman should be independent. The Combined Code (2006) states:

A chief executive should not go on to be chairman of the same company. If exceptionally a board decides that a chief executive should become chairman, the board should consult major shareholders in advance and should set out its reasons to shareholders at the time of the appointment and in the next annual report (para A.2.2).

As well as a lack of independence, there is a feeling that it might cause problems for any incoming CEO if the retired CEO is still present at a senior level in the company (in the role of chairman) because he may tend to try to become more involved in the running of the company rather than the running of the board (his new role as chairman).

Various institutional bodies have made their views known on this issue: for example, Research Recommendations Electronic Voting (RREV), a joint venture between the NAPF and Institutional Shareholder Services (ISS), states that 'the normal application of the NAPF policy is to vote against the re-election of a director with the roles of both chief executive and chairman'. Hermes, in its Corporate Governance Principles, states that it is generally opposed to a chief executive officer becoming chairman of the board at the same company.

Chairman

The Chairman is responsible for the running of the board and for ensuring that the board meets frequently, that directors have access to all the information they need to make an informed contribution at board meetings, and that all directors are given the opportunity to speak at board meetings.

As Sir Adrian Cadbury (2002) observed:

the primary task of chairmen is to chair their boards. This is what they have been appointed to do and, however the duties at the top of a company may be divided, chairing the board is their responsibility alone (p. 78).

He also succinctly highlights an important difference between CEOs and chairmen:

the difference between the authority of chairmen and that of chief executives is that chairmen carry the authority of the board, while chief executives carry the authority delegated to them by the board. Chairmen exercise their authority on behalf of the board; chief executives have personal authority in line with the terms of their appointment (p. 99).

The Chairman should hold meetings with the non-executive directors without the executives present. The Combined Code (2006) states that no individual should hold more than one chairmanship of a FTSE 100 company.

Senior independent director

The Combined Code (2006) provides for the appointment of a Senior Independent Director (SID) who should be one of the independent non-executive directors. The Combined Code (2006) states:

the senior independent director should be available to shareholders if they have concerns which contact through the normal channels of chairman, chief executive or finance director has failed to resolve or for which such contact is inappropriate (para A.3.3).

The Hermes Corporate Governance Principles also see the SID as providing an additional communication channel to shareholders and also state:

if the chairman of the board is not independent, then the board should appoint a senior independent director whose role would include reviewing the performance of the chairman (para 3.4).

The non-executive directors should meet without the chairman present at least annually in order to appraise the chairman's performance, and on other occasions as necessary. At these times, the SID would lead the meeting.

Company secretary

The Company Secretary, like the directors, must act in good faith and avoid conflicts of interest. The Company Secretary has a range of responsibilities including facilitating the work of the board by ensuring that the directors have all the information they need for the main board and also for the board sub-committees (commonly audit, remuneration, nomination), and that such information flows well between the various constituents. The Company Secretary advises the board, via the chairman, on all governance matters and will assist with the professional development needs of directors and induction requirements for new directors.

The dismissal of the Company Secretary is a decision for the board as a whole and not just the CEO or Chairman.

Board sub-committees

The board may appoint various sub-committees, which should report regularly to the board, and although the board may delegate various activities to these sub-committees, it is the board as a whole that remains responsible for the areas covered by the sub-committees. Charkham (2005) states:

committees of the board are used for various purposes, the main one being to assist the dispatch of business by considering it in more detail than would be convenient for the whole board . . . the second purpose is to increase objectivity either because of inherent conflicts of interest such as executive remuneration, or else to discipline personal preferences as in the exercise of patronage.

The Cadbury Report recommended that an audit committee and a remuneration committee should be formed, and also stated that a nomination committee would be one possible way to make the board appointments process more transparent.

The Higgs Review (2003) reported that most listed companies have an audit committee and a remuneration committee. Only one FTSE 100 company did not have an audit committee or remuneration committee, whilst 15 per cent of companies outside the FTSE 350 did not have an audit committee. Adoption of nomination committees has tended to be less prevalent with the majority (71 per cent) of companies outside the FTSE 350 not having a nomination committee. FTSE 100 companies have tended to adopt nomination committees with the exception of six companies. The Combined Code (2006) states that there should be a nomination committee to lead the board appointments process.

Audit committee

The audit committee is arguably the most important of the board sub-committees.

The Smith review of audit committees, a group appointed by the Financial Reporting Council, reported in January 2003. The review made clear the important role of the audit committee 'while all directors have a duty to act in the interests of the company, the audit committee has a particular role, acting independently from the executive, to ensure that the interests of shareholders are properly protected in relation to financial reporting and internal control' (para 1.5). The review defined the audit committee's role in terms of 'oversight', 'assessment', and 'review', indicating the high-level overview that audit committees should take – they need to satisfy themselves that there is an appropriate system of controls in place but they do not undertake the monitoring themselves.

It is the role of the audit committee to review the scope and outcome of the audit, and to try to ensure that the objectivity of the auditors is maintained. This would usually involve a review of the audit fee and fees paid for any non-audit work, and the general independence of the auditors. The audit committee provides a useful 'bridge' between both internal and external auditors and the board, helping to ensure that the board is fully aware of all relevant issues related to the audit. The audit committee's role may also involve reviewing arrangements for whistle-blowers (staff who wish confidentially to raise concerns about possible improper practices in the company). In addition, where there is no risk management committee (see below), the audit committee should assess the systems in place to identify and manage financial and non-financial risks in the company.

The Combined Code (2006) states that 'the board should establish an audit committee of at least three, or in the case of smaller companies, two, members, who should all be independent non-executive directors. The board should satisfy itself that at least one member of the audit committee has recent and relevant financial experience' (para C.3.1).

Spira (2002) provides a useful insight into the processes and interactions of audit committees, and highlights the importance of the composition of audit committees. The audit committee should comprise independent non-executive directors who are in a position to ask appropriate questions so helping to give assurance that the audit committee is functioning properly.

Remuneration committee

The area of executive remuneration is always a 'hot issue' and one that attracts a lot of attention from investors and so, perhaps inevitably, the press. Executive remuneration itself is covered in some detail in a separate chapter, whilst the structure of the remuneration committee is detailed below.

The Combined Code (2006) states that 'the board should establish a remuneration committee of at least three, or in the case of smaller companies, two, members, who should all be independent non-executive directors' (para B.2.1). The remuneration committee should make recommendations to the board, within agreed terms of reference, on the company's framework of executive remuneration and its cost; it should determine on their behalf specific remuneration packages for each of the executive directors, including pension rights and any compensation payments.

The establishment of a remuneration committee (in the form recommended by the Combined Code) prevents executive directors from setting their own remuneration levels. The remuneration committee mechanism should also provide a formal, transparent procedure for the setting of executive remuneration levels including the determination of appropriate targets for any performance-related pay schemes. The members of the remuneration committee should be identified in the annual report. The remuneration of non-executive directors is decided by the chairman and the executive members of the board. The company chairman may serve on – but should not chair – the remuneration committee where he is considered independent on appointment as the chairman.

Nomination committee

In the past, directors were often appointed on the basis of personal connections. This process often did not provide the company with directors with appropriate business experience relevant to the particular board to which they were appointed. The board would also not have a balance in as much as there would be a lack of independent non-executive directors.

The Combined Code (2006) advocates a formal, rigorous, and transparent procedure for the appointment of new directors and states that 'there should be a nomination committee which should lead the process for board appointments and make recommendations to the board. A majority of members of the nomination committee should be independent non-executive directors' (para A.4.1). The chair of the committee may be the chairman of the company or an independent non-executive director.

The nomination committee should evaluate the existing balance of skills, knowledge, and experience on the board, and utilize this when preparing a candidate profile for new appointments. The nomination committee should throw its net as wide as possible in the search for suitable candidates to ensure that it identifies the best candidates. In an often rapidly changing business environment, the nomination committee should also be involved with succession planning in the company, noting challenges that may arise and identifying possible gaps in skills and knowledge that would need to be filled with new appointments. As with the other key board committees, the members of the nomination committee should be identified in the annual report.

It is important that the board has a balanced composition, both in terms of executive and non-executive directors, and in terms of the experience, qualities, and skills that individuals bring to the board. The Institute of Directors (IoD) has published some useful guidance in this area. Below is an extract from Standards for the Board (1999) in relation to an action list for deciding board composition.

ACTION LIST FOR DECIDING BOARD COMPOSITION

- Consider the ratio and number of executive and non-executive directors.
- Consider the energy, experience, knowledge, skill and personal attributes of current and prospective directors in relation to the future needs of the board as a whole, and develop specifications and processes for new appointments, as necessary.
- Consider the cohesion, dynamic tension and diversity of the board and its leadership by the chairman.
- Make and review succession plans for directors and the company secretary.
- Where necessary, remove incompetent or unsuitable directors or the company secretary, taking relevant legal, contractual, ethical, and commercial matters into account.
- Agree proper procedures for electing a chairman and appointing the managing director and other directors.
- Identify potential candidates for the board, make selection and agree terms of appointment and remuneration. New appointments should be agreed by every board member.

continues

- Provide new board members with a comprehensive induction to board processes and policies, inclusion to the company and to their new role.

- Monitor and appraise each individual's performance, behaviour, knowledge, effectiveness and values rigorously and regularly.

- Identify development needs and training opportunities for existing and potential directors and the company secretary.

Source: Standards for the Board (Institute of Directors, 2006)

Risk committee

Risk of various types features significantly in the operation of many businesses. Although not a recommendation of the Combined Code, many companies either set up a separate risk committee or establish the audit committee as an audit and risk committee. Of course, it is essential that directors realize that they are responsible for the company's system of internal controls and have mechanisms in place to ensure that the internal controls of the company and risk management systems are operating efficiently.

Equally, many companies, particularly larger companies or those with significant transactions overseas, may find that they have interest or currency exposures that need to be covered. The misuse of derivatives through poor internal controls and lack of monitoring led to the downfall of Barings Bank (as detailed in Chapter 1) and other companies may be equally at risk. A risk committee should therefore comprehend the risks involved by, inter alia, using derivatives, and this would necessitate quite a high level of financial expertise and the ability to seek external professional advice where necessary.

In a study of the changing role of boards, Taylor, Stiles, and Tampoe (2001) identified three major challenges facing company boards over the forthcoming five-year period. These challenges were to build more diverse boards of directors, to pay more attention to making their boards more effective, and to be able to react appropriately to any changes in the corporate governance culture. By building better boards, innovation and entrepreneurship should be encouraged and the business driven to perform better. The board will focus on the value drivers of the business to give the firm competitive advantage. Clearly, the composition of the board will play a key role in whether a company can successfully meet these challenges. The presence of the most suitable non-executive directors will help the board in this task. The role and appointment of non-executive directors is discussed in more detail below.

Non-executive directors

Non-executive directors are a mainstay of good governance. The non-executive director's role essentially has two dimensions. One dimension – which has been given much emphasis in the last decade – is as a control or counterweight to executive directors so that the presence of non-executive directors helps to ensure that an individual person or group cannot unduly influence the board's decisions. The second dimension is the contribution that non-executive directors can make to the overall leadership and development of the company. Some argue that there may be a conflict in these two roles because non-executive directors are expected both to monitor executive directors' actions and to work with executive directors as part of the board. This idea of a potential conflict in the roles is an area discussed by Ezzamel and Watson (1997).

The Cadbury Report stated that 'given the importance of their distinctive contribution, non-executive directors should be selected with the same impartiality and care as senior executives' (para 4.15). Non-executives should ideally be selected through a formal process and their appointment should be considered by the board as a whole.

The Cadbury Report also emphasized the contribution that independent non-executive directors could make, stating 'the Committee believes that the calibre of the non-executive members of the board is of special importance in setting and maintaining standards of corporate governance' (para 4.10). The importance of non-executive directors was echoed in the OECD Principles: 'Boards should consider assigning a sufficient number of non-executive board members capable of exercising independent judgement to tasks where there is a potential for conflict of interest. Examples of such key responsibilities are financial reporting, nomination and executive and board remuneration.'

The Combined Code (2006) also recognizes the important role to be played by independent non-executive directors:

as part of their role as members of a unitary board, non-executive directors should constructively challenge and help develop proposals on strategy...[they] should scrutinize the performance of management in meeting agreed goals and objectives and monitor the reporting of performance...they should satisfy themselves on the integrity of financial information and that financial controls and systems of risk management are robust and defensible (para A.1).

Independence of non-executive directors

Although there is a legal duty on all directors to act in the best interests of the company, this does not of itself guarantee that directors will act objectively. To try to ensure objectivity in board decisions, it is important that there is a balance of independent non-executive directors. This idea of independence is emphasized again and again in various codes and reports: for example, Cadbury (1992) stated that 'apart from their directors' fees and shareholdings, they (NEDs) should be independent of management and free from any business or other relationship which could materially interfere with the exercise of their independent judgement' (para 4.12). The OECD (1999) also considered this issue: 'Board independence usually requires that a sufficient number of board members not be employed by the company and not be closely related to the company or its management through significant economic, family or other ties. This does not prevent shareholders from being board members.' Subsequently, the OECD (2004) stated that 'board independence . . . usually requires that a sufficient number of board members will need to be independent of management'. The Higgs Review (2003) stated that 'a board is strengthened significantly by having a strong group of non-executive directors with no other connection with the company. These individuals bring a dispassionate objectivity that directors with a closer relationship to the company cannot provide' (para 9.5).

The Combined Code (2006) states that 'the board should identify in the annual report each non-executive director it considers to be independent. The board should determine whether the director is independent in character and judgement and whether there are relationships or circumstances which are likely to affect, or could appear to affect, the director's judgement' (para A.3.1.).

'Independence' is generally taken as meaning that there are no relationships or circumstances that might affect the director's judgement. Situations where a non-executive director's independence would be called into question include: where the director was a former employee of the company or group within the last five years; where additional remuneration (apart from the director's fee) was received from the company; where the director had close family ties with the company's other directors and advisers; where he had a material business relationship with the company in the last three years; where he had served on the board for more than ten years; where he represented a significant shareholder.

There is some discussion as to whether the number of non-executive directorships that any one individual can hold should be defined. Of course, if an individual were to hold many non-executive directorships, for example, ten or more, then it is arguable whether that individual could devote enough time and consideration to each of the directorships. On the other hand, it may be perfectly feasible for an individual to hold, for example, five non-executive directorships. It really depends on the time that an individual has available, on the level of commitment, and whether any of the multiple non-executive directorships might lead to the problem of interlocking directorships whereby the independence of the non-executive director is compromised. An interlocking relationship might occur through any of a number of circumstances including family relationship, business relationship, or a previous advisory role (such as auditor), which would endanger the fundamental aspect of independence. However, the independence of non-executive directors is an area of corporate governance that institutional investors and their representative groups monitor very carefully and disclosure of biographical information about directors and increasing use of databases of director information should help to identify potential problems in this area. The Combined Code (2006) states that 'non-executive directors should undertake that they will have sufficient time to meet what is expected of them' and 'their other significant commitments should be disclosed to the board before appointment, with a broad indication of the time involved' (para A.4.4). It is recommended that a full-time executive director should not take on 'more than one non-executive directorship in a FTSE 100 company nor the chairmanship of such a company' (para A.4.5).

Contribution of non-executive directors

The necessity for the independence of the majority of non-executive directors has been established above, and the 'right' non-executive directors can make a significant contribution to the company. When non-executive directors are being sought, the company will be looking for the added value that a new appointment can make to the board. The added value may come from a number of facets: their experience in industry, the City, public life, or other appropriate background; their knowledge of a particular functional specialism (for example, finance or marketing); their knowledge of a particular technical process/system; their reputation; their ability to have an insight into issues discussed at the board and to ask searching questions. Of course, these attributes should be matched by the non-executive director's independence and integrity. The Cadbury Code of Best Practice (1992) stated that 'non-executive directors should bring an independent judgement to bear on issues of strategy, performance, resources, including key appointments, and standards of conduct' (para 2.1).

As well as their contribution to the board, non-executive directors will serve on the key board committees (audit, remuneration, nomination) as described earlier. However it is not recommended that any one non-executive director sit on all three of these board committees. The Combined Code (2003) refers to the benefits of 'ensuring that committee membership is refreshed and that undue reliance is not placed on particular individuals' (para A.3).

Higgs Review

The Higgs Review, chaired by Derek Higgs, was established by the Department of Trade and Industry (DTI) in 2002 to review the role and effectiveness of non-executive directors. The Higgs Review was discussed in more detail in Chapter 3. Its recommendations caused much discussion but most of them were incorporated into the Combined Code (2003, 2006) although some in a modified form.

In 2006, the Financial Reporting Council published 'Good Practice Suggestions from the Higgs Report'. These include guidance on the role of the chairman and the non-executive director, and a summary of the principal duties of the remuneration committee and nomination committee.

Director evaluation

In the Hampel Committee Final Report (1998), it was suggested that boards consider the introduction of formal procedures to 'assess both their own collective performance and that of individual directors' (para 3.13). In a widely cited report of institutional investor opinion, McKinsey (2002) defined 'good' board governance practices as encompassing a majority of outside (non-executive) directors, outside directors who are truly independent with no management ties, and under which *formal director evaluation is in place.*

The evaluation of directors has two dimensions, which are the evaluation of the board as a whole and the evaluation of individual directors serving on the board. Most annual reports are not forthcoming on how these evaluations may be carried out in their business, and indeed KPMG (2002) found, in a survey of corporate governance in Europe, that only 39 per cent of UK respondents had a regular process for the evaluation of the board. However, this was considerably better than the figure for the European countries as a whole which was only 17 per cent.

In terms of the evaluation of the board as a whole, there are several approaches that might be utilized. These approaches include, first, a structured questionnaire to evaluate how the board is performing in key areas such as achieving key goals that have been set, and second, informal discussion between the chairman of the board and the directors which would cover a wide range of strategic and operational issues (such as how well do the board dynamics work, and how well do the board sub-committees work).

The evaluation of individual directors provides individual directors with the opportunity to discuss key areas with the chairman on a one-to-one basis. It is an important process for finding out just how comfortable an individual director is, what areas he/she might be able to contribute to more effectively, and whether there are any barriers to full participation in the board's activities (for example, lack of information to enable an informed discussion).

These evaluations will contribute to the establishment of the performance criteria that will help to achieve the corporate objectives and which are used in helping to align the performance of directors with the interest of shareholders.

It does seem clear that, in order to determine whether boards of directors as a whole, and directors as individuals, are performing to the best of their ability, there should be evaluation of the board as a whole, the board leadership, and the individual directors. Many boards are silent on this issue, indicating either that they do not have evaluation procedures in place or that they do not wish to disclose them if they have. If the latter is the case, then one has to ask whether the reluctance to disclose is because the evaluation process is not robust enough to stand up to scrutiny. If the former is the case, that is, that there are no evaluation or assessment procedures in place, then equally one has to ask: 'Why not?' This information will be very helpful in setting performance-related pay for directors and helping to eliminate the unease that many investors feel about executive remuneration levels.

The area of board evaluation has been taken up by the Combined Code (2006), which includes the principle that 'the board should undertake a formal and rigorous annual evaluation of its own performance and that of its committees and individual directors' (para A.6). The board should disclose in the annual report the way in which the performance evaluations have been carried out.

Van den Berghe and Levrau (2004), in a study of the boards of directors of thirty companies listed on Euronext Brussels and Nasdaq Europe, found that there were a number of areas where better understanding was needed of elements that determined board effectiveness. They also found that board evaluation was not as widespread as might be hoped. Epstein and Roy (2006) state that it is important to evaluate both the board as a whole and individual directors, as this may help highlight deficiencies, Metrics for evaluation should be relevant and linked to the inputs, such as attendance at board meetings, and outputs such as stock price. A balanced scorecard approach, derived from the work of Kaplan and Norton (1992, 2000) is an appropriate tool for director evaluation.

Conclusions

In this chapter, the different types of board structure, unitary or dual, have been discussed. We have seen that the UK has a unitary board structure and that the predominant form of board structure in Europe is also the unitary board structure. The roles and responsibilities of the board, including those of the chair, chief executive officer, senior independent director and company secretary, have been reviewed.

The increasing emphasis on the importance of the role of non-executive (outside) directors is shown, and the definition of the important criterion of the 'independence' of non-executive directors is analysed, together with the role that non-executive directors play on a company's key board sub-committees: audit, remuneration, and nomination.

In future, it is likely that non-executive directors will be called upon to play an ever more important role as investors look to the audit committees, in particular, to restore and enhance confidence in companies.

■ SUMMARY

- Board structure may be unitary (single tier) or dual (two tier). In a dual structure, there is a supervisory board as well as an executive board of management. Usually, both the unitary board of directors and the supervisory board (in a dual system) are elected by shareholders.

- The board of directors leads and controls the company and is the link between managers and investors.

- It is desirable to split the roles of chair and CEO so that there is not too much power invested in one individual. The chair is responsible for the running of the board, whilst the CEO is responsible for running the business.

- The board may delegate various activities to board sub-committees, the most common being the audit committee, the remuneration committee, and the nomination committee.

- The board should include an appropriate number of independent non-executive (outside) directors. The non-executive directors bring a balance to the board and their experience and knowledge can add value to the board. The non-executive directors make a key contribution through their membership of the board sub-committees.

Example: BP plc

This is an example of a company that has comprehensive corporate governance disclosures. Disclosure is considered to be an important aspect of a company's governance, indicative of a transparent approach and outlook by the directors.

BP's high quality disclosures are recognized as an example of best practice in the UK. BP states: 'Governance lies at the heart of all the board does and it is the task our owners entrust to the board.' A review of the company's annual report and accounts shows detailed corporate governance disclosures covering BP's relationship with shareholders, board process, board/executive relationships, non-executive remuneration, report on executive remuneration, compliance with the Combined Code and a section on how BP's corporate governance practices differ from those followed by domestic US companies listed on the New York Stock Exchange. The board's governance policies were adopted in 1997 and regulate its relationship with shareholders, the conduct of board affairs and its relationship with the group chief executive.

BP also uses electronic communications to facilitate the exercise of shareholder voting rights, and also states: 'Presentations given at appropriate intervals to representatives of the investment community are available simultaneously to all shareholders by live Internet broadcast or open conference call.'

Example: Wm Morrison Supermarkets

This is an example of an exception to the rule: a large UK company that, for many years, did not have a corporate governance structure that was in line with accepted best practice as defined by the Combined Code. However, recent changes to its corporate governance structure have been made.

Wm Morrison Supermarkets was a successful company with an impressive track record of 35 years of successive increases in turnover and pre-tax profits. However, in terms of its corporate governance structure, Wm Morrison was lacking many of the key features that would normally be expected: there were no non-executive directors on the board, no audit committee, and no remuneration committee (as at early 2003). The company had been so successful despite its lack of a typical corporate governance structure because Sir Ken Morrison had seen the firm grow from a small family-owned business into a company listed in the FTSE 100. The family still had a significant shareholding in the company and, as the chairman, Sir Ken Morrison had kept a close eye on all developments in the company.

Things began to change when, in 2003, Sir Ken Morrison decided to bid for the Safeway chain. Funds needed to be raised from shareholders and it was stipulated that at least two independent non-executive directors should be appointed. For some time, Morrisons did not comply with the Combined Code regarding composition of the board and its key board committees. However, significant board changes were made in March 2005 with Sir Ken Morrison stepping down as chairman and the promised appointment of a further four non-executive directors.

Mini case study: Marks and Spencer plc

This is a good example of a well-known 'blue chip' company that had good financial performance over a number of years but then hit a downturn. There were several aspects of its corporate governance that were not ideal, but the market turned a blind eye to these whilst the company was doing well. However, once the company's sales and profitability fell, there was more of a spotlight on Marks and Spencer's corporate governance. Several issues were highlighted as being less than satisfactory and, under pressure from the City, action was taken to improve these.

Marks and Spencer plc enjoyed an enviable reputation for many years, performing well and giving its shareholders a good return on their investment. However, there was some criticism of its corporate governance, in particular that there was a lack of sufficient independent non-executive directors. This meant that the board lacked a real balance between executive and non-executive directors, and appropriate questions might not be asked of the executive directors by the non-executive directors: for example, questions relating to the strategic direction that the company was taking, and the market it was aiming for.

In the late 1990s, Marks and Spencer found that its plummeting sales and declining profits resulted in a lot of pressure to reform its corporate governance. As well as the criticism regarding non-executive directors, there was also much criticism of the pay-offs made to departing directors in the late 1990s and early 2000/01. The annual report for 2005 shows how Marks and Spencer's corporate governance has improved. The board now comprises half non-executive directors with a wide range of experience who can exercise their independent judgement on key issues. The main board committees (audit, remuneration, and nomination) are comprised of non-executive directors. There is also a Corporate Social Responsibility Committee to provide an overview of social and environmental and ethical impacts of the group's activities.

Given the greater emphasis on corporate governance and the appointment in 2002 of non-executive directors such as Paul Myners (chair of the government-sponsored Myner's review of institutional investment), investors can have much more confidence in Marks and Spencer. Improved corporate governance will help the company to re-establish itself and give investors the confidence that various viewpoints are heard on issues of strategy, performance, and resources at board meetings.

■ QUESTIONS

The discussion questions below cover the key learning points of this chapter. Reading of some of the additional reference material will enhance the depth of the students' knowledge and understanding of these areas.

1. What function does a board perform and how does this contribute to the corporate governance of the company?

2. What are the main sub-committees of the board and what role does each of these sub-committees play?

3. What are the main differences between a unitary board system and a dual board system?

4. In what ways might directors be appointed to the board, and what advantages and disadvantages might there be in these methods?

5. How might the 'independence' of non-executive (outside) directors be defined?

6. 'Non-executive directors are a waste of time. They often have little involvement with a company and are not aware of what is really going on.' Critically discuss this statement.

■ **FT ARTICLE**

Misys separates chairman and chief roles

By Maija Palmer, IT Correspondent

Misys bowed to shareholder pressure yesterday when it announced that it would separate the roles of chairma and chief executive two years earlier than planned.

Sir Dominic Cadbury, a senior independent director of the software company, has been appointed non-executive chairman. He will hold the role on an interim basis while Misys searches for a more permanent replacement. Kevin Lomax is to remain chief executive. Misys had planned to separate the roles in 2008 when Mr Lomax would have given up the chief role to focus on the chairmanship.

However, the company had come under pressure to accelerate the timetable this summer after facing shareholder anger over a profit warning and a deeply unpopular proposal of a £2 4m "retention" bonus scheme for two senior executives.

Misys was forced to retract the bonus proposal just days before the company's annual meeting in September after the Association of British Insurers, the shareholder activist group, advised its members to vote against the scheme.

The company also faced shareholder anger when it warned about a "significant" shortfall in profit at the annual meeting.

"There was a lot of frustration caused by the trading statement, which was more pessimistic than we had anticipated and shareholders wanted the governance issue addressed," Sir Dominic said. "It was becoming a distraction. I think this will get rid of the slight cloud we have been under."

Shareholders, who have been in discussions with Misys over the issue throughout the autumn, welcomed yesterday's move.

Peter Montagnon, director of investment affairs at the ABI, said the events of the summer "had resulted in a positive dialogue".

"We have talked to Misys and welcome this step as a permanent strengthening of its board structure," he said.

Shares in Misys, which have been slowly regaining ground after falling more than 20 per cent on the profit warning, rose $1\frac{1}{4}$p to $215\frac{1}{4}$p yesterday.

Financial Times Friday 4 November 2005

■ **REFERENCES**

Cadbury, Sir Adrian (1992), *Report of the Committee on the Financial Aspects of Corporate Governance*, Gee & Co. Ltd., London.

——— (2002), *Corporate Governance and Chairmanship: A Personal View*, Oxford University Press, Oxford.

Charkham, J. (2005), *Keeping Better Company: Corporate Governance Ten Years On*, Oxford University Press, Oxford.

Combined Code (2006), *The Combined Code on Corporate Governance*, Financial Reporting Council, London.

Company Law Reform Bill (2005), *Company Law Reform Bill (HL)*, Her Majesty's Stationery Office, London.

Epstein M.J. and Roy, M.J. (2006), 'Measuring the Effectiveness of Corporate Boards and Directors' in *The Accountable Corporation*, M.J. Epstein and K.O. Hanson (eds.), Praeger Publishers, Westport, USA.

Ezzamel, M. and Watson, R. (1997), 'Wearing Two Hats: The Conflicting Control and Management Roles of Non-Executive Directors' in *Corporate Governance: Economic, Management and Financial Issues*, K. Keasey, S. Thompson, and M. Wright (eds.), Oxford University Press, Oxford.

Financial Reporting Council (2006), *Good Practice Suggestions from the Higgs Report*, Financial Reporting Council, London.

Hampel, Sir Ronnie (1998), *Committee on Corporate Governance: Final Report*, Gee & Co. Ltd., London.

Hermes (2006), *The Hermes Corporate Governance Principles*, Hermes Investment Management Limited, London.

Higgs, D. (2003), *Review of the Role and Effectiveness of Non-Executive Directors*, Department of Trade and Industry, London.

Institute of Directors (2006), *Standards for the Board*, IoD and Kogan Page, London.

Kaplan R.S. and Norton, D.P. (1992), 'The Balanced Scorecard – Measures that Drive Performance', *Harvard Business Review*, January–February, pp. 71–79.

____ (2000), 'Having trouble with your strategy? Then map it', *Harvard Business Review*, September–October, pp. 167–176.

KPMG (2002), *Corporate Governance in Europe KPMG Survey 2001/02*, KPMG, London.

McKinsey & Co. (2002), *Investor Opinion Survey on Corporate Governance*, McKinsey & Co., London.

OECD (1999), Principles of Corporate Governance, OECD, Paris.

____ (2004), Principles of Corporate Governance, OECD, Paris.

Smith, Sir Robert (2003), *Audit Committees Combined Code Guidance*, Financial Reporting Council, London.

Spira, L. (2002), *The Audit Committee: Performing Corporate Governance*, Kluwer Academic Publishers, Dordrecht.

Taylor, B., Stiles, P. and Tampoe, M. (2001), *The Future for the Board*, Director and Board Research, Institute of Directors, London.

Van Den Berghe L.A.A. and Levrau, A.P.D. (2004), 'Evaluating Boards of Directors: What Constitutes a Good Corporate Board?', *Corporate Governance: An International Review*, Vol. 12, No. 4, October 2004.

■ USEFUL WEBSITES

http://asp.thecorporatelibrary.net The website of the Corporate Library contains many interesting references to articles on directors and board structure.

www.dti.gov.uk The website of the UK Department of Trade and Industry has a number of references to interesting material relating to directors.

www.icsa.org.uk The website of the Institute of Chartered Secretaries and Administrators has useful references to matters relating to boards and directors including board effectiveness.

www.independentdirector.co.uk The Independent Director website promotes the role and understanding of the work of non-executive directors.

www.iod.co.uk The website of the Institute of Directors has information relating to a wide range of topics relating to directors.

<table>
<tr><td>

9

</td><td>

Directors' Performance and Remuneration

</td></tr>
</table>

LEARNING OBJECTIVES

- To be aware of the main features of the directors' remuneration debate
- To know the key elements of directors' remuneration
- To assess the role of the remuneration committee in setting directors' remuneration
- To understand the different measures used to link directors' remuneration with performance
- To know the disclosure requirements for directors' remuneration
- To be aware of possible ways of evaluating directors

The directors' remuneration debate

The last decade has seen considerable shareholder, media, and policy attention given to the issue of directors' remuneration. The debate has tended to focus on four areas: (i) the overall level of directors' remuneration and the role of share options; (ii) the suitability of performance measures linking directors' remuneration with performance; (iii) the role played by the remuneration committee in the setting of directors' remuneration; (iv) the influence that shareholders are able to exercise on directors' remuneration.

 The debate about directors' remuneration spans continents and is a topic that is as hotly debated in the USA as it is in the UK. Indeed, the UK's use of share options as long-term incentive devices has been heavily influenced by US practice. Countries that are developing their corporate governance codes are aware of the ongoing issues relating to directors' remuneration and try to address these issues in their own codes. In the UK, the debate was driven in the early years by the remuneration packages of the directors of the newly privatized utilities. The perception that directors were receiving huge remuneration packages – and often, it seemed, with little reward to the shareholders in terms of company performance – further fuelled the interest in this area on both sides of the Atlantic. The level of directors' remuneration continues to be a worrying trend and as Lee (2002) commented 'the evidence in the US is of many companies having given away 10 per cent, and in some cases as much as 30 per cent, of their equity to executive directors and other staff in just the last five years or so. That is clearly not sustainable into the future: there wouldn't be any companies left in public hands if it were'.

It is interesting to note that a comparison of remuneration pay and incentives of directors in the USA and the UK gives a useful insight. Conyon and Murphy (2000) documented the differences in CEO pay and incentives in both countries for 1997. They found that chief executive officers in the USA earned 45 per cent higher cash compensation and 190 per cent higher total compensation. The implication is that, in the USA, the median CEO received 1.48 per cent of any increase in shareholder wealth compared to 0.25 per cent in the UK. The difference being largely attributable to the extent of the share option schemes in the USA.

The directors' remuneration debate clearly highlights one important aspect of the principal–agent problem discussed at length in Chapter 2. In this context, Conyon and Mallin (1997) highlight that shareholders are viewed as the 'principal' and managers as their 'agents' and that the economics literature, in particular, demonstrates that the compensation received by senior management should be linked to company performance for incentive reasons. Well-designed compensation contracts will help to ensure that the objectives of directors and shareholders are aligned, and so share options and other long-term incentives are a key mechanism by which shareholders try to ensure congruence between directors' and shareholders' objectives.

However, the debate is far from over and Bebchuk and Fried (2004) highlight that there are significant flaws in pay arrangements, which 'have hurt shareholders both by increasing pay levels and, even more important, by leading to practices that dilute and distort managers' incentives'.

Key elements of directors' remuneration

Directors' remuneration can encompass six elements:

- base salary;
- bonus;
- stock options;
- restricted share plans (stock grants);
- pension;
- benefits (car, healthcare, etc.).

However, most discussions of directors' remuneration will tend to concentrate on the first four elements listed above and this text will also take that approach.

Base salary

Base salary is received by a director in accordance with the terms of his contract. This element is not related either to the performance of the company nor to the performance of the individual director. The amount will be set with due regard to the size of the company, the industry sector, the experience of the individual director, and the level of base salary in similar companies.

Bonus

An annual bonus may be paid, which is linked to the accounting performance of the firm.

Stock options

Stock options give directors the right to purchase shares (stock) at a specified exercise price over a specified time period. Directors may also participate in long-term incentive plans (LTIPs). UK share options generally have performance criteria attached, and much discussion is centred around these performance criteria, especially as to whether they are appropriate and demanding enough.

Restricted share plans (stock grants)

Shares may be awarded with limits on their transferability for a set time (usually a few years), and various performance conditions should be met.

Role of the remuneration committee

The Combined Code (2006) recommends that 'there should be a formal and transparent procedure for developing policy on executive remuneration and for fixing the remuneration packages of individual directors' (principle B.2). In practice, this normally results in the appointment of a remuneration committee.

The remuneration committee's role and composition was discussed in Chapter 8. However, in this chapter on directors' performance and remuneration, we consider the effect of remuneration committees on directors' remuneration levels in recent years. Sykes (2002) points out that, although remuneration committees predominantly consist of a majority, or more usually entirely, of non-executive directors, these non-executive directors 'are effectively chosen by, or only with the full agreement of, senior management'. Given that the non-executive directors of one company may be executive directors of another (unrelated) company, they may not be willing to stipulate demanding performance criteria because they may have a self-interest in ensuring that they themselves can go on earning a high salary without unduly demanding performance criteria being set by their own companies' remuneration committees. There is also another aspect, which is that remuneration committees will generally not wish the executive directors to be earning less than their counterparts in other companies, so they will be more inclined to make recommendations that will put the directors into the top or second quartile of executive remuneration levels. It is certainly the case that executive remuneration levels have increased fairly substantially since remuneration committees were introduced which, of course, was not the intended effect. Sykes (2002) makes the pertinent point that all the remuneration packages now so widely criticized as flawed and inappropriate were once approved by an 'independent' remuneration committee.

The performance measures that the remuneration committee decides should be used are therefore central to aligning directors' performance and remuneration in the most appropriate way. Remuneration committees are offered some general guidance by the Combined Code (2006) recommendation that 'levels of remuneration should be sufficient to attract, retain and motivate directors of the quality required to run the company successfully, but a company should avoid paying more than is necessary for this purpose' (principle B.1).

In the UK, both the National Association of Pension Funds (NAPF) and the Association of British Insurers (ABI) have been involved in the debate about executive remuneration and have issued guidance in this area. The ABI (2002) guidelines on executive remuneration include the recommendations that: remuneration packages should have a balance between fixed and variable pay and between long- and short-term incentives; performance-based remuneration arrangements should be demonstrably clearly aligned with business strategy and objectives; the remuneration committee should have regard to pay and conditions generally in the company, taking into account business size, complexity, and geographical location and should also consider market forces generally; share option schemes should link remuneration to performance and align the long-term interests of management with those of shareholders; performance targets should be disclosed in the Remuneration Report within the bounds of commercial confidentiality considerations.

In December 2005, the ABI issued its Principles and Guidelines on Remuneration, which have a two-fold aim of providing 'a practical framework and reference point for both shareholders in reaching voting decisions and for companies in deciding upon remuneration policy'. The Principles and Guidelines emphasize that remuneration (committee) reports should provide a clear and full explanation of remuneration policy, showing a clear link between reward and performance and that 'shareholders believe that the key determinant for assessing remuneration is performance in the creation of shareholder value'.

Performance measures

Performance criteria will clearly be a key aspect of ensuring that directors' remuneration is perceived as fair and appropriate for the job and in keeping with the results achieved by the directors. Performance criteria may differentiate between three broadly conceived types of measures: (i) market-based measures, (ii) accounts based measures, and (iii) individual based measures. Some potential performance criteria are:

- shareholder return;
- share price (and other market based measures);
- profit-based measures;
- return on capital employed;

- earnings per share;
- individual director performance (in contrast to corporate performance measures).

Sykes (2002) highlights a number of problems with the way in which executive remuneration is determined: (i) management is expected to perform over a short period of time and this is a clear mismatch with the underlying investor time horizons; (ii) management remuneration is not correlated to corporate performance; (iii) earnings before interest, tax, and amortisation (EBITA) is widely used as a measure of earnings and yet this can encourage companies to gear up (or have high leverage) because the measure will reflect the flow of earnings from high leverage but not the service (interest) charge for that debt. He suggests that the situation would be improved if there were: longer term tenures for corporate management; more truly independent non-executive directors; the cessation of stock options and in their place a generous basic salary and five-year restricted shares (shares that could not be cashed for five years).

The ABI (2002, 2005) guidelines state that total shareholder return relative to an appropriate index or peer group is a generally acceptable performance criterion. The guidelines also favour performance being measured over a period of at least three years to try to ensure sustained improvements in financial performance rather than the emphasis being placed on short-term performance. Share incentive schemes should be available to employees and executive directors but not to non-executive directors (although non-executive directors are encouraged to have shareholdings in the company, possibly by receiving shares in the company, at full market price, as payment of their non-executive director fees).

Another area that has attracted attention, and which is addressed in joint ABI/NAPF guidance, is the area of 'golden goodbyes'. This is another dimension to the directors' remuneration debate because it is not only ongoing remuneration packages that have attracted adverse comment but also the often seemingly excessive amounts paid to directors who leave a company after failing to meet their targets. Large pay-offs or 'rewards for failure' are seen as inappropriate because such failure may reduce the value of the business and threaten the jobs of employees. Often the departure of underperforming directors triggers a clause in their contract that leads to a large undeserved pay-off, but now some companies are cutting the notice period from one year to, for example, six months where directors fail to meet performance targets over a period of time, so that a non-performing director whose contract is terminated receives six months' salary rather than one year's salary.

The ABI/NAPF guidance emphasizes the importance of ensuring that the design of contracts should not commit companies to payment for failure; the guidance also suggests that phased payments are a useful innovation to include in directors' contracts. A phased payment involves continuing payment to a departing director for the remaining term of the contract but payments cease when the director finds fresh employment. An alternative suggested by the Myners Report (2001) is that compensation for loss of office should be fixed as a number of shares in the company (and hence the value of the compensation would be linked to the share price performance of the company).

It does seem that the days of lucrative payments for underperforming directors are drawing to a close. Furthermore, the UK's Department of Trade and Industry issued a consultation document in summer 2003, 'Rewards for Failure: Directors' Remuneration – Contracts, Performance and Severance', which invites comment on ways in which severance pay might be limited by: restricting notice periods to less than one year; capping the level of liquidated damages; using phased payments; limiting severance pay where a company has performed poorly.

Remuneration of non-executive directors

The remuneration of non-executive directors is decided by the board, or where required by the articles of association, or the shareholders in general meeting. Non-executive directors should be paid a fee commensurate with the size of the company, and the amount of time that they are expected to devote to their role. Large UK companies would tend to pay in excess of £40,000 (often considerably more) to each non-executive director. The remuneration is generally paid in cash although some advocate remunerating non-executive directors with the company's shares to align their interests with those of the shareholders. However, it would not be a good idea to remunerate non-executive directors with share options (as opposed to shares) because this may give them a rather unhealthy focus on the short-term share price of the company.

Disclosure of directors' remuneration

There has been much discussion about how much disclosure there should be of directors' remuneration and how useful detailed disclosures might be. The Greenbury report, issued in the UK in 1995, was established on the initiative of the CBI because of public concern about directors' remuneration. Whilst the work of the Greenbury report focused on the directors of public limited companies, it hoped that both smaller listed companies and unlisted companies would find its recommendations useful.

Central to the Greenbury report recommendations were the strengthening of accountability and enhancing the performance of directors. These two aims were to be achieved by (i) the establishment of remuneration committees comprised of independent non-executive directors who would report fully to the shareholders each year about the company's executive remuneration policy, including full disclosure of the elements in the remuneration of individual directors, and (ii) the adoption of performance measures linking rewards to the performance of both the company and individual directors, so that the interests of directors and shareholders were more closely aligned.

One of the Turnbull Committee recommendations (1999, revised 2005) was that boards should consider whether business objectives and the risk management/control systems of a business are supported by the performance-related reward system in operation in a company.

As part of the accountability/transparency process, the remuneration committee membership should be disclosed in the company's annual report, and the chairman of the remuneration committee should attend the company's annual general meeting to answer any questions that shareholders may have about the directors' remuneration.

The Department of Trade and Industry published its Directors' Remuneration Report Regulations 2002. These regulations require, inter alia, that:

- quoted companies must publish a detailed report on directors' pay as part of their annual reporting cycle. This report must be approved by the board of directors;
- a graph of the company's total shareholder returns over five years, against a comparator group, must be published in the remuneration committee report
- names of any consultants to the remuneration committee must be disclosed, including whether they were appointed independently, along with the cost of any other services provided to the company;
- companies must hold a shareholder vote on the directors' remuneration report at each general meeting.

The stipulation that companies must hold a shareholder vote on the directors' remuneration report is an interesting one, and something that various shareholder representative groups have campaigned for over a long period of time. However, the vote is an advisory shareholder vote, but it will serve a useful purpose ensuring that the shareholders can vote specifically on directors' remuneration, which has caused so much heated debate for so long. The other provisions will help to strengthen the role of the remuneration committee and enhance both the accountability and transparency of the directors' remuneration-setting process. The disclosures relating to the consultants used by the remuneration committee may also lead to interesting questions relating to any other services they may provide to a company to try to determine their independence.

International guidance on executive remuneration

International Corporate Governance Network

The International Corporate Governance Network (ICGN) issued its recommendations on best practice for executive remuneration in 2003. It was hoped that the recommendations would create a consensus amongst both companies and investors around the world about the structure of remuneration packages.

The ICGN recommendations stated that the 'fundamental requirement for executive remuneration reporting is transparency'. This was the starting point: that there should be disclosure of the base salary, short-term and long-term incentives, and any other payments or benefits to each main board director. The remuneration committee should publish statements on the expected outcomes of the remuneration structures, in terms of ratios between base salaries, short-term bonuses, and long-term rewards, making both 'high' and 'low' assumptions as well as the 'central' case. Whilst recognizing that share options are probably here to stay, the ICGN recommendations supported the International Accounting Standards Board (IASB) proposal to expense share options through the profit and loss account.

The remuneration committee report should be presented as a separate voting item at every annual meeting (this would depend on local practice). The ICGN also urged institutional investors to devote more resources to the analysis of remuneration resolutions.

In 2004, the ICGN published statements about the compliance of each of the UK, USA, and Australia with the ICGN's Executive Remuneration Principles. Each of these countries generally complied with the principles, although each had strengths and weaknesses on particular issues.

In 2006, the ICGN approved the updated ICGN Remuneration Guidelines. Three principles underpin the new Guidelines: transparency; accountability; and the performance basis. The Guidelines state that there should also be thought given to the reputational aspects of remuneration.

The Conference Board

In the USA, the Conference Board Commission on Public Trust and Private Enterprise was established to address widespread abuses that led to corporate governance scandals and a resulting lack of confidence in the markets.

One area that the Commission looked at was executive compensation. The Commission reported in 2002 with principles, recommendations, and specific best practice suggestions. The seven principles relate to: the compensation (remuneration) committee and its responsibilities; the importance of performance-based compensation; the role of equity-based incentives; creating a long-term focus; accounting neutrality; shareholders' rights; transparency and disclosure. The principles serve to clarify several areas and identify that the compensation committee, which should be comprised of directors who are free of any relationships with the company and its management, should be primarily responsible for ensuring that there is a fair and appropriate compensation scheme in place. In order to aid them in this role, the compensation committee may appoint outside consultants who should report solely to the committee. Performance-based remuneration incentives should 'support and reinforce the corporation's long-term strategic goals set by the board (for example, cost of capital, return on equity, economic value added, market share, quality goals, compliance goals, environment goals, revenue and profit growth, cost containment, cash management, etc)'. In relation to the role of equity incentives, such as share options, the compensation committee should ensure that disclosure is made of any costs to shareholders associated with equity-based compensation such as dilution; the earnings per share after dilution should be shown. Key executives and directors should be encouraged to build up a reasonable shareholding in the corporation and hold that shareholding for the longer term.

The Commission's report is likely to influence policy in many countries, especially those countries that have already followed the US-style remuneration package and adopted share option schemes.

Conclusions

The debate on executive directors' remuneration has rumbled on through the last decade, but with the increase in institutional investor activism and the scandals and subsequent collapses associated with a number of large corporations in the UK, USA, and elsewhere, the focus is well and truly on curtailing excessive and undeserved remuneration packages. The emphasis is on remuneration committees, comprised of independent non-executive directors, to try to ensure that executive directors' remuneration packages are fairly and appropriately constructed, taking into account long-term objectives. Central to this aim is the use of performance indicators that will incentivize directors but at the same time align their interests with those of shareholders, to the long-term benefit of the company.

■ SUMMARY

- The debate on executive directors' remuneration has been driven by the view that some directors are being overpaid to the detriment of the shareholders, the employees, and the company as a whole. The perception that high rewards have been given without corresponding performance has caused concern, and this area has increasingly become the focus of investor activism and media coverage.

- The components of executive directors' remuneration are base salary, bonuses, stock options, stock grants, pension, and other benefits.

- The remuneration committee, which should be comprised of independent non-executive directors, has a key role to play in ensuring that a fair and appropriate executive remuneration system is in place.

- There are a number of potential performance criteria that may be used to incentivize executive directors. These are market-based measures (such as share price), accounts-based measures (such as earnings per share), and individual director performance measures.

- It is important that there is full disclosure of directors' remuneration and the basis on which it is calculated.

- There seems to be a trend towards convergence internationally in terms of the recommendations for the composition, calculation, and disclosure of executive directors' remuneration.

Example: GlaxoSmithKline plc

This is an example of a company that had to reconsider its executive remuneration package in the light of pressure from investors.

In late 2002, GlaxoSmithKline proposed a remuneration package for its chief executive that was reputedly worth some £11 million. The proposed package would have resulted in a basic salary of over £990,000 and the granting of options exercisable over a five-year period and estimated at being worth just under £9 million.

   The proposed package caused widespread concern amongst the company's largest shareholders at a time when there were concerns being expressed over various aspects of the company's strategy. In addition, the performance targets associated with the package were not viewed as being particularly stretching. A number of the company's largest shareholders met with the company's chairman to discuss the matter. After several days of discussion and debate, the company finally agreed to drop the proposed package and to maintain the chief executive's existing remuneration package for another year, whilst considering what revised proposal might be put forward in the future. In late December 2003, GlaxoSmithKline announced new executive remuneration arrangements with:

the link between pay and performance strengthened with robust EPS and TSR hurdles; contracts for executive directors reduced from 24 months to 12 months without compensation; remuneration aligned with other global pharmaceutical companies; and the new policy closely aligned with UK shareholder best practice guidelines.

Example: Unilever plc

This is an example of a company that has regard to continental European remuneration packages as well as UK packages. In addition, it reviews remuneration packages in the US market when considering the remuneration package of its USA-based director.

The remuneration package of the directors consists of a base salary, allowances and benefits in kind (for example, healthcare, company cars), annual performance bonus, long-term incentive arrangements, and pension provision. The remuneration committee links a significant proportion of directors' remuneration to key measures of company performance. The three main measures are earnings per share growth, underlying sales growth in the leading brands, and total shareholder return generated by Unilever in comparison with a group of twenty relevant competitors. If the target levels of performance are achieved, this will mean that the performance-related elements will account for some 60 per cent of the directors' total remuneration. There is an upper limit so that, in the case of outstanding results, the overall value of the incentive awards can increase to no more than three quarters of the directors' total remuneration. (Equally, if performance were unsatisfactory, then there would be no variable incentive award paid.)

Interestingly, any remuneration and fees earned by directors from outside directorships are paid over to Unilever.

Unilever proposed that the existing executive share option plans be replaced with a new Global Performance Share Plan from 2005 onwards. The performance criteria relating to the annual bonus of executive directors is being revised to align their targets to the business plans leading up to 2010.

Mini case study: ICI plc

ICI is one of a number of companies that has extensive disclosure on remuneration issues in its annual report. The full annual report and accounts for 2004 has a 12-page report from the chairman of the remuneration committee.

An analysis of the Remuneration Report highlights some interesting features:

• first, the role and composition of the remuneration committee is defined; importantly it is comprised exclusively of independent non-executive directors. The remuneration committee received advice from three independent external groups of consultants during the year;

- ICI has a policy that executive directors and senior executives are expected to build up personal shareholdings of ICI ordinary shares through the retention of shares acquired from company share-based plans. The target value of the shareholdings is two times base salary for the chief executive and one times base salary for executive directors;

- non-executive directors are paid an annual fee with an additional fee if they chair a board committee or are the senior non-executive director;

- the remuneration package for executive directors comprises four elements: base salary, annual incentive plan, long-term incentives, and retirement/other benefits. The performance-related elements, when valued at target performance levels, comprise more than 50 per cent of the package (excluding pension and other benefits);

- the annual incentive plan motivates executive directors towards the achievement of annual financial and strategic goals of the business. In ICI, the achievement of this is based on the delivery of economic profit (profit after tax, less a charge for the use of capital), a measure that encourages profitable growth and the efficient use of capital to generate sustainable shareholder value;

- the performance growth plan drives and rewards longer term business improvement making conditional awards of ICI shares linked to performance over a fixed three-year period. Depending on which executive directors are being assessed, the measures include economic profit and total shareholder return, the latter measure rewards the relative outperformance of ICI versus its global competitors;

- share option grants are made under a plan approved by shareholders in 2004. Options will be granted provided demanding EPS performance conditions are met. EPS was selected as it is the 'quantifiable outcome of the key targets set by the board in the areas of sales growth, trading profit margin and return on capital employed';

- retirement benefits take account of local practices in the countries in which ICI operates;

- executive directors are encouraged to have one external non-executive directorship, such appointments to be approved by the remuneration committee and the board.

■ **QUESTIONS**

The discussion questions below cover the key learning points of this chapter. Reading of some of the additional reference material will enhance the depth of the students' knowledge and understanding of these areas.

1. What factors have influenced the executive directors' remuneration debate?

2. Why is the area of executive directors' remuneration of such interest to investors, and particularly to institutional investors?

3. What are the main components of executive directors' remuneration packages?

4. Critically discuss the role of the remuneration committee in setting executive directors' remuneration.

5. Critically discuss the performance criteria that may be used in determining executive directors' remuneration.

6. Critically discuss the importance of executive director remuneration disclosure.

■ **FT ARTICLE**

Compass faces criticism over executive pay

By Salamander Davoudi

Compass shareholders yesterday expressed concern that a proposed pay package of up to £5m for the company's incoming chief executive was insensitive given the recent loss of shareholder value at the troubled contract caterer.

One investor said: "Many shareholders will be upset, about this. That is an awful lot of money in terms of extra compensation."

But, in spite of shareholder reservations, some pointed out that the pay package might be the only way to attract a high-quality candidate.

Richard Cousins, the former chief executive of BPB, the plasterboard maker, is believed to be a strong candidate for the chief executive position.

Anne Fraser, head of corporate governance at Scottish Widows Investment Partnership, said: "We are supportive of the new incentive proposals. What matters is that the incentive awards are structured to align the interests of executives with those of shareholders. Where that's the case, shareholders will benefit, too."

However, Mrs Fraser said SWIP would be voting against part of the remuneration report relating to compensation being paid to Alan Dupuis, former chief executive of Compass's eastern operations. "Mr Dupuis has received significant compensation following his resignation from the board and yet has been re-engaged on a new three year contract with an upfront pension payment," she said. "We can not support this arrangement."

The new executive pay package includes a base salary of about £1m, a performance-related bonus which could be up worth up to 150 per cent of basic salary, a long-term incentive plan equal to 200 per cent of basic salary and potential share options.

If a director takes half his or her bonus in shares after three years, the company will match them.

Paul Kelly, spokesman for Compass, said: "The pay package is now more linked to performance and the amount an executive director can receive is actually reducing. In 2006, the maximum award under the long-term incentive plan has been capped at 150 per cent and share options are unlikely."

Compass has been dogged by corruption allegations since last September and several investigations into the company are under way.

Samuel Johar, chairman of headhunter Buchanan Harvey, said: "The priority should be for them to get the best guy. What is insensitive is when an underperforming company pays its long-time executives too much."

The company's shares yesterday fell $1/4$p to 221$1/4$p.

Additional reporting by Kate Burgess

Financial Times Saturday 4 February 2006

■ **REFERENCES**

Association of British Insurers (2002), *Guidelines on Executive Remuneration*, ABI, London.

____ (2005), *Principles and Guidelines on Remuneration*, ABI, London.

Association of British Insurers and National Association of Pension Funds (2002), *Best Practice on Executive Contracts and Severance – A Joint Statement by the Association of British Insurers and National Association of Pension Funds*, ABI/NAPF, London.

Bebchuk L. and Fried, J. (2004), *Pay Without Performance: The Unfulfilled Promise of Executive Compensation*, Harvard University Press, USA.

Combined Code (2003), *The Combined Code on Corporate Governance*, Financial Reporting Council, London.

Conference Board (2002), *Commission on Public Trust and Private Enterprise Findings and Recommendations Part 1: Executive Compensation*, Conference Board, New York.

Conyon, M.J. and Mallin, C.A. (1997), *Directors' Share Options, Performance Criteria and Disclosure: Compliance with the Greenbury Report*, ICAEW Research Monograph, London.

____ and Murphy, K.J. (2000), 'The Prince and the Pauper? CEO Pay in the United States and United Kingdom', *The Economic Journal* 110.

Department of Trade and Industry (2002), *The Directors' Remuneration Report Regulations 2002* (SI No. 2002/1986), DTI, London.

Greenbury, Sir R. (1995), *Directors' Remuneration: Report of a Study Group Chaired by Sir Richard Greenbury*, Gee Publishing Ltd., London.

International Corporate Governance Network (2003), *Best Practices for Executive and Director Remuneration*, ICGN, London.

____ (2004), *Australian Compliance 2004 with ICGN's Executive Remuneration Principles*, ICGN, London.

____ (2004), *UK Compliance 2004 with ICGN's Executive Remuneration Principles*, ICGN, London.

____ (2004), *US Compliance 2004 with ICGN's Executive Remuneration Principles*, ICGN, London.

____ (2006), Remuneration Guidelines, ICGN, London.

Lee, P. (2002), 'Not Badly Paid But Paid Badly', *Corporate Governance: An International Review*, Vol. 10(2).

Myners, P. (2001), *Institutional Investment in the UK: A Review*, HM Treasury, London.

Sykes, A. (2002), 'Overcoming Poor Value Executive Remuneration: Resolving the Manifest Conflicts of Interest', *Corporate Governance: An International Review*, Vol. 10(4).

Turnbull Committee (1999), *Internal Control: Guidance for Directors on the Combined Code*, ICAEW, London.

■ USEFUL WEBSITES

www.abi.org.uk The website of the Association of British Insurers has guidelines on executive remuneration issues.

http://asp.thecorporatelibrary.net The website of the Corporate Library has a useful range of articles/references relating to directors' remuneration.

www.conference-board.org/ The Conference Board website gives details of its corporate governance activities and publications.

www.dti.gov.uk The website of the Department of Trade and Industry contains a range of information including material on aspects of directors' remuneration.

www.icgn.org The website of the International Corporate Governance Network contains various reports it has issued in relation to directors' remuneration.

www.napf.co.uk The website of the National Association of Pension Funds has guidelines on various corporate governance issues.

Part Three case study: Hollinger International

This case study draws together a number of the issues covered in this section of the book relating to a dominant CEO and the lack of a sufficient number of independent non-executive directors on the board.

The Hollinger group comprises the holding company, Hollinger Inc. and its subsidiary Hollinger International Inc. Hollinger's principal asset is its approximately 66.8 per cent voting and 17.4 per cent equity interest in Hollinger International, a newspaper publisher with many newspaper and media assets.

Conrad Black was instrumental in Hollinger's expansion so that, by the early 1990s, Hollinger controlled over four hundred newspapers in the USA and Canada and had acquired the UK *Daily Telegraph* newspaper. By the late 1990s, Conrad Black had built up an impressive newspaper empire, with Hollinger having more than five hundred titles covering various continents. Black had ultimate control of both Hollinger International and its parent company, Hollinger Inc. In 2001, Conrad Black became a British subject and subsequently became Lord Conrad Black.

Lord Black was the CEO and dominant shareholder of Hollinger International and the board seemed to comprise many of his nominees, so there was a combination of a powerful individual coupled with a lack of a balanced board because there was an insufficient number of independent non-executive directors.

Hollinger International reported large losses in 2001 and 2002; investors became restless about the losses that were being incurred, and there was speculation that Hollinger International faced a financial crisis. Tweedy Browne, a US investment firm and activist investor that owns around 18 per cent of Hollinger International, drew attention to the various doubtful transactions in which the board of Hollinger International seem to have engaged. It was alleged that millions of dollars had been diverted from the company for the benefit of Lord Black and certain other directors. Under pressure, a committee of independent directors was set up and, in November 2003, confirmed many unauthorized payments seemingly of a personal nature, including opera tickets and expensive restaurant meals, to Lord Black. Lord Black subsequently resigned as CEO.

The case of Hollinger illustrates how a dominant individual whose power is not effectively balanced by a board with a majority of independent non-executive directors can lead to apparent significant weaknesses in corporate governance so that the assets of the firm are not safeguarded and the firm is not run in the interests of the majority of shareholders. One implication of a lack of a sufficient number of independent non-executive directors is that key board committees, such as the audit committee, may not be in a position to ask the searching questions that need to be asked on issues such as related party transactions.

The case shows how a powerful institutional investor can intervene to try to ensure that its investment is safeguarded and that the weaknesses in the corporate governance structure that have led to this situation are improved.

PART FOUR

International Corporate Governance

10 Corporate Governance in Continental Europe

LEARNING OBJECTIVES

- To understand the background to the development of corporate governance codes in Europe
- To be aware of the main differences in corporate governance in Continental European countries
- To have a detailed knowledge of the corporate governance codes for a range of Continental European countries
- To be able to evaluate whether corporate governance codes are converging or diverging

Background

As in other countries across the globe, the interest in corporate governance in Continental European countries has grown considerably in the last decade. Its importance for the development of capital markets and investor confidence has been widely appreciated. The realization that the barriers between different countries' capital markets are declining with the adoption of the euro, the internationalization of cross-border portfolios, and technological advances means that corporate governance practices of individual countries increasingly need to satisfy certain perceived core principles of accepted good practice. We have seen that the Cadbury Code (1992) and the OECD Principles (1999, 2004) have been influential in the determination of these core principles.

The increase in both privatizations of former state-owned enterprises and mergers and acquisitions in many countries has also led to a need for better corporate governance as wider shareholder groups are created and providers of finance need to be sure that their investment will be protected.

The work of La Porta et al. (1998) suggests that countries that have a civil law/code often have a limited protection of minority shareholders; in addition, these countries often have a concentrated share ownership structure rather than a more dispersed shareholder base such as that in the UK or the USA. This aspect should be borne in mind when analysing the corporate governance of Continental European countries.

Franks and Mayer (1995) used the terms 'insider' and 'outsider' systems to differentiate between two types of ownership and control structures. In the **outsider** system, there is dispersed ownership of corporate equity amongst a large number of outside investors (as in both the UK and the USA), whereby institutional investor ownership is predominant although the institutional investors do not tend to hold large shareholdings in any given company, hence they have little direct control. In contrast, in an **insider** system, such as in many Continental European countries, ownership tends to be much more concentrated, with shares often being owned either by holding companies or families (although the state still plays an important role in France, for example).

Sometimes, a corporate governance system may also be termed 'bank-oriented' or 'market-oriented'. A **bank-oriented** system implies that banks play a key role in the funding of companies and so may well be able to exercise some control via the board structure (for example, bank representatives may have seats on the supervisory board in German companies); on the other hand, a **market-oriented** system is one where banks' influence is not prevalent in the same way and does not infiltrate the corporate structure. Becht and Mayer (2001) make an interesting observation about this distinction: they state that the balance of evidence provided by various studies shows that 'the distinction between bank- and market-oriented financial systems is therefore fragile. In contrast, the differences in ownership and control of corporations . . . are pronounced'.

It is likely too that, over time, the remaining influence of banks in terms of direct influence in a company will become less and it will be the distinction between ownership and control that helps to drive and shape corporate governance reform. Of course, such reform will be within the context of the legal and capital market structure of the various countries. Needless to say, as EU reforms lead to more 'common' requirements of countries and hence to more harmonization, companies and where appropriate, their corporate governance systems, will need to provide for certain of these aspects. EU directives may have an immediate or a more long-term effect on corporate governance. Two examples are the European Works Councils Directive 94/95 ([1994] OJ L254/64), which is concerned with the establishment of European Works Councils for informing and consulting employees, and the Large Holdings Directive (EEC 88/627) whereby voting blocks of 10 per cent or more in companies have to be disclosed.

More recently, the EU Accounts Modernization Directive was intended to produce more comparability across the financial reporting of its Member States. By its provisions, companies in various countries in the EU are subject to common standards of both the level and content of disclosures. The Directive was discussed in more detail in Chapter 4.

However, there have also been developments in relation to the Action Plan on Modernizing Company Law and Enhancing Corporate Governance in the EU, which was presented in 2003. The EU Commissioner, Charlie McCreevy, launched a consultation on the Action Plan with responses due at the end of March 2006. Various aspects of company law are examined such as the different legal forms of enterprise including the European Company (*Societas Europaea*), the European Private Company and the European Foundation. Particular issues in relation to corporate governance include shareholder rights, such as 'one share, one vote', which is prevalent in some Member States but not in others, the process for the nomination and dismissal of directors, and the extent to which institutional investors should disclose their policies. The consultation document is available at: **http://europa.eu.int/comm/internal_market**.

As already mentioned, apart from ownership structure, the main differences in corporate governance codes amongst Continental European countries stem from companies law and securities regulation. Gregory and Simmelkjaer (2002) identify the main differences as being: employee representation; social/stakeholder issues; shareholder rights and participation mechanics; board structure, roles, and responsibilities; supervisory body independence and leadership; board committees; disclosure.

Table 10.1 highlights the predominant board and leadership structure in a number of European countries. The table shows that most European countries have a unitary board structure although the majority also have the option of a dual structure. A number of countries provide for employee representation on, or a role in, the supervisory board; there is separate supervisory and managerial leadership in the companies in countries where the board structure is dual.

Table 10.2 indicates the key distinctions between the supervisory board and the management board. The supervisory board is elected by shareholders and employees, and it in turn appoints the management board. The supervisory board has a control function whereas the management board manages the business.

The next sections will look at several countries in more detail: Germany, Denmark, France, and Italy. These countries have been chosen because they represent different board structures and ownership patterns – Germany and Denmark each have a two-tier

Table 10.1 Predominant board and leadership structure

Member State	Board structure	Employee role in supervisory body
Austria	*Two-tier*	Yes
Belgium	Unitary*	No
Denmark	*Two-tier*	Yes
Finland	Unitary*	Articles may provide
France	Unitary*	Articles may provide (and Advisory)
Germany	*Two-tier*	Yes
Greece	Unitary*	No
Ireland	Unitary	No
Italy	Unitary**	No
Luxembourg	Unitary	Yes
Netherlands	*Two-tier*	Advisory
Portugal	Unitary***	No
Spain	Unitary	No
Sweden	Unitary	Yes
United Kingdom	Unitary	No

*Other structure also available   **Board of auditors also required
Source: Gregory and Simmelkjaer (2002)
©European Communities 2002, Internal Market Directorate General

Table 10.2 Summary of key differences between supervisory and management boards

Supervisory board	Management board
Members (shareholder representatives) are elected by the shareholders in general meeting; members (employee representatives) are nominated by the employees	Members are appointed by the supervisory board
Controls the direction of the business	Manages the business
Oversees the provision of information and that appropriate systems have been put in place by the management board	Provides various financial information and reports; and installation of appropriate systems, e.g. a risk management system

board structure but with different corporate ownership structures; France has a unitary board structure but the other structure is also available; Italy has a unitary board structure but a board of auditors is also required.

Germany

Charkham (1994) stated that 'if there were a spectrum with "confrontation" at one end and "co-operation" at the other, we would confidently place German attitudes and behaviour far closer to the "co-operation" end than, say, those of the British or Americans'. This is an important statement in the context of understanding the philosophy of the German approach to business and to companies, whereby the shareholders are but one of a wider set of stakeholder interest with the employees and customers being given more emphasis. Charkham (1994) finds this approach evidenced in the industrial relations of German companies: 'Good industrial relations . . . would not be prominent in works on corporate governance systems in most countries, or at best would be regarded as peripheral. In Germany, however, good industrial relations are much nearer centre stage.' This is evidenced in the Works Constitution Act 1972, which sets out the rights of the works council and, broadly speaking, deals with all matters pertaining to the employees' conditions of employment. Works councils are part of the co-operative process between workers and employers, the idea being that **co-determination** (the right to be kept informed about the company's activities and to participate in decisions that may affect the workers) means that there is a basis for more trust and co-operation between workforce and employers. The Co-determination Act 1976 defines the proportion of employee and shareholder representatives on the supervisory board (*Aufsichtsrat*) and also stipulates that a director on the management board has special responsibility for labour-related matters.

The business structure in Germany is detailed in Wymeersch (1998) where he identifies the most used business types in various Continental European states. In Germany, as far as the larger business entities are concerned, the business types tend to be either public (*Aktiengesellschaft, AG*) or private companies limited by shares (*Gesellschaft mit beschrankter Haftung, GmbH*). However, he identifies a hybrid that is also used in Germany – specifically, a hybrid of the *GmbH & Co. KG*, combining the advantages of the unincorporated *Kommanditgesellschaft* and the limited liability of *GmbH*.

In Germany, as in many Continental European countries and the UK, there is a trend away from individual share ownership. The most influential shareholders are financial and non-financial companies, and there are significant cross-holdings, which mean that when analysing share ownership and control in Germany, one needs to look also at the links between companies. Banks, and especially a few large banks, play a central role in German corporate governance with representation on the supervisory boards of companies and links with other companies. Charkham (1994) identifies a number of reasons as to why banks are influential in Germany. First, there is direct ownership of company shares by banks; second, German shareholders generally lodge their shares with banks authorized to carry out their voting instructions (deposited share voting rights, or DSVR); third, banks tend to lend for the long term and hence develop a longer term relationship with the company (relationship lending); fourth, banks offer a wide range of services that the company may find it useful to draw upon. Given these factors, banks tend to build up a longer term, deeper relationship with companies, and their expertise is welcomed on the supervisory boards. Hence the German corporate governance system could be termed an 'insider' system. A more detailed analysis is beyond the scope of this text but a comprehensive analysis is provided in Prigge (1998).

The German corporate governance system is based around a dual board system, and essentially, the dual board system comprises a management board (*Vorstand*) and a supervisory board (*Aufsichtsrat*). The management board is responsible for managing the enterprise. Its members are jointly accountable for the management of the enterprise and the chairman of the management board co-ordinates the work of the management board. On the other hand, the supervisory board appoints, supervises, and advises the members of the management board and is directly involved in decisions of fundamental import- ance to the enterprise. The chairman of the supervisory board co-ordinates the work of the supervisory board. The members of the supervisory board are elected by the share- holders in general meetings. The co-determination principle provides for compulsory employees representation. So, for firms or companies which have more than five hundred or two thousand employees in Germany, employees are also represented in the supervis- ory board which then comprises one-third employee representative or one-half employee representative respectively. The representatives elected by the shareholders and repres- entatives of the employees are equally obliged to act in the enterprise's best interests.

The idea of employee representation on boards is not always seen as a good thing because the employee representatives on the supervisory board may hold back decisions being made that are in the best interests of the company as a whole but not necessarily in the best interests of the employees as a group. An example would be where a company wishes to rationalize its operations and close a factory but the practicalities of trying to get such a decision approved by employee representatives on the supervisory board, and the repercussions of such a decision on labour relations, prove too great for the strategy to be made a reality.

The committee on corporate governance in Germany was chaired by Dr Gerhard Cromme and is usually referred to as the Cromme Report or Cromme Code. The code

online resource centre

Table 10.3 Key characteristics influencing German corporate governance

Feature	Key characteristic
Main business form	Public or private companies limited by shares
Predominant ownership structure	Financial and non-financial companies
Legal system	Civil law
Board structure	Dual
Important aspect	Compulsory employee representation on supervisory board

harmonizes a wide variety of laws and regulations and contains recommendations and also suggestions for complying with international best practice on corporate governance.

The Cromme Code was published in 2002 and is split into a number of sections, starting with a section on shareholders and the general meeting. The Cromme Code also reflects some of the latest developments in technology and these are discussed below. The Cromme Code was amended in 2005. Whilst it remains substantially the same, there are some significant changes, which are shown in bold in the relevant sections (i)–(vi) below.

(i) Shareholders and the general meeting

At the general meeting, the management board submits the annual, and consolidated, financial statement, and the general meeting decides on the appropriation of net income and approves the decisions of the management board and the supervisory board. An important aspect of the general meeting is that it elects the shareholders representatives to the supervisory board and also, generally, the auditors.

Interestingly, the Cromme Code makes explicit provision that the management board shall not only provide the report and accounts and other documents required by law for the general meeting but should also publish them on the company's website together with the agenda. Similarly, the use of technology is encouraged as the general meeting should be capable of being followed on the Internet or similar media.

The shareholders' right to vote is facilitated in a number of ways, including by the personal exercise of shareholders voting rights, and by the use of proxies.

(ii) Co-operation between the management board and the supervisory board

It is essential that the management board and the supervisory board co-operate closely for the benefit of the enterprise. The Cromme Code defines the management board's role as to co-ordinate the enterprise's strategic approach with the supervisory board and to discuss the implementation of strategy with the supervisory board at regular intervals. There are certain situations, such as those relating to the enterprise's planning, business development, risk situation, and risk management, when the management board should inform the supervisory board immediately of any issues.

The supervisory board is able to specify the management board's information and reporting duties in more detail. It is essential that there is open discussion between the management board and supervisory board as well as amongst the members within each of those two boards. The management board and the supervisory board report each year on the enterprise's corporate governance in the annual report and they should explain any deviations from the Cromme Code. **The company shall keep previous declarations of conformity with the Code available for viewing on its website for five years.**

(iii) Management board

The composition of the management board is determined by the supervisory board, and should be reported in the notes to the accounts. Any conflict of interest should be disclosed to the supervisory board. The Cromme Code states that 'the management board is responsible for independently managing the enterprise' with a view to acting in the enterprise's best interest, and endeavouring to increase the sustainable value of the enterprise. As mentioned earlier, the management board develops the enterprise's strategy and co-ordinates with the supervisory board on this issue.

The Cromme Report provides for the compensation to be comprised of a fixed salary and variable component. As in many other countries, the variable compensation element should be linked to the business performance as well as long-term incentives. Stock options are mentioned as one possible element of variable compensation components and these should be linked to certain performance criteria such as the achievement of predetermined share prices.

(iv) Supervisory board

It is important that the composition of the supervisory board reflects a suitable level of knowledge, ability, and experience to be able properly to carry out the tasks relevant to the business. **There should be an adequate number of independent members. 'Independence' will mean no business or personal relations with the company or its management board which cause a conflict of interest.** To help maintain its independence, not more than two former members of the management board should be members of the supervisory board. **The former management board chairman or a management board member should not generally become supervisory board chairman or chairman of a supervisory board committee.** Supervisory board members should not have directorships or similar positions or indeed have advisory roles with important competitors of the enterprise.

The supervisory board carries out a number of important functions as follows:

(i) it provides independent advice and supervision regularly to the management board on the management of the business;

(ii) the management board and the supervisory board should ensure that there is a long-term succession plan in place;

(iii) the supervisory board may delegate some duties to other committees, which include compensation and audit committees;

(iv) the chairman of the supervisory board, who should not be the chairman of the audit committee, co-ordinates work within the supervisory board and chairs its meetings and **attends to the affairs of the supervisory board externally.**

It is worth elaborating on the committees that may be formed with a remit for various delegated areas. These may include the audit committee (the chairman of the audit committee should not be a former member of the management board of the company); **the chairman of the audit committee should have specialist knowledge and experience in the application of accounting principles and internal control processes**, and a compensation committee to look at the compensation of the management board. This committee may also look at the appointment of members of the management board.

The Cromme Code also states that members of the management board of a listed company should not be on more than five supervisory boards in non-group listed companies. The compensation of members of the supervisory board is specified either by a resolution of the general meeting or in the articles of association. Members of the supervisory board may receive performance-related compensation as well as fixed compensation. **The compensation of the supervisory board members should be disclosed in the Corporate Governance Report**.

An interesting disclosure required by the Cromme Code is that if a supervisory board member takes part in less than half of the meetings of the supervisory board in a financial year, then this will be noted in the report of the supervisory board. Any conflicts of interest should be reported to the supervisory board and the supervisory board would then inform the general meeting of any conflicts of interest together with how these conflicts have been treated.

(v) Transparency

The code provides that the management board should disclose immediately any facts that might affect the enterprise's activities and which are not publicly known. The report emphasizes that all shareholders should be treated equally in respect of information disclosure and that the company may use appropriate media, such as the internet, to inform the shareholders and investors in an efficient and timely manner. There is disclosure required in terms of the shareholdings, including options and derivatives, that are held by individual management board and supervisory board members. These must be reported if they directly or indirectly exceed 1 per cent of the shares issued by the company. The code also states: 'If the entire holdings of all members of the management board and supervisory board exceed 1 per cent of the shares issued by the company, these shall be reported separately according to the management board and supervisory board.' **These disclosures should all be included in the Corporate Governance Report.**

(vi) Reporting and audit of the annual financial statements

The code states that the supervisory board or the audit committee should obtain a statement from the proposed auditor clarifying whether there are any 'professional, financial or other relationships' that might call the auditor's independence into question. Interestingly, this statement should include the extent to which other services have been performed for the company in the past year, especially in the field of consultancy, or which are contracted for the following year. It is the supervisory board that concludes agreement on the auditors fee.

From the discussion above, it can be seen that the defining feature of Germany's corporate governance system is the significant role played by the supervisory board. In addition, the supervisory board has compulsory representation of workers via the co-determination rules. This can have an important impact on key strategic decisions, for example, if a German company decides that it needs to close one of its subsidiaries, then it may prefer to close down a subsidiary overseas, in a country such as the UK, which has a unitary board structure and hence no supervisory board with employee representation. Employees in the UK would therefore be in a weaker position than their German counterparts, and have less influence over any closure decision.

It is interesting to note that Charkham (2005), in reviewing corporate governance developments in Germany, is of the opinion that

Internal and external developments have put pressure on it, but its main provisions remain intact. The factors for change have been the diminishing role of the banks, the international governance codes and principles, and the international capital markets

In November 2005, Germany abolished the requirement for shares to be blocked in advance of a shareholder meeting. Blocking had meant that shares could not be traded for a period of time before a company's general meeting, if the holder of the shares wished to be able to vote on the resolutions tabled for the general meeting. Therefore, it had effectively been a deterrent to voting because institutional investors often could not afford to be in a position whereby they were unable to trade their shares.

Recent legal changes now require companies to disclose pay details for executive directors, effective for annual reports for 2006 onwards. However, company management may propose that disclosure is limited and if the proposal is approved by 75 per cent of its shareholders, then the additional disclosure does not have to be given. An amended version of the German Corporate Governance Code was published in 2006 and recommended that various executive remuneration disclosures should be made in the Corporate Governance Report. Companies would be obliged to disclose if they were to deviate from these recommendations.

Denmark

Denmark has a quite different ownership structure to that of, say, the USA, the UK, or most of other European countries. The ownership is quite concentrated and there is a widespread existence of foundation ownership. This means that some of the largest Danish companies are controlled by a foundation (a foundation being a legal entity without owners often created to administer a large ownership stake in a particular company). There is also significant institutional investor share ownership in Denmark, with institutional investors owning approximately 35 per cent of market value of Danish equity. Like Germany, corporate governance in Denmark is focused on a dual board structure. The Danish Companies Act provides that half the members elected by the shareholders, or by other parties entitled to appoint directors, will be elected by the employees, with a minimum of two (this provision applies to companies with at least 35 employees).

The Nørby Committee's report was published in 2001 and made recommendations for corporate governance in Denmark. The foreword to the report very much emphasized

online
resource
centre

Table 10.4 Key characteristics influencing Danish corporate governance

Feature	Key characteristic
Main business form	Public or private companies limited by shares
Predominant ownership structure	Institutional investors and foundation ownership
Legal system	Civil law
Board structure	Dual
Important aspect	Many shares have multiple voting rights

that this was a voluntary code and that it was really up to the individual companies as to whether they actually followed it, but that the Nørby Committee believed that it was in companies' best interests to do so. The committee tried to make the recommendations operationally practical, although it emphasized that the recommendations be followed by companies of their own accord, so these were non-binding recommendations. However, the Committee felt that it was in the companies' own interests to follow the recommendations and did think it important that companies stated to what extent they had followed the recommendations. The report built on the OECD basic values of openness, transparency, responsibility, and equality. The Nørby Committee felt that because of the growing interest internationally in corporate governance and because, internationally, investors demand more and better information about managements' actions and the companies' long-term goals and strategy, it was important that Denmark also had a set of corporate governance recommendations. The committee believed that there should be more demands on listed companies than on unlisted companies; it also recommended that state companies complied with the recommendations, where relevant. The Nørby report was split into seven sections.

The Nørby Committee's (2001) recommendations formed the basis for further corporate governance developments in Denmark. In late 2002, the Copenhagen Stock Exchange appointed an independent corporate governance committee to develop further corporate governance for Danish listed companies. Various international initiatives occurred that impacted on corporate governance thinking in Denmark. These included the US Sarbanes–Oxley Act (2002), the UK Combined Code (2003), and EU initiatives such as the Action Plan (2003) to modernize company law and to enhance corporate governance in the EU (see earlier for more detail). In the light of these various international developments, it was decided to revisit the original Nørby recommendations to see what revisions might be needed.

In December 2003, the Copenhagen Stock Exchange Committee on Corporate Governance issued its report, hereafter referred to as Nørby (2003). The report stated that the Nørby (2001) recommendations were fundamentally appropriate and that their effect was as intended, therefore sweeping changes to the recommendations were not needed, but only revision or elaboration of existing recommendations. The Committee felt that some of the recommendations for corporate governance could be amended to try to ensure that the focus was on companies using relevant principles and ideas in a way that would be most appropriate for a particular company's needs. It also bore in mind that 'comply or explain' principles adopted in the UK were likely to become more widespread in the EU. The recommendations covered eight main areas, adding one more to the original Nørby recommendations: audit. Comments were invited on the proposed changes to the recommendations and subsequently, in August 2005, the final report was issued, hereafter referred to as Nørby (2005).

An important development was that the Copenhagen Stock Exchange has incorporated the Nørby (2005) Committee's revised recommendations for corporate governance into the disclosure requirements for listed companies 'obliging the companies, in accordance with the "comply or explain" principle, to include in their future annual reports a statement on how they address the Recommendations'. The fundamentally important aspect here is transparency. As in the UK, companies may comply by explaining how and why they do not comply with a particular recommendation. It is the disclosure and transparency aspects that enable shareholders and other stakeholders to understand better what is going on in the company.

The focus of the original Nørby (2001) recommendations plus the additional recommendation, and the revisions to these by subsequent committees, are outlined below, these being the recommendations as at August 2005.

(i) The role of the shareholders and their interaction with the management of the company

The report emphasizes the importance of communication and dialogue between management and shareholders, in order to ensure that the company's funds are appropriately utilized and that the company continues to be competitive and to create value. The report lays great importance on the role of the annual general meeting as a medium for communication and decision. The report recommends that the shareholders should be facilitated in using their rights, both in terms of communications and also in terms of voting rights. Denmark has a dual voting system, in other words, some shares have multiple voting rights, but the report states that voting rights differentiation or restricting the number of votes that an individual shareholder can cast or restricting the number of shares that an individual shareholder may own in the company are not recommended. If any of these restrictions already apply, then the board should look at these and decide whether it is possible to revoke them. Shareholders should receive sufficient notice of the AGM.

(ii) The role of the stakeholders and their importance to the company

The report emphasizes the importance of dialogue with stakeholders – a stakeholder being anyone who 'is directly affected by the company's decisions and business'. The interaction is emphasized as being of great importance and the company should have policies or guidelines in appropriate areas such as environmental and social issues.

(iii) Openness and transparency

Openness and transparency are seen as essential in providing continuous and timely information to the shareholders and other stakeholders of the company. The report recommends that investor relations should be based on continuous dialogue and that investor relations might be enacted in various ways such as investor meetings, use of information technology, use of the Internet, etc. The company should prepare its company report according to the relevant Danish rules but it is also recommended to apply international accounting standards.

(iv) The tasks and responsibilities of the supervisory board

The report states that 'the supervisory board is responsible for safeguarding the interests of the shareholders, with care and due consideration of the interests of the other stakeholders'. There is an emphasis on the development, and implementation of strategies for the company and the board's essential tasks are concerned with this area, as well as with areas such as risk management, appointing a qualified management, and trying to ensure good relations with a company's stakeholders. The chairman's task is to run the board and to ensure that these meetings are run effectively and efficiently, and it is recommended that a deputy chairman is also appointed. There should be established procedures as to how management reports to the board and the communications between the board and management.

(v) Composition of the supervisory board

The board should be comprised of directors who have the relevant and necessary knowledge and professional experience to contribute positively to the board, so that the strategic and managerial tasks of the board can be effectively carried out. When nominations are made to the AGM, then certain information should be provided about the directors, including the requirements of professional qualifications, international experience, and so on. It is recommended that when directors join the board they, in collaboration with the chairman, decide on any relevant or supplementary training that may be necessary. Every year, the supervisory board should assess whether the competence and expertise of its members needs to be updated.

The board size is recommended to be such that it allows for constructive debate and effective decision-making and ensures that the supervisory board members' experience and capabilities match the company's requirements. The independence of directors is emphasized, directors should be able to act independently of special interests and hence at least half of the supervisory board members should be independent. In this context, independent means that the director should not have been an employee in the company or someone who has been employed by the company within the past five years; nor should he be or have been a member of the executive board of the company; nor a professional consultant to the company; nor have any other strategic interest in the company other than that of a shareholder. The annual report would contain information about the directors elected by the general meeting including the directors' occupations, their other managerial positions or directorships in Danish as well as foreign companies, and how many shares, options, and warrants each director owns in the company. It is recommended that the board meets at regular intervals. Individual directors should be able to allocate sufficient time for their duties and it is recommended that a supervisory board member who is also a member of the executive board of an active company should not fill more than three ordinary directorships, or one chairmanship and one ordinary directorship, in companies that are not part of the group. Directors should retire at an age agreed by the supervisory board.

The supervisory board should consider whether to establish board committees such as audit, remuneration, and nomination committees. If such committees are established, terms of reference should be drawn up for each committee. Members' names would be listed in the annual report in relation to each committee. Where such committees are established, it is important to ensure that information relevant to the whole supervisory board is made available to all its members and not just to the members of an individual committee. There should be self-assessment of the board's work on an annual basis and this should take account of the strategic goals and plans, and whether these are being realized. The procedures for self-assessment should be included in the annual report.

(vi) Remuneration of the members of the supervisory board and the executive board

The report emphasizes the importance of a competitive remuneration scheme for attracting, and keeping, competent directors and managers. It is important that principles and guidelines are established and that there should be incentives that reflect the interests of the shareholders and the company. Whilst stating that the remuneration of the directors may include incentive schemes (including bonus schemes and shares at market price), the report does not recommend that it consists of share option schemes. However, where share or subscription options are used, these should be set up as roll-over schemes (the options are allocated and expire over a number of years). There should be transparency in this important area and directors' remuneration should be published in the annual report. Information about severance schemes should be disclosed in the company's annual report.

(vii) Risk management

It is important that the board considers risk management and that the company has an efficient risk management system. The board should monitor this area and ensure that the systems are working efficiently. The annual report should contain information about risk management activities.

(viii) Audit

An essential part of the supervisory board's work is to ensure a competent and independent audit. The framework for the auditor's work should be decided upon by the supervisory board and the executive board. Each year, the supervisory board should also detail the scope of any non-audit services provided by the auditor to help ensure the auditor's independence. At least annually, the supervisory board should review and assess the internal control systems of the company. The supervisory board should discuss with the auditor the accounting policies, together with important accounting estimates. The result of the audit should be discussed at meetings with the supervisory board.

From the discussion above, it can be seen that the Danish corporate governance system is developing rapidly, with a move to a 'comply or explain' basis. Finally, as with Germany, the dual board system may mean that Danish employees are at an advantage if the company's strategy requires that part of the company be closed down – the closure is more likely to hit part of the company located in a country with a unitary board structure, where employees have less influence.

France

The corporate governance system in France is set in a civil law context and, traditionally, does not offer good protection to minority investors. The French government has been an important stakeholder, partly because of its direct shareholdings in French industry (although this has declined with the privatizations in recent years) and also because of the fact that many civil servants are appointed to corporate boards. Wymeersch (1998) states that takeovers, particularly of recently privatized firms, are prevented by the *noyaux durs* (hard core), which comprise a series of holdings by financial institutions, banks, and insurance companies to help stabilize the French industrial sector. In addition, control may be enhanced by multiple voting rights attaching to shares, a construct that is against generally accepted corporate governance best practice.

There are various business forms available in France of which the two we are most concerned with are the *Sociétés anonymes (SAs)*, which is essentially like a public company in the UK, and the *Sociétés à responsibilité limitée (SARL)*, which is a limited liability company along the lines of a limited company in the UK. The French corporate governance system places a lot of emphasis – and power – on the *président directeur-général (PDG)* of a company. This is in line with the French tradition of centralized leadership and power.

France has a predominantly unitary board system, although the option to have a dual board exists. Similarly, there is provision for employee involvement where this is provided for by the articles of the company. French corporate governance codes therefore need to take account of this diversity of structure.

The first French corporate governance report was the Viénot Committee report in 1995. The Viénot Committee was established by two employers' federations (MEDEF and AFEP-AGREF) and with the support of leading private sector companies; it was chaired by Marc Vienot, head of Société Generale. The second Viénot report (Viénot II) was issued in 1999. Subsequent to Viénot II, the corporate governance environment became further complicated by the introduction of 'new economic regulations' in 2001 that gave companies with a unitary board structure the choice of separating the functions of chairman and chief executive officer or keeping them joint. The corporate governance report of a working group chaired by Daniel Bouton (President of Société Generale) was then issued in October 2002.

Table 10.5 Key characteristics influencing French corporate governance

Feature	Key characteristic
Main business form	Public or private companies limited by shares
Predominant ownership structure	State, institutional investors, individuals
Legal system	Civil law
Board structure	Unitary (but other structure possible)
Important aspect	Many shares have multiple voting rights

Bouton Report (2002)

The Bouton Report recommended incremental improvement rather than any radical reform. Part 1 of the report was split into six areas: the role and operation of the board of directors; the board of directors' composition; evaluation of the board of directors; the audit committee; the compensation committee; the nominating committee. Part 2 of the report contained some recommendations on strengthening the independence of statutory auditors (with specific reference of the importance of this area in the context of the Enron affair). Part 3 covered financial information, accounting standards and practices, and discussed the importance of high quality financial information and disclosures and the means to achieve them. Let us now look at Part 1 of the Bouton report in more detail.

(i) Role and operation of the board of directors

In line with the earlier Viénot reports, the Bouton Report emphasized that there should be specialized committees to undertake work in the areas of:

- reviewing the financial statements;
- monitoring the internal audit function;
- selection of statutory auditors;
- deciding a policy on remuneration and stock options;
- appointing of directors and corporate officers (chairman, chief executive officer, and chief operating officer in a unitary board system; chairman and members of the management board in a dual board system).

The report highlighted the importance of strategy and stated that the directors' internal rules of operation should specify board procedures for dealing with key strategic issues, such as issues relating to the company's financial position.

The importance of directors' access to information on a timely basis was also emphasized as an 'essential requirement for the satisfactory performance of their duties'. The report stated that information of a negative nature (if such arises) should also be supplied to the directors. A crucial feature relating to the interpretation of any information by directors was that newly appointed directors should have the facility to obtain additional training concerning specific facets of the company (such as its lines of business and markets). There was also provision for the directors to meet key executives of the company without, if they so wish, the corporate officers being present.

(ii) Board of directors' composition

The report recognized that the quality of the board is dependent on its membership and that directors should be sound characters with integrity, be knowledgeable about the business, be active in their role as directors (competently discussing strategy and other issues in board meetings), and should have regard to the interest of all shareholders.

The report advocated that half of the board be comprised of independent directors in companies that have a dispersed ownership structure and no controlling shareholders.

This was an increase on the Viénot II report, which had called for boards to be comprised of one-third independent directors. The report defined 'independence' as: 'A director is independent when he or she has no relationship of any kind whatsoever with the corporation, its group or the management of either that is such as to color his or her judgement.' This is a fairly encompassing, yet at the same time succinct, definition.

(iii) Evaluation of the board of directors

The report recommended annual evaluations via a debate at board level about its operation each year; at least every three years, there should be a formal evaluation, possibly under the leadership of an independent director, with help from an appropriate consultant. Shareholders would be kept informed each year via the annual report of evaluations carried out and the steps taken as a result.

(iv) The audit committee

The report recommended that the audit committee should be comprised of two-thirds independent directors and that there should not be any corporate officers as members. As well as any financial or accounting expertise that the audit committee members may already possess, they should also be informed of 'the company's specific accounting, financial and operating procedures'.

The audit committee should draw up rules of operation detailing responsibilities and operating procedures, and these should be approved by the board, to which the audit committee should also report so that the board is fully informed. Furthermore, the annual report should describe the work carried out by the audit committee. It is expected that the audit committee should interview the external auditors (whose appointment process they should drive) and the head of internal audit, and be able to call upon outside experts as necessary. The audit committee should also monitor auditor independence, including the amount of fees paid to the audit firm and what proportion those fees represent in relation to the audit firm's total billings.

(v) Compensation committee

The report recommended that the compensation committee should be comprised of a majority of independent directors and that there should not be any corporate officers as members. The compensation committee should draw up rules of operation, detailing responsibilities and operating procedures, and these should be approved by the board, to which the compensation committee should also report so that the board is fully informed. Furthermore, the annual report should describe the work carried out by the compensation committee.

Under French law, the annual report should include a discussion of the principles and processes applied in the setting of the corporate officers' compensation. The Bouton report required that the compensation committee defines how the variable element of directors' compensation will be set and ensures that this is consistent with the annual performance evaluation of the corporate officers and with the company's medium-term strategy.

The Bouton Report highlighted some significant differences relating to stock options under French law, compared to some other countries. First, 'only the general meeting of shareholders has the power to authorize the granting of options, to set their maximum number and to determine the main conditions of the granting process'; second, 'the exercise price of the options, which is set based on stock prices at the time of granting, cannot subsequently be revised or altered regardless of stock price trends'; third, 'the holding period of options ... is directly determined in practice by tax rules', being five years' minimum period from the date of grant for options granted prior to April 2000 (four years' minimum for options granted subsequently); fourth, 'directors who are neither corporate officers nor employees are barred by law from receiving stock options'.

(vi) Nominating committee

The Bouton Report emphasized the importance of the nominating committee, which should include the chairman of the board as a member, because it 'plays an essential role in shaping the future of the company, as it is in charge of preparing the future membership of leadership bodies'. There should be a formal procedure in place to select future independent directors, and the annual report should include a description of the work of the nominating committee.

The Bouton Report recommended that its proposals be implemented as soon as possible, but at the latest, by the end of 2003 (see below). Companies should include a discussion in their annual report of the extent to which the recommendations have been implemented. The events at Enron, in particular, were clearly in the minds of the Bouton working group when they stated: 'Although procedural rules and recommendations concerning the operation of the board and its committees are essential corporate governance standards, any procedure will only be as good as the people implementing it. ENRON complied formally with all these rules and was even considered a model of corporate governance!' It is really a case of substance over form: companies may comply with the letter of a code but do they comply with the spirit of it too? That will be the ultimate decider as to whether there are more Enrons in the future.

On a separate note, France published a decree in February 2002 setting out mandatory disclosure by companies in their annual report and accounts of the social and environmental impact of their activities. It came into force in 2003 for all annual reports.

(vii) Social and environmental issues

Areas where disclosures take place are community indicators, which are primarily qualitative, and these would focus on companies' integration with local communities and engagement with stakeholder groups. Labour standards are also addressed with disclosure required on how subsidiaries respect International Labor Organization (ILO) conventions and how the company promotes them with its sub-contractors. Environmental indicators cover areas such as emissions to air, water, and ground, implementation of management systems, and compliance with mainstream standards of practice or certification. Whilst these provisions are comprehensive, the question remains as to what could be done if a company did not comply and therefore the effectiveness of this legislation may, in practice, be limited.

In August 2003, France enacted new laws relating to financial security with the aim of restoring the trust of investors in French markets. The changes included that there should be improved transparency with more information provided to shareholders, including a separate report on the internal control procedures of the company, and a new procedure for the appointment of external auditors.

In October 2003, AFEP and MEDEF published 'The Corporate Governance of Listed Corporations', a document that provided a set of principles of corporate governance based on consolidation of the 1995, 1999 (Viénot 1 and 11) and 2002 (Bouton) AFEP and MEDEF reports. The report does not add to the Viénot and Bouton reports, the substance of which is retained; rather, it collates the recommendations into a single set of principles. The principles cover various aspects of the: board of directors; independent directors; board evaluation; meeting of the board and the committees; board committees such as audit, compensation, nominations; directors' compensation. The principles utilize a 'comply or explain' approach with regard to which recommendations a company has adopted.

In conclusion, France's corporate governance system gives companies the option of either the unitary or dual board structure. As in Denmark, there are still multiple voting rights in existence. A very positive move by the French government is the mandatory disclosure requirements for companies of the social and environmental impact of their activities, which is very encouraging.

Italy

Bianchi et al. (2001) identify seven different company types in Italy. However, the main business forms are the *societa di persone*, or partnership, which generally has unlimited liability, and the *societa di capitali*, or limited liability companies. Furthermore, their analysis of direct ownership for both listed and unlisted companies in Italy finds that 'a major role is played by families, coalitions, the State and above all by other companies. The largest stake in listed and unlisted companies is held by other non-financial or holding companies. Contrary to other European countries, the amount held by financial institutions is limited' (p. 154). They do, however, comment that the situation is changing as pyramidal private groups are simplifying, and hence both banks and institutional investors are starting to play a more important role.

Italy has a unitary board structure but a board of auditors is also required. The corporate governance situation in Italy has been subject to a number of revisions in recent years. In 1998, the Director General of the Italian Treasury, Mario Draghi, introduced corporate governance rules, a series of legislative measures, which became known as the Draghi Law. These rules enhanced transparency of listed companies, discussed the structure for decision-making within companies, and also looked at the area of internal control. Minority shareholders benefited from this legislation and it also strengthened the position of Italian companies with reference to the confidence with which they were perceived by international investors.

The Draghi Law also required the establishment of a board of auditors comprised of at least three individuals, all of whom should be independent of the company's directors and employees. Members of the board of auditors have to fulfil experience

Table 10.6 Key characteristics influencing Italian corporate governance

Feature	Key characteristic
Main business form	Limited liability companies; partnerships
Predominant ownership structure	Non-financial/holding companies; families
Legal system	Civil law
Board structure	Unitary
Important aspect	Board of auditors required

and other criteria. The role of the board of auditors includes reviewing the company's organizational structure, its internal control system, its accounting system, and its administrative system.

In 1998, the Borsa Italiana introduced a corporate governance report that became known as the Preda Report, named after its chairman. The Preda code introduced recommendations regarding the composition of the board, the formation of key board committees, the roles of chairman and CEO, and the independence of directors. However, the code was a voluntary code and companies could disclose the extent to which they had adopted or complied with the code. It must be said that the code was not as comprehensive as, for example, the UK's Combined Code. For example, it said that the majority of a company's remuneration committee members should be non-executive but it did not really talk about their independence. So, given the current climate where there is a lot of focus and emphasis on corporate governance, in 2002, there was another report issued. This was a revision of the Preda report. This report is known as Preda 2.

The Preda 2 report deals with a number of areas relating to corporate governance: the role of the board of directors; the composition of the board of directors; independent directors; the chairman of the board of directors; information to be provided to the board of directors; appointment and remuneration of directors; internal control; related party transactions; relations with institutional investors and other shareholders; shareholders meetings; members of the board of auditors.

online resource centre

(i) Role of the board of directors

The Preda code identifies the role of the board of directors as, inter alia, to examine and approve the company's strategic operational and financial plans; to establish appropriate committees, which should report regularly to the board of directors; to consult with the board of auditors on the remuneration for directors recommended by the special committee (remuneration committee); to allocate the total amount to which the members of the board and the executive committee are entitled; to supervise the general performance of the company; to report to the shareholders at shareholders meetings. The code defines the objective as creating value for the shareholders. The report mentions that the emphasis placed on shareholder value, apart from reflecting an internationally prevalent approach, is in conformity with Italian law, which sees the interest of the shareholders as the main point of reference for the directors.

The code emphasizes that it is important for listed companies to be governed by a board that meets at regular intervals and that has an efficient way of operating. The directors are expected to exercise independent judgement (regardless of whether they are executive or non-executive).

When directors accept a board appointment, they should do so on the basis that they have the requisite skills and knowledge and that they can devote the appropriate amount of time to the directorship. They should also take into account how many other directorships they might actually have. Each year, the annual report should publish details of other positions held by the directors on other boards of companies or as auditors of listed companies.

(ii) Composition of the board of directors

The board is made up of executive directors and non-executive directors and the report emphasizes the role that non-executive directors can play. Normally, non-executive directors in Italy will outnumber the executive directors and the contribution that non-executive directors bring is in terms of their expertise of a general strategic or specific technical nature, which has been acquired outside the company. The other area where non-executive directors can be particularly helpful is where the interests of the executive directors and the shareholders might not coincide, and in that case, the non-executive directors can help to assess proposals with greater detachment.

(iii) Independent directors

There should be an adequate number of independent non-executive directors and the definition that is given in the code broadly encompasses the generally accepted definition of what an independent director is: for example, they should not be engaged in business relationships with the company or its subsidiaries, or with the executive directors or shareholders or group of shareholders who control the company in such a way as would influence their own judgement. They should not be immediate family members of the executive directors of the company. In terms of owning shares, they may own shares, but not such a quantity that would enable them to have control over the company or to exercise significant influence. A new provision, which is quite an interesting one, is that the directors' independence would be periodically assessed by the board on the basis of information provided and the results of that test of independence will then be communicated to the market. The presence of independent directors is recognized as one way of trying to represent the interest of all shareholders, whether majority or minority shareholders.

(iv) The chairman of the board of directors

The chairman is responsible for calling meetings of the board and for ensuring that the activities of the board are co-ordinated, and for chairing the meetings effectively and efficiently. The board may delegate power to the chairman and that should be disclosed in the annual report, i.e. which powers have actually been delegated. In Italy, it is quite common that the chairman and managing director roles may be combined into one position or, alternatively, they may be separate positions with their own tasks.

(v) Information to be provided to the board of directors

The executive committee and managing directors should periodically report to the board of directors on activities performed in the exercise of their delegated powers; they are asked to provide the board of directors and the board of auditors with the same information.

(vi) Confidential information

The report emphasizes the confidentiality of information that directors receive in the performance of their work and asks them to comply with procedures for communicating such information to third parties as appropriate. The code recommends the adoption of internal procedures so that the disclosure of transactions carried out by 'relevant persons' (insider dealings) is appropriately dealt with. Further, the code states that, if a nomination committee is established, which is one way of ensuring a transparent selection procedure, then that committee should be comprised of a majority of non-executive directors. Nomination committees will also be particularly appropriate where the shareholder base is quite diverse. Any proposals for potential directors should be accompanied by details of the personal traits and professional qualifications of the candidates, and this information should be deposited at the company's registered office at least ten days before the date fixed for the shareholders meeting or at the time the election lists, if provided for, are deposited.

(vii) Remuneration of directors

It is recommended that the board of directors form a remuneration committee that is comprised of the majority of non-executive directors. The remuneration committee would make recommendations to the board of directors regarding remuneration issues. It is also recommended that, of the total remuneration, a part should be linked to the company's profitability and maybe to the achievement of certain objectives. However, the Preda code does give companies a lot of flexibility in this area and states that it is really up to the board of directors acting on the remuneration committee's recommendations as to whether they do actually use systems of remuneration that are linked to results, which might include stock options, and setting the objectives for managing directors.

(viii) Internal control

The report recognizes the importance of internal controls and that the responsibility for an internal control system lies with the board of directors. The board of directors is therefore tasked with the duty of instituting a system of internal control and periodically checking that that system is functioning as expected. An internal control committee may be established and this would be made up of non-executive directors, the majority being independent. The head of internal audit may also head up the internal control system. It is important that the internal control system is monitored and that there are appropriate reports to enable any inadequacies to be remedied. The internal control committee would assess the proposals of audit firms (external auditors), and also report to the board of directors on its activity and the adequacy of the internal control system at least once every six months.

(ix) Transactions with related parties

Transactions with related parties should comply with criteria of substantial and procedural fairness and the board should be informed in detail of the existence, potential or actual, of the interest that has arisen. Any directors concerned with the related party transaction would have to leave the board meeting when the issue is actually being discussed.

(x) Relations with institutional investors and other shareholders

The chairman of the board of directors and the managing director should actively endeavour to develop a dialogue with shareholders and institutional investors based on recognition of their reciprocal roles. They might designate a person or create a corporate structure that would be responsible for this function, which would presumably be along the lines of an investor relations department. The report recognizes the importance of continuous communication with shareholders and that it is important to both present and prospective shareholders.

(xi) Shareholders meetings

The report recognizes the importance of shareholders meetings and believes that directors should encourage and facilitate as broad a participation in the meetings as possible. All directors should usually attend shareholders meetings, which are seen as an opportunity to provide shareholders with information about the company. It is important that a procedure is set in place to ensure that the meeting is conducted in an orderly manner and effectively, and also to guarantee that each shareholder may speak on matters on the agenda, meaning that the rights of each shareholder are guaranteed.

(xii) Members of the board of auditors

Any proposals for appointment to the position of auditor should be accompanied by detailed information regarding the personal traits and professional qualifications of the candidates (a similar process to the appointment of the independent directors). The members of the board of auditors act autonomously with respect to shareholders, including those that elected them. In other words, they would actually represent the interest of the generality of shareholders rather than those who actually appointed them specifically. Any documents and information that come their way in the performance of their duties must be treated with confidentiality.

In 2006, Borsa Italiana issued a new corporate governance code to take account of changes in good governance practices internationally. Whilst the order of contents is similar to that of the 2002 code, the structure has changed: principles are elaborated on with application criteria and comments, which help to define the range of the principles and criteria, and also give examples. New features include: the introduction of recommendations on the limit of roles held by each director and annual self-assessment by the board; the introduction of a lead independent director; recommendations on the internal control system; promotion of initiatives to encourage shareholder participation in shareholders' meetings and the exercise of their rights.

Convergence or divergence

We have seen that the main differences in corporate governance codes amongst Continental European countries stem from companies law and securities regulation. The ownership structure varies across Continental European countries and those countries with a civil law/code tend to have poorer protection of minorities, which is not attractive for smaller shareholders or for those investing from overseas. Van den Berghe (2002) concludes that 'a serious tension is growing between capital markets, which are gradually globalising, and the economic and legal environments (like the company models involved, the governance recommendations and legal rules) that are still quite divergent. This gap creates pressure on firms that want to enter the capital market with structures and governance environments that are not up to the global standards of the capital markets' (p. 167). Gregory (2005) reviews the various developments in international corporate governance, highlighting both the commonalities and the remaining differences, which indicate that there is a move towards convergence, albeit gradual and incomplete.

Whilst recognizing that 'one size does not fit all' in terms of corporate governance, institutional investors are increasingly converging on the basic characteristics of good corporate governance, encompassing such areas as basic shareholder rights, independence of directors, and presence of key board committees. Therefore it is likely that, over time, there will be convergence on the fundamental aspects of good corporate governance, notwithstanding that ownership structures and legal systems may vary. The EU Action Plan, with its implications for a more consistent approach to issues such as shareholder rights across EU Member States, will be a powerful force towards convergence on various aspects of corporate governance.

Conclusions

This chapter has shown how corporate governance has developed in a number of Continental European countries. Spurred by the development of capital markets, the influence of institutional investors, and a growing desire for more transparency and disclosure following various high-profile financial scandals across the globe, Continental Europe has responded by improving its corporate governance to provide increased disclosure and accountability. Although corporate ownership structures may differ across Europe, and some countries have a unitary board whilst others have a dual board, there does seem to be agreement on some of the fundamental aspects of corporate governance that is leading towards a convergence of corporate governance in key areas.

■ **SUMMARY**

- Corporate governance codes in Continental Europe have developed against a backdrop of varying legal and ownership structures. Whilst idiosyncratic features of countries influence the development of individual codes, there seems to be a consensus on certain key issues, for example, more transparency and disclosure, accountability of the board, and the independence of at least a portion of the directors.

- Most European countries have a unitary board structure, although the majority also have the option of a dual structure.

- Germany has a dual board structure and co-determination means that employees are represented on the supervisory board. Banks are quite influential in the German corporate governance system. The Cromme Code harmonized a wide variety of laws and regulations and contained recommendations and suggestions for complying with international best practice on corporate governance. The amended Corporate Governance Code (2006) updates the earlier provisions of the Cromme Code.

- Denmark also has a dual board structure. Its ownership structure is unusual because there is widespread foundation ownership. The Nørby Code and subsequent updates made recommendations on corporate governance in Denmark and a 'comply or explain' approach is now followed.

- France has a predominantly unitary board system although the option to have a dual board exists. Building on the earlier Viénot reports, the Bouton Report recommended incremental improvements rather than any radical reform. AFEP–MEDEF produced a single set of corporate governance principles that drew together the earlier recommendations of Viénot and Bouton. France has some comprehensive recommendations regarding disclosure of social and environmental indicators.

- Italy has a unitary board structure but a board of auditors is also required. The Preda Codes (1 and 2) make recommendations regarding corporate governance. The Corporate Governance Code (2006) adapts the earlier principles in the light of international best practice in corporate governance.

- There is much debate about whether corporate governance systems are converging or diverging. There does seem to be agreement on some of the fundamental characteristics of a sound corporate governance system, indicative of a move towards convergence. Developments such as the EU Action Plan will play a key role in convergence on key aspects of corporate governance.

Example: Euro Disney, France

Many French companies have traditionally had poor disclosure of their corporate governance practices. This is changing gradually over time but good disclosure is still the exception rather than the rule. An example of good corporate governance practice and disclosure is Euro Disney.

Euro Disney is a young company. It was floated on the London, Brussels, and Paris bourses in 1989 and Disneyland Park opened in 1992. The Euro Disney website contains financial and other information in several languages. The corporate governance statement clarifies the governance structure of the company as being comprised of a management team and a supervisory board. The supervisory board has a 'Supervisory Board Members' Charter', which sets out the fundamental obligations that should be met. Some of the obligations in the Charter are innovative and go beyond the company's by-laws, such as requiring each board member to own at least some of the company's shares.

Example: Telecom Italia, Italy

This is an example of an Italian company that has very good corporate governance practices and disclosures, and is recognized as one of the best in Italy.

Telecom Italia is heavily involved in most aspects of the telecommunications industry. The largest stake is owned by Olimpia SpA, which owns over 18 per cent; the second largest stake is held by international institutional investors (26 per cent), whilst Italian institutional investors own 20 per cent (all percentages as at 30 June 2005).

The website contains excellent information on the principles and codes that the company abides by and the 'Self-Regulatory Code (2003)' is comprised of more than a dozen sections, including sections on the role, powers, and duties of the board of directors, independent directors, meetings of the board of directors, the chairman of the board of directors, Internal Control and Corporate Governance Committee, meetings of shareholders, and relations with shareholders. An annual corporate governance report is produced and contains a comprehensive review of Telecom Italia's corporate governance. For example, in 2004, the board of directors met 12 times with on average more than 90 per cent of the directors present (and independent directors recording an attendance rate of 94 per cent). Telecom Italia's by-laws stipulate that the board of directors should comprise between 7 and 23 members; it is presently 19 members with 10 of these being independent. There is also detailed disclosure of directors' remuneration.

Mini case study: Deutsche Bank, Germany

As with the examples cited from France and Italy, Deutsche Bank has very good corporate governance practices and disclosure.

In contrast to the French example of Euro Disney, Deutsche Bank is a long-established business that has effectively survived two world wars, and today is an efficient and forward-looking business.

Again, as with the earlier examples of Euro Disney and Telecom Italia, Deutsche Bank makes excellent use of its website to inform interested parties of its corporate governance. It incorporated most of the German Corporate Governance Code recommendations into its own Corporate Governance Principles. These state that 'effective corporate governance in accordance with high international standards is a part of our identity'. This really crystallizes the philosophy that Deutsche Bank has. The Principles are contained in a substantial document, which includes relations with shareholders, board of managing directors and supervisory board, performance-related compensation, and reporting and transparency.

An area worthy of special comment is the emphasis on electronic media conveying information relating to the general meeting and associated areas such as voting. The supervisory board has established four standing committees, being the chairman's committee, the audit committee, the risk committee, and the mediation committee.

■ **QUESTIONS**

The discussion questions below cover the key learning points of this chapter. Reading of some of the additional reference material will enhance the depth of the students' knowledge and understanding of these areas.

1. What factors have influenced the development of board structure in Continental European countries?

2. How might the employees' interests be represented in a company's corporate governance structure?

3. To what extent is there an emphasis on the role of non-executive directors in Continental European countries?

4. To what extent are the needs of various stakeholder groups satisfied by corporate governance structures in Continental Europe?

5. Critically discuss the case for a unitary board structure versus a dual board structure.

6. Critically discuss the extent to which you believe that corporate governance systems are converging or diverging.

■ **FT ARTICLE**

Scandals prompt Italy to toughen governance code

By Ian Limbach and Adrian Michaels in Milan

Borsa Italiana, the Milan stock exchange, yesterday tightened its corporate governance guidelines for listed companies, bringing in tougher standards for director independence and financial literacy.

Prominent heads of Italian businesses have complained that their governance and transparency are often viewed unfavourably in other countries in the wake of scandals at companies such as Parmalat and in the banking industry.

Yesterday's revamped voluntary code brought Italian governance into line with international best practices, said Massimo Capuano, stock exchange chief executive. The code replaced one written in 1999 and revised in 2002. Consob, Italy's market regulator, will verify company disclosures.

The most significant changes regard director independence and internal controls. The criteria defining the independence of a director are more thorough, in an effort to tackle superficial compliance. Mr Capuano said: "We're calling for a realistic, pragmatic definition of independence, not just a formal one."

A company's board will be responsible for ensuring that directors are independent in substance as well as form, and application of the rules will be verified by independent auditors.

Companies with executive chairmen will have to nominate a lead independent director and the board's independent directors will meet separately at least once a year.

The new code also imposes conditions on some board committees such as the remuneration committee, with membership restricted to non-executive members, the majority of whom must be independent. At least one member of the audit committee must have financial expertise.

Board members will also be prohibited from holding an excessive number of other directorships. But no specific limit has been given and the board will decide if directors devote enough time to their duties.

The exchange expects companies to observe the guidelines from next year. Mr Capuano said: "We are looking for ways to press companies to be more exhaustive in demonstrating compliance."

'We're calling for a realistic, pragmatic definition of independence, not just a formal one' – MASSIMO CAPUANO, EXCHANGE HEAD

Italian governance guidelines still will not require a majority of board members to be independent, as in the US. The Italian economy is slowly evolving from being dominated by private family-run enterprises and Mr Capuano said it would not be realistic to expect families to take their companies public and relinquish control at the same time.

The exchange is in the process of going public and has hired investment bank UBS to advise it. There is a meeting of its shareholders at the end of next month and a report from UBS should be ready by then.

Financial Times Wednesday 15 March 2006

■ **REFERENCES**

AFEP and MEDEF (2003), *The Corporate Governance of Listed Corporations*, Paris.

Association Française des Entreprises Privées (AFEP) and Mouvement des Enterprises de France (MEDEF) (1999), *Report of the Committee on Corporate Governance (Vienot II)*, Paris.

Becht, M. and Mayer, C. (2001), 'Introduction' in *The Control of Corporate Europe*, F. Barca and M. Becht (eds.), Oxford University Press, Oxford.

Bianchi, M., Bianco, M. and Enriques, L. (2001), 'Pyramidal Groups and the Separation Between Ownership and Control in Italy' in *The Control of Corporate Europe*, F. Barca and M. Becht (eds.), Oxford University Press, Oxford.

Bouton, D. (2002), *Promoting Better Corporate Governance in Listed Companies*, Report of the working group chaired by Daniel Bouton, AFEP/MEDEF, Paris.

Cadbury, Sir Adrian (1992), *Report of the Committee on the Financial Aspects of Corporate Governance*, Gee & Co. Ltd., London.

Centre for European Policy Studies (1995), *Corporate Governance in Europe*, Brussels.

Charkham, J. (1994), *Keeping Good Company: A Study of Corporate Governance in Five Countries*, Oxford University Press, Oxford.

——(2005), *Keeping Better Company: Corporate Governance Ten Years On*, Oxford University Press, Oxford.

Conseil National du Patronat (CNPF) and Association Française des Entreprises Privées (AFEP) (1995), *The Board of Directors of Listed Companies in France (Vienot I)*, Paris.

Corporate Governance Committee (2006) *Corporate Governance Code*, Borsa Italiana.

Cromme Code (2002), *Corporate Governance Code* as contained in the Transparency and Disclosure Act German Government Commission.

——(2005), *German Corporate Governance Code, as amended 2 June 2005*, Government Commission, Germany.

——(2006) *German Corporate Governance Code, as amended 12 June 2006*, Government Commission, Germany.

EU Commission (2003), *Modernising Company Law and Enhancing Corporate Governance in the European Union*, EU Commission, Brussels.

Franks, J. and Mayer, C. (1995), 'Ownership and Control' in H. Siebert (ed.), *Trends in Business Organization: Do Participation and Co-operation Increase Competitiveness?*, Mohr (Siebeck) Tubingen.

Gregory, H. (2005), 'International Corporate Governance: A Gradual If Incomplete Convergence' in *The Accountable Corporation*, M.J. Epstein and K.O. Hanson (eds.), Praeger Publishers, Westport, USA.

Gregory, H J. and Simmelkjaer, R.T. (2002), *Comparative Study of Corporate Governance Codes Relevant to the European Union and Its Member States*, on behalf of the European Commission, Internal Market Directorate General, Weil Gotshal & Manges, New York. http://europa.eu.int/comm/internal_market/en/company/company/news/corp-gov-codes-rpt_en.htm

La Porta, F., Lopez de Silvanes, F., Shleifer, A. and Vishny, R. (1998), 'Law and Finance', *Journal of Political Economy*, 106(6).

McKinsey & Co. (2000), *Investor Opinion Survey on Corporate Governance*, McKinsey & Co., London.

Mertzanis, H. (1999), *Principles on Corporate Governance in Greece: Recommendations for its Competitive Transformation*, Committee on Corporate Governance in Greece, Athens.

Nørby Commission (2001), *Recommendations for Good Corporate Governance in Denmark*.

Nørby Committee (2003), *Report on Corporate Governance in Denmark – the Copenhagen Stock Exchange Committee on Corporate Governance*, Copenhagen Stock Exchange, Denmark.

—— (2005), *Revised Recommendations for Corporate Governance in Denmark – the Copenhagen Stock Exchange Committee on Corporate Governance*, Copenhagen Stock Exchange, Denmark.

OECD (1999), *Principles of Corporate Governance*, OECD, Paris.

——(2004), *Principles of Corporate Governance*, OECD, Paris.

Preda (2002), *Self Regulatory Code*, Committee for the Corporate Governance of Listed Companies, Borsa Italiana.

Prigge, S. (1998), 'A Survey of German Corporate Governance' in *Comparative Corporate Governance: The State of the Art and Emerging Research*, K.J. Hopt, H. Kanda, M.J. Roe, E. Wymeersch, and S. Prigge (eds.), Oxford University Press, Oxford.

Van den Berghe, L. (2002), *Corporate Governance in a Globalising World: Convergence or Divergence? A European Perspective*, Kluwer Academic Publishers.

Wymeersch, E. (1998), 'A Status Report on Corporate Governance in Some Continental European States' in *Comparative Corporate Governance: The State of the Art and Emerging Research*, K.J. Hopt, H. Kanda, M.J. Roe, E. Wymeersch, and S. Prigge (eds.), Oxford University Press, Oxford.

■ USEFUL WEBSITES

www.borsaitalia.it The website of the Italian Stock Exchange, Borsa Italia, contains information about corporate governance in Italy.

www.corporategovernance.dk This website contains the Nørby Committee Report on Corporate Governance in Denmark.

www.ecgi.org The website of the European Corporate Governance Institute has comprehensive information about corporate governance, including downloadable codes/guidelines for most countries.

www.gccg.de The German Code of Corporate Governance (Berlin Initiative) can be downloaded from this website.

www.icgn.org The website of the International Corporate Governance Network contains information relating to corporate governance issues globally.

www.oecd.org The website of the Organization for Economic Co-operation and Development has information about various corporate governance guidelines.

11

Corporate Governance in Central and Eastern Europe

LEARNING OBJECTIVES

- To understand the implications of the privatization process for ownership structure in countries moving towards a market economy
- To be aware of the effect on the development of corporate governance of different privatization processes
- To have a detailed knowledge of the corporate governance systems in several Central and Eastern European countries

---

Introduction

More than a decade has passed now since the USSR began to dissolve into constituent countries. The move from a command economy to a market economy is not an easy one and the countries that comprised the former USSR have achieved this transition with varying degrees of success. In general, the companies have moved from a situation where, as state-owned enterprises, they were most probably not expected to make a profit because the objective of the business was not really defined in those terms but rather in terms of socialist goals such as full employment. This meant that, very often, the companies were highly inefficient: often using old machinery, having too large a workforce to be justified, and access to funds from the Central Bank without having to produce any repayment plans.

The success of the various countries can often be linked to the type of privatization that was followed to take businesses from state-owned enterprises to joint stock companies to public corporations. It is important to note that, in some countries, the term 'joint stock company' describes a company that has share capital which is traded on the stock exchange (essentially a public company); in other countries, the term may refer to a stage in the privatization process whereby a state-owned enterprise issues share capital to become a joint stock company, but that share capital is owned by the state with the next stage in the process being to sell the shares on to the public so that the company becomes a public corporation.

In general, there are three types of privatization process: the first is a mass privatization model, state-owned assets being distributed free of charge to the general public through vouchers that can be traded for ownership shares in state-owned firms. This model is sometimes referred to as the 'voucher privatization method' and was used in the Czech Republic and Russia. The second model allowed management and employees to buy company assets. This method was the method adopted in Poland. The third model, and arguably the one that produced the most successful results, involved selling majority control to an outside investor. The outside investor was often a foreign investor and this tended to lead first of all to higher expectations of the companies in which they invested and, secondly, in the companies that these outside investors bought into, the corporate governance is generally better. This third method was followed in Hungary and also in Estonia.

In this chapter, we will look at four countries: the Czech Republic, Poland, Russia, and Hungary. We will look at the process of privatization that each of these countries followed and the framework for corporate governance that exists in these countries. There is clearly a link between the method of privatization used, the resultant ownership structure, and the degree or level of corporate governance that is being adopted. The method of privatization has tended to have more of an immediate impact on the development of corporate governance than the legal framework in these countries. Whilst the legal framework has been based on a command economy with state-owned enterprises, as the owners of the privatized industries find their voice, it can be expected that they will push for improved corporate governance including better protection of minority rights. As Coffee (2002) points out:

online resource centre

the more plausible explanation is that economic changes have produced regulatory changes, rather than the reverse…Mass privatization came overnight to the Czech Republic, and its securities market soon crashed, at least in part because of the absence of investor protections. Only then, several years later, were statutory reforms adopted to protect minority shareholders. Pistor (2000) has generalized that the same responsive reaction of law to economic change has characterized the adoption of common law reforms by transitional economies.

Privatization process and its implications

Boeri and Perasso (1998), in a study of the Czech Republic, Hungary, Poland, and Russia, highlight the effects of each of the three privatization methods on a number of outcomes. They outline the outcomes, or performance indicators, as:

the *speed* of privatization, that is, the proportion of former state enterprises which has changed ownership within the first four years of the privatization process, the relevance of *outside ownership* (percentage of privatized enterprises with dominant outside ownership) in the resulting ownership structure of firms, and finally, the degree of *control* exerted over managerial decisions by the owners of the firm. The latter indicator is proxied by the involvement in privatization of foreign and domestic companies.

They find that the Czech Republic's speed of privatization was very rapid, resulted in significant outside ownership, but a rather weak control structure; Hungary's

Table 11.1 Ownership structures of companies in selected transition countries (unweighted)

No. of companies	Czech Republic %	Hungary %	Poland %	Romania %	Russia %	Ukraine %
Insiders	3	11	10	15	40	45
State	51	53	26	46	8	21
Outsiders	46	29	55	39	45	28
Individuals/families	6	8	31	20	40	22
Institutional outsiders	40	21	24	20	5	6
Others/no answer	0	7	9	0	7	6
Number of enterprises	35	38	84	41	214	87

Source: EBRD/World Bank Business Environment Survey 1999 (only medium-sized and larger companies with more than 100 employees are included here)

privatization process was less rapid but resulted in a stronger control structure and more outside ownership; Poland's process was slower but achieved a reasonable level of outside ownership and control; Russia's privatization process was quite rapid but resulted in much less outside control and a poor control structure, given the initial concentration of ownership into the hands of insiders.

Looking in more detail at the ownership structure of a sample of Central and Eastern European countries, Table 11.1 shows the dominant owners of companies in selected transition countries. The broad categories of owners are: insider owners (managers and workers); outsider owners (individuals and families, and institutional outsiders such as investment funds and banks); the state. It can be seen that the dominant owners vary across the transition countries, with the state still influential; outsiders are also influential, either in the form of individuals/families, or as institutional outsiders. It should be remembered that the privatization process will have been instrumental in determining the basic ownership structure in each of the countries, but that the data in Table 11.1 is based on a 1999 survey, several years after the initial privatization processes in each country. Nonetheless, the influence of the different privatization processes on ownership structure is still very much in evidence as, for example, in Russia, where insider ownership still retains a lot of influence.

Berglof and Pajuste (2003) highlight the fact that whilst the level of state ownership differs across countries in Central and Eastern Europe, private ownership is becoming more dominant, with ownership being increasingly concentrated. Strong insider ownership and control, combined with poor protection of minority shareholders, makes companies less attractive to foreign investors and minority shareholders.

The Czech Republic

As discussed earlier, the Czech Republic used the voucher privatization method to privatize state-owned enterprises. Coffee (1998) details how the voucher system entitled each Czechoslovak adult to purchase a booklet of 1000 voucher points for a cost equating to about 25 per cent of the average monthly wage at the end of 1991. For the second privatization wave in 1993/94, the price was raised by a modest amount but, by then, this accounted for less than 18 per cent of the average monthly wage. By the end of the second privatization wave, Coffee (1998) notes that 'over 80 per cent of adult Czech citizens had become shareholders in the 1849 companies that were privatized (in whole or in part)'.

The investment privatization funds (IPFs) were established shortly after the first privatization wave and bought the vouchers from individual citizens. The Czech government legislated to ensure that IPFs appointed a bank as their depository and deposited all securities and funds with it; IPFs were also required to appoint managing and supervisory boards. However, substantial holdings were still controlled by the state via the National Property Fund (NPF), which contained holdings awaiting sale, and holdings of strategic companies that may be sold at some point, such as utilities. The NPF also exercised influence via the IPFs. As Boeri and Perasso (1998) point out: 'The largest IPFs are controlled by banks, especially the big four banks, whose main shareholder, but not majority except in one case, is the state, via NPF.' Claessens et al. (1997) show that at the end of 1995, the top five IPFs owned, on average, just under 49 per cent of a firm privatized in the first wave and just under 41 per cent of a firm privatized in the second wave.

Unfortunately, the Czech voucher privatization process led to two significant shortcomings post-privatization: one was a high level of cross-ownership, resulting in a consolidation of control in the Czech banking sector; the other was the situation where, although many individuals held shares as a result of the voucher system, they formed a minority interest which had no effective legal protection. This lack of legal protection and a downturn in the Czech Republic stock market led overseas institutional investors to sell their shares and leave the market. An improved corporate governance system will be one way to try to ensure that foreign investment is lured back to invest in the Czech Republic.

From 1 January 2001, an extensive package of changes was introduced into the Czech Republic. These changes involved the Commercial Code, the Securities Act, and the Auditing Act. Many of the changes altered the responsibilities and rights of companies, board members, shareholders, and auditors, and so they were fairly wide ranging and far reaching.

A revised Corporate Governance Code (2001), hereinafter 'the Code', set out corporate governance best practice for companies in the Czech Republic and was based on the OECD Principles, but reference was also made to other codes, including the Combined Code of the London Stock Exchange. The focus was on transparency and accountability because these elements are essential to encourage investor confidence. The Prague Stock Exchange recommended that companies adopted as many of the Code's provisions as they could straight away, and then explained in their annual report why they were not adopting other provisions and when they anticipated being able to do so. Hopefully, companies would be able to comply fully within a couple of years. Additionally, it encouraged all companies listed on the second market to do the same.

The Code stated that the principles on which it was based are those of openness, integrity, and accountability, and that acceptance of these concepts would do much to remove some of the more unethical behaviour and practices prevalent in various parts of the Czech business world, and so restore an environment conducive to both strategic

Table 11.2 Summary of key characteristics influencing corporate governance in the Czech Republic

Feature	Key characteristic
Privatization method	Mass privatization via voucher
Predominant ownership structure	State; institutional outsiders (investment funds and banks)
Legal system	Civil law
Board structure	Dual
Important aspect	Influence of investment privatization funds (IPFs)

and portfolio investment. The Code recognized that 'good corporate governance is particularly important in the Czech Republic and other transition countries where there was no long term, continuous experience of non-state ownership of companies and the associated corporate practices'. Good corporate governance provides a framework for setting corporate objectives, and monitoring the progress towards achieving those objectives.

As in other countries around the globe, the observance and adoption of good corporate governance is an increasingly important factor for attracting investment in the Czech Republic, and much needed to be done to rebuild the confidence of investors, because many investors had lost substantial amounts due to poor management practices, and to address the lack of investor protection, particularly of minority interests.

An important aspect of the revised Code was the emphasis on shareholder value, with the corporate governance principles contained in the Code being based on the acceptance of the improvement of shareholder value as the corporate objective.

The main provisions of the Code included the following.

(i) 'The Company should be headed by an effective board of directors and supervisory board which should lead it and account to the shareholders. The board of directors should meet no less than once each month and the supervisory board should meet no less than ten times each year'

This part of the report covered various aspects relating to the boards. All members of the board of directors and supervisory board members are expected to bring an independent judgement to bear on issues of strategy, performance, resources. There should be an appropriate and timely flow of information between the two boards.

There is an emphasis on independent non-executive directors. The Code stated that the supervisory board should include members of sufficient calibre and number for their views to carry significant weight. Not less than 25 per cent of the members of the supervisory board should be independent of management and free from any business or other relationship, whether with the majority shareholders or the company, which could materially interfere with the exercise of their independent judgement. Members of the supervisory board considered to be independent should be identified in the annual report. A decision to combine the role of general director and chairman of the board of directors should be explained. In either case, whether the posts are held by different people or by the same person, there should be a strong and independent non-executive element on the board, with a recognized senior member other than the chairman. These individuals should be identified in the annual report.

Companies should establish three committees, with a majority of independent members, responsible for the independent audit of the company and the remuneration (including other financial incentives) and nomination of directors and key executives.

Members of the supervisory board should be appointed by the annual general meeting for specified terms and reappointment should not be automatic: members should be subject to re-election at intervals of no more than five years. Shareholders should be invited, specifically at the annual general meeting, to approve all new long-term incentive schemes (including share option schemes), whether payable in cash, in kind, or shares in which members of the executive or supervisory board and senior executives will participate (as detailed in section 66, paras 2 and 3 of the Commercial Code).

This section of the Code also contains provisions that may help the members of the boards to be more competent in their job. These provisions include: members of the board of directors and the supervisory board should be able to take independent professional advice if necessary, in the context of their corporate duties, at the company's expense; they should also have access to the advice and services of the company lawyer; they should be given appropriate training on first being appointed to the executive or supervisory board.

(ii) 'The Company should protect shareholders' rights'

Companies should make sure that there is a secure method of ownership registration, and that registered shares can be conveyed or transferred efficiently.

This part of the Code also included the recommendation that companies should inform shareholders of the date, time, and location of the annual general meeting and provide them with appropriate information relating to agenda items. The Code emphasized that there should be early disclosure of the data on dividend and coupon payments. Companies should include a specific agenda item providing for shareholders to ask questions of the directors. Questions may be submitted in advance and there should be enough time allowed for full discussion. In the general meeting, the shareholders will elect the members of both the board of directors and the supervisory board (unlike the German model, in which the shareholders in general meeting elect the supervisory board members only).

The Code discussed the importance of voting, and stated that shareholders should be able to vote in person or in absentia (by proxy), and encouraged companies to use modern technology, such as electronic communications and electronic voting (pending the introduction of a new law sanctioning the latter), to enable as many shareholders as possible to participate. The use of electronic media would be particularly beneficial for overseas investors.

(iii) **'The Company should ensure disclosure of all capital structures and any arrangements that enable certain shareholders to obtain a degree of control disproportionate to their equity ownership. Some capital structures allow a shareholder to exercise a degree of control over the company disproportionate to the shareholders' equity ownership in the company'**

The Code cited as an example cases of FDI through privatization or joint ventures, where shareholder agreements give high levels of control to the foreign shareholder. The important thing is that there is full disclosure of such arrangements.

(iv) **'The Company should ensure that all shareholders, including minorities and foreign shareholders, are treated equitably'**

This principle is important to all shareholders but particularly overseas investors who are seeking assurances that they will be treated equitably. All shareholders of the same class should be treated equally: for example, within any class, all shareholders should have the same voting rights.

Members of the board and managers should be required to disclose any material interests in transactions or matters affecting the company; insider trading and abusive self-dealing should be prohibited.

Companies were encouraged to develop good relationships with their shareholders. In this context, the company's general meeting was seen as a good opportunity to develop investor relations with investors. The Code set out a 'protocol' for the general meeting, which included companies: arranging for the notice of the general meeting and related papers to be sent to shareholders at least 30 working days before the meeting; proposing a separate resolution at the general meeting on each substantially separate issue and allowing reasonable time for the discussion of each resolution; counting all proxy votes and announcing the proxy count on each resolution; arranging for the chairmen of the audit, remuneration, and nomination committees to be available to answer questions at the general meeting.

(v) **'The Company should ensure that timely and accurate disclosure is made on all material matters regarding the company, including the financial situation, performance, ownership, and governance of the company. In particular the company should observe the standards of best practice issued by the Czech Securities Commission on the contents of the annual report, half-year report and ongoing disclosure requirements'**

There should be disclosure of appropriate information to enable shareholders to make decisions and assessments in relation to their investment, and to enable them to exercise their voting rights. The information should include information about: the financial and operating results of the company; the company objectives; the ownership structure of the company including disclosure of major shareholders; the individual board members and key executives and their remuneration; material foreseeable risk factors such as industry-specific or geographical risks, financial market risks; material issues regarding employees and other stakeholders. The channels for disseminating information should provide for fair, timely, and cost-efficient access to relevant information by users, and includes the use of electronic media.

Companies were also encouraged to report on how they apply relevant corporate governance principles in practice. The board is accountable to the shareholders and should ensure that there is a proper system of internal controls and auditing procedures.

(vi) 'The board of directors should undertake all key functions in the management of the company and the supervisory board should effectively supervise such functions'

The key functions of the board include setting and reviewing corporate strategy, monitoring corporate performance, reviewing board remuneration, monitoring and managing potential conflicts of interest, ensuring the integrity of the company's accounting systems, and overseeing the process of disclosure and communications.

The Code highlighted a situation in many companies where the supervisory board and the board of directors each meet only once or twice a year, and delegates the direction of the company to a general manager who appoints his own management board. The Code highlighted that this is unacceptable because the general manager is an employee without official directorial responsibilities and hence not accountable to shareholders. As an interim step, the Code suggested that the general manager must be a member of the board of directors but that, within three years, companies should adopt 'a more usual structure'.

The Code stated that the corporate governance framework should ensure the strategic guidance of the company, the effective monitoring of management by the board of directors, and the board of directors' accountability to the supervisory board, company, and the shareholders. Members of both boards should act in good faith with due diligence and care, in the best interests of the company and shareholders. The Code also mentioned that both boards should consider the interests of the wider stakeholder group including employees, creditors, customers, suppliers, and local communities.

(vii) 'Institutional shareholders should act responsibly in their dealings with the company'

As with the rest of the Code, the section on institutional investors seemed to reflect what was essentially internationally recognized best practice. It is recommended that institutional investors may have a constructive dialogue with the companies in which they invest, that they should make considered use of their votes, and that they should disclose their own policies with respect to the companies in which they invest. Institutional shareholders should also, if requested, make available to their clients information on the proportion of resolutions on which votes were cast and non-discretionary proxies lodged.

(viii) 'Shareholders should have certain rights and exercise certain responsibilities in connection with the company'

This section of the Code emphasized the fact that shareholders will have more confidence in investing if there is a mechanism to ensure that they have effective redress for violation of their rights. In addition, shareholders are reminded that they have responsibilities, such as attending general meetings and voting their shares, as well as rights.

(ix) 'The role of stakeholders in corporate governance'

The role of stakeholders is recognized in this part of the Code, which stated 'the corporate governance framework should recognise the rights of stakeholders as established by law and encourage active co-operation between companies and stakeholders in creating wealth, jobs, and the sustainability of financially sound companies'. The Code cited various mechanisms that enable stakeholder participation, including employee representation on boards and employee stock ownership plans.

The Czech Code (2001) was fairly comprehensive and adoption of the recommendations by Czech companies should have helped to restore investor confidence, both that of domestic investors and also foreign investors.

However, when the revised OECD Principles were published in 2004, the Czech Securities Commission decided to update its corporate governance code as well, and in June 2004, the Czech Securities Commission issued the Corporate Governance Code based on the OECD Principles (2004). The majority of the ideas contained in the 2001 Code discussed above were retained; however, the working group of the Securities Commission decided to follow the structure as well as the content of the OECD Principles (2004). By mapping the content and structure of the OECD Principles so closely, it was felt that this would lead to easier communication about the corporate governance of the Czech Republic with organizations such as the World Bank and with those that are familiar with the OECD Principles. Also, given various developments in corporate governance and in capital markets generally, such as the EU Action Plan discussed earlier, it was felt appropriate to update the Code. One such development relates to the EU Commission's decision to leave European companies with a choice of either the unitary board or dual board structure. Whereas the Code (2001) tended to prefer the unitary board structure (Anglo-Saxon model), the Code (2004) leaves it up to companies as to whether they choose a dual board (German style) or unitary board (Anglo-Saxon). The Code (2004) also places more emphasis on the independence of board members.

As mentioned, the revised Czech Code (2004) mirrors both structure and content of the OECD Principles (2004) (for the detail of the OECD Principles (2004), please see Chapter 3). However, it is useful to highlight some of the additions to the revised Czech Code (2004), which include:

- facilitating the exercise of shareholders' rights, including participation in key corporate governance decisions such as nomination and election of board members;
- institutional investors acting in a fiduciary capacity should disclose their corporate governance and voting policies;
- amendment to the Commercial Code to permit distance voting by electronic means;
- minority shareholders must be protected from abusive actions by, or in the interest of, controlling shareholders and should have effective means of redress;
- members of the board of directors, supervisory board, and key executives are

required to disclose to the board if they have a material interest in a transaction or matter affecting the corporation;

- the rights of stakeholders, whether established in law or through mutual agreements, must be respected;

- the development of performance-enhancing mechanisms for employee participation must be allowed;

- stakeholders, including employees and their representative bodies, must be able freely to communicate their concerns about illegal or unethical practices to the supervisory board without their rights being compromised;

- the corporate governance framework must be complemented by an effective, efficient insolvency framework and by effective enforcement of creditor rights;

- the remuneration policy for members of the board of directors and supervisory board and key executives, and information about board members, including their qualifications, the selection process, other company directorships, and whether they are regarded as independent, must be disclosed;

- disclosure about the content of any corporate governance code and the process by which it is implemented;

- an annual audit must be carried out by an independent, competent, and qualified auditor to provide assurance that the financial statements fairly represent the financial position and performance of the company;

- the external auditor is accountable to shareholders and owes a duty to the company to exercise due professional care in the conduct of the audit;

- the corporate governance framework must be complemented by an effective approach that addresses and promotes the provision of analysis or advice by analysts, brokers, etc. that is relevant to decisions by investors, free from material conflicts of interest that might compromise the integrity of their analysis or advice;

- appropriate and full disclosure about directors' remuneration;

- companies should publish in their annual reports a declaration of how they apply in practice the relevant principles of corporate governance contained in the Czech Code (2004);

- three separate committees responsible for the independent audit of the company, the remuneration of directors and key executives, and the nomination of directors and key executives should be established, and the mandate, composition, and working procedures of these committees must be disclosed.

The Czech Code (2004) is a comprehensive code with many explanatory notes in each section to aid the companies and investors. Adoption of the Czech Code (2004) should help to ensure that investor confidence is maintained, that shareholders' rights can be exercised more easily, and that minority shareholders are better protected.

Poland

The second model used in the privatization process was one that allowed management and employees to buy company assets. This method was the method adopted in Poland. Poland had a slower start to privatization than did the Czech Republic, with Poland starting the process in 1995. State-owned enterprises targeted for privatization first became joint stock companies. In this instance, the joint stock company's ownership did not change, but the control structure changed to include a board of directors and the Workers' Councils, which were previously quite powerful, were disbanded, so reducing workers' power.

A defining feature of the Polish privatization process was that shares had to be included in one of 15 National Investment Funds (NIFs) established in 1995. NIFs were essentially established to manage shares that were purchased in the various privatized companies in Poland as part of the mass privatization programme. NIFs have strategic 33 per cent holdings in some firms but much smaller shares in other firms. Coffee (1998) points out that the NIFs 'remain indirectly under governmental control'. The Polish government did not allow its citizens to have vouchers that could be exchanged directly for shares in the privatized companies; rather the vouchers were exchanged for shares in the NIFs. The state also retained a significant shareholding of 25 per cent in some companies, with another 15 per cent being allotted free of charge to the workers. The investor base includes foreign investors as well as domestic, institutional investors, and retail investors.

Some of the firms that the NIFs are invested into require major restructuring but, sometimes, there is disagreement between the NIFs and the supervisory board as to when and how this restructuring might be undertaken. Coffee (1998) points out that 'if a proposed restructuring is politically sensitive or cuts deeply into local employment, one must suspect that labor interests and others with political clout will know how to protest effectively. Because the initial board of each NIF is governmentally appointed, there is little reason to believe that individual NIFs will feel insulated from such protests'. Therefore the state continues to have an influential role in many companies, despite the fact that the companies are now privatized.

Poland is a country that has a civil law system. The legal framework for listed companies comprises the Commercial Code of 1934 and the Code of Commercial Companies (2000). In the summer of 2002, there were two publications on corporate governance: the Corporate Governance Code for Polish Listed Companies and the Best Practices in Public Companies guidance. Both of these are now discussed in more detail.

Poland has a predominantly two-tier board structure comprising a supervisory board and a management board. As is usual, the supervisory board supervises the management board and oversees the company's financial statements, it also reports to the shareholders on the activities of the company. The management board conducts the day-to-day business of the company and is responsible for issues that are not the area of the supervisory board or the shareholders meeting. The company's articles of association will often expand on the areas to be covered by the management board.

The final proposal of the Corporate Governance Code for Polish Listed Companies (hereinafter the Code) was published in June 2002. The Code was drawn up under

Table 11.3 Summary of key characteristics influencing Polish corporate governance

Feature	Key characteristic
Privatization method	Management and employees buy company assets
Predominant ownership structure	Institutional outsiders (NIFs); state; individuals/families
Legal system	Civil law
Board structure	Dual
Important aspect	Role of National Investment Funds (NIFs)

the initiative of the Polish Forum for Corporate Governance established by the Gdansk Institute for Market Economics, and may also be referred to as the Gdansk Code.

The Code recognizes the problems that have occurred in the past with the violation of minority rights and seeks to address these in order to help restore confidence in the Polish market. The Code largely reflects the OECD Principles, the Cadbury Code, and other benchmarks of international best practice. It is recommended that the Code's provisions be included in a company's articles of association. The Code expects companies to report on compliance combining annual descriptive reports and the 'comply or explain' mechanism.

The Code has seven Principles, which cover various areas of good corporate governance practice as follows.

(i) 'The main objective of the company should be to operate in the common interest of all shareholders, which is to create shareholder value'

The company's objectives should be publicized. It is important for the company to respect the rights of stakeholder groups as well. Employees are an important stakeholder group and may be offered representation on the supervisory board or the right to put forward their opinions on various matters.

(ii) 'The composition of the supervisory board should facilitate objective oversight of the company and reflect interests of minority shareholders'

The Code does not lay down the minimum number of members for the supervisory board although it envisages that there should be five or more members (except for smaller companies or where other justification exists). It is recommended that at least two of the supervisory board members should be independent (should not be linked to the company or its controlling shareholder) and should be elected without any decisive influence of the controlling shareholder. Details of candidates for supervisory board membership should be published prior to the general meeting in a timely manner to enable shareholders to vote in an informed way.

(iii) 'The powers of the supervisory board and the company by-laws should ensure an effective supervisory board process and duly secure interests of all shareholders'

The operation of the supervisory and management boards should be regulated by appropriate by-laws, and the articles of association of the company, which should be available from the company website. Members of the management board and the supervisory board should disclose any conflicts of interest; there should be regulated trading of the shares of the company in respect of the members of the management and supervisory board members (and any other person with privileged access to information) to ensure that there is no violation of the interests of shareholders and investors. Where there are transactions between the company and related parties, then these should be subject to supervisory board approval and require at least two independent board members' approval.

The supervisory board should have sufficient administrative support and also be able to hire external experts at the company's expense in pursuance of its duties. The Code also refers to the fact that many codes overseas recommend appropriate training particularly on first appointment to the board.

(iv) 'The shareholders' meeting should be convened and organised so as not to violate interests and rights of any shareholders. The controlling shareholder should not restrict the other shareholders in the effective exercise of their corporate rights'

There should be adequate notice of the meeting to enable shareholders to attend; shareholders should be able to submit questions prior to the meeting to which the answers should be provided both in the meeting and subsequently published, where possible, on the company's website. The Code states that 'to participate in the general meeting is an inalienable right of any shareholder and should not be restricted... [T]his... gains special importance in Poland where participation in the general meeting by the way of voting by correspondence or by audio-visual means is not allowed'. Two independent supervisory board members may request that a shareholders' meeting be called, whilst company law provides for shareholders representing at least 10 per cent of the share capital to call a meeting (the company can lower this level if it thinks it appropriate). The chairman of the meeting should be impartial, and so be independent from the company and the controlling shareholder.

(v) 'The company should not apply anti-takeover defences against shareholders' interests. Changes in the company share capital should not violate interests of the existing shareholders'

The company should not use various anti-takeover devices including: acquiring its own shares for that purpose; voting caps which might limit the use/number of votes by large shareholders. Management and employee stock option plan arrangements should not involve the issuance of more than 10 per cent of the total number of the company's shares over any five-year period.

(vi) 'The company should provide effective access to information, which is necessary to evaluate the company's current position, future prospects, as well as the way in which the company operates and applies the corporate governance rules'

The disclosure recommendations cover quite a comprehensive range of areas including publishing a report, on an annual basis, providing detail of: the corporate governance framework, and the extent of compliance with the Code (or explain the reasons for non-compliance); the company's financial position and prospects, and its system of internal controls; information about the members of the management board and the supervisory board, including positions held with other companies, links with shareholders, and information about remuneration. The Code recommends that information should also be disclosed on the company's website whenever possible. The company should also disclose information about its ownership and control structure, including where there is a difference between the amount of shares owned and the amount of control, and where there are any agreements of which the company is aware that mean that shareholders might act together to vote in concert.

(vii) 'The appointment process of the company's auditor should ensure independence of the auditor's opinion'

The auditor is appointed by the supervisory board or recommended by them to the shareholders' general meeting. At least two independent board members should support the appointment resolution. The supervisory board may appoint an audit committee, comprised mainly of independent members of the supervisory board, to monitor the company's financial situation and its accounting system. There are some interesting provisions to help ensure auditor independence, which include appointing a new auditor every five years, and publishing the value of services provided by the auditor, or its subsidiaries/affiliates, in the accounting year. However, it should be noted that instead of appointing a new audit firm, the company may continue to use the same firm but with a change of personnel to a completely different audit team.

The Best Practices in Public Companies in 2002 publication came out of the Best Practices Committee at Corporate Governance Forum, who stated that 'this set of best practices, established for the needs of the Polish capital market, presents the core of corporate governance standards in a public joint stock company'. There were a number of 'general rules' including: the objective of the company; the concept of majority rule and protection of the minority; the ideas of honest intentions and no abuse of rights; court control, which may apply to some issues in a company; that when expert services/opinions are sought, the experts should be independent. In addition to these general rules, there were specific guidelines relating to best practices including: the notification and running of general meetings, and associated voting issues; the role of the supervisory board and its members; role of the management board and its members; relations with third parties including the auditors. The Best Practices 2002 are not elaborated upon further here because the Gdansk Code, detailed above, also covered these areas.

The Best Practices were reviewed and amended in the light of practical experience and opinions of market participants and Best Practices in Public Companies 2005 were issued. The amended practices now include recent EU recommendations, for example, the emphasis on independence aimed at strengthening the role of non-executive or supervisory directors.

The corporate governance recommendations introduced by the Gdansk Code and the Best Practices will undoubtedly have strengthened the corporate governance of Polish companies and helped to encourage investment by restoring confidence in the market. As Rozlucki (2003) stated: 'In Poland, corporate governance has become an additional and indispensable guarantee of system stability to the financial market.'

Russia

The collapse of the communist system in Russia heralded a wave of privatizations, with the privatization programme in Russia itself based on a voucher system. Pistor and Turkewitz (1996) indicate that, between January 1993 and June 1994, some 14,000–15,000 companies were sold in voucher auctions. They state that 'privatization regulations required companies with more than a thousand employees and a book value of at least 50 million rubles to set up a privatisation plan'. They highlight that there were substantial benefits available to the managers of enterprises, including subsidized equity stakes and the right to buy further shares in voucher auctions. Frydman, Pistor, and Rapaczynski (1996) highlight the high participation levels of the Russian people in the voucher privatization process: 'The program did bring out a very high degree of popular participation: by July 1994, 132.7 million Russians made some use of their vouchers (even if only to sell them on the open market), and this number represents 87.8 per cent of the 151 million voucher recipients.' The privatization programme also saw the participation of privatization investment funds, which either bought shares directly or through intermediaries. After privatization, many managers bought shares from the workers. These factors contributed to a high level of ownership by insiders (managers and workers), such that managerial entrenchment became a real threat as it meant that outside, and particularly overseas investors, would be reluctant to invest in companies where management control was high and protection of minority rights low.

Ownership in Russia is documented by Sprenger (2002), who cites some interesting surveys carried out by the Russian Economic Barometer. Table 11.4 shows the ownership change in Russian industry over the period 1995–99. What emerges is that, over time, the ownership by insiders (managers and workers) is declining whilst the ownership by outsiders is increasing, particularly ownership by individuals and financial firms, holdings, foreign investors. Sprenger's (2005) study of 530 Russian manufacturing firms confirms the gradually decreasing ownership stakes of firms' insiders over time.

Russia, in common with other transition economies, is moving towards a market economy and has joint stock companies and limited liability companies. Minority rights have traditionally not been well looked after in Russia, so that the role and the relevance of shareholders in a company have not generally held much sway. Many foreign investors who invested in Russia post-privatization lost a lot of money as managers of the companies misused their funds and there was little effective redress. The Russian corporate governance code therefore sees it as very important to restore investor confidence in the market and to ensure that future foreign investment is encouraged by building more confidence in Russian companies.

The Russian Code of Corporate Governance was issued by the Federal Securities Commission in late 2001. It has the support of both government officials and private groups and it is hoped that compliance with the code will be at a high level. Given that the code has government support, it is likely that any company where the state has influence will have to comply and also large companies that are still subject to political influence and decisions will want to comply. Also, in order to attract external

Table 11.4 Ownership change in Russia

Category of owner	1995	1997	1999
Insiders	54.8	52.1	46.2
Managers	11.2	15.1	14.7
Workers	43.6	37.0	31.5
State	9.1	7.4	7.1
Outsiders	35.2	38.9	42.4
Individuals	10.9	13.9	18.5
Non-financial firms	15.0	14.6	13.5
Financial firms, holdings, foreign investors	9.3	10.3	10.4
Others	0.9	1.6	4.3
Sample size	136	135	156

Source: Russian Economic Barometer in Kapelyushnikov (2000), cited in Sprenger (2002)

direct investment, companies will want to comply with the new Corporate Governance Code. This is particularly important given that, in the 1990s, the external investors who invested money into Russia had their fingers badly burnt when the money was pocketed by various corrupt individuals involved in companies. In order to restore confidence and to encourage more foreign investment, compliance with a corporate governance code is of prime importance.

Essentially, the code is based on the OECD Corporate Governance Principles, but has also drawn from other international codes and guidelines. The Russian Corporate Governance Code (hereinafter the Code) has ten sections or chapters and these are dealt with below. online resource centre

(i) Principles of corporate governance

This chapter sets out the key principles of corporate governance and draws heavily on the OECD principles. There should be equal treatment of shareholders, including minority and foreign investors. The key rights of shareholders are discussed, including the right to reliable registration of shares and disclosure of shares, the right to participate in profit distribution, the right to participate in managing the company by taking part in key decisions, and the right to have access to full, reliable, and timely information about the

Table 11.5 Summary of key characteristics influencing Russian corporate governance

Feature	Key characteristic
Privatization method	Mass privatization via voucher
Predominant ownership structure	Insiders (managers and workers) although outsiders increasing
Legal system	Civil law
Board structure	Dual
Important aspect	Covers dividend payments

company. In terms of the protection of minority shareholders, minority shareholders have the legal right to vote on all matters of importance, including mergers and sale of substantial assets. Shareholders may vote and attend meetings both personally and by proxy.

The board of directors is responsible for the strategic management of the company and for effective control over the executive bodies of the company. The board of directors is accountable to the shareholders, with members of the board of directors being elected through a transparent procedure taking into account diverse shareholders' opinions. There should be 'a sufficient number' of independent directors. Various committees, including a strategic planning committee, an audit committee, personnel and remuneration committee, corporate conflicts committee, risk management committee, and ethics committee, may be established. A managerial board should be established to manage the day-to-day activities of the company; its members should be elected by a transparent procedure.

(ii) General shareholders meetings

The Code states: 'For a minority shareholder, the annual general shareholders meeting is often the only chance to obtain information on the company's operations and ask the company management questions regarding the company's administration. By participating in a general shareholders meeting, a shareholder exercises its right to be involved in the company's management.'

The Code states that shareholders should have sufficient time to prepare for an annual general meeting (AGM) and to see the resolutions to be voted on. It is recommended that notice of the meeting should be given 30 days before the AGM, which is an improvement over the 20-day minimum notice mandated by law. The place, time, and location of the AGM should facilitate shareholders' attendance, and the Code recommends that an AGM should not start earlier than 9am, nor later than 10pm local time.

At the AGM, the chairman should 'act reasonably and in good faith, without using his authority to limit the rights of shareholders'. There should be a clearly formulated agenda, with all information necessary to make voting decisions. Shareholders have the right to propose agenda items and they may correspond with the company by traditional means or by electronic means. During the meeting, all shareholders have an equal right to ask questions of the directors. In the past, companies have occasionally resorted to deceitful behaviour such as moving meetings at the last minute in order to stop shareholders from voting, or using technical loopholes to prevent outside shareholders from voting. In this way, they have been able to focus attention on the interest of insiders and controlling shareholders. It is hoped that the new recommendations will help to ensure that these situations do not recur.

(iii) Board of directors

The key functions of the board are defined in this section. They include strategic aspects ensuring effective control over management, resolving corporate conflict, and ensuring the effective work of the executive body. Board members should actively participate in board meetings and the board is required to meet regularly and to set up committees to discuss important issues: the Code explicitly lists a strategic planning committee, audit committee, human resources and remuneration committee, and corporate conflicts resolution committee. The compensation for board managers decided by the annual general meeting should reflect the company's operational performance.

The Code also proposes a transparent procedure for nomination and election of board members and requires that 25 per cent of the board be independent (it is also recommended that the company's Charter should provide for the board to include at least three independent directors). The 25 per cent is a lower level than one would like to see and also the definition of an independent director is often contentious in Russia. In Russia, the relationship between managers, controlling shareholders, and board members has sometimes been very close, with the result that board members may be largely selected by controlling shareholders and hence under their influence, even if, in theory, they qualify as being independent.

(iv) Executive bodies

The Code refers to the executive bodies of the company, which encompass the managerial board (or management board) and the director general (akin to a chief executive officer). The executive bodies are responsible for the day-to-day operations of the company and compliance with financial and business plans of the company. The managerial board should approve transactions involving more than 5 per cent of a company's assets, with timely notification of such transactions to the board of directors. The managerial board, like the board of directors, should work in the interests of all shareholders, and not use confidential information for personal benefit. It should take into account the interests of various stakeholder groups to try to ensure the efficient operation of the company. In particular, it should take account of the interests of employees by maintaining contact with the trade unions/professional organizations.

There is no clear recommendation regarding the size of the managerial board, rather that 'the company should proceed from the requirement that the number of members of the managerial board be optimal for productive, constructive discussion, and making prompt, informed decisions'. However, it is important that there is a transparent process for election of the director general and members of the managerial board, including making available appropriate information about the candidates.

The remuneration of the director general and managerial board members should reflect their skills and their actual contribution to the success of the company's operations.

(v) Company secretary

Perhaps one of the most radical proposals in the Code is the creation of the post of Company Secretary, which is a new concept for Russia. The secretary's functions would be to: prepare for AGMs and board meetings; ensure the appropriate provision of information disclosure and maintenance of corporate records; consider shareholders' requests and resolve any infringement of investors' rights. The Company Secretary would be appointed by the board of directors and should be granted adequate powers to perform these duties. The Company Secretary should inform the board chairman if anything prevents him from carrying out his duties.

(vi) Major corporate actions

The Code states that major corporate actions include reorganizations of the company and acquisition of 30 per cent or more of the outstanding shares of the company or those actions deemed to be of significant importance for the company's capital structure and financial situation. Such major corporate actions should be approved by the board of directors or extraordinary general meeting before being finalized, and also be evaluated by an independent auditor. In the case of a takeover attempt, the board of directors should inform the shareholders about its position but should not present the takeover if this would be against the shareholders' interests or would have a negative effect on the company.

(vii) Information disclosure

The Code states that the company information policy should make available to current and potential shareholders appropriate information. The Code lists information that should be disclosed in prospectuses, and the annual and quarterly reports: the report for the final quarter should outline the company's corporate governance policies and state whether or not it complies fully with the Code.

It is possible that there may be a potential conflict in that some information relating to 'trade or professional secrets' may be withheld if there is a need to strike a balance between transparencies and the protection of a company's interest, and this may effectively cast a shadow over disclosure.

(viii) Supervision of operations

In order to ensure that the company is operating according to plan and that the board and management mechanisms are appropriate and transparent, and that any risks are being limited, there needs to be adequate supervision. The Code recommends that supervision is carried out by the board of directors and its audit committee, the audit commission of the company, the control and audit service of the company, and the external auditor of the company. The Code prefers the audit committee to be comprised of only independent directors.

(ix) Dividends

Traditionally, dividends have been problematic in Russia and so the Code states that, if net profit is used to calculate the dividend, then this number must be the net profit figure that is reported in the company's accounts. Dividends should be paid in cash only and the company has to set a clear deadline for payment, which cannot exceed 60 days after the announcement. If announced dividends are delayed or not paid, then the board of directors has the right to reduce the director general's compensation and/or that of the managerial board members, or to dismiss them completely.

(x) Resolution of corporate conflicts

The company secretary is identified as the key person for determining and monitoring conflict between the company and its shareholders. Any response to shareholders must be based on the law and also the company can serve as an intermediary if there is a conflict between two shareholders.

It can be seen that the provisions of the Russian Code are quite far reaching. In some ways, the provisions are as much about educating the Russian corporate sector so that they understand what good corporate governance actually is. Whilst some companies are already complying, others have been slower to comply and the Code's provisions are not legally binding. However, the companies may not wish to incur the disapproval of the government and many still rely heavily on political influence: for example, they may be denied the right to state tender or, alternatively, pension funds might be prohibited from investing in companies that do not comply.

Kostikov (2003) stated: 'Poor corporate governance in Russian companies makes them much less attractive as investment objects.' Initiatives to encourage more truly independent directors onto Russian boards are essential to help ensure improved corporate governance and to encourage investors. As Belikov (2004) stated: 'The challenge is to attract conservative portfolio investors who are willing to commit to long-term investments and who view good corporate governance as a vital part of an investment decision.' Legislation introduced in 2006 should help ensure that boards have more independent directors and hence that board committees have a higher proportion of independent directors.

Hungary

The third model, and arguably the one that produced the most successful results, involved selling majority control to an outside investor. This model was followed in Hungary and resulted in a high level of outside ownership and control. It is useful to mention various changes that occurred in Hungary in the late 1980s/early 1990s, as described in Pistor and Turkewitz (1996). A change in Hungarian law led, in the late 1980s, to a wave of manager-initiated organizational restructuring of enterprise assets and the right to form a limited liability company or joint stock company. Whilst the state retained ownership of a large proportion of these assets, state officials were unable to keep up with the pace of change and so were unable to keep up with the changes in the ownership structures. In 1989, the majority of state-owned companies were transferred to the State Property Agency (SPA), and over the next five years many of these were privatized. However, some of the assets were transferred to the State Holding Company (Av.Rt.). The state still retains significant holdings and influence, one way being through 'golden shares', which were issued to the state during the privatization process enabling the state to have control over key strategic issues. The World Bank–IMF ROSC 2003 report on corporate governance in Hungary identifies that ten of the 56 listed companies have issued a golden share that can only be held by the state.

For some time, Hungary did not have a published corporate governance code, although the Budapest Stock Exchange started to draft a corporate governance code in mid-2002. However, many areas relating to corporate governance were covered in the Companies Law and these areas are described below.

Table 11.6 Summary of key characteristics influencing Hungarian corporate governance

Feature	Key characteristic
Privatization method	Privatization via selling majority control to outside investor, often foreign
Predominant ownership structure	State; institutional outsiders (foreign)
Legal system	Civil law
Board structure	Dual
Important aspect	State influence but potential influence of foreign investor activism waiting to happen.

The World Bank–IMF ROSC 2003 report identified that, whilst Hungary had a robust legislative and regulatory framework to deal with corporate governance issues, there were shortcomings in the system, including the lack of a corporate governance code of best practice. The report identified the various sections of the Companies Act 1997 relating to corporate structure and governance.

(i) Board structure

Public companies should have a two-tier (dual) structure consisting of a board of directors (management board) and a supervisory board. The shareholders in general meeting usually appoint the directors of both boards and approve their remuneration. However, the company's Charter may provide that the supervisory board appoint and set the remuneration of the management board.

The management board may comprise between 3 and 11 members, whilst the supervisory board can have as many as 15 members, with employees appointing one-third of the supervisory board members.

(ii) Operation of the boards

The management board is responsible for the day-to-day running of the company, whilst the supervisory board exercises control over the management board on behalf of the shareholders. The management board's responsibilities include reporting on operational issues, including the company's financial position, at the AGM and also quarterly to the supervisory board, and maintaining the books and records of the company, etc.

Board meeting minutes are not required to be kept, but board members participate and report at the AGM. Both boards are accountable to the AGM and, in theory, to all shareholders; in practice, some directors appointed on the votes of large shareholders may effectively represent the interests of those large shareholders. Board members may seek expert opinions as appropriate.

(iii) Independence

There is no specific reference to independence, although the Companies Act does refer to the objectivity of board members so that close family members are not allowed to be members of the supervisory and management board at the same company.

Board members may not be employees (except in their capacity as employee representatives on the supervisory board); board members should disclose any conflict of interest.

(iv) Disclosure

Hungary's disclosure of information relevant to investors was generally quite good. Disclosure requirements are contained in the Capital Markets Act 2002 and the Budapest Stock Exchange listing rules. The areas that companies must provide disclosure on include: the corporate objectives; major ownership and voting rights; the financial and operating results of the company; remuneration of board members; details of loans to board members; information relating to employees such as the average number of employees employed. Investors must have access to the company's annual report and many companies post this information on their website.

As mentioned earlier, the Budapest Stock Exchange began work on its Corporate Governance Recommendations in 2002, and the final document was published in 2004. The recommendations suggest applicable practices but are not mandatory for companies listed on the Stock Exchange. However, the publication of a declaration, whereby the corporate issuers provide information on their management practices in comparison with the contents of the recommendations, will be mandatory and confirmed in the Stock Exchange rules. If an issuer does not comply with a recommendation or applies it in a different manner, then an explanation should be provided, i.e. the 'comply or explain' approach.

The Budapest Stock Exchange has split the recommendations into corporate governance recommendations and recommendations on shareholders' meetings. The corporate governance recommendations are laid out in a three-column format, with the first column being the recommendations themselves, then the middle column, the relevant Hungarian legal regulations, and the final column, explanations and in-depth suggestions relating to each recommendation. The corporate governance recommendations are outlined below.

Corporate governance recommendations

(i) Competences of the board of directors and of the supervisory board

The Code emphasizes that the most important role of the board is the overall stewardship of the company. The responsibilities of the board encompass:

- developing the strategy, supervision of business and financial plans, setting corporate objectives and overseeing corporate performance;
- ensuring the integrity of accounting reports;
- managing conflicts of interest and drafting a code of ethics;
- succession planning;
- risk management;
- mechanisms for nomination and remuneration of directors;

- guidelines for transparency and disclosure of corporate information, and timely communication with shareholders;
- continuous oversight of the effectiveness of corporate governance;
- communication with, and reporting to, the supervisory board.

The board should carry out its responsibilities with due diligence in the best interest of the company, having regard to the rights of shareholders and stakeholders, and as far as possible also in the best interest of stakeholders.

The supervisory board, on behalf of shareholders, monitors the activities of the board of directors and ensures its duties are carried out with due care. The supervisory board has a Charter, which determines its mandate, and a work schedule.

Members of both boards should be notified well in advance of the meetings of the respective boards and of the agenda items, and all relevant information should be made available on a timely basis.

In terms of board membership, the board of directors and the supervisory board need to submit nominations for officers to the shareholders' meeting. The nominees should be competent and qualified and have sufficient time to devote to their duties. The board of directors should contain an appropriate number of independent members to ensure that resolutions can be passed objectively in the interest of shareholders and not be subject to the influence of executive management or individual shareholders. Interestingly, the Code explains that the presence of a strategic investor is typical in Hungarian companies and so it is not considered a violation of the board's independence if a member of the board is delegated by one of the owners. The supervisory board members should be independent and not employees of the company, save for the employees' representatives.

In relation to the duties of the chairman and the CEO, these shall be outlined separately in the basic documents (such as articles of association or board Charter).

In terms of remuneration, the board of directors should establish guidelines and rules relating to the performance review and remuneration of directors and of executive management. These guidelines and rules should be approved by the shareholders' general meeting, taking into account the views of the supervisory board. The remuneration scheme should support the long-term strategic interests of the company (and hence the shareholders). For members of the supervisory board, a fixed remuneration is recommended.

Board committees, including a remuneration committee, audit committee, and nomination committee, may be established and should be comprised of at least three members, the majority of whom are independent, and who are appropriately experienced and qualified to perform their duties. Committees, like the board of directors and the supervisory board, are entitled to consult with external advisers.

The board of directors should ensure that there is in place a reliable system of internal controls. Internal audit departments should be established and these will report regularly to the board of directors or supervisory board.

Succession planning is important in any business, so companies should identify potential successors to key figures in the company. Finally, the business should have appropriate co-ordination of corporate affairs to ensure appropriate and timely exchange of views between various parties.

(ii) Transparency and disclosure

There should be adequate and timely disclosure of information about the operations of the company and circumstances that may influence its share price. Information shall be made available to the public about the company's corporate strategy, its main business activities, business ethics, and its policies regarding other stakeholders. The company will disclose information on a range of issues including:

- the background of directors and supervisory board members, the guidelines for the evaluation of their performance and the establishment of their remuneration;
- the risk management guidelines;
- the extent to which the company adopts the Hungarian corporate governance recommendations;
- its guidelines on insider trading.

It is also recommended that disclosures are made in English as well as the official language of the company.

(iii) Shareholders' rights and treatment of shareholders

All voting practices and treatment of shareholders should comply with laws and regulations and with the company's formal documents (for example, articles of association). Shareholders should have the right to participate in key decisions about the company, via the shareholders' meeting, and should be notified of the time, location, and agenda of the shareholders' meeting. Minutes of the meeting should be made available to shareholders within 30 days of the meeting. An investor relations department should be established.

(iv) Role of stakeholders in corporate governance

The board of directors should respect the rights of all stakeholders and it is believed that shareholder interests are best served if the interests of other stakeholders are equally respected. The board shall strive to perform its duties in a socially responsible manner. It is recommended that companies publish a code of ethics, which defines the ethical guidelines of the company.

Recommendations on shareholders' meetings

The recommendations on shareholders' meetings are designed to establish principles to provide a basis for future shareholders' meetings, which support the validation of shareholders' interests, take into account the interests of potential investors, and facilitate the decision-making process. These recommendations are a supplement to the corporate governance recommendations and have three sections relating to the preliminary procedures prior to meetings, conducting the shareholders' meetings, and concluding the shareholders' meetings.

As can be seen from the analysis above, the Hungarian corporate governance recommendations are quite comprehensive.

Earle, Kucsera, and Telegdy (2005) found that high-quality data available on companies listed on the Budapest Stock Exchange enabled them to undertake a study of ownership concentration and corporate performance. They found that the size of the largest block of shares increases profitability and efficiency but that the effects of the total block-holdings are much smaller. In other words: 'The marginal costs of concentration [of share ownership] may outweigh the benefits when the increased concentration involves "too many cooks".'

Conclusions

In this chapter, we have reviewed the three different approaches that were used in the privatization of state-owned enterprises in the former USSR. The effect of each of these approaches on the resultant ownership and control of privatized companies, and the implications for corporate governance developments, have been discussed. In particular, it has been noted that the countries in Central and Eastern Europe are keen to improve protection of minority shareholder rights, and to establish more confidence in their capital markets to attract foreign direct investment. All of the countries have already published corporate governance codes of best practice.

■ SUMMARY

- Three main privatization methods were used to privatize state-owned enterprises in the former USSR: (i) the voucher privatization method was used in the Czech Republic and Russia and enabled the public to own shares in privatized firms; (ii) management and employees were allowed to buy company assets, and this method was used in Poland; (iii) selling majority control to an outside investor was the method used in Hungary.

- The different privatization methods resulted in different ownership and control structures. In practice, the state retained considerable influence in many firms, either directly or indirectly.

- The four countries reviewed all have a dual board structure (supervisory board and management board).

- The Czech Republic has an ownership structure that includes predominantly the state and institutional outsiders (investment funds and banks). The investment privatization funds (IPFs) can be quite influential.

- Poland has an ownership structure that includes: predominantly institutional outsiders; the state; individuals/families. The national investment funds (NIFs) play an important role.

- Russia has an ownership structure that includes predominantly insiders (managers and workers), although outsiders are increasing. The Russian Corporate Governance Code is comprehensive at over 90 pages and includes sections on the company secretary and on dividends.

- Hungary has an ownership structure that includes predominantly the state and institutional outsiders (foreign investors). Whilst Hungary has many good practices, especially in the area of corporate disclosures, its corporate governance infrastructure could be improved in a number of ways and its comprehensive code of corporate governance should encourage this.

Example: Agora SA

This is an example of a media company in Poland that demonstrates good corporate governance.

Agora SA is a company involved in the media business. Agora emphasizes in its annual report, that building shareholders' confidence is a key issue, and an important aspect of this is the implementation of corporate governance. The company's annual report details the structure of the company: there is a supervisory board with five members, at least three of whom are independent to help ensure the protection of minority rights, and presently four members are independent. The management board has between three and six members. The supervisory board decides on the remuneration of the management board and has elected two committees: the Human Resources & Remuneration Committee, and the Audit Committee. Agora was the first Polish listed company to introduce limitations in the trading of its securities by the management board, based on regulations in London and New York.

The company has an investor relations department and is active in following an open communications policy with its investors, which includes roadshows, presentation meetings, and a corporate website. It believes that transparency and openness are the keys to building investor confidence.

In September 2005, Agora received, for the second time in a row, the 'Grand Prix Corporate Governance' title. This is awarded by the Polish Institute of Directors on recommendations of institutional investors who evaluate public companies on various criteria including transparency of ownership, financial transparency, shareholders' meetings, access to company information, and the effectiveness of the supervisory board, as well as remuneration of the management board.

Mini case study: VimpelCom

This is a good example of a Russian company that is recognized as having probably the best corporate governance amongst Russian companies.

VimpelCom is a leading provider of telecommunications services in Russia, with its 'Bee Line' brand being well known and highly regarded in Russia. VimpelCom is a market leader and at the forefront of some of the latest technology, such as wireless Internet access and other services, mobile portals, etc.

VimpelCom was the first Russian company to list its shares on the New York Stock Exchange in 1996. VimpelCom's annual report is informative and includes a 'letter to shareholders', which reviews the company's financial performance and operations. The annual report emphasizes that its founders have inspired it with the values of 'transparency, strong corporate governance, quality, innovation and a pioneering spirit'. VimpelCom was awarded the 'Best Corporate Governance Award 2002' by the Russian Association for the Protection of Investor Rights. There has been recognition from overseas as well, with *BusinessWeek* naming VimpelCom as number six in its list of the top 100 IT companies in the world for 2002; its $250 million 10.45 per cent bond issue was cited by *Euroweek* as third in the Best Corporate Deals in Emerging Europe. More recently Vimpelcom was named the winner of the Best Corporate Governance Award at the Frist Annual IR Magazine Russia Conference in 2004. Vimpelcom was also awarded the Grand Prix for Best Overall Investor Relations.

The key to VimpelCom's success, in terms of its attractiveness to investors both domestically and overseas, is attributable to its openness and transparency, and to its regard for good corporate governance practices. It has an investor relations department with an investor relations website and, during 2005, it took part in various roadshows, conferences, and meetings with its investors. It had more than 150 one-to-one investor meetings in 2005; it also held quarterly conference calls regarding its earnings, which broadcast via the web.

The Institute of Corporate Law and Corporate Governance (ICLG) have produced a corporate governance rating (CORE-Rating) for Russian companies. The CORE-Rating takes into account information disclosure, ownership structure, board of directors and management structure, basic shareholder rights, absence of expropriation risks, and corporate governance history. VimpelCom performed very well and scored the highest overall rating (as it had done in the previous year). VimpelCom is therefore an exemplary company in terms of having a good corporate governance structure that gives confidence to investors and helps to restore confidence in the Russian market more generally.

■ QUESTIONS

The discussion questions below cover the key learning points of this chapter. Reading of some of the additional reference material will enhance the depth of the students' knowledge and understanding of these areas.

1. What do you think was the rationale behind the different privatization methods employed in various countries?

2. What effect did each of the privatization methods have on the ownership structure and control of privatized companies?

3. Which method of privatization do you think has resulted in the best structure in which to nurture good corporate governance?

4. What do you think that a foreign investor would be looking for when it comes to investing in a country in Central and Eastern Europe?

5. Critically discuss the role of National Investment Funds and Investment Privatization Funds.

6. Do you think there is a role to be played by institutional investors, both domestic and foreign, in the corporate governance of privatized companies?

■ **FT ARTICLE**

Dicey Russian flotations challenge London investors' appetite for risk

By Kate Burgess, Joanna Chung, Arkady Ostrovsky and Helen Thomas, Financial Times

The flotation this month of Russia's Novolipetsk Steel and the entry into the FTSE 100 index of Kazakhmys, Kazakhstan's biggest copper miner, have drawn attention to some of the risks associated with the London market's more exotic new members.

The pages of Novolipetsk's prospectus contain more drama than a Dostoevsky plot. Like some of the other companies that have come to London from Russia and its neighbouring states, they present a spectacular opportunity for the London market and a challenge to its appetite for risk.

The 26 pages of risk factors contained in Novolipetsk's prospectus, published last week ahead of its £5.2bn listing, include details of a price-fixing investigation, potential conflicts of interest and substantial commitments to fund public services in its home town of Lipetsk.

They also include the fact that "our privatisation or the title to any privatized company that we acquired may be challenged". The company also lists extensive political and economic risks, including uncertainties over stock ownership rights.

Many of these risks would apply to any company emerging from Russia or one of its neighbouring states and will not alarm old hands. Seven companies from the region have listed on London's main market this year, bringing the total to 13.

Some of what is in the prospectus, though, is more specific. For example, a Novolipetsk non-executive director resigned last month after being charged in a criminal case. It goes on to say that Novolipetsk gave an $85m (£49m) interest-free loan to a company, LKB Invest, which used the money to buy Novolipetsk shares.

It also paid more than $2m in consultancy fees in each of the past three years to Rumelco, a company owned and controlled by Vladimir Lisin, Novolipetsk's controlling shareholder.

In 2003 Rumelco bought LKB Invest the year after it had bought Novolipetsk shares, the prospectus says, and now indirectly owns 7.52 per cent of Novolipetsk. The loan to LKB Invest was fully repaid.

Interest-free loans crop up at Kazakhmys as well. Vladimir Ni, a 72-year-old mining engineer who has been on the board since 1999, is also a director of HOZU Corporation. In the latest accounts of Kazakhmys, HOZU is shown as having a secured interest free loan of $14.2m from Kazakhmys, due to mature on December 31 this year.

Kazakhmys's prospectus said the privatisation of some of its assets had been challenged, although this did not have "any substance" and the State Property and Privatisation Committee had confirmed that the assets were acquired "in accordance with applicable law".

Kazakhmys, whose membership of the FTSE 100 will mean many institutional investors are obliged to own its stock, throws up other issues that may make some London's corporate governance experts wince.

Non-executive director David Monro, formerly of mining group BHP Billiton, was paid $400,000 for services rendered in relation to the London listing. Fellow non-executive director Lord Renwick, the former diplomat, is vice-chairman of investment banking at JPMorgan Cazenove, financial adviser to Kazakhmys. Some non-executives are also paid £120,000 a year, which is generous by UK standards.

Tracey Pierce, the London Stock Exchange's head of international business development, says: "It is a balance between having appropriate levels of protection but not undermining the UK's position as a leading financial centre." Most former Soviet companies coming to the UK list their shares in the form of Global Depositary Receipts, which can only be bought by professional investors and are not part of stock market indices.

However, Ms Pierce says companies such as Kazakhmys, which has a primary listing for its shares in London, must meet the same high standards as UK companies, or explain why they do not.

For the LSE, the opportunity is huge. The demand for access to western capital comes at just the time that tougher regulations make New York less attractive than it hitherto was to foreign companies.

Few of the Russian companies that have listed shares in London in the past year had a pressing need for cash. Gaining respectability and establishing their property rights is more important for many of their owners than raising new funds.

In light of the recent attack on Yukos, once Russia's biggest oil company, a London listing has become a form of political insurance against growing state interference in private business. A London listing may not make a company untouchable, but having foreign shareholders makes it harder for the Russian state to go after it. Many Russian companies see a flotation in London as part of their exit strategy ahead of the 2008 presidential elections.

The fast and wild evolution of Russian companies, and the lawless environment in which they operated for much of the 1990s, mean most Russian businesses have skeletons in their closets. Nevertheless, investors looking for higher yields have a strong appetite for companies from the former Soviet Union.

Some investment bankers say the pricing still does not reflect the risks these companies represent, both in terms of their past and in terms of their political vulnerability at home.

A senior investment banker in Moscow says glossy prospectuses and road shows prepared by international banks make these companies look normal. But beneath the surface lurk risks that are different from those of western companies and are not always properly evaluated.

There is some leeway on key corporate governance guidelines that set out best practice on board composition, remuneration and shareholder relations. Overseas companies must explain annually how they comply with corporate governance codes in their own countries and how that practice might differ from the UK's corporate governance code.

However, says Anita Skipper, Morley Fund Management's head of corporate governance, there is room for considerable interpretation of the rules.

Richard Singleton, director of corporate governance at F&C Asset Management, which is leading calls for tougher tests on overseas companies, says: "There are those who feel a brief listing of differences satisfies the requirements but we, and many other investors, feel that we need more explanations. If companies are coming to London for the London market's money, then the quid pro quo should be behaving by local standards".

Anyone investing in emerging markets must do the research, get to know the management and work out whether he or she trusts them, Mr Singleton says. Those companies that do not abide by the same rules should be valued at a discount to UK companies, he adds.

So it was last month for Amtel-Vredestein, one of Russia's largest tyre makers. The company raised about a third less than planned from its initial public offering partly because poor results from a rival group made investors baulk at the price. Amtel placed 18.3m shares in the form of global depositary receipts at $11 each, below the $13-16 range previously expected.

Ms Pierce of the LSE believes investors are quite capable of making their own judgments of value.

She said: "The comply or explain model is appropriate in the UK. It enables investors to obtain full disclosure of all facts and decide whether they want to invest."

In fact, Amtel is a rarity. Its shares are among a handful of stocks that have fallen since flotation.

Sistema, the consumer conglomerate, is up 27 per cent from listing; Pyaterochka, the food retailer, is up 92 per cent; Evraz, the steel group, has gained 22 per cent.

Kazakhmys, despite the interest-free loan and the issues surrounding the way it pays its directors, is up 26 per cent from flotation.

Ms Pierce says: "The fact that the [former Soviet] IPOs have done so well shows the investor demand for these stocks."

Moreover, the fact that this demand is present despite the issues that are so graphically highlighted in some of these companies' prospectuses suggests that investors, for now at least, are comfortable with those risks.

Financial Times Tuesday 6 December 2005

■ REFERENCES

Belikov, I. (2004), *Corporate Governance in Russia: Who Will Pay For It and How Much?* Economic Reform Feature Service, Center for International Private Enterprise (Article adapted from a longer article originally appearing in Russian in the magazine *Rynok Tsennikh Bumag* (2004, No. 5).

Berglof, E. and Pajuste, A. (2003), 'Emerging Owners, Eclipsing Markets? Corporate Governance in Central and Eastern Europe' in *Corporate Governance and Capital Flows in a Global Economy*, P.K. Cornelius and B. Kogut (eds.), Oxford University Press, Oxford.

Best Practices Committee at Corporate Governance Forum (2002), *Best Practices in Public Companies 2002*, Best Practices Committee at Corporate Governance Forum, Warsaw.

___ (2005), *Best Practices in Public Companies 2005*, Best Practices Committee at the Corporate Governance Forum, Warsaw.

Boeri, T. and Perasso, G. (1998), 'Privatization and Corporate Governance: Some Lessons from the Experience of Transitional Economies' in *Corporate Governance, Financial Markets and Global Convergence*, M. Balling, E. Hennessy, and R. O'Brien (eds.), Kluwer Academic Publishers, Dordrecht.

Budapest Stock Exchange (2004), *Corporate Governance Recommendations*, Budapest Stock Exchange, Budapest.

Cadbury, Sir Adrian (1992), *Report of the Committee on the Financial Aspects of Corporate Governance*, Gee & Co. Ltd., London.

Centre for European Policy Studies (1995), *Corporate Governance in Europe*, Brussels.

Claessens S., Djankov, S. and Pohl, G. (1997), *Ownership and Corporate Governance: Evidence from the Czech Republic*, World Bank Policy Research Working Paper, No. 1737.

Coffee, J.C. (1998), 'Inventing a Corporate Monitor for Transitional Economies' in *Comparative Corporate Governance, the State of the Art and Emerging Research*, K.J. Hopt, H. Kanda, M.J. Roe, E. Wymeersch, and S. Prigge (eds.), Oxford University Press, Oxford.

___ (2002), 'Convergence and its Critics' in *Corporate Governance Regimes, Convergence and Diversity*, J.A. McCahery, P. Moerland, T. Raaijmakers, and L. Renneboog (eds.), Oxford University Press, Oxford.

Co-ordination Council for Corporate Governance (2001), *The Russian Code of Corporate Conduct*, Federal Securities Commission, Moscow.

Czech Securities Commission (2004), *Corporate Governance Code based on the OECD Principles (2004)*, Czech Securities Commission, Prague.

Dzierzanowski, M. and Tamowicz, P. (2002), *The Corporate Governance Code for Polish Listed Companies*, Gdansk Institute for Market Economics/Polish Corporate Governance Forum, Gdansk.

Earle J.S., Kucsera, C. and Telegdy, A. (2005), 'Ownership Concentration and Corporate Performance on the Budapest Stock Exchange: Do Too Many Cooks Spoil the Goulash?', *Corporate Governance: An International Review*, Vol. 13, No. 2, March 2005.

European Bank of Reconstruction and Development/World Bank (1999), *Business Environment Survey*, EBRD.

Frydman, R., Pistor, K. and Rapaczynski, A. (1996), 'Investing in Insider Dominated Firms: Russia' in *Corporate Governance in Central Europe and Russia: Volume 1 Banks, Funds, and Foreign Investors*, R. Frydman, C.W. Gray, and A. Rapaczynski (eds.), CEU Press, Budapest.

Kostikov, I. (2003), 'Governance in an Emerging Financial Market, The Case of Russia' in

Corporate Governance and Capital Flows in a Global Economy, P.K. Cornelius and B. Kogut (eds.), Oxford University Press, Oxford.

KCP (2001), *Revised Corporate Governance Code*, KCP/Czech Securities Commission, Prague.

La Porta, F., Lopez de Silvanes, F., Shleifer, A., and Vishny, R. (1998), 'Law and Finance', *Journal of Political Economy*, 106(6).

McKinsey & Co. (2002), *Investor Opinion Survey on Corporate Governance*, McKinsey & Co., London.

OECD (1999), *Principles of Corporate Governance*, OECD, Paris.

—— (2004), *Principles of Corporate Governance*, OECD, Paris.

Pistor, K. and Turkewitz, J. (1996), 'Coping with Hydra – State Ownership after Privatization: A Comparative Study of the Czech Republic, Hungary and Russia' in *Corporate Governance in Central Europe and Russia: Volume 2 Insiders and the State*, R. Frydman, C.W. Gray, and A. Rapaczynski (eds.), CEU Press, Budapest.

Rozlucki, W. (2003), 'Governance in an Emerging Financial Market, The Case of Poland' in *Corporate Governance and Capital Flows in a Global Economy*, P.K. Cornelius and B. Kogut (eds.), Oxford University Press, Oxford.

Sprenger, C. (2002), *Ownership and Corporate Governance in Russian Industry: A Survey*, European Bank for Research and Development, Working Paper No. 70.

Sprenger, C. (2005), 'The Determinants of Ownership After Privatisation – The Case of Russia' (August), EFA 2005 Moscow Meetings.

World Bank–IMF (2003), *Report on the Observance of Standards and Codes (ROSC) Corporate Governance Country Assessment Hungary February 2003*, drafted by O. Fremond and A. Berg, Corporate Governance Unit Private Sector Advisory Services, World Bank, Washington DC.

■ USEFUL WEBSITES

www.cipe.org The website of the Centre for International Private Enterprise has numerous articles of relevance to corporate governance.

www.corp-gov.org The website of Corporate Governance in Russia contains information about corporate governance in the Russian market.

www.ecgi.org The website of the European Corporate Governance Institute contains articles relating to corporate governance, and lists of corporate governance codes, guidelines, and principles.

www.iclg.ru The website of the Institute of Corporate Law and Corporate Governance has information about corporate governance developments in Russia.

Corporate Governance in the Asia-Pacific

LEARNING OBJECTIVES

- To understand the background to the development of corporate governance codes in the Asia-Pacific
- To be aware of the different ownership structures in the Asia-Pacific
- To be aware of the main differences in corporate governance codes in various countries in the Asia-Pacific
- To have a detailed knowledge of the corporate governance codes for a range of countries in the Asia-Pacific

---

Introduction

This chapter gives an overview of the development of corporate governance in the Asia-Pacific countries. The 1990s saw the meteoric rise and subsequent catastrophic collapse of many markets in the Asia-Pacific countries, in most of the so-called 'tiger economies'. Many investors, both local and overseas, had poured money into the stock markets to benefit from the vast gains that could be made. Equally, many investors lost large amounts when the markets crashed, when the bubble burst following on from Japan's prolonged recession in the early 1990s. By the late 1990s, it had spread to South Korea and several countries in the Asia-Pacific region. Following the crash, there was much soul-searching and questioning as to how and why this financial crisis could have happened. Many people expressed the view that the lack of transparency in companies' financial reports had been largely to blame, together with a lack of accountability of directors of companies. No one had really seemed to notice this situation, or if they had, they had not seemed to care about it, as long as the share prices were increasing and there were profits to be made from the stock market. However, once the markets crashed, it became a different story, and governments and stock exchanges sought to restore investor confidence in their countries by increasing transparency and accountability, and instituting better corporate governance.

In the context of the Asian countries with weak institutions and poor property rights (including protection of minority shareholders' rights), Claessens and Fan (2000) state that 'resulting forms of crony capitalism, i.e. combinations of weak corporate governance and government interference, not only lead to poor performance and risky financing patterns, but also are conductive to macro-economic crises'.

Following the financial downturn of the 1990s, many countries in South-East Asia, issued revised – and strengthened – corporate governance codes, and countries that previously had not had corporate governance codes introduced them.

The countries discussed in this chapter cover a range of ownership structures and influences that have impacted on the corporate governance structures. The countries discussed are: Japan, with the dominant shareholders being typically main banks of industrial groups or *keiretsu*; South Korea, with its *chaebol* representing the interests of dominant shareholders, often family groups; Malaysia, with families often being a dominant shareholder; China, where despite ongoing reforms, the state still has significant influence in companies; Australia, which has a common law system and widespread institutional investor share ownership.

In a study of nine Asian countries (including Malaysia, South Korea, and Japan but not China), Claessens et al. (2000) find that 'in all countries, voting rights frequently exceed cash flow rights via pyramid structures and cross-holdings'. This is indicative of the power that the dominant shareholders are able to build up. However, an encouraging and positive sign is that the countries examined in detail in this chapter have in common that they have felt the need to improve their corporate governance to provide greater transparency and enhance protection of minority shareholders' rights.

Japan

Japan's economy developed very rapidly during the second half of the twentieth century. Particularly during the period 1985–89, there was a 'bubble economy', characterized by a sharp increase in share prices and the value of land; the early 1990s saw the bubble burst as share prices fell and land was devalued. As well as shareholders and landowners finding themselves losing vast fortunes, banks found that they had severe problems too. During the bubble period, the banks had lent large amounts of money against the value of land and, as the price of land fell, borrowers found themselves unable to make the repayments and the banks were left with large non-performing loans. The effect of the fall in share prices and land values spread through the Japanese economy, which became quite stagnant, and the effects spread to other countries' economies, precipitating a regional recession.

The Japanese government wished to restore confidence in the Japanese economy and in the stock market, and to attract foreign direct investment to help regenerate growth in companies. Improved corporate governance was seen as a very necessary step in this process.

Japan's corporate governance system is often likened to that of Germany because banks can play an influential role in companies in both countries. However, there are fundamental differences between the systems, driven partly by culture and partly by the Japanese shareholding structure with the influence of the *keiretsu* (broadly, associations of companies). Charkham (1994) sums up three main concepts that affect Japanese attitudes towards corporate governance: obligation, family, and consensus. The first of these, obligation, is evidenced by the Japanese feeling of obligation to family, a company, or country; the second, family, is the strong feeling of being part of a 'family' whether this is a family *per se*, or a company; finally, the third concept, consensus, means that there is an emphasis on agreement rather than antagonism. These three concepts deeply influence the Japanese approach to corporate governance.

The *keiretsu* sprang out of the *zaibatsu*. Okumura (2002) states: 'Before World War II, when *zaibatsu* (giant pre-war conglomerates) dominated the Japanese economy, individuals or families governed companies as major stockholders. By contrast, after the war, by virtue of corporate capitalism, companies in the form of corporations became large stockowners, and companies became major stockholders of each other's stock.' The companies forming the *keiretsu* may be in different industries, forming a cluster often with a bank at the centre. Charkham (1994) states that 'banks are said to have encouraged the formation and development of groups of this kind, as a source of mutual strength and reciprocal help'. Indeed, banks themselves have a special relationship with the companies they lend to, particularly if they are the lead or main bank for a given company. Banks often buy shares in their customer companies to firm up the relationship between company and bank. However, they are limited to a 5 per cent holding in a given company but, in practice, the combination of the traditional bank relationship with its client and the shareholding mean that they can be influential, and often very helpful, if the company is in financial difficulties, viewing it as part of their obligation to the company to try to help it find a way out of its difficulties.

When compared to the German system, it should be noted that there is no automatic provision for employees to sit on the supervisory board. However, employees have traditionally come to expect that they will have lifelong employment with the same company – unfortunately, in times of economic downturn, this can no longer be guaranteed.

The Japan Corporate Governance Committee published its revised Corporate Governance Code in 2001. The Code had six chapters, which contained a total of 14 principles. The Code had an interesting introduction, part of which stated 'a good company maximizes the profits of its shareholders by efficiently creating value, and in the process contributes to the creation of a more prosperous society by enriching the lives of its employees and improving the welfare of its other stakeholders'. Hence the Code tried to take a balanced view of what a company is all about, and clearly the consideration of stakeholders is seen to be an important aspect. The foreword to the Code discussed and explained some of the basic tenets of corporate governance to help familiarize readers of the Code with areas including the role and function of the board of directors, the supervisory body, independent directors, incentive-based compensation, disclosure, and investor relations.

online resource centre

(i) Mission and role of the board of directors

This first chapter contained five principles relating to: the position and purpose of the board of directors; the function and powers of the board of directors; the organization

Table 12.1 Summary of key characteristics influencing Japanese corporate governance

Feature	Key characteristic
Main business form	Public limited company
Predominant ownership structure	*Keiretsu*; but institutional investor ownership is increasing
Legal system	Civil law
Board structure	Dual
Important aspect	Influence of *keiretsu*

of the board of directors; outside directors and their independence; the role of the leader of the board of directors.

The board should be comprised of outside directors (someone who has never been a full-time director, executive, or employee of the company) – preferably a majority – and inside directors (executives or employees of the company). Independent directors are outside directors who can make their decisions independently. The board of directors' role is seen as one of management supervision including approving important strategic decisions, nominating candidates for director positions, appointment and removal of the CEO, and general oversight of accounting and auditing. The board of directors may also be required to approve certain decisions made by the CEO.

(ii) Mission and role of the committees established within the board of directors

The board is recommended to establish various committees including an audit committee, compensation committee, and nominating committee. Each committee established should comprise at least three directors, and an outside director appointed as chair of each committee. The majority of directors on the audit committee should be independent directors, whilst the majority of directors on the audit committee should be independent directors, whilst the majority of directors on the other two committees should be outside directors, of whom at least one should be an independent director.

The roles of the various committees are broadly defined and cover the usual areas that one would expect for each of these committees.

(iii) Leadership responsibility of the CEO

The CEO's role is to formulate management strategies with the aim of maximizing corporate value in the long term. The CEO is supervised by the board of directors. The CEO may set up an executive management committee to assist him in conducting all aspects of the business. The CEO may not be a member of the committees listed above in (ii).

(iv) Addressing shareholder derivative litigation

A litigation committee, comprised a majority of independent directors, may be established to determine whether litigation action should be made against directors or executives against whom the company/shareholders may have a claim.

(v) Securing fairness and transparency for executive management

Two important areas were covered in this section of the Code: internal control and disclosure. The CEO should ensure that there is an effective corporate governance system with adequate internal control. The audit committee should evaluate the CEO's policies on internal audit and control. The CEO should prepare an annual report about the internal audit and control, which should preferably be audited by a certified public accountant.

Disclosure should be made by the CEO of any information that may influence share prices; also information should be disclosed to the various stakeholder groups as appropriate.

(vi) Reporting to the shareholders and communicating with investors

The shareholders' general meeting is seen as an opportunity for shareholders to listen to the reports of the directors and executives, and to obtain further information about the company through asking questions. Should the questions go unanswered in the general meeting, then the answer should be put on the company's website subsequent to the general meeting.

The company's executives are encouraged to meet analysts and others who can convey information to investors and shareholders about the company. Information should also be posted on the Internet to try to ensure equality of access to information amongst the various investors.

The Commercial Code in Japan provides for the appointment of statutory auditors to monitor the various aspects of the company's activities. However, in 2002, there was an extensive revision of the Commercial Code essentially providing companies with the option of adopting a 'US-style' corporate governance structure. The US-style structure would have a main board of directors to carry out the oversight function, and involve the establishment of audit, remuneration, and nomination committees, each with at least three members, a majority of whom should be non-executive. A board of corporate executive officers would also be appointed who would be in charge of the day-to-day business operations. Under the US-style structure, the board of statutory auditors would be abolished. It can be seen that the Japanese Corporate Governance Committee's Code's recommendations dovetailed with the revised Commercial Code.

In 2004, the Tokyo Stock Exchange issued the Principles of Corporate Governance for Listed Companies. In the preface, the purpose of the Principles is described as being 'to provide a necessary common base for recognition, thereby enhancing corporate governance through the integration of voluntary activities by listed companies and demands by shareholders and investors'. The five principles are based around the OECD Principles of Corporate Governance.

The first principle relates to exercising various rights of shareholders, including the right to participate and vote in general meetings, voting on such issues as the election and dismissal of directors and auditors, and fundamental corporate changes, the basic right to share various profits such as dividends, and the special right to make derivative lawsuits and injunction of activities in contravention of laws, regulations, and other rules. The voting environment should be developed and improved so that shareholders can exercise their votes appropriately and participate in general meetings of shareholders.

The second principle relates to the equitable treatment of shareholders, including minority and foreign shareholders. To this end, there should be an adequate system to prohibit transactions through the abuse of officers, employees, and controlling shareholders, which are against the primary interests of the company or shareholders. There should be enhanced disclosure where it seems that such actions might occur, and there should be prohibition of special benefits to specified shareholders.

The third principle is the relationship with stakeholders in corporate governance. Whilst corporate governance should help to create corporate value and jobs, the fact that companies sustain and improve their strengths and enhance value over time is 'the result of the provision of company resources by all stakeholders', so the establishment of good relationships with stakeholders is important. To this end, companies should cultivate a corporate culture and internal systems, which respect the various stakeholder groups and ensure timely and accurate disclosure of information relating to them.

The fourth principle relates to disclosure and transparency. Companies should ensure timely and accurate disclosure on all material matters, including the financial state and performance of the company and ownership distribution, through both quantitative and qualitative disclosures. The company should seek to ensure that investors can access information easily and that there is equal access to information. Internal systems should seem to ensure the accuracy and timeliness of disclosure.

The final principle relates to the responsibilities of the board of directors, auditors, board of corporate auditors, and other relevant groups. Corporate governance should enhance the supervision of management by the aforementioned groups and ensure their accountability to shareholders. Systems should be developed, or enhanced, to ensure that these requirements can be met.

Finally, it is important to note that the legal framework in Japan, via the Commercial Code Revision on Boards (2003), provides for two corporate governance structures: a corporate auditors' system, consisting of general meetings with shareholders, the board of directors, representative directors, executive directors, corporate auditors, and the board of corporate auditors, and a committees system, where there are general meetings of the shareholders, the board of directors, and committees composed of members of the board of directors (nomination committee, audit committee, and compensation committee), representative executive officers, and executive officers. It is up to the company which system it chooses. In each case, the general meeting of shareholders is the decision-making body on matters of fundamental importance to the company. A key difference between the two structures is that companies with a committee system need to re-elect their directors annually through the general meeting of shareholders, because the board of directors has the authority regarding the definitive plan for the distribution of profit, whereas in the corporate auditors' system, this power lies with the general meetings of shareholders.

Charkham (2005) discusses the various changes that have taken place in the context of corporate governance in Japan and states:

The important part the banks played has greatly diminished. In its place there are now better structured boards, more effective company auditors, and occasionally more active shareholders.

An increase of interest, and, where appropriate, action on their part, might restore the balance that the banks' withdrawal from the scene has impaired.

South Korea

The downturn in the Japanese economy soon affected the Korean economy, which suffered similar consequences. Balino and Ubide (1999), amongst others, stated that poor corporate governance was an important contributory factor to the extent of the financial crisis in 1997. The poor corporate governance was characterized by a lack of transparency and disclosure, ineffective boards, and the activities of the *chaebols*.

The *chaebols* are large Korean conglomerates that wield considerable power through their cross-holdings of shares in various companies. The *chaebols* often constitute powerful family interests in Korea, and families may be able to exert more control in a particular company than their shareholdings on paper would merit. They often have little regard for the rights and interests of minority shareholders. However, in recent years, the People's Solidarity for Participatory Democracy (PSPD) has been established as an influential minority shareholder activist group that has campaigned for better corporate governance in a number of Korea's top companies. Jang and Kim (2002) emphasize the influence and power of families via the *chaebols*: 'Ownership by the controlling families in listed Korean *chaebol* companies has been only a fraction and their controlling power derives from their ownership through affiliated companies . . . personal stakes, particularly in listed companies, are minimized but control is maintained by an extensive matrix of circuitous cross-ownership among affiliated companies.'

online resource centre

The Korean Committee on Corporate Governance was established in March 1999, with funding from the Korea Stock Exchange, the Korea Securities Dealers' Association, the Korea Listed Companies Association, and the Korea Investment Trust Companies Association. It reported six months later in September 1999, with a Code of Best Practice (hereinafter the Code), which tries to take into account both internationally accepted corporate governance principles and also the 'unique managerial circumstances faced by Korean companies'. The purpose of the Code is stated as being to maximize corporate value by enhancing transparency and efficiency of corporations for the future. It is recognized

Table 12.2 Summary of key characteristics influencing South Korean corporate governance

Feature	Key characteristic
Main business form	Public limited company
Predominant ownership structure	Controlling shareholder (family, corporate cross-holdings)
Legal system	Common law
Board structure	Unitary
Important aspect	Influence of *chaebol*

that, in order to attract and retain both domestic and foreign investment, there needs to be more transparency and more regard to the rights of minority shareholders.

The Code applies to listed companies and other public companies but it is also advised that non-public companies follow the Code where practicable. The Code has five sections relating to shareholders, the board of directors, audit systems, stakeholders, and management monitoring by the market.

(i) Shareholders

Shareholders possess basic rights, such as the right to attend and vote at general shareholder meetings, and to receive relevant information in a timely way, that should be protected. Shareholders shall be treated equitably: for example, shares of the same class shall have the same voting and other rights.

As well as rights, shareholders have responsibilities and so should try to exercise their voting rights. Controlling shareholders have the corresponding responsibilities when they exercise any influence toward the corporate management other than the exercise of voting rights.

(ii) Board of directors

The board of directors should make the corporation's key management policy decisions and shall supervise the activities of directors and management. Its activities should include: setting corporate goals and the strategies to achieve them; approving business plans and budgets; supervising risk management activities and associated controls; ensuring appropriate information disclosure. Board meetings of the full board (inside and outside directors) should be held regularly, and at least once a quarter.

The board/directors should perform their duties faithfully in the best interests of the corporation and its shareholders; they shall also perform their social responsibilities and consider the interests of various stakeholders. The board shall observe the related statutes and the articles of incorporation when performing its duties, and shall ensure that all members of the corporation also observe them. If a director breaches the law or the company's articles of incorporation, or has neglected his duties, he may be liable for damages to the corporation.

The board may set up internal committees such as audit, operation, and remuneration committees, comprised of directors with relevant expertise in the area. The remuneration of directors may be covered by a remuneration committee and should be related to an evaluation of their contribution to the company.

There should be outside directors who are 'capable of performing their duties independently from the management, controlling shareholders and the corporation'. The outside directors should comprise 25 per cent of the board (50 per cent for financial institutions and large-scale public corporations). It is recommended that there are also regular meetings between the outside directors only and the management to enable both to gain a fuller perspective of corporate management issues.

Directors should be appointed through a transparent process and it is recommended that a nomination committee be established, comprised one-half outside directors. There should be sufficient information disclosed about the director appointment nominees to enable shareholders to vote in an informed way.

(iii) Audit systems

Companies such as public corporations, government-invested institutions, and financial institutions, should establish an audit committee composed of at least three board members, of which at least two-thirds, including the audit committee chair, should be outside directors; at least one member should have professional auditing knowledge. When a company has an audit committee, it does not need to have an auditor as well (that is, an auditor appointed permanently in the company), but large firms (those with total assets of more than US$5.8 million) must have an annual accounting audit by an external firm.

The audit committee remit includes: evaluating the internal control system; evaluating the external auditors; reviewing the accuracy of the company's financial reports; reviewing management's operations. The audit committee should be provided with sufficient information to enable it to perform its role properly. The audit committee should meet at least once a quarter and draft appropriate detailed minutes, which shareholders are allowed to read.

The external audit shall be performed by those independent from stakeholders in the corporation, such as the management or controlling shareholder, and by those who specialize in auditing. External auditors should attend the company's general shareholder meeting and answer shareholders' questions on the audit report.

(iv) Stakeholders

The Code states that the rights of stakeholders, and appropriate means of redress for infringement of their rights, shall be protected. Companies need to take account of their social responsibilities too, such as consumer protection and environmental protection. Stakeholders may monitor management as appropriate (in the context of their particular stakeholder interest) and have access to relevant information to protect their rights.

There is no provision for employee representation as such (it is a unitary board system rather than dual), but the Act on Worker Participation and Promotion of Co-operation stipulates that employees and management have consultative meetings whereby the employees are informed of the company's plans, quarterly performance, personnel plans, etc.

(v) Management monitoring by the market

Corporations shall actively disclose matters of material importance to the decision-making of shareholders, creditors, and other interested parties. Anything that could lead to a change in corporate control, including takeovers, mergers, acquisitions, and business splits, should be carried out through a transparent and fair procedure. The board is entitled to defend against hostile takeovers but not to the detriment of the company's profits to help maintain control for only some shareholders or for management.

The company should explain in its annual report any differences between its corporate governance and the recommendations laid down in the Code. An interesting recommendation is that where there is a minimum of 20 per cent foreign ownership, then companies should make disclosures in both Korean and English languages for audit reports and 'material timely disclosures'.

Finally, and of some significance, is the recommendation that companies disclose detailed information on the share ownership status of controlling shareholders because 'the actual controlling shareholder of the corporation is one at the core of corporate governance'.

Black, Jang and Kim (2005), in a study of firms' corporate governance practices in Korea, found that regulatory factors are very important, largely because Korean rules impose special governance requirements on large firms (as mentioned earlier). They found that industry factors, firm size, and firm risk are important, with larger firms and riskier firms being better governed.

Malaysia

Malaysia was one of the fastest growing of the tiger economies in the early 1990s. The government had introduced a succession of five-year plans with the aim of full industrialization in the twenty-first century. The government had also introduced the New Economic Policy (NEP) in 1970 to implement affirmative actions in favour of the Bumiputera (the indigenous Malay people). These types of affirmative action were designed to increase Bumiputera involvement in the corporate sector. The government also set up trusts to hold shares on behalf of the Bumiputera, and Bumiputera, whether as companies, individuals, or trusts, tend to be one of the largest shareholder groups in Malaysian companies. The corporate governance code in Malaysia concentrates on the principles and best practice of corporate governance, drawing largely on the UK corporate governance recommendations.

In Malaysia, many of the listed companies are family-owned or controlled, with many companies having evolved from traditional family-owned enterprises. This means that the directors may not be responsive to minority shareholders' rights and better corporate governance would help to remedy this and ensure that minority shareholders' rights are protected. In addition, transparency should be improved to help restore investor confidence.

Malaysia established its High Level Finance Committee on Corporate Governance in 1998, following on from the drastic downturn of the Malaysian economy the previous year. The Committee reported in March 2000, with a detailed corporate governance

Table 12.3 Summary of key characteristics influencing Malaysian corporate governance

Feature	Key characteristic
Main business form	Public limited company
Predominant ownership structure	Controlling shareholder (family, corporation, or trust nominee)
Legal system	Common law
Board structure	Unitary
Important aspect	Influence of Bumiputera shareholders; emphasis on director training

code: the Malaysian Code of Corporate Governance (hereinafter the Code). The Kuala Lumpur Stock Exchange has adopted the Code's recommendations and, with effect from 2002, listed companies have had to include a statement of their compliance with the Code and explain any areas of the Code that they do not comply with (i.e. a 'comply or explain' mechanism).

The Code has four parts: first, broad principles of good corporate governance; second, best practices for companies, which gives more detail for each of the broad principles; third, a section aimed at investors and auditors discussing their role in corporate governance; fourth, various explanatory notes are provided. As mentioned, the first part of the Code is devoted to the principles of corporate governance, which cover directors, directors' remuneration, shareholders, and accountability and audit, whilst the second part essentially expands on the principles with examples of best practice, or guidelines as to how best to implement the principles.

(i) Directors

Every listed company should have an effective balanced board comprised of executive and non-executive directors. Independent non-executive directors should comprise at least one-third of the board. Where the company has a significant shareholder (a shareholder with the ability to exercise a majority of votes for the election of directors), then the board should disclose annually whether it fairly reflects, through board representation, the investment of the minority of shareholders. There is a preference for the chairman and the chief executive officer's roles to be separate to ensure that power is not centred in one individual. The roles can be combined but then the presence of an independent element on the board would be particularly important, and a decision to combine the roles would need to be publicly explained.

The board should have appropriate relevant information supplied in a timely fashion. Its responsibilities will include: the strategic direction of the company; ensuring proper management of the company; identifying risks and ensuring an appropriate risk management system; reviewing the overall effectiveness of the internal control systems of the company; succession planning and training of directors; the investor relations programme. The board should meet regularly and disclose the attendance record of individual directors at board meetings.

The board should have access to a company secretary who should ensure that the board provides all appropriate information for corporate and statutory requirements. The board should also have access to independent professional advice as and when needed at the company's expense.

Directors should be appointed by a transparent nominations process by a nominating committee comprised exclusively of non-executive directors, a majority of these being independent. The nominating committee should review the mix of skills and experience on the board each year and identify any gaps that might need to be filled. The nominating committee should assess, on an annual basis, the effectiveness of the board, the committees of the board, and individual directors. Re-election should take place regularly (minimum every three years).

An important aspect is the emphasis on the importance of director training. The Code describes orientation and education of new directors as 'an integral element of the process of appointing new directors'.

(ii) Directors' remuneration

There should be a remuneration committee, comprised wholly or mainly of non-executive directors, to recommend the remuneration levels for the executive directors. Remuneration packages should reflect levels of both corporate and individual performance. The remuneration of non-executive directors should be decided by the board as a whole and should reflect each non-executive's experience and responsibilities in the company. The remuneration of each director should be disclosed in the company's annual report.

(iii) Accountability and audit

An audit committee should be established, comprised of at least three directors with the majority being independent. It should be chaired by an independent non-executive director. The audit committee's role includes: reviewing the year-end and quarterly financial statements of the company; considering the appointment of the external auditor, his fee, and the nature and scope of the audit; reviewing the scope, programme, and results of the internal audit. The activities of the audit committee, the number of meetings held each year, and the attendance by individual directors should be disclosed. Internal audit should be independent of the activities they audit.

(iv) Shareholders

The board should ensure that there is an effective communications strategy between the board, management, shareholders, and stakeholders. There should be 'a dialogue based on the mutual understanding of objectives' between the company and its institutional investors, whilst the AGM is a way to communicate with private investors and encourage their participation.

The third part of the Code is aimed at investors and auditors and their role in corporate governance. The role of institutional investors is emphasized: they should engage in constructive dialogue with companies; they should evaluate companies' corporate governance arrangements; they should vote in a considered way at companies' AGMs. For their part, auditors should independently report to shareholders in accordance with statutory and professional requirements.

The Corporate Law Reform Committee was established in 2004 to lead a programme of corporate law reform in Malaysia. Corporate governance reforms are the focus of one of the working groups, which is looking at issues of corporate governance and shareholders' rights. A consultation document on engagement with shareholders was issued in February 2006, with comments invited for later in the spring. The review is seeking to find an appropriate balance between providing a framework for effective shareholder engagement and ensuring that this framework is cost efficient, flexible, and facilitative for business. The focus is on general meetings and associated issues such as voting.

China

The Peoples' Republic of China (PRC) has introduced a number of changes to develop its stock market. In the early 1990s, the Shanghai and Shenzhen Stock Exchanges were launched, with the aim of raising finance from domestic and foreign investors to provide listed companies with new funds. The 1990s saw many businesses move from being state-owned enterprises (SOEs) to joint stock companies, and then to companies listed on one of the stock exchanges. The PRC government wished to modernize its industry and other sectors, and to expand the economy, to move towards a socialist market economy.

However, many of the former SOEs were lumbering giants with outdated machinery, and employing far too many people to make them viable as commercially run businesses with the aim of increasing profits. They were used to receiving loans from the state-owned commercial banks, which the banks very often knew they had little chance of repaying, these being non-performing loans that, in turn, were a real drain on the resources of the state-owned banks. The SOEs were also subject to the influence of party members at a number of levels: as employees, as local government officials in the district in which they operate, and at national level. This situation is changing over time but the old influences still exist. The situation was exacerbated by unfortunate incidents of corruption, which meant that the assets of the business were not safeguarded, and by a lack of transparency, disclosure, and accuracy of information. All in all, this was not a state of affairs that was going to build confidence in the stock market.

The government's desire to build a socialist market economy, to modernize, and to become part of the World Trade Organization all fuelled the move to try to improve shareholders' rights and protection of those rights, the insulation of company boards from inappropriate influence, and greater transparency and disclosure: in essence, the building of a corporate governance system. However, although many of the provisions are there on paper for an effective corporate governance system (as will be shown below), in practice, the state still owns large shareholdings in many companies (often more than half), minority shareholders' rights are sometimes ignored, and companies in the PRC are liable to have influence exerted over them from a number of different sources. Nonetheless, steps have been taken in the right direction and the government will be aware that if it wishes to attract foreign institutional investors, it will need to have a corporate governance system that protects minority rights and encourages confidence in the corporate structure and operations, and companies will need to provide accurate and timely information. As On Kit Tam (1999) stated: 'The task of establishing functional and appropriate corporate governance arrangements [in China] is necessarily a long-term and continually changing one.'

In the PRC, corporate governance developments involve a number of regulatory bodies, including the China Securities Regulatory Commission (CSRC), the Ministry of Finance (MOF), the State Economic and Trade Commission (SETC), and the People's Bank of China (PBOC), which is essentially the Central Bank of China.

A series of corporate scandals came to light in 2001, including that of Lantian Co. Ltd. Lantian Co. Ltd. was the first publicly listed ecological agricultural company in China.

online resource centre

Table 12.4 Summary of key characteristics influencing Chinese corporate governance

Feature	Key characteristic
Main business form	State-owned enterprises, joint stock companies
Predominant ownership structure	State
Legal system	Civil law
Board structure	Dual
Important aspect	Influence of Communist Party

However, investors grew suspicious of its high profit growth because its business could not have underpinned such growth. Subsequently, inaccuracies in its financial reporting came to light and it is estimated that Lantian overstated net profits by up to US$60 million. Scandals such as Lantian have helped fuel the drive for corporate governance reforms and, in January 2001, the CSRC issued a Code of Corporate Governance For Listed Companies in China (hereinafter the Code).

The Code is broadly based on the OECD Principles of Corporate Governance. The Code is aimed at listed companies and addresses 'the protection of investors' interests and rights, the basic behaviour rules and moral standards for directors, supervisors, managers, and other senior management members of listed companies'. The Code is seen as the yardstick by which a company is able to measure its corporate governance, and if there are deficiencies in the corporate governance of a company, then the securities supervision and regulatory authorities may instruct the company to correct its corporate governance to comply with the Code.

The Code contains seven main chapters dealing with: shareholders and shareholders' meetings; the listed company and its controlling shareholders; directors and the board of directors; the supervisors and the supervisory board; performance assessments and incentive and disciplinary systems; stakeholders; information disclosure and transparency.

(i) Shareholders and shareholders' meetings

The Code states that the company should ensure that all shareholders are treated fairly, especially minority shareholders. Shareholders should have equal rights and, if their rights are infringed, then they should have redress through legal action. Directors, supervisors, and managers of companies will be liable to pay compensation if they breach laws and regulations.

Companies should establish communications channels with shareholders and shareholders should be informed of significant matters that affect the company. Shareholders should be notified in good time of a shareholders' meeting and agenda items should be given an appropriate amount of time in the meeting. Electronic communications may be used to help increase the number of shareholders participating. Shareholders may vote in person or may appoint a proxy to vote on their behalf. The role of institutional investors is specifically mentioned in the appointment of directors, remuneration, and other major decisions.

In related party transactions, these transactions should, in principle, be at market value.

(ii) Listed company and its controlling shareholders

This section of the Code deals with a protocol for how the controlling shareholders should behave when an enterprise is being restructured or reorganized prior to listing. Certain aspects of the enterprise, such as its non-operational institutions and welfare institutions, will not be transferred to the listed company, but may continue to provide services to the listed company in the capacity of a separate company based on commercial principles. Reform of labour, personnel, and distribution systems may occur. However, the controlling shareholders should not act in a way detrimental to the listed company's or shareholders' legal rights and interests by adversely restructuring assets or otherwise taking advantage of their position.

The controlling shareholders initially nominate the candidates for directors and supervisors on the basis of their professional skills, knowledge, and experience. The shareholders' meeting or the board of directors will approve appointments as appropriate. The listed company should be able to act independently of the controlling shareholders, including its personnel, and also the financial and accounting management systems of the listed company should be independent from the controlling shareholders. Logically, the board of directors and supervisory committee should operate in an independent manner and indeed the Code states that 'a listed company's business shall be completely independent from that of its controlling shareholders'.

(iii) Directors and board of directors

In order to enable shareholders to make an informed choice as to which candidate to vote for in director elections, there should be detailed disclosure of information about the candidate. The emphasis is on appointments being made through a transparent process.

Directors should attend appropriate training sessions to familiarize themselves with their directorial duties and responsibilities. They should be suitably qualified with appropriate skills and knowledge. They should 'faithfully, honestly, and diligently perform their duties for the best interests of the company and all shareholders', and they should also devote adequate time to their role as director and to attending board meetings. The board of directors is accountable to shareholders and 'shall treat all shareholders equally and shall be concerned with the interests of stakeholders'.

The board of directors should meet periodically and have a pre-set agenda, with timely and clear information about the agenda items being sent to all the directors. If two or more independent directors feel that the information is unclear or inadequate, then they may apply to postpone the meeting or the discussion of the relevant agenda item. Minutes of the board meetings should be carefully maintained.

Independent directors should be independent of the company and its major shareholders and should act in good faith and perform their duties diligently. They 'shall protect the overall interests of the company, and shall be especially concerned with protecting the interests of minority shareholders from being infringed'.

It is recommended that various committees of the board be established, such as a corporate strategy committee, a remuneration and appraisal committee, an audit committee, and a nomination committee. Independent directors should be in the majority on these committees and the audit committee, nomination committee, and remuneration/appraisal committee should be chaired by an independent director. In relation to the audit committee, at least one independent director should be an 'accounting professional'.

(iv) Supervisors and supervisory board

The supervisory board should comprise individuals with 'professional knowledge or work experience in such areas as law and accounting'. The supervisory board's members need to be able to supervise effectively the directors and managers and to examine knowledgably the company's financial matters.

The supervisory board is accountable to shareholders and its duties include supervising corporate finance, the directors' and managers' performance, and protecting the company's and shareholders' legal rights and interests. The supervisory board's members should be provided with appropriate information to enable them to do their job effectively. The supervisory board's meetings should be minuted.

(v) Performance assessments and incentive and disciplinary systems

Directors, supervisors, and management's performance should be assessed through a fair and transparent procedure, with directors and management being evaluated by the board of directors or by the remuneration/appraisal committee. When any individual's performance is being reviewed, then the director being discussed should leave the meeting. Independent directors and supervisors should be evaluated by a combination of self-assessment and peer review. The performance and compensation of the directors and supervisors should be reported to the shareholders' meeting.

The Code has an interesting provision in the context of the selection and appointment of management personnel, as it states 'no institution or individual shall interfere with a listed company's normal recruiting procedure for management personnel'. One problem with appointments in Chinese companies is that the state still wields a lot of influence and a mechanism is needed to isolate, as far as possible, the appointments process from the influence of political appointments. The Code seeks to make this an explicit point in the selection process.

Similarly, there is much demand from employees in Chinese companies, particularly at the higher levels where an awareness of Western practices is more apparent, to link compensation with performance. The Code states that the compensation for management personnel should be linked to both the company's performance and the individual's work performance.

(vi) Stakeholders

The section of the Code that deals with stakeholders states that 'while maintaining the listed company's development and maximizing the benefits of shareholders, the company shall be concerned with the welfare, environmental protection and public interests of the community in which it resides, and shall pay attention to the company's social responsibilities'.

The Code also mentions that the company should respect the legal rights of the various stakeholder groups and provide them with information as appropriate. In particular, employees are encouraged to provide feedback on various issues that might affect them by direct communication with the board of directors, the supervisory board, and management personnel.

(vii) Information and disclosure and transparency

The importance of the provision of timely and accurate information is emphasized; as well as any mandatory disclosures, the company should disclose other information that may impact on the decisions of shareholders or stakeholders. The same access to information should be available to all shareholders.

There should be specific disclosures relating to the company's corporate governance (as already mentioned in the individual sections above), plus the company should make disclosure about its state of corporate governance and the reasons why it may differ from the Code. It should also mention any plans to improve its corporate governance.

The company should disclose information relating to the shareholding distribution in the company: for example, detail of shareholders who own 'a comparatively large percentage of the shares' (what level this might be is not specified in the Code), shareholders who can control the company by acting in concert (that is, acting together), and the shareholders who actually control the company.

In the summer of 2001, the CSRC produced 'Guidelines for Introducing Independent Directors to the Board of Directors of Listed Companies'. The guidelines mandate all domestically listed companies to amend their articles as necessary to comply with the guidelines and to appoint, by 30 June 2002, at least two independent directors to the board of directors; by 30 June 2003, at least one-third of the board should be independent directors.

Neoh (2003) stated there are at least two areas that must be addressed for the market to move away from short-termism and for good governance to take root. One is for investors to have a longer term time horizon and the second is for the system of management succession to be addressed, so that politics is separated from the enterprise. The legal system also needs to support important bankruptcy laws and company law reform.

In February 2006, China moved towards convergence with global standards with the release by the Ministry of Finance of 39 standards based on International Financial Reporting Standards (IFRS), which will, inter alia, improve the quality of financial information and boost investor confidence. Given that transparency, disclosure, and accountability are at the heart of sound corporate governance, this is a most welcome development.

Australia

Whilst not suffering financial crisis in the same way as many countries in the region, Australia was nonetheless affected by the ripples from the various crises that occurred. It was, and is, vital for Australia's economic growth and well-being that the countries in the Asia-Pacific region are economically and financially sound, and politically stable. Australia therefore contributed to various IMF initiatives to help Asia-Pacific Economic Co-operation (APEC) economies to recover from the crises and strengthen their economic and financial management.

In terms of its corporate governance, Australia has a common law system and, certainly at first glance, its corporate governance system seems to have developed along the lines of the Anglo-Saxon model, having features that would usually be typical of a UK unitary board structure. However, on closer inspection, Australia seems to have features of both an insider and an outsider system. Dignam and Galanis (2004) summarize the various features in Australia that might lead to doubt as to which corporate governance system, insider or outsider, it has, or indeed whether it is moving from one system and towards another. These features include the political system, which is socialist and so would usually be associated with an insider system, and yet the corporate governance system does not fit this proposition; ownership of listed company shares is another interesting area because there are both dispersed shareholdings in listed companies and the presence of a significant non-institutional shareholder, or blockholder, in others. The former pattern of ownership is typical of an outsider system, whilst the latter is more commonly associated with an insider system.

Dignam and Galanis (2004) conclude their study by stating that the listed market in Australia is characterized by

significant blockholders engaged in private rent extraction; institutional investor powerlessness; a strong relationship between management and blockholders, which results in a weak market for corporate control; and a historical weakness in public and private securities regulation, which allows the creation and perpetuation of crucial blocks to information flow.

They feel that these characteristics make it more like an insider system than an outsider system.

Farrar (2005) also provides some interesting insights into corporate governance developments in Australia in his book about these developments in both Australia and New Zealand.

Turning now to look in more detail at the regulatory and corporate governance systems in Australia, in this context, it is important to realize that Australia's present regulatory infrastructure is relatively young. The Australian Securities and Investments Commission (ASIC), an independent Australian government body, has regulated financial markets, securities, futures, and corporations since January 1991. The Australian Stock Exchange (ASX) was formed in 1987 through the amalgamation of six independent stock exchanges that formerly operated in the state capital cities. Each of those exchanges had a history of share trading dating back to the nineteenth century.

online resource centre

Table 12.5 Summary of key characteristics influencing Australian corporate governance

Feature	Key characteristic
Main business form	Public corporations
Predominant ownership structure	Institutional investors; non-institutional shareholders (corporate or family)
Legal system	Common law
Board structure	Unitary
Important aspect	More emphasis on shareholder rights in recent years

The Bosch Report on *Corporate Practice and Conduct* was first issued in 1991 with further issues in 1993 and 1995. It covered a range of corporate governance issues including: board structure and composition; appointment of non-executive directors; directors' remuneration; risk management; financial reporting and auditing; conflicts of interest; the role of the company secretary. In many ways, it was the equivalent of the Cadbury Report in the UK.

A number of corporate governance codes and guidelines followed, including the Hilmer Report (1998), which had an emphasis on issues such as board composition, executive remuneration, and disclosure.

In 2003, the ASX Corporate Governance Council issued the Principles of Good Corporate Governance and Best Practice Recommendations. The introduction states

good corporate governance structures encourage companies to create value (through entrepreneurism, innovation, development and exploration) and provide accountability and control systems commensurate with the risks involved [and] demonstrably good corporate governance practices are increasingly important in determining the cost of capital in a global capital market. Australian companies must be equipped to compete globally and to maintain and promote investor confidence both in Australia and overseas.

Ten core principles are identified: 'the essential corporate governance principles', which are detailed below. Each of the principles has one or more recommendations associated with it that act as implementation guidance. The recommendations are not mandatory; rather, they are guidelines to help ensure the desired outcome.

(i) Lay solid foundations for management and oversight – recognize and publish the respective roles and responsibilities of board and management

The company should have in place a framework to enable the board to provide strategic guidance and effective oversight; the roles and responsibilities of board members and senior executives should be clarified and this will help with accountability, and no single individual should have too much power. One recommendation supports this principle – recommendation 1.1: to formalize and disclose the functions reserved to the board and those delegated to management.

(ii) **Structure the board to add value** – have a board of an effective composition, size and commitment to discharge adequately its responsibilities and duties

The board should be structured so that it has an understanding of the current and future issues affecting the business, and can review and challenge the performance of management and exercise independent judgement. Five recommendations support this principle, which are that: the majority of the board should be independent directors; the chairperson should be an independent director; the roles of chairperson and chief executive officer should not be exercised by the same individual; the board should establish a nomination committee; various information relating to the directors including their skills, experience and expertise, and the names of the members of the nomination committee and their attendance at the meetings thereof, should be included in the corporate governance section of the company's annual report.

(iii) **Promote ethical and responsible decision-making** – actively promote ethical and responsible decision-making

The company should clarify the standards of ethical behaviour required of company directors and key executives and encourage the observance of standards, and publish its policy as regards board and employee trading in company securities and related products. Three recommendations support this principle, which include that there should be a code of conduct to guide the directors, the CEO, the chief financial officer (CFO) and any other key executives in relation to practices necessary to maintain confidence in the company's integrity, and the responsibility and accountability of individuals for reporting and investigating reports of unethical practices. There should also be disclosure of the policy concerning trading in company securities by directors, officers, and employees, and provision of information in relation to any departures from the aforesaid recommendations.

(iv) **Safeguard integrity in financial reporting** – have a structure to independently verify and safeguard the integrity of the company's financial reporting

Five recommendations support this principle. The CEO and the CFO (or their equivalents) should be required to state in writing to the board that the company's financial reports present a true and fair view, in all material respects, of the company's financial state and that the operational results are in accordance with relevant accounting standards. The board should establish an audit committee, which should consist of at least three members and these should comprise only non-executive directors of whom the majority are independent directors. The audit committee should be chaired by an independent chairperson who is not the chairperson of the board. The audit committee should have a formal Charter. Information should be disclosed including the names of qualifications of those appointed to the audit committee, the number of meetings of the audit committee, and the names of those attending the meetings.

(v) Make timely and balanced disclosure – promote timely and balanced disclosure of all material matters concerning the company

Disclosures should be made in such a way that all investors have equal and timely access to information about the company, including its financial situation, performance, ownership, and governance. The concept of balance requires disclosure of both positive and negative information. Two recommendations support this principle: firstly, that written policies and procedures designed to ensure compliance with ASX Listing Rule disclosure requirements and to ensure accountability at a senior management level for that compliance be established; secondly, certain information should be disclosed including explanation from any departures.

(vi) Respect the rights of shareholders – respect the rights of shareholders and facilitate the effective exercise of those rights

A company should empower its shareholders by effective communication with them, enabling their access to balanced and comprehensible information, and facilitating their participation in general meetings. Two recommendations support this principle: firstly, the company should design and disclose a communications strategy to promote effective communication with shareholders and encourage effective participation at general meetings; secondly, the company should request the external auditor to attend the annual general meeting and to be available to answer shareholder questions about the conduct of the audit and preparation and content of the auditor's report.

(vii) Recognise and manage risk – establish a sound system of risk oversight and management and internal control

The system should identify, assess, monitor, and manage risk, and inform investors of material changes to the company's risk profile. Three recommendations support this principle: the board or appropriate board committee should establish policies on risk oversight and management; the CEO and CFO (or equivalents) should state to the board in writing that they have made their statement about the integrity of the financial statements based on a sound system of risk management and internal control and compliance, and that that system is operating efficiently and effectively; explanations should be provided of any departures from the aforesaid best practice recommendations.

(viii) Encourage enhanced performance – fairly review and actively encourage enhanced board and management effectiveness

Directors and key executives should have the knowledge and information to discharge their responsibilities effectively, and individual and collective performance should be regularly and fairly reviewed. There is one supporting recommendation, which is that there should be disclosure of the process for performance evaluation of the board, its committees and individual directors, and key executives.

(ix) Remunerate fairly and responsibly – ensure that the level and composition of
   remuneration is sufficient and reasonable and that its relationship to corporate and individual
   performance is defined

There are five recommendations relating to the principle: disclosure should be provided
of the company's remuneration policies to enable investors to understand the costs and
benefits of those policies, and the link between remuneration and corporate performance; the board should establish a remuneration committee; there should be a clear
distinction between the structure of non-executive directors' remuneration from that of
executives (non-executive directors should receive fees but not options or bonus payments); payment of equity-based executive remuneration should be made in accordance
with thresholds set in plans approved by shareholders; there should be disclosure of
various aspects including the remuneration policies, and the names of the remuneration
committee members and their attendance at meetings.

(x) Recognize the legitimate interests of stakeholders – recognize legal and other
   obligations to all legitimate stakeholders

There is recognition that, by better managing various stakeholder groups, value can
be created. Companies therefore need to have commitment to appropriate practices to
achieve this end. There is one recommendation supporting this principle, which is that
companies should establish and disclose a code of conduct to guide compliance with
legal and other obligations to legitimate stakeholders.

Under the ASX listing rules, companies are required to provide a statement in their
annual report disclosing the extent to which they have followed the best practice
recommendations. Where companies have not followed all the recommendations, they
must identify the recommendations that have not been followed and give reasons for
not following them, i.e. the 'if not, why not?' approach.

In October 2004, the Investment and Financial Services Association Limited (IFSA)
in Australia published *Corporate Governance: A Guide for Fund Managers and Corporations*,
which is commonly known as the IFSA Blue Book. This was the fifth edition, the
first one having been published in 1995. The IFSA's members manage investments on
behalf of superannuation funds and retail clients, and the Blue Book is intended to
guide the IFSA's members in monitoring the corporate governance of their investee
companies, so that good governance can be encouraged to the benefit of shareholders
and stakeholders.

The guidelines comprise two sections: one for fund managers and one for corporations.
The section for fund managers encourages constructive communications and emphasizes the importance of voting and of having a corporate governance policy, which has
a section on voting policy; fund managers should report back to the client on voting.
In relation to corporations, the guidelines cover: the annual disclosures that a company
should make in relation to corporate governance; the composition of the board of directors in terms of competency and independence; the number of permissible directorships
an individual may hold; that the chairperson should be an independent director; key
board committees and committees generally; the election of directors; performance evaluation; equity participation by non-executive directors; the respective roles of the board

and management; board and executive remuneration policy and disclosure; company meetings; the disclosure of beneficial shareholder information; major corporate changes; the company code of ethics.

In August 2005, the Australian Council of Super Investors issued its revised Corporate Governance Guidelines. These guidelines are for superannuation trustees in their monitoring of Australian listed companies. The guidelines reinforce the accountability of corporate boards and management teams to shareholders, and also emphasize the importance of having an ethical governance culture.

In addition to the above codes and guidelines, the Corporate Law Economic Reform Program (CLERP) has made a number of changes to Australia's corporate regulatory framework. Maintaining investor protection and confidence in the market is important, and issues such as director liability, disclosure, and shareholder participation have received attention.

Conclusions

The financial downturn that affected countries in the Asia-Pacific in the 1990s came as a great shock. The so-called 'tiger economies' had seen their stock markets experience meteoric rises and then that golden situation was wiped out. This change in fortunes led to many questions as to how and why this could have happened, but also as to how they would be able to rebuild themselves and attract investment back into their stock markets. As we have seen, the lack of transparency and disclosure, the misuse of corporate assets by dominant shareholders, and the lack of protection for minority shareholders' interests, have all been seen as contributory factors to the demise, and as areas that need to be improved in order to rebuild economies and attract both domestic and overseas investment.

The countries looked at in detail in this chapter have all strengthened their corporate governance codes. Without exception, the codes now recommend: fuller disclosure and accountability; transparency of process; the appointment of independent directors; recognition and protection of minority shareholders' rights. It is encouraging that these countries all seem to be moving in the right direction, and these changes should encourage more foreign direct investment and greater confidence in their stock markets.

■ **SUMMARY**

- The financial downturn that occurred in the Asia-Pacific countries in the 1990s acted as a trigger for improved corporate governance structures to be developed. The proposed changes encompassed fuller disclosure and transparency, the appointment of independent directors, and better protection of minority shareholders' rights.

- The dominant form of ownership structure in many Asia-Pacific countries tends to be concentrated either in families, or in cross-holdings. The state still exercises significant influence in a number of countries.

- In Japan, the *keiretsu*, associations of companies with holdings of shares one in the other, are slowly beginning to loosen their grip on corporate ownership but are still very influential. New corporate governance provisions provide Japanese companies with more flexibility and encourage more disclosure and the appointment of independent directors.

- In Korea, the *chaebol*, large conglomerates with extensive cross-holdings of shares, still wield enormous power. The corporate governance code emphasizes transparency and the protection of minority shareholders' rights.

- In Malaysia, companies are largely family-owned or controlled. The Malaysian corporate governance code emphasizes more transparency and disclosure, and also the importance of director training.

- China is moving towards a 'socialist market economy' and many of the state-owned enterprises have become joint stock companies with shares to be more widely held. Much of the corporate reporting in China remains quite opaque and greater reliable disclosure is generally required. However, the Corporate Governance Code's recommendations are encouraging and, furthermore, listed companies are now required to appoint an appropriate number of independent directors.

- Australia has an interesting corporate governance system that has been strengthened in recent years to give more emphasis to shareholders' rights and to the ethical conduct of corporations.

Example: Kookmin Bank, South Korea

This is an example of a South Korean bank that is recognized both domestically and internationally as having good corporate governance.

Kookmin Bank is a well-established world-class retail bank. It has a good corporate governance structure as evidenced by the fact that, in addition to other committees such as the audit committee, it has established a risk management committee and a compensation committee, which are comprised exclusively of outside directors.

Kookmin Bank has a 'Code of Ethics' that covers various aspects of the business. These aspects encompass the fundamental principles including the objective of the bank ('maximization of shareholder values and customer satisfaction'), the bank management, the social responsibility of the bank, and work ethics for officers and employees of the bank. Kookmin Bank views itself as a 'good corporate citizen' with a role in helping to improve the community.

The confidence in Kookmin Bank is evidenced by the fact that over 70 per cent of its shares are in the hands of foreign ownership.

In late 2004, Kookmin Bank was ranked fifth in Asia and best in Korea in terms of corporate governance by CLSA Asia-Pacific Markets.

Mini case study: Tokyo Electron

This is a good example of a Japanese company that has been proactive in implementing reforms to its corporate governance structure. It has been presented with awards for its good corporate governance and for its disclosure.

Tokyo Electron is a leading supplier of semiconductor and LCD production equipment globally. It had invested heavily in new technology and product development and seen its overseas sales jump nearly 30 per cent during the latter half of the 1990s.

In 1998, it decided that it needed to reform its management structure to become more transparent, to enable decisions to be made quickly and appropriately, and to delineate clear lines of responsibility. As part of this reform, the board of directors was streamlined and its role defined as 'protecting shareholders' interests and optimising corporate value'; a compensation committee was established, a director was appointed to oversee the establishment of comprehensive corporate ethics, and the oversight function of the statutory auditors was strengthened. There were also a number of reforms in relation to the strategic aspects of business structure and composition. All in all, the restructuring enabled Tokyo Electron to respond quickly and at the appropriate level to key business events, and led to increased transparency and accountability.

This proactive approach has continued and, most recently, Tokyo Electron has made changes to its disclosure in relation to directors' remuneration. In Japan, there has traditionally been little disclosure about directors' remuneration, whereas Tokyo Electron notifies its shareholders before the shareholders' meeting of the individual compensation received by a number of executives. Most Japanese companies have been reluctant to disclose information about directors' remuneration so Tokyo Electron stands out as being at the forefront of good corporate governance practice in this area too.

■ QUESTIONS

The discussion questions below cover the key learning points of this chapter. Reading of some of the additional reference material will enhance the depth of the students' knowledge and understanding of these areas.

1. What factors contributed to the financial collapse in the Asia-Pacific region in the early 1990s? How did this affect corporate governance developments?

2. How might improving corporate governance help to restore investor confidence in countries affected by financial collapse?

3. What are the defining features of the Japanese corporate governance system? Critically compare and contrast with the Korean corporate governance system.

4. How has corporate governance developed in China and what are the main obstacles to be overcome to improve effectively corporate governance?

5. Critically discuss corporate governance developments in Malaysia.

6. Critically discuss the impact of ownership structure on the development of corporate governance in the Asia-Pacific region.

■ FT ARTICLE

Korea sees rise of domestic activists

By Song Jung-a in Seoul

A $200m equity fund aims to create value in mid-sized companies by improving governance

The first domestic activist fund is being launched in South Korea, as Korean companies face increasing calls from domestic and foreign investors to improve corporate governance.

Lazard Asset Management is jumping on the South Korea shareholder activism bandwagon with a $200m equity fund, which it plans to set up in April with local shareholder activists.

The Korea Corporate Governance Fund will be managed by John Lee, a managing director at Lazard, and advised by Jang Ha-sung, a South Korean corporate governance veteran, and the Centre for Good Corporate Governance (CGCG), a local civic group calling for improved transparency at Korean companies.

Lazard and Mr Jang plan to invest in "undervalued" mid-sized Korean companies with a strong growth potential, unlike previous foreign shareholder activists who focused on big companies such as SK Corp, the country's largest oil refiner.

"We will target medium-sized companies, which are profitable and technologically competitive, but are undervalued beause of weak governance. We can create value by improving their governance," says Mr Jang, adding that the CGCG is already looking at 20 domestic firms.

Mr Jang is a director of the Asian Institute of Corporate Governance and the dean of the Korea University's business school. He has long advocated minority shareholders' rights and called for more transparency at *chaebol,* South Korea's family-run conglomerates, which still dominate the Korean economy.

His investment partner, John Lee, previously worked as the manager of the Korea Fund, the first overseas fund investing in Korean companies, in the wake of the Asian financial crisis. Mr Lee was unavailable for comment.

A briefing for potential investors was held last month in Tokyo and another event is planned in Seoul this month. A number of potential investors, including University of Virginia, Georgetown University, and Hana Financial Group, have expressed interest. Mr Jang stresses his fund will be a "long-term value investor" with a minimum lock-up period of two years. The fund will be offshore, based in Ireland.

"Korean companies are still undervalued, compared with their assets and earnings. One of the main reasons for the 'Korea Discount' is the governance risk," he says. "So we aim to create additional returns by getting rid of governance risks."

Shareholder activists have claimed that opaque management practices and a complex ownership structure contribute to the "Korea Discount" – the 20 per cent or so reduction investors price into Korean stocks because of concerns over corporate governance and geopolitical risks involving North Korea.

For example, Sovereign Asset Management, a Dubai-based investment fund, has led a high-profile attempt to oust the chairman of SK Corp, who was convicted for accounting fraud, claiming that improved governance will boost SK shares.

Mr Jang's new fund will be launched amid renewed concerns about increasing foreign influence over Korea Inc, with US financier Carl Icahn pressing KT&G to boost value through asset sales and share buybacks.

Lazard, the advisory investment bank, served as an advisor for Sovereign's investment in SK Corp. It also advised Mr Icahn on his six-month attempt to shake up Time Warner in the US. Mr Icahn is now taking on management of KT&G, South Korea's largest tobacco and ginseng company with a $10bn hostile takeover bid.

Kim Sun-woong, head of the CGSG, expects shareholder activism to get stronger in coming years, now that minority shareholders are more aware of their rights and more companies are exposed to foreign investors, who own about 40 per cent of Korean shares.

Financial Times Monday 6 March 2006

■ REFERENCES

Australian Council of Super Investors Inc. (2005), *Corporate Governance Guidelines: A Guide for Superannuation Trustees to Monitor Listed Australian Companies*, ACSI, Melbourne.

Australian Stock Exchange Corporate Governance Council (2003), *Principles of Good Corporate Governance and Best Practice Recommendations*, Australian Stock Exchange, Sydney.

Balino, T.J.T. and Ubide, A. (1999), *The Korean Financial Crisis of 1997 – A Strategy of Financial Sector Reform*, International Monetary Fund Working Paper No. WP/99/28.

Black B.S., Jang, H. and Kim, W. (2005), 'Predicting Firms' Corporate Governance Choices: Evidence from Korea', *Journal of Corporate Finance*, Vol. 12, No. 3, pp. 660–691.

Bosch (1995), *Corporate Practice and Conduct*, Woodslane Pty Ltd., Australia.

Charkham, J. (1994), *Keeping Good Company: A Study of Corporate Governance in Five Countries*, Clarendon Press, Oxford.

____ (2005), *Keeping Better Company: Corporate Governance Ten Years on*, Oxford University Press, Oxford.

China Securities Regulatory Commission (2001), *Code of Corporate Governance For Listed Companies in China*, China Securities Regulatory Commission, State Economic Trade Commission, Beijing.

____ (2001), *Guidelines for Introducing Independent Directors to the Board of Directors of Listed Companies*, China Securities Regulatory Commission, State Economic Trade Commission, Beijing.

Claessens, S., Djankov, S. and Lang, L.H.P. (2000), 'The Separation of Ownership and Control in East Asian Corporations', *Journal of Financial Economics*, 58.

____ and Fan, J.P.H. (2003), 'Corporate Governance in Asia: A Survey', *University of Amsterdam and Hong Kong University of Science and Technology Working Paper*.

Dignam, A.J. and Galanis, M. (2004), 'Australia Inside/Out: The Corporate Governance System of the Australian Listed Market', *Melbourne University Law Review*, Vol. 28, No. 3, December 2004.

Farrar, J. (2005), *Corporate Governance in Australia and New Zealand*, Oxford University Press, Oxford.

Finance Committee on Corporate Governance (2000), *Malaysian Code on Corporate Governance*, Ministry of Finance, Kuala Lumpur.

Hilmer, F.A. (1998), *Strictly Boardroom: Enhancing Governance to Improve Company Performance*, Report of the Independent Working Party into Corporate Governance, 2nd edn, Information Australia.

Investment and Financial Services Association Limited (2004), *Corporate Governance, A Guide for Fund Managers and Corporations*, IFSA, Sydney.

Jang, H. and Kim, J. (2002), 'Nascent Stages of Corporate Governance in an Emerging Market: Regulatory Change, Shareholder Activism and Samsung Electronics', *Corporate Governance: An International Review*, Vol. 10, No. 2.

Japan Corporate Governance Committee (2001), *Revised Corporate Governance Principles*, Japan Corporate Governance Forum, Tokyo.

Korean Committee on Corporate Governance (1999) *Code of Best Practice for Corporate Governance*, Korean Committee on Corporate Governance, Seoul.

Neoh, A. (2003), 'Corporate Governance in Mainland China: Where Do We Go from Here?' in *Corporate Governance and Capital Flows in a Global Economy*, P.K. Cornelius and B. Kogut (eds.), Oxford University Press, Oxford.

Okumura, H. (2002), 'Corporate Governance in Japan' in *Japanese Economy and Society under Pax-Americana*, H. Shibuya, M. Maruyama, and M. Yasaka (eds.), University of Tokyo Press, Tokyo.

On Kit Tam (1999), *The Development of Corporate Governance in China*, Edward Elgar, Cheltenham.

Schweitzer H. and Kumpan, C. (2005), 'Changes of Governance in Europe, Japan, and the US: Discussion Report' in *Corporate Governance in Context, Corporations, States and Markets in Europe, Japan and the US*, K.J. Hopt, E. Wymeersch, H. Kanda and H. Baum (eds.), Oxford University Press, Oxford.

Tokyo Stock Exchange (2004), *Principles of Corporate Governance for Listed Companies*, Tokyo Stock Exchange, Tokyo.

■ USEFUL WEBSITES

www.acsi.org.au The website of the Australian Council of Super Investors Inc., a not-for-profit organization, which provides independent research and education services to superannuation funds in relation to the corporate governance practices of investee companies.

www.asa.asn.au The website of the Australian Shareholders' Association, which has a range of material relevant to investors.

www.asx.com.au The website of the Australian Stock Exchange, which contains information relating to corporate governance, companies, and investors.

www.csrc.gov.cn The website of the China Securities Regulatory Commission has information about corporate governance developments in China.

www.jcgf.org The website of the Japan Corporate Governance Forum has information about coporate governance issues in Japan.

www.maicsa.org.my The website of the Malaysia Corporate Law Reform Programme has details of the progress of the reform programme and copies of consultative documents.

www.pspd.org The People's Solidarity for Participatory Democracy website has information about corporate governance developments and issues in South Korea.

www.sc.com.my The website of the Securities Commission in Malaysia has a range of material relating to corporate governance issues in Malaysia.

13 | Corporate Governance in South Africa, India, and Brazil

LEARNING OBJECTIVES

- To understand the background to the development of corporate governance codes in a range of countries globally

- To be aware of the different ownership structures in a global context

- To be aware of the main differences in corporate governance codes in various countries in a global context

- To have a detailed knowledge of the corporate governance codes for a sample of countries in a global context

Introduction

In this chapter, corporate governance developments in a sample of countries in a global context are examined. The countries are diverse in their cultural and legal backgrounds, in their ownership structures, and in their corporate governance structures. Nonetheless, we can see that certain core principles, seen in earlier chapters, are evident in the corporate governance codes of these countries. These core principles will help build or restore confidence in stock markets, help to ensure more transparency and disclosure, enhance protection of minority shareholders' rights, and help to ensure that the company is managed in the interests of shareholders and stakeholders, as appropriate.

Of course, as well as the existence of a corporate governance code, the firm-level corporate governance is very important – that is, to what extent a firm itself actually has good governance. Klapper and Love (2002) undertook a study of firm-level governance in 14 emerging market countries, including South Africa, India, and Brazil. They find that 'firm-level corporate governance provisions matter more in countries with weak legal environments' and their results 'suggest that firms can partially compensate for ineffective laws and enforcement by establishing good corporate governance and credible investor protection'. Hence, a firm with good corporate governance in a country with a generally weaker corporate governance will stand out from the crowd and be able to obtain capital at a lower cost, and generally be more attractive to investors.

Each of the selected countries has interesting characteristics that make it a good choice to include in this penultimate chapter to illustrate that corporate governance is relevant to all countries, whatever their ownership structure and whatever their stage of development.

South Africa has a well-developed corporate governance code. In fact, its revised Code published in 2002 is the most comprehensive in the world, and leading edge in terms of its outlook and recommendations. India's corporate governance code aims to differentiate between mandatory recommendations and non-mandatory, whilst recognizing that both categories of recommendations will result in the most effective corporate governance system. Brazil is trying to encourage compliance with its corporate governance code but the progress seems quite slow, with controlling groups still exercising disproportionate influence.

South Africa

South Africa has had a troubled and turbulent past. In the latter half of the twentieth century, there was considerable social unrest and inequality exacerbated by the policy of apartheid (racial segregation). Extensive legislation was introduced in the 1990s, which led to social and political transformation; this included the Employment Equity Act (No. 55 of 1998) and the National Environmental Management Act (No. 107 of 1998).

In 1992, a Committee on Corporate Governance was established in South Africa. Chaired by Mervyn King, the Committee produced the King Report on Corporate Governance late in 1994. The King Report (1) contained some of the most far-reaching recommendations at that time. Some eight years later, the King Report (2) (hereinafter the King Report) was published in 2002. Between the dates of the two reports (1994–2002), there was extensive legislation as mentioned above, and the King Report needed to take account of these developments. In common with its earlier version, the King Report is one of the most comprehensive and most innovative reports published to date anywhere in the world. It takes an 'inclusive' approach, in other words, the company should not develop its strategies and carry out its operations without considering the wider community, including employees, customers, and suppliers. An interesting cultural aspect is mentioned in the context of labour relations and people management, which is the tradition of consultation practised by African chiefs; clearly, consultation is part and parcel of the African psyche and so a company should take this into account in its relationship with employees and people generally.

As well as addressing what might be perceived as the traditional areas of corporate governance, such as the role and function of boards of directors, and internal audit, the King Report pays significant attention to integrated sustainability reporting including stakeholder relations, ethical practices, and social and transformation issues. The whole report is a comprehensive 354 pages, which includes detailed appendices covering areas such as board self-evaluation and developing a code of ethics. In addition, the appendices include details about the United Nations Global Compact and the Global Sullivan Principles.

Table 13.1 Summary of key characteristics influencing South African corporate governance

Feature	Key characteristic
Main business form	Public limited company
Predominant ownership structure	Institutional investors
Legal system	Common law
Board structure	Unitary
Important aspect	Inclusive approach

The King Report identifies what can be regarded as seven characteristics of good corporate governance: discipline, transparency, independence, accountability, responsibility, fairness, and social responsibility. Discipline in the context of proper and appropriate behaviour, includes acceptance of good governance, at senior management level. Transparency is the extent to which, and how easily, investors can know the true picture of what is happening in the company. Independence is the existence of appropriate mechanisms to ensure that there are no conflicts of interest at board/management level. Decision-makers in the company must be accountable for their decisions and actions, and there should be mechanisms to ensure this accountability. Management have a responsibility for their actions and should correct inappropriate actions. Fairness should exist in the consideration of the rights of various parties with an interest in the company. Finally, social responsibility is characteristic of a good corporate citizen, and companies should give a high priority to ethical standards.

The King Report contains the Code of Corporate Practices and Conduct (hereinafter the Code), which contains principles in a number of areas.

(i) Boards and directors

This section of the Code covers board best practice, the responsibilities of the directors, and director remuneration. The board is viewed as 'the focal point of the corporate governance system' and so the constitution of the board and the operation of the board and its sub-committees are of fundamental importance. The Code recommends that the board should preferably comprise a majority of non-executive directors, with sufficient of these being independent to enable shareowner interests, including minority interests, to be protected.

The roles of chair and CEO should be separate, and it is recommended that the chair is an independent non-executive director.

There should be an audit committee and a remuneration committee, and other committees as appropriate for the particular company and its operations. In relation to director remuneration, there should be a transparent process to develop policy in this area and companies should form a remuneration, or similar, committee to make recommendations on directors' pay to the board. This committee, comprised wholly or mainly of independent non-executive directors, should also be chaired by an independent non-executive director.

(ii) Risk management

The board has responsibility for the overall risk management process, with management being accountable to the board for the actual day-to-day risk management. It is the board's responsibility to form an opinion on the effectiveness of the risk management process.

It stands to reason that the board should identify areas where the business may be particularly vulnerable, and utilize accepted risk management internal controls and frameworks to ensure that such risks are appropriately monitored. A board committee may be established, possibly as a dedicated risk management committee, to help the board with reviewing risk management issues. The Code points out that risk management, rather than perhaps being viewed as only a negative process, may also give rise to opportunities to create competitive advantage.

(iii) Internal audit

Companies should establish an internal audit function with a reporting line directly between the head of internal audit and the CEO. However, if a company does not establish an internal audit function, then it must disclose this in its annual report together with why it has not done so and, in its absence, also how assurance in internal controls can be made.

Internal audit should have a plan that delineates its scope and function. The audit committee should approve the internal audit work agenda, and internal audit should report at all audit committee meetings. In addition, internal audit should liaise with the external auditors.

(iv) Integrated sustainability reporting

The Code states that each company should report every year 'on the nature and extent of its social, transformation, ethical, safety, health and environmental management policies and practices'. The board, therefore, is reporting both on the policies it has in place, and on the implementation of those policies and the resultant changes and benefits.

The company's integrity is seen as something that should be company-wide, and which should also involve the stakeholders in terms of developing appropriate standards of ethical behaviour for the company. The company should disclose the extent of its compliance with its code of ethics. Similarly, companies should think twice before doing business with those who do not seem so committed to integrity.

(v) Accounting and auditing

An audit committee should be established, comprising a majority of independent non-executive directors, the majority of whom are 'financially literate'. It should be chaired by an independent non-executive director. There should be written terms of reference, and the company should disclose in its annual report if the audit committee has adopted formal terms of reference and whether these have been complied with. The audit committee prepare a recommendation for the appointment of the external auditors, in addition to their other duties.

(vi) Relations with shareowners

There is encouragement for companies to have a meaningful dialogue with institutional investors. Companies should ensure adequate information is provided in advance to all shareowners about annual general meeting agenda items, and there should be reasonable time for discussion of items. The results of decisions made at annual general meetings should be made available to shareowners to enable particularly those who could not attend to be aware of the outcomes.

(vii) Communications

There is an emphasis on the company providing a balanced view of the company's position to stakeholders. Reporting should be clear and include non-financial as well as financial matters.

Companies listed on the Johannesburg Securities Exchange and all public sector entities are expected to abide by the recommendations of the Code on a 'comply or explain' basis. Directors therefore need to provide a statement in the annual report about compliance with the Code or give reasons for non-compliance.

India

Following on from a period of economic downturn and social unrest in 1990–91, the Indian government introduced a programme of reforms to open up the economy and encourage greater reliance on market mechanisms and less reliance on government. Further reforms were aimed at making the public sector more efficient and divestment of government holdings was initiated. There were also reforms to the banking sector to bring it into line with international norms, and to the securities market, with the Securities and Exchange Board of India (SEBI) becoming the regulator of the securities market.

The securities market was transformed as disclosure requirements were brought in to help protect shareholder's interests. Kar (2001) mentions how 'foreign portfolio investment was permitted in India since 1992 and foreign institutional investors also began to play an important role in the institutionalisation of the market'. All of the reforms above led to a much-improved environment in which corporate governance was able to develop.

India has a range of business forms, including public limited companies, which are listed on the stock exchange, domestic private companies and foreign companies. Ownership data is difficult to find because the number of studies carried out in this area is few, however it is clear that, as the economy has opened up, so the institutional investors are increasing their share of the market.

The Confederation of Indian Industries published a 'Desirable Code of Corporate Governance' in 1998 and a number of forward-looking companies took its recommendations on board. However, many companies still had poor governance practices, which led to concerns about their financial reporting practices, their accountability, and ultimately

Table 13.2 Summary of key characteristics influencing Indian corporate governance

Feature	Key characteristic
Main business form	Public limited company
Predominant ownership structure	Corporate bodies; families; but institutional investors' ownership increasing
Legal system	Common law
Board structure	Unitary
Important aspect	Some aspects of the Code are mandatory recommendations

to losses being suffered by investors, and the resultant loss of confidence that this caused.

SEBI formally established the Committee on Corporate Governance in May 1999, chaired by Shri Kumar Mangalam Birla. The Report of the Kumar Mangalam Birla Committee on Corporate Governance (hereinafter the Report) was published in 2000.

The Report emphasizes the importance of corporate governance to future growth of the capital market and the economy. Three key aspects underlying corporate governance are defined as accountability, transparency, and equality of treatment for all stakeholders. The impact of corporate governance on both shareholders and stakeholders is mentioned, although the corporate objective is seen as one of maximizing shareholder value, and indeed the Committee views the fundamental objective of corporate governance as 'enhancement of shareholder value, keeping in view the interests of other stakeholders'. The Committee feels that companies should see the Code as 'a way of life'. The recommendations apply to all listed private and public sector companies, and are split into mandatory requirements (ones that the Committee sees as essential for effective corporate governance) enforceable via the listing rules, and non-mandatory (but nonetheless recommended as best practice).

(i) Board of directors

This section of the Code covers the composition of the board, and independent directors. The board provides leadership and strategic guidance for the company and is at all times accountable to the shareholders. The Code recommends that not less than 50 per cent of the board is comprised of non-executive directors; where there is a non-executive chairman, then at least one-third of the board should comprise independent directors, but where there is an executive chairman, then at least half of the board should be independent. The latter recommendation is mandatory.

(ii) Nominee directors

The Indian system allows for nominee directors to be put forward by financial or investment institutions to safeguard their investment in the company. The Code decided to allow this practice to continue, but stated that such nominees should have the same responsibility as other directors and be accountable to the shareholders generally.

(iii) Chairman of the board

Whilst recognizing that the roles of chairman and chief executive are different, the Code recognizes that the roles may be combined and performed by one individual in some instances.

(iv) Audit committee

There are a number of mandatory recommendations in the Code in relation to audit committees, including the recommendation that a qualified and independent audit committee is established to help to enhance confidence in the company's disclosures. The committee should comprise a minimum of three members, all of whom are non-executive, with a majority being independent; it should be chaired by an independent director. At least one director should have appropriate financial knowledge. The audit committee is empowered to seek external advice as appropriate, and interestingly, to seek information from any employee.

(v) Remuneration committee

A remuneration committee should be established to make recommendations on executive directors' remuneration. The committee should be comprised of at least three non-executive directors, and chaired by an independent director. A mandatory requirement is that there should be disclosures in the annual report relating to 'all elements of remuneration package of all the directors, i.e. salary, benefits, bonuses, stock options, pension, etc.' together with 'details of fixed component and performance-linked incentives, along with performance criteria'. Finally, another mandatory requirement is that the board of directors should decide the remuneration of the non-executive directors.

(vi) Board procedures

Mandatory requirements in relation to board meetings are: first, that they should be held at least four times a year with a maximum of four months between any two meetings; second, that a director should not be involved in more than ten committees or act as chairman of more than five committees across all companies with which he is a director.

(vii) Management

The role of the management of the company (chief executive, executive directors, and key management personnel) in ensuring the smooth running of the day-to-day activities of the company is emphasized. A mandatory recommendation is that there should be disclosure in the annual report, either as part of the directors' report, or as a 'management discussion and analysis' report, about the company's position, its outlook, performance, and other relevant areas of interest to shareholders. There should also be disclosure of any material financial/commercial transactions in which management has a personal interest that may have a potential conflict with the interest of the company.

(viii) Shareholders

Shareholders are entitled to be able to participate effectively in the annual general meeting. Therefore, in support of this aim, it is a mandatory recommendation that, on the appointment of new, or reappointment of existing, directors, the shareholders are provided with relevant information about the director(s). Similarly, companies are mandated to disclose information, including their quarterly results and presentations, to company analysts which may be made available via the internet.

The growing influence of institutional investors is recognized, along with the fact that they have a responsibility to exercise their votes.

(ix) Manner of implementation

There are mandatory recommendations that a company should have a separate section on corporate governance in its annual report, including a detailed compliance report. Non-compliance with any mandatory recommendations should be highlighted, as should the level of compliance with non-mandatory recommendations. A company should obtain a certificate from its auditors in relation to compliance with the mandatory recommendations and it should be attached to the directors' report, which is sent each year to all the shareholders, and to the Stock Exchange.

The Indian Code is clearly rather complex having as it does a series of mandatory and non-mandatory recommendations. The feasibility of this approach will lie in a number of areas: first, the extent to which companies are willing to implement the recommendations; second, the growing influence of shareholders and how effectively they can exercise their voice; third, the approach taken by the Stock Exchange in India in terms of enforcing compliance.

Chakrabarti (2005) provides an interesting review of the evolution of corporate governance in India and highlights the fact that, whilst India has good corporate governance codes/guidelines, there is poor adoption of the recommendations in many companies.

Brazil

The economies of various countries in South America were also affected adversely by the world economic downturn in the 1990s. As with many other countries around the globe, this led to a demand for more transparency and accountability, and the need to restore and build confidence in the stock market.

Many businesses in South America are dominated by a controlling group, often representing family interests. This pattern can be seen in Brazil, Mexico, and Chile, for example. In this section, we will look in more detail at the corporate governance of Brazil.

As with most South American countries, in Brazil, the protection of minority interests has traditionally been a weak area, with minority shareholders lacking both access to information and the means to take appropriate action. In the past, companies have often issued preferred shares as a means of raising capital. Although preferred shares carry a dividend, they do not usually have voting rights except in certain specific circumstances. Therefore holders of preferred shares are often in a weak position and vulnerable to the whims of controlling shareholders.

The Sao Paulo Stock Exchange (BOVESPA) has introduced a new index: the ICG (Index of Shares under Special Corporate Governance Registration). Companies can

Table 13.3 Summary of key characteristics influencing Brazilian corporate governance

Feature	Key characteristic
Main business form	Public limited company
Predominant ownership structure	Controlling owner (corporations or individuals)
Legal system	Civil law
Board structure	Dual
Important aspect	Fiscal councils

register at different levels: Level 1 and Level 2. Level 1 requirements include 'compliance with disclosure regulations for transactions involving shares issued by the company's controlling shareholders or directors' and 'disclosure of shareholder agreements and stock option programs'.

The Brazilian Institute of Corporate Governance (BICG) published a Code of Best Practice of Corporate Governance in 2001. The BICG was established as a civil not-for-profit association to act as a leading forum for corporate governance in Brazil. The Code identifies transparency, accountability, and fairness as the 'pillars' of corporate governance. The Code is very helpful in identifying some of the key features of Brazilian companies, such as the fact that the majority have controlling owners. It also recommends that family-controlled businesses should establish a family council 'to settle family issues and keep them apart from the governance of the company'.

The corporate governance structure is essentially a two-tier, or dual, structure because Brazilian companies have a board of directors and also a fiscal council. The fiscal council is elected by, and accountable to, the owners. The BICG Code states that the fiscal council 'is created because the minorities and the owners of non-voting stock have no influence and little information. The Fiscal Council is a partial remedy to this. It has access to information and can express its opinion in the annual general meeting'. Its access to information is quite extensive because its members can have access to copies of board of directors' meeting minutes, financial statements, and other information. They may also have access to the independent auditors.

The Comissao de Valores Mobiliarios (CVM) is the Securities and Exchange Commission of Brazil, and in June 2002, the CVM issued recommendations on corporate governance. The Code covers four main areas: transparency of ownership and control, and shareholder meetings; structure and responsibilities of the board of directors; minority shareholder protection; accounting and auditing. It is interesting that there is a specific section dedicated to minority shareholder protection.

(i) Transparency of ownership and control, shareholder meetings

All shareholders should be provided with full information about agenda items to be discussed at the general shareholders' meeting. The meeting should be arranged on a date/time that will not preclude attendance by shareholders; where there are complex agenda items, then the company should give at least 30 days' notice of the meeting.

A list of shareholders, together with the amount of their shareholdings, should be available on request by shareholders. There should be clear regulations laid down about the process for voting on general meeting agenda items.

(ii) Structure and responsibilities of the board of directors

The board of directors should safeguard the assets of the business whilst ensuring that the company's goals and objectives are met. There is an emphasis on maximizing return on investment.

The roles of chair and CEO should not be carried out by the same person. The board should comprise five to ten directors, at least two of whom should have appropriate experience of finance/accounting practices. There are three categories of director: internal, being officers or employees of the company; external, being those who do not work in the company but are not classed as independent; independent directors. The Code states that 'as many board members as possible should be independent of company management'.

Board sub-committees may be set up to focus on certain aspects, for example, an audit committee. Board members are entitled to appropriate information to enable them to fulfil their function and also to take external advice as necessary.

An interesting recommendation is that holders of preferred shares should be entitled to nominate and elect a representative to the board of directors. This would give holders of preferred shares a voice and would be particularly helpful where there is a group of controlling shareholders who might otherwise not consider the views of holders of preferred shares.

(iii) Minority shareholder protection

Recent changes to legislation have instructed Brazilian public companies not to issue more than 50 per cent of their capital as preferred shares. Preferred shares (as in the UK) have limited voting rights, usually to vote only on issues that directly affect them rather than on all general meeting agenda issues. This part of the Code recommends that there should be no voting restrictions for preferred shares in relation to decisions being made on a number of areas, including alteration of the company's activities, and mergers/spin-offs, as these areas impact on all shareholders.

There is a specific recommendation that, if dividends are not paid to shares with the right to fixed or guaranteed dividends, then those shares immediately acquire the right to vote; also, if the company does not pay dividends for three years, then any non-voting shares will acquire the right to vote. These are particularly important recommendations in situations where controlling shareholders may try to deprive minority shareholders of their right to the company's cash flows in the form of dividends.

There are a number of recommendations that relate to utilizing the idea of 'tag-along', including that, if there is a change in control, then both controlling shareholders and minority shareholders should be paid the same price for their shares. Disagreements between either the company and its shareholders, or the controlling shareholders and the minority shareholders, may be solved by arbitration.

(iv) Accounting and auditing

Quarterly financial statements should be published, along with details of the factors that have affected business performance over the quarter.

This section of the Code also contains recommendations in relation to the fiscal board, which should have between three and five members. The Code states: 'Holders of preferred shares and holders of common shares, excluding shareholders in the controlling group, should have the right to elect an equal number of members as the controlling group. The controlling group should renounce the right to elect the last member (third or fifth member), who should be elected by the majority of share capital, in a shareholders' meeting at which each share represents one vote, regardless of its type or sort, including controlling shares.' The Code emphasizes that all appropriate information should be made available to members of the fiscal board so that their 'supervisory capacity shall be the broadest possible'.

An audit committee should be established, comprising board members with knowledge of finance, and there should be at least one member representing minority shareholders. The audit committee will oversee the relationship with the auditor; the fiscal board and the audit committee should meet with the auditors.

The Code recommends that the board should either prohibit or restrict the amount of non-audit services provided to the company by the company's auditor in order to try to ensure that the auditor retains independence.

The CVM requires that public companies include in their annual report the level to which they comply with the recommendations, utilizing a comply or explain approach.

In 2004, the Brazilian Institute of Corporate Governance published an updated and enlarged edition of the Code of Best Practice of Corporate Governance. The Code aims to provide guidelines to all types of company, ranging from publicly or privately held corporations to non-governmental organizations, with the aim of increasing company value, improving corporate performance, facilitating access to capital at lower costs and contributing to the long-term survival of the company.

The Code has six sections: ownership, the board of directors, management, independent auditing, the fiscal council, and conduct and conflicts of interest.

(i) Ownership

A number of points are covered under this section, including: that every shareholder is a company owner, commensurate with his/her respective share in the company's capital; the 'one share, one vote' concept is advocated; there is discussion of the general assembly and the powers it has; a minimum of 30 days' notice of the annual general meeting (AGM) of the company should be given; the agenda and documentation for the AGM should be circulated to all shareholders well in advance of the meeting itself; the responsibilities of the family council are outlined, such as differentiating between family and company interests, preserving family values, succession planning, and establishing criteria to appoint members to the board of directors.

(ii) Board of directors

This section includes the recommendations that every organization should have a board of directors, of between five and nine members, elected by its owners, and it should take into account other stakeholders, corporate objectives, and corporate sustainability. An advisory board is recommended, particularly in certain companies such as family companies and private companies; the mission of the board is to protect and add value to the company and maximize the return on investment. The responsibilities of the board are detailed, together with the recommendation that there are internal regulations laid down for the activities of the board. The roles of chair and CEO should be split. Board committees including an audit committee may be set up and the latter should be made up preferably of independent directors; criteria for independent directors are discussed as are director qualifications. There should be an annual formal performance evaluation of the board and of individual directors; directors' compensation should reflect their experience and the time and effort they put in. Succession planning should be in place, and there should be induction training for new directors and continuing education thereafter. Risk management should be undertaken, and the company's policies on social, environmental, occupational, and health safety practices should be disclosed at least annually.

(iii) Management

The CEO is accountable to the board of directors; the CEO and corporate officers are accountable for a transparent relationship with stakeholders. There should be adequate disclosure, which should be clear and well balanced, and the annual report should include mention of the company's corporate governance practices, shareholdings, and compensation of directors, and be prepared in accordance with international accounting standards. There should be a system of internal controls, a code of conduct, an appropriate structure for management compensation, and access to information for the directors and fiscal council.

(iv) Independent auditing

Every organization should have an independent auditor who should express clearly their opinion on the financial statements. The board of directors and/or the audit committee should establish a work plan and the fees of the independent auditors. The independent auditors should report issues of concern to the audit committee, or in its absence, to the board, and the independence of auditors is discussed in relation to the length of their contract and to the provision of non-audit services.

(v) The Fiscal Council

The Fiscal Council is described in the Code as 'an essential part of the Brazilian companies' governance system', although it is, however, non-mandatory. Its purpose is to oversee the actions of the companies' administrative bodies and to give its opinion on certain matters to the owners. It acts as a tool 'designed to add value to the company, since it works as an independent control for the owners of the company'. The controlling and minority shareholders should discuss the composition of the Fiscal Council prior to its election, at the assembly meeting, in order to ensure an appropriate mix of professional backgrounds.

(vi) Conduct and conflicts of interest

Each organization should have a code of conduct, covering such areas as conflicts of interest, discrimination in the workplace, political activities, community relations, company share-trading policies, loans between related parties, and lawsuits/arbitration, which is followed by everyone in the company.

There are four basic principles of the Code: transparency, fairness, accountability, and corporate responsibility. With regard to the last principle, the Code states:

corporate responsibility is a broader view of corporate strategy, contemplating all kinds of relations with the community where the company operates. The 'social role' of the company should include the creation of wealth and job opportunities, work force skills and diversity, promotion of scientific advancements through technology, and improved standards of living through educational, cultural, social, and environmental initiatives. This principle should include preferred treatment of local people and resources.

Conclusions

In this chapter, the corporate governance of three very different countries has been discussed. We have seen that South Africa, India, and Brazil have different cultural influences, legal systems, and corporate governance structures (the first two have a unitary board system, the last a two-tier board system). However, there appears to be a certain commonality of approach to their corporate governance codes, with an emphasis on transparency and accountability, and the desire to enhance the protection of minority shareholders' rights. There is an emphasis on the importance of having a balanced board with an appropriate proportion of independent directors, and also recognition that a company cannot operate in isolation but should consider the interests of its various stakeholder groups.

These countries, diverse as they are in many respects, illustrate that corporate governance is relevant and valuable to countries around the globe. Over time, it is to be expected that corporate governance will improve, as countries seek to attract international investment and maintain investor confidence.

■ **SUMMARY**

- The financial downturn that occurred in many countries in the 1990s has had an impact in driving forward corporate governance globally. Countries are seeking to improve their corporate governance to help to restore confidence in the markets by increasing transparency and disclosure, and ensuring better protection of minority shareholders' rights.

- South Africa arguably has the most comprehensive corporate governance code in the world. The Code takes an inclusive approach, paying significant attention to integrated sustainability reporting including stakeholder relations, ethical practices, and social and transformation issues.

- India has a unitary board system. The corporate governance code splits recommendations into mandatory and non-mandatory recommendations. Both are desirable but the mandatory recommendations are seen as core to effective corporate governance.

- Brazil is fairly typical of South American countries, with controlling groups and a lack of effective mechanisms for minority shareholders' protection of rights. Brazil has a two-tier structure, with a fiscal board acting as a balance to the board of directors.

Example: Petrobras, Brazil

This is a good example of a Latin American company, Petrobras, which has good corporate governance. It has been the recipient of several awards and has a corporate governance code, and a comprehensive website with disclosures relating to corporate governance, environmental and social policy.

Founded in 1953, Petrobras specializes in the oil, gas, and power industry, and is involved in various aspects including production, refining, and distribution. It is one of the largest oil companies in the world.

Petrobras made significant changes to improve its corporate governance structure in the late 1990s, to include reducing the size of the board of directors from 12 to 9 members to be elected by the shareholders in general meeting, and establishing the right of minority shareholders to elect one board member. There is a Fiscal Council comprised of five members elected by the annual general meeting. Three members represent the Federal Government; one represents the minority shareholders owning common (ordinary) shares and one the shareholders of preferred shares. There is also an Executive Board and a Business Committee. The former consists of a president and six members elected by the board of directors, and is responsible for the integrated management of the company's business; the latter is comprised of the president of the company and executive directors, and its purpose is to encourage integration and greater efficiency in the management of the business. In addition, Management Committees function as forums for discussion and in-depth study of issues to be discussed by the Business Committee. The three Management Committees are the Investment Committee, Business Area Committee, and Corporate and Services Committee. These committees are comprised the main managers of the departments involved, and should preferably have at least one member belonging to the Business Committee. It is also recommended that they should not have more than 12 members.

Petrobras has a Code of Ethics and one of its principles states 'our daily concern with efficiency, competitiveness and profitability cannot take the place of ethical behaviour'. It states also that 'the Code of Ethics acts as a link and base for the mechanisms of good corporate governance'.

Mini case study: SABMiller, South Africa

SabMiller has both a South African and a UK listing. It has good corporate governance and disclosure practices, and displays a good awareness of stakeholders' interests.

In 2002, SAB plc, a company with brewing interests dating back to the 1880s, acquired Miller Brewing, and the company became known as SABMiller plc. SABMiller plc is the world's leading brewer in developing markets.

SABMiller views corporate governance as a 'process through which its shareholders may derive assurance that, in protecting and adding value to SABMiller's financial and human investment, the group is being managed ethically, according to prudently determined risk parameters'.

The board of directors comprises two executive directors and 11 non-executive directors with four of the non-executive directors classed as independent. The company has an audit committee, nomination committee, remuneration committee, and corporate accountability and risk assurance committee (CARAC). SABMiller gives comprehensive disclosure of the function/role of each of the key board committees, including the CARAC, established in 2001, with the main objective being 'to assist the board in the discharge of its duties relating to corporate accountability and associated risk and opportunities in terms of direction, assurance and reporting for the group. The committee also provides independent and objective oversight'.

The company aims to engage in appropriate dialogue with institutional investors and encourages its shareholders to attend annual general meetings and ask questions as appropriate.

SABMiller provides good disclosure of its company values, which 'guide us in our relations with all those who have a direct interest in the business – our stakeholders – and inform the Guiding Principles which govern those relationships'. The company values include respecting the rights and dignity of individuals, being a responsible corporate citizen, and respecting the values and cultures of the communities in which they operate.

SABMiller was named 'best company to work for' in South Africa, and is seeking to encourage diversity in its workforce globally. The company published information on its website relating to its policies on, and measurement of, environmental impacts and social impacts, Environmental measures include measures of the efficient use of water and CO_2 emissions; social impacts relating to the workforce include accident rates and days allocated to training.

■ QUESTIONS

The discussion questions below cover the key learning points of this chapter. Reading of some of the additional reference material will enhance the depth of the students' knowledge and understanding of these areas.

1. Critically discuss the potential advantages and disadvantages of an 'inclusive' approach to corporate governance.

2. To what extent do you think it appropriate that stakeholders' interests should be taken into consideration?

3. Critically discuss the problems that minority shareholders may face in the presence of controlling shareholders.

4. What might be the advantages or disadvantages of a corporate governance code that splits recommendations into mandatory and non-mandatory?

A responsible balancing act

Global companies must be sensitive to different concerns of consumers worldwide but must avoid double standards, writes **Alison Maitland**

To Chinese consumers, the hallmark of a socially responsible company is safe, high-quality products. For Germans, it is secure employment. In South Africa, what matters most is a company's contribution to social needs such as healthcare and education.

Public expectations of companies are rising everywhere – but consumers' top concerns vary substantially between countries and regions, according to a new study by GlobeScan, an international opinion research company.

There are common threads: consumers in the US, France, Italy, Switzerland, the Philippines and much of South America agree that the most important thing a company must do if it wants to be regarded as socially responsible is to treat employees fairly.

But the differences stand out – and they mean that multinationals cannot hope to build public trust with a single global message that ignores specific concerns in Canada or Chile, Italy or India.

"This is not an argument for cultural relativism, but rather for a careful balance of global and local responsibility," says Lord Holme, chairman of GlobeScan and a former director of Rio Tinto. "The principles and the corporate commitment ought to be the same everywhere, otherwise you get straight into double standards," he says.

"But you should very carefully consult with local communities [in order] to make sure that, in applying universal principles, you are not minimising what matters to them."

Time and again, GlobeScan found that people in different countries had a different perception of what constitutes good corporate responsibility.

In Turkey, the most important demonstration of corporate responsibility is charitable donations.

In Australia, Canada, Indonesia and the UK, respondents most often mentioned environmental protection.

In China, India and Russia, good service and product quality were listed as crucial. "For Chinese people, a company should first of all be honest and not deceive customers," says Huixin Ke, GlobeScan's research partner in China.

"This applies particularly to the food and electronics industries. In the past year, several food companies were exposed for not strictly following national production standards." She suggests that these concerns will shift over time. "With the development of the economy, Chinese people will expect more and more of a good company in terms of CSR." Indeed, perceptions do vary not only between countries but also within them, especially over time. Today in Argentina, for example, consumers put job creation and fair treatment of employees top of their list of expectations of big companies, reflecting high unemployment and concern about poverty.

But back in the 1980s, when there was high inflation, their main concern was that companies keep prices down, says Ricardo Hermelo of TNS Gallup Argentina, GlobeScan's research partner in the country.

People in different countries had a different perception of what constitutes good corporate responsibility

"The opinion that citizens have about what a firm should do to be considered socially responsible is a dynamic perception related to the social agenda.''

While consumers' expectations of companies have grown, their ratings of corporate performance have fallen in the last four years. Even industries such as computers and telecommunications, which have the highest ratings for social and environmental performance, have slipped in the public's perception.

Only banking and finance has a slightly higher rating than two years ago.

In the minds of consumers, companies' responsibilities fall into two categories, says GlobeScan's 2005 Corporate Social Responsibility Monitor.

First, there are "operational" responsibilities, which include product safety, environmental protection, fair treatment of employees and ensuring an ethical supply chain. More than 70 per cent of consumers in the 21 countries surveyed by GlobeScan hold companies completely responsible for these. Operational responsibilities are a matter of risk management: failure to fulfil them can seriously damage a company's reputation.

Second, there are so-called "citizenship" responsibilities: solving social problems, reducing the divide between rich and poor or tackling human rights abuses. These are actions that companies do not have to undertake as part of their normal business operations. Fewer than half of consumers hold them fully responsible for these.

Companies that take on "citizenship" responsibilities can differentiate themselves and boost their reputation. But there is a health warning: a company that is tempted to pursue reputation enhancement at the expense of risk management is wasting its time.

"Our findings show that the lack of CSR at the operational level cannot be compensated for by more socially oriented citizenship activities," says Chris Coulter, vice-president of GlobeScan. "The public is more likely to punish companies seen as performing poorly on the operational side than reward companies that exceed their expectations on the citizenship side."

There is, however, a north-south divide. Consumers in South America and South Africa, in particular, place greater emphasis on companies fulfilling social responsibilities, while those in North America and Europe have very high expectations in terms of product safety and the environment.

What lessons should companies draw from the research? Bob Langert, senior director for corporate responsibility at McDonald's, one of the most global of all brands, says that the findings are already being channelled to country managers "so that they can get the pulse of what's important in their countries". He is struck by the finding that consumers hold companies more responsible for the things over which they have direct influence. In particular, he points to high expectations about the way people are treated – both direct employees and those further down the supply chain. Corporate responsibility and employee loyalty are intimately linked, he notes. "Employees want to work for a company that has these values."

McDonald's is one of a handful of global brands including Coca-Cola, Nestle and PepsiCo, that have the dubious honour of being named by some respondents as the most socially responsible company they can think of and by others as the most irresponsible.

This can be explained by the fact that consumers fall into distinct categories. According to GlobeScan's analysis, the biggest segment comprises "demanding regulators", who tend to be female, low-income consumers in developing countries. They have a good opinion of corporate social performance but also strongly favour government regulation of companies. This category has been shrinking since 2001.

"Inactive capitalists", the next biggest segment, tend to be high-earners, male and employed by large companies.

They view industry favourably and are ethically inactive consumers and shareholders. But they increasingly expect companies to meet their operational responsibilities.

Third in size, and growing since 2001, are "mainstream activists". These, too, tend to be men on high incomes; they have the highest level of internet access of any group. Unlike inactive capitalists, however, they are very critical of business and are ethically active consumers and shareholders.

Executives attempting to get their heads around these different, and often demanding, consumer groups face another big challenge: the scepticism that often greets corporate communications about social and environmental initiatives.

The study finds that consumers in Brazil, China, Indonesia, the Philippines, South Africa and the US are most receptive to the formal kinds of corporate messages.

Scepticism remains high, however, in Mexico, Canada, Australia and Europe. Globescan concludes: "Building trust and formulating more informal communication strategies will be necessary to win over consumers in these markets."

Financial Times Wednesday 1 June 2005

5. What commonalities seem to be emerging in various corporate governance codes?

6. Critically discuss the drivers to corporate governance reform in a global context.

■ REFERENCES

Brazilian Institute of Corporate Governance (2001), *Code of Best Practice of Corporate Governance*, BICG, Sao Paulo.

____ (2004), *Code of Best Practice of Corporate Governance*, BICG, Sao Paulo.

Chakrabarti R. (2005), *Corporate Governance in India – Evolution and Challenges*. Available at SSRN: http://ssrn.com/abstract=649857.

Comissao de Valores Mobiliarios (2002), *CVM Recommendations on Corporate Governance*, CVM, Rio de Janeiro.

Confederation of Indian Industry (1998), *Desirable Corporate Governance in India – A Code*, Delhi.

Kar P. (2001), 'Corporate Governance in India' in *Corporate Governance in Asia, A Comparative Perspective*, OECD, Paris.

King, M. (2002), *King Report on Corporate Governance*, Institute of Directors, Johannesburg.

Klapper, L.F. and Love, I. (2002), 'Corporate Governance, Investor Protection, and Performance in Emerging Markets', *World Bank Policy Research Working Paper 2818*, World Bank, Washington DC.

Kumar Mangalam Birla (2000), *Report of the Kumar Mangalam Birla Committee on Corporate Governance*, Securities and Exchange Board of India, Delhi.

■ USEFUL WEBSITES

www.ciionline.org The Confederation of Indian Industry website has information about corporate governance issues in India.

www.ecgi.org The website of the European Corporate Governance Institute contains codes from around the world.

http://econ.worldbank.org The World Bank website has comprehensive information about various corporate governance issues and reports.

www.ibgc.org.br The website of the Institute of Brazilian Corporate Governance has information about various corporate governance issues in Brazil.

www.jse.co.za The website of the JSE Securities Exchange South Africa contains useful information relating to South Africa.

www.sebi.gov.in The website of the Securities and Exchange Board of India has information about various issues in India.

14 | Conclusions

This chapter is a useful point to review the main themes that have been covered in this book and to sum up developments that have occurred in corporate governance in the last decade. We have seen that various corporate collapses and financial scandals have been the impetus for many companies to improve their corporate governance. The loss of confidence produced by corporate failures can be truly devastating, reverberating not just in the country where the collapse occurs but around the globe. We are all too aware of the consequences of Enron, Royal Ahold, and Parmalat – their effects have been felt across the world and, in some cases, their fallout continues. Yet that does not seem to stop new scandals from occurring and one thing we can be sure of is that there will be more, and maybe bigger, scandals in the future. Therefore, corporate governance has a heavy load on its shoulders if it is to be effective in trying to stop financial scandals and collapses. It may be that it can only, at best, partially succeed, but then it will still have been a worthwhile investment because investor confidence will be higher, corporations will be in better shape, investors will be more active and involved, and the views and interests of stakeholder groups will be given more consideration.

As we have seen, corporate governance is concerned with both the internal aspects of the company, such as internal control and board structure, and the external aspects, such as the company's relationship with its shareholders and other stakeholders. Corporate governance is also seen as an essential mechanism to help the company to attain its corporate objectives and monitoring performance is a key element in achieving the objectives. Corporate governance is fundamental to well-managed companies and to ensuring that they operate at optimum efficiency.

Interestingly, despite the recognition that one model of corporate governance cannot be applied to all companies in all countries, there does seem to be convergence on certain common core principles, usually based around the OECD Principles of Corporate Governance (1999) and their subsequent revision in 2004, and often influenced by the Cadbury report (1992) recommendations. However, the growing influence of other organizations has also been noted, with the World Bank and OECD providing the impetus for the Global Corporate Governance Forum, the Commonwealth Association for Corporate Governance doing a sterling job in promoting corporate governance, and the International Corporate Governance Network (ICGN) proving an influential group that has issued its own guidelines and reports on a number of corporate governance issues, ranging from global corporate governance principles, to executive remuneration, to barriers to cross-border voting. The ICGN's ongoing programme includes work on shareholders' responsibilities and shareholders' rights. The former aspect is updating the ICGN's statement on shareholder responsibility and developing a set of best practice guidance for the internal governance of institutional investors, whilst the latter aspect maintains a 'watching brief' on shareholder rights globally and informs the work of other committees.

Corporate governance is indeed truly international. As mentioned previously, a corporate collapse in one country can have knock-on effects around the globe, the fallout rippling like waves in a pool. The impact of Enron, for example, has been felt across the world, not least because of the Sarbanes–Oxley Act, which the US legislature has decreed applies to all companies listed on a US stock exchange, including non-US firms that have a US listing. The EU is currently looking at reforms that will impact on the corporate governance of Member States. Notable amongst the proposed EU reforms is a directive to facilitate shareholder voting in EU countries, including ensuring shareholders have all relevant information in a timely manner, the facilitation of postal and proxy voting, and the abolition of share blocking. Practically every month, a new corporate governance code, or revision to an existing one, is produced somewhere in the globe with the aim of increasing transparency, disclosure, or accountability.

Corporate governance is just as applicable to a family-owned business as to one with a diverse shareholder base, and just as applicable to a public limited company as to a state-owned enterprise. Whatever the form of business organization, a good corporate governance structure can help ensure the longevity of the organization by means of appropriate internal controls, management structures, performance measures, succession plans, and full consideration of shareholder and wider stakeholder interests. The role of independent non-executive directors is a crucial one in helping to ensure that good governance is present, both in form – and in substance.

We have seen too that the legal and ownership structures, whilst influencing the corporate governance structure, in no way negate the necessity for such a structure to be in place. Legal systems based on common law tend to give greater protection of shareholders' rights, including minority shareholders' rights, whereas legal systems based on civil law tend to give less protection. This has influenced the way that ownership structures have developed, with common-law system countries tending to have more public companies with widely dispersed share ownership, and civil law system countries tending to have more ownership by families or blockholders. In each system, however, a strong case can be made for the benefits of good corporate governance.

The growing trend in a number of countries for institutional investors to be the dominant shareholder group has had an impact on the development of corporate governance in those countries, such as the UK and the USA. The role that institutional investors can play in corporate governance is significant, although they have been criticized for not being active enough, not really caring about the companies in which they invest, not trying to change things for the better, in short not acting as owners. However, there now seems to be a change of mindset, partly spurred on by the institutional investors themselves, partly by governments, and partly by the ultimate beneficiaries whom they represent. Institutional investors are coming under increasing pressure to be more activist in corporate governance matters, and to be proactive in their rights and responsibilities as shareholders. This has led to some highly visible changes including more institutional investors being prepared to vote against management, for example, on executive directors' remuneration packages. The level of voting overall by institutional investors is also increasing, albeit slowly, as they recognize that the vote is an asset of share ownership with an economic value and that they should therefore exercise their votes. Institutional investors are gradually exercising their 'voice' more effectively by constructive dialogue with management, by voting, and by focus lists, to name but a few ways. Equally, institutional investors are themselves now coming under more scrutiny and there seems to be a desire to 'round the circle' and to have more transparency and disclosure from institutional investors, and more accountability to their ultimate beneficiaries: ordinary men and women who have an interest in what institutional investors are doing. The ultimate beneficiaries may be contributing to a pension scheme, or may already be retirees, or may simply be investing into the market. Whatever their interest, the institutional investors are wielding large amounts of power by virtue of millions of individuals who essentially are the roots from which the tree of institutional investment grows. Institutional investors should be acting as owners and they should also themselves be more accountable to the suppliers of their funds, the investors and policyholders whom they ultimately represent. There is also now an increasing emphasis on the role and responsibilities of the trustees of pension funds, with more emphasis being placed on trustees being appointed with appropriate experience and the facility to undertake training specifically related to their role.

With the change in 2000 to the UK Pensions Act, pension fund trustees had to state their policy on social, environmental, and ethical issues. There seems now to be a growing awareness of these issues and companies themselves will have to consider their stance on corporate social responsibility issues more fully with the growing recognition that a company cannot act in isolation from its wider stakeholder groups, including employees, customers, suppliers, and the local community, but must take account of their interests too.

Many of the 'hot issues' of corporate governance, including directors' remuneration, directors' performance; the role and independence of non-executive directors; the internal governance of institutional shareholders, the role of pension fund trustees, and the social responsibilities of companies, will no doubt continue as the most debated issues for some time to come. At the same time, in both developed and developing markets, there will continue to be a focus on improving corporate governance, especially in relation to transparency and disclosure, for without that, one cannot determine how well a company is performing, whether it is acting in a socially responsible way, and whether it is being run and managed appropriately. There is an old saying that 'knowledge is power' and shareholders must have knowledge about companies to enable them to fulfil their role as owners. Part of that role is to try to ensure that companies perform to their best capabilities, and the evidence increasingly points to the fact that good corporate governance and corporate performance are linked. This is yet another reason why corporate governance will continue to have a high profile across the globe.

Corporate governance, and corporate social responsibility, can be seen as areas that can help to make lives better: not just the corporate lives, the directors, managers, and shareholders, but the lives of the various stakeholder groups too. Society at large may, in the longer term, become better off in a holistic sense, not only commercially but in terms of overall well-being. Charkham (1994) summed this up with his usual intuitive insight when he said it is

vital to keep a system of corporate governance under review. It is as important to a nation as any other crucial part of its institutional framework, because on it depends a good portion of the nation's prosperity; it contributes to its social cohesion in a way too little recognized. A proper framework for the exercise of power is an economic necessity, a political requirement, and a moral imperative.

Corporate governance therefore seems likely to continue its high-profile growth and will no doubt evolve to meet new challenges to be faced in the future, some of which we are already aware of, some hinted at, and some still, as yet, unknown.

■ **REFERENCES**

Cadbury, Sir Adrian (1992), *Report of the Committee on the Financial Aspects of Corporate Governance*, Gee & Co. Ltd, London.

Charkham, J. (1994), *Keeping Good Company: A Study of Corporate Governance in Five Countries*, Oxford University Press, Oxford.

OECD (1999), *Principles of Corporate Governance*, OECD, Paris.

___ (2004), *Principles of Corporate Governance*, OECD, Paris.

Sarbanes–Oxley Act (2002), US Legislature.

THE COMBINED CODE
ON CORPORATE
GOVERNANCE

ISBN1 84140 406 3

Electronic copies of this volume and related material are available on the
FRC website:http://www.frc.org.uk/combined.cfm.

Printed copies may be ordered from CCH Information, tel 0870 777 2906
or ordered online at: www.asbpublications.com

THE COMBINED CODE ON
CORPORATE GOVERNANCE

June 2006

CONTENTS

Pages

The Combined Code on Corporate Governance

Preamble			277–279
Section	1	COMPANIES	280–301
	A	Directors	280–290
	B	Remuneration	291–294
	C	Accountability and Audit	295–298
	D	Relations with Shareholders	299–301
Section	2	INSTITUTIONAL SHAREHOLDERS	301–305
	E	Institutional Shareholders	301–302
Schedule A		Provisions on the design of performance related remuneration	303–304
Schedule B		Guidance on liability of non-executive directors: care, skill, and diligence	304–305
Schedule C		Disclosure of corporate governance arrangements	306–309

CODE ON CORPORATE GOVERNANCE

PREAMBLE

1. This Code supersedes and replaces the Combined Code issued in 2003. It follows a review by the Financial Reporting Council of the implementation of the Code in 2005 and subsequent consultation on possible amendments to the Code.

2. The Financial Services Authority, as the UK Listing Authority, is obliged by statute to carry out a separate consultation before listed companies can be formally required under the Listing Rules to disclose how they have applied this new version of the Combined Code. This consultation is expected to begin in September 2006 and, subject to views received, the Listing Rules would be expected to apply to the new version of the Combined Code with effect from some time in the second quarter of 2007.

3. In the meantime, in view of the limited nature of the changes and the strong support that they have received, the FRC would encourage companies and investors to apply the revised Code voluntarily for reporting years beginning on or after 1 November 2006.

4. The Code contains main and supporting principles and provisions. The Listing Rules require listed companies to make a disclosure statement in two parts in relation to the Code. In the first part of the statement, the company has to report on how it applies the principles in the Code. This should cover both main and supporting principles. The form and

content of this part of the statement are not prescribed, the intention being that companies should have a free hand to explain their governance policies in the light of the principles, including any special circumstances applying to them which have led to a particular approach. In the second part of the statement the company has either to confirm that it complies with the Code's provisions or – where it does not – to provide an explanation. This 'comply or explain' approach has been in operation for over ten years and the flexibility it offers has been widely welcomed both by company boards and by investors. It is for shareholders and others to evaluate the company's statement.

5. While it is expected that listed companies will comply with the Code's provisions most of the time, it is recognised that departure from the provisions of the Code may be justified in particular circumstances. Every company must review each provision carefully and give a considered explanation if it departs from the Code provisions.

6. Smaller listed companies, in particular those new to listing, may judge that some of the provisions are disproportionate or less relevant in their case. Some of the provisions do not apply to companies below the FTSE 350. Such companies may nonetheless consider that it would be appropriate to adopt the approach in the Code and they are encouraged to consider this. Investment companies typically have a different board structure, which may affect the relevance of particular provisions.

7. Whilst recognising that directors are appointed by shareholders who are the owners of companies, it is important that those concerned with the evaluation of governance should do so with common sense in order to promote partnership and trust, based on mutual understanding. They should pay due regard to companies' individual circumstances and bear in mind in particular the size and complexity of the company and the nature of the risks and challenges it faces. Whilst shareholders have every right to challenge companies' explanations if they are unconvincing, they should not

be evaluated in a mechanistic way and departures from the Code should not be automatically treated as breaches. Institutional shareholders and their agents should be careful to respond to the statements from companies in a manner that supports the 'comply or explain' principle. As the principles in Section 2 make clear, institutional shareholders should carefully consider explanations given for departure from the Code and make reasoned judgements in each case. They should put their views to the company and be prepared to enter a dialogue if they do not accept the company's position. Institutional shareholders should be prepared to put such views in writing where appropriate.

8.   Nothing in this Code should be taken to override the general requirements of law to treat shareholders equally in access to information.

CODE ON BEST PRACTICE

SECTION 1   COMPANIES

A.   DIRECTORS

A.1   The Board

Main Principle

Every company should be headed by an effective board, which is collectively responsible for the success of the company.

Supporting Principles

The board's role is to provide entrepreneurial leadership of the company within a framework of prudent and effective controls which enables risk to be assessed and managed. The board should set the company's strategic aims, ensure that the necessary financial and human resources are in place for the company to meet its objectives and review management performance. The board should set the company's values and standards and ensure that its obligations to its shareholders and others are understood and met.

All directors must take decisions objectively in the interests of the company.

As part of their role as members of a unitary board, non-executive directors should constructively challenge and help develop proposals on strategy. Non-executive directors should scrutinise the performance of management in meeting agreed goals and objectives and monitor the reporting of performance. They should satisfy themselves on the integrity of financial information and that financial controls and systems of risk management are robust and defensible. They are responsible for determining appropriate levels of remuneration of executive directors and have a prime role in appointing, and where necessary removing, executive directors, and in succession planning.

Code Provisions

A.1.1 The board should meet sufficiently regularly to discharge its duties effectively. There should be a formal schedule of matters specifically reserved for its decision. The annual report should include a statement of how the board operates, including a high-level statement of which types of decision are to be taken by the board and which are to be delegated to management.

A.1.2 The annual report should identify the chairman, the deputy chairman (where there is one), the chief executive, the senior independent director, and the chairmen and members of the nomination, audit, and remuneration committees. It should also set out the number of meetings of the board and those committees and individual attendance by directors.

A.1.3 The chairman should hold meetings with the non-executive directors without the executives present. Led by the senior independent director, the non-executive directors should meet without the chairman present at least annually to appraise the chairman's performance (as described in A.6.1) and on such other occasions as are deemed appropriate.

A.1.4 Where directors have concerns which cannot be resolved about the running of the company or a proposed action, they should ensure that their concerns are recorded in the board minutes. On resignation, a non-executive director should provide a written statement to the chairman, for circulation to the board, if they have any such concerns.

A.1.5 The company should arrange appropriate insurance cover in respect of legal action against its directors.

A.2   Chairman and chief executive

Main Principle

There should be a clear division of responsibilities at the head of the company between the running of the board and the executive responsibility for the running of the company's business. No one individual should have unfettered powers of decision.

Supporting Principle

The chairman is responsible for leadership of the board, ensuring its effectiveness on all aspects of its role and setting its agenda. The chairman is also responsible for ensuring that the directors receive accurate, timely, and clear information. The chairman should ensure effective communication with shareholders. The chairman should also facilitate the effective contribution of non-executive directors in particular and ensure constructive relations between executive and non-executive directors.

Code Provisions

A.2.1 The roles of chairman and chief executive should not be exercised by the same individual. The division of responsibilities between the chairman and chief executive should be clearly established, set out in writing and agreed by the board.

A.2.2[1] The chairman should on appointment meet the independence criteria set out in A.3.1 below. A chief executive should not go on to be chairman of the same company. If, exceptionally,

---

[1]   Compliance or otherwise with this provision need only be reported for the year in which the appointment is made.

a board decides that a chief executive should become chairman, the board should consult major shareholders in advance and should set out its reasons to shareholders at the time of the appointment and in the next annual report.

A.3   Board balance and independence

Main Principle

The board should include a balance of executive and non-executive directors (and in particular independent non-executive directors) such that no individual or small group of individuals can dominate the board's decision taking.

Supporting Principles

The board should not be so large as to be unwieldy. The board should be of sufficient size that the balance of skills and experience is appropriate for the requirements of the business and that changes to the board's composition can be managed without undue disruption.

To ensure that power and information are not concentrated in one or two individuals, there should be a strong presence on the board of both executive and non-executive directors.

The value of ensuring that committee membership is refreshed and that undue reliance is not placed on particular individuals should be taken into account in deciding chairmanship and membership of committees.

No one other than the committee chairman and members is entitled to be present at a meeting of the nomination, audit, or remuneration committee, but others may attend at the invitation of the committee.

Code provisions

A.3.1 The board should identify in the annual report each non-executive director it considers to be independent.[2] The board should determine whether the director is independent in character and judgement and whether there are relationships or circumstances which are likely to affect, or could appear to affect, the director's judgement. The board should state its reasons if it determines that a director is independent notwithstanding the existence of relationships or circumstances which may appear relevant to its determination, including if the director:

- has been an employee of the company or group within the last five years;

- has, or has had within the last three years, a material business relationship with the company either directly, or as a partner, shareholder, director, or senior employee of a body that has such a relationship with the company;

- has received or receives additional remuneration from the company apart from a director's fee, participates in the company's share option or a performance-related pay scheme, or is a member of the company's pension scheme;

- has close family ties with any of the company's advisers, directors, or senior employees;

- holds cross-directorships or has significant links with other directors through involvement in other companies or bodies;

- represents a significant shareholder; or

- has served on the board for more than nine years from the date of their first election.

---

[2] A.2.2 states that the chairman should, on appointment, meet the independence criteria set out in this provision, but thereafter the test of independence is not appropriate in relation to the chairman.

A.3.2 Except for smaller companies,[3] at least half the board, excluding the chairman, should comprise non-executive directors determined by the board to be independent. A smaller company should have at least two independent non-executive directors.

A.3.3 The board should appoint one of the independent non-executive directors to be the senior independent director. The senior independent director should be available to shareholders if they have concerns which contact through the normal channels of chairman, chief executive, or finance director has failed to resolve or for which such contact is inappropriate.

A.4   Appointments to the Board

Main Principle

There should be a formal, rigorous, and transparent procedure for the appointment of new directors to the board.

Supporting Principles

Appointments to the board should be made on merit and against objective criteria. Care should be taken to ensure that appointees have enough time available to devote to the job. This is particularly important in the case of chairmanships.

The board should satisfy itself that plans are in place for orderly succession for appointments to the board and to senior management, so as to maintain an appropriate balance of skills and experience within the company and on the board.

Code Provisions

A.4.1 There should be a nomination committee which should lead the process for board appointments and make recommen-

---

[3]   A smaller company is one that is below the FTSE 350 throughout the year immediately prior to the reporting year.

dations to the board. A majority of members of the nomination committee should be independent non-executive directors. The chairman or an independent non-executive director should chair the committee, but the chairman should not chair the nomination committee when it is dealing with the appointment of a successor to the chairmanship. The nomination committee should make available[4] its terms of reference, explaining its role and the authority delegated to it by the board.

A.4.2 The nomination committee should evaluate the balance of skills, knowledge, and experience on the board and, in the light of this evaluation, prepare a description of the role and capabilities required for a particular appointment.

A.4.3 For the appointment of a chairman, the nomination committee should prepare a job specification, including an assessment of the time commitment expected, recognising the need for availability in the event of crises. A chairman's other significant commitments should be disclosed to the board before appointment and included in the annual report. Changes to such commitments should be reported to the board as they arise, and included in the next annual report. No individual should be appointed to a second chairmanship of a FTSE 100 company.[5]

A.4.4 The terms and conditions of appointment of non-executive directors should be made available for inspection.[6] The letter of appointment should set out the expected time commitment. Non-executive directors should undertake that they will have sufficient time to meet what is expected of them. Their other significant commitments should be disclosed to the

---

[4]   The requirement to make the information available would be met by including the information on a website that is maintained by or on behalf of the company.
[5]   Compliance or otherwise with this provision need only be reported for the year in which the appointment is made.
[6]   The terms and conditions of appointment of non-executive directors should be made available for inspection by any person at the company's registered office during normal business hours and at the AGM (for 15 minutes prior to the meeting and during the meeting).

board before appointment, with a broad indication of the time involved and the board should be informed of subsequent changes.

A.4.5 The board should not agree to a full-time executive director taking on more than one non-executive directorship in a FTSE 100 company nor the chairmanship of such a company.

A.4.6 A separate section of the annual report should describe the work of the nomination committee, including the process it has used in relation to board appointments. An explanation should be given if neither an external search consultancy nor open advertising has been used in the appointment of a chairman or a non-executive director.

A.5   Information and professional development

Main Principle

The board should be supplied in a timely manner with information in a form and of a quality appropriate to enable it to discharge its duties. All directors should receive induction on joining the board and should regularly update and refresh their skills and knowledge.

Supporting Principles

The chairman is responsible for ensuring that the directors receive accurate, timely, and clear information. Management has an obligation to provide such information but directors should seek clarification or amplification where necessary.

The chairman should ensure that the directors continually update their skills and the knowledge and familiarity with the company required to fulfil their role both on the board and on board committees. The company should provide the necessary resources for developing and updating its director's knowledge and capabilities.

Under the direction of the chairman, the company secretary's responsibilities include ensuring good information flows within the board and its committees and between senior management and non-executive directors, as well as facilitating induction and assisting with professional development as required.

The company secretary should be responsible for advising the board through the chairman on all governance matters.

Code Provisions

A.5.1 The chairman should ensure that new directors receive a full, formal, and tailored induction on joining the board. As part of this, the company should offer to major shareholders the opportunity to meet a new non-executive director.

A.5.2 The board should ensure that directors, especially non-executive directors, have access to independent professional advice at the company's expense where they judge it necessary to discharge their responsibilities as directors. Committees should be provided with sufficient resources to undertake their duties.

A.5.3 All directors should have access to the advice and services of the company secretary, who is responsible to the board for ensuring that board procedures are complied with. Both the appointment and removal of the company secretary should be a matter for the board as a whole.

A.6   Performance evaluation

Main Principle

The board should undertake a formal and rigorous annual evaluation of its own performance and that of its committees and individual directors.

Supporting Principle

Individual evaluation should aim to show whether each director continues to contribute effectively and to demonstrate commitment to the role (including commitment of time for board and committee meetings and any other duties). The chairman should act on the results of the performance evaluation by recognising the strengths and addressing the weaknesses of the board and, where appropriate, proposing new members be appointed to the board or seeking the resignation of directors.

Code Provision

A.6.1 The board should state in the annual report how performance evaluation of the board, its committees, and its individual directors has been conducted. The non-executive directors, led by the senior independent director, should be responsible for performance evaluation of the chairman, taking into account the views of executive directors.

A.7   Re-election

Main Principle

All directors should be submitted for re-election at regular intervals, subject to continued satisfactory performance. The board should ensure planned and progressive refreshing of the board.

Code Provisions

A.7.1 All directors should be subject to election by shareholders at the first annual general meeting after their appointment, and to re-election thereafter at intervals of no more than three years. The names of directors submitted for election or re-election should be accompanied by sufficient biographical details and any other relevant information to enable shareholders to take an informed decision on their election.

A.7.2 Non-executive directors should be appointed for specified terms subject to re-election and to Companies Acts provisions relating to the removal of a director. The board should set out to shareholders in the papers accompanying a resolution to elect a non-executive director why they believe an individual should be elected. The chairman should confirm to shareholders when proposing re-election that, following formal performance evaluation, the individual's performance continues to be effective and to demonstrate commitment to the role. Any term beyond six years (e.g. two three-year terms) for a non-executive director should be subject to particularly rigorous review, and should take into account the need for progressive refreshing of the board. Non-executive directors may serve longer than nine years (e.g. three three-year terms), subject to annual re-election. Serving more than nine years could be relevant to the determination of a non-executive director's independence (as set out in provision A.3.1).

B. Remuneration

B.1 The Level and Make-up of Remuneration

Main Principles

Levels of remuneration should be sufficient to attract, retain, and motivate directors of the quality required to run the company successfully, but a company should avoid paying more than is necessary for this purpose. A significant proportion of executive directors' remuneration should be structured so as to link rewards to corporate and individual performance.

Supporting Principle

The remuneration committee should judge where to position their company relative to other companies. But they should use such comparisons with caution, in view of the risk of an upward ratchet of remuneration levels with no corresponding improvement in performance. They should also be sensitive to pay and employment conditions elsewhere in the group, especially when determining annual salary increases.

Code Provisions

Remuneration policy

B.1.1 The performance-related elements of remuneration should form a significant proportion of the total remuneration package of executive directors and should be designed to align their interests with those of shareholders and to give these directors keen incentives to perform at the highest levels. In designing schemes of performance-related remuneration, the remuneration committee should follow the provisions in Schedule A to this Code.

B.1.2 Executive share options should not be offered at a discount save as permitted by the relevant provisions of the Listing Rules.

B.1.3 Levels of remuneration for non-executive directors should reflect the time commitment and responsibilities of the role. Remuneration for non-executive directors should not include share options. If, exceptionally, options are granted, shareholder approval should be sought in advance and any shares acquired by exercise of the options should be held until at least one year after the non-executive director leaves the board. Holding of share options could be relevant to the determination of a non-executive director's independence (as set out in provision A.3.1).

B.1.4 Where a company releases an executive director to serve as a non-executive director elsewhere, the remuneration report[7] should include a statement as to whether or not the director will retain such earnings and, if so, what the remuneration is.

Service Contracts and Compensation

B.1.5 The remuneration committee should carefully consider what compensation commitments (including pension contributions and all other elements) their directors' terms of appointment would entail in the event of early termination. The aim should be to avoid rewarding poor performance. They should take a robust line on reducing compensation to reflect departing directors' obligations to mitigate loss.

B.1.6 Notice or contract periods should be set at one year or less. If it is necessary to offer longer notice or contract periods to new directors recruited from outside, such periods should reduce to one year or less after the initial period.

B.2   Procedure

Main Principle

There should be a formal and transparent procedure for developing policy on executive remuneration and for

---

[7]   As required under the Directors' Remuneration Report Regulations 2002.

fixing the remuneration packages of individual directors. No director should be involved in deciding his or her own remuneration.

Supporting Principles

The remuneration committee should consult the chairman and/or chief executive about their proposals relating to the remuneration of other executive directors. The remuneration committee should also be responsible for appointing any consultants in respect of executive director remuneration. Where executive directors or senior management are involved in advising or supporting the remuneration committee, care should be taken to recognise and avoid conflicts of interest.

The chairman of the board should ensure that the company maintains contact as required with its principal shareholders about remuneration in the same way as for other matters.

Code Provisions

B.2.1 The board should establish a remuneration committee of at least three, or in the case of smaller companies[8] two, independent non-executive directors. In addition the company chairman may also be a member of, but not chair, the committee if he or she was considered independent on appointment as chairman. The remuneration committee should make available[9] its terms of reference, explaining its role and the authority delegated to it by the board. Where remuneration consultants are appointed, a statement should be made available[10] of whether they have any other connection with the company.

B.2.2 The remuneration committee should have delegated responsibility for setting remuneration for all executive directors and

---

[8]   See footnote 3.
[9]   See footnote 4.
[10] See footnote 4.

the chairman, including pension rights and any compensation payments. The committee should also recommend and monitor the level and structure of remuneration for senior management. The definition of 'senior management' for this purpose should be determined by the board but should normally include the first layer of management below board level.

B.2.3 The board itself or, where required by the Articles of Association, the shareholders should determine the remuneration of the non-executive directors within the limits set in the Articles of Association. Where permitted by the Articles, the board may, however, delegate this responsibility to a committee, which might include the chief executive.

B.2.4 Shareholders should be invited specifically to approve all new long-term incentive schemes (as defined in the Listing Rules) and significant changes to existing schemes, save in the circumstances permitted by the Listing Rules.

C.   Accountability and Audit

C.1   Financial Reporting

Main Principle

The board should present a balanced and understandable assessment of the company's position and prospects.

Supporting Principle

The board's responsibility to present a balanced and understandable assessment extends to interim and other price-sensitive public reports and reports to regulators as well as to information required to be presented by statutory requirements.

Code Provisions

C.1.1 The directors should explain in the annual report their responsibility for preparing the accounts and there should be a statement by the auditors about their reporting responsibilities.

C.1.2 The directors should report that the business is a going concern, with supporting assumptions or qualifications as necessary.

C.2   Internal Control[11]

Main Principle

The board should maintain a sound system of internal control to safeguard shareholders' investment and the company's assets.

---

[11]   The Turnbull guidance suggests means of applying this part of the Code. Copies are available at www.frc.org.uk/corporate/internalcontrol.cfm

Code Provision

C.2.1 The board should, at least annually, conduct a review of the effectiveness of the group's system of internal controls and should report to shareholders that they have done so. The review should cover all material controls, including financial, operational, and compliance controls and risk management systems.

C.3   Audit Committee and Auditors[12]

Main Principle

The board should establish formal and transparent arrangements for considering how they should apply the financial reporting and internal control principles and for maintaining an appropriate relationship with the company's auditors.

Code provisions

C.3.1 The board should establish an audit committee of at least three, or in the case of smaller companies[13] two, members, who should all be independent non-executive directors. The board should satisfy itself that at least one member of the audit committee has recent and relevant financial experience.

C.3.2 The main role and responsibilities of the audit committee should be set out in written terms of reference and should include:

- to monitor the integrity of the financial statements of the company, and any formal announcements relating to the company's financial performance, reviewing significant financial reporting judgements contained in them;

---

[12]   The Smith guidance suggests means of applying this part of the Code. Copies are available at www.frc.org.uk/corporate/combinedcode.cfm.
[13]   See footnote 3.

- to review the company's internal financial controls and, unless expressly addressed by a separate board risk committee composed of independent directors, or by the board itself, to review the company's internal control and risk management systems;

- to monitor and review the effectiveness of the company's internal audit function;

- to make recommendations to the board, for it to put to the shareholders for their approval in general meeting, in relation to the appointment, re-appointment, and removal of the external auditor and to approve the remuneration and terms of engagement of the external auditor;

- to review and monitor the external auditor's independence and objectivity and the effectiveness of the audit process, taking into consideration relevant UK professional and regulatory requirements;

- to develop and implement policy on the engagement of the external auditor to supply non-audit services, taking into account relevant ethical guidance regarding the provision of non-audit services by the external audit firm; and to report to the board, identifying any matters in respect of which it considers that action or improvement is needed and making recommendations as to the steps to be taken.

C.3.3 The terms of reference of the audit committee, including its role and the authority delegated to it by the board, should be made available.[14] A separate section of the annual report should describe the work of the committee in discharging those responsibilities.

C.3.4 The audit committee should review arrangements by which staff of the company may, in confidence, raise concerns about possible improprieties in matters of financial reporting or other matters. The audit committee's objective should be to ensure

---

[14] See footnote 4.

that arrangements are in place for the proportionate and independent investigation of such matters and for appropriate follow-up action.

C.3.5 The audit committee should monitor and review the effectiveness of the internal audit activities. Where there is no internal audit function, the audit committee should consider annually whether there is a need for an internal audit function and make a recommendation to the board, and the reasons for the absence of such a function should be explained in the relevant section of the annual report.

C.3.6 The audit committee should have primary responsibility for making a recommendation on the appointment, reappointment, and removal of the external auditors. If the board does not accept the audit committee's recommendation, it should include in the annual report, and in any papers recommending appointment or re-appointment, a statement from the audit committee explaining the recommendation and should set out reasons why the board has taken a different position.

C.3.7 The annual report should explain to shareholders how, if the auditor provides non-audit services, auditor objectivity and independence is safeguarded.

D. Relations with Shareholders

D.1 Dialogue with Institutional Shareholders

Main Principle

There should be a dialogue with shareholders based on the mutual understanding of objectives. The board as a whole has responsibility for ensuring that a satisfactory dialogue with shareholders takes place.[15]

Supporting Principles

Whilst recognising that most shareholder contact is with the chief executive and finance director, the chairman (and the senior independent director and other directors as appropriate) should maintain sufficient contact with major shareholders to understand their issues and concerns.

The board should keep in touch with shareholder opinion in whatever ways are most practical and efficient.

Code Provisions

D.1.1 The chairman should ensure that the views of shareholders are communicated to the board as a whole. The chairman should discuss governance and strategy with major shareholders. Non-executive directors should be offered the opportunity to attend meetings with major shareholders and should expect to attend them if requested by major shareholders. The senior independent director should attend sufficient meetings with a range of major shareholders to listen to their views in order to help develop a balanced understanding of the issues and concerns of major shareholders.

D.1.2 The board should state in the annual report the steps they have taken to ensure that the members of the board, and

---

[15] Nothing in these principles or provisions should be taken to override the general requirements of law to treat shareholders equally in access to information.

in particular the non-executive directors, develop an understanding of the views of major shareholders about their company, for example through direct face-to-face contact, analysts' or brokers' briefings and surveys of shareholder opinion.

D.2 Constructive Use of the AGM

Main Principle

The board should use the AGM to communicate with investors and to encourage their participation.

Code Provisions

D.2.1 At any general meeting, the company should propose a separate resolution on each substantially separate issue, and should in particular propose a resolution at the AGM relating to the report and accounts. For each resolution, proxy appointment forms should provide shareholders with the option to direct their proxy to vote either for or against the resolution or to withhold their vote. The proxy form and any announcement of the results of a vote should make it clear that a 'vote withheld' is not a vote in law and will not be counted in the calculation of the proportion of the votes for and against the resolution.

D.2.2 The company should ensure that all valid proxy appointments received for general meetings are properly recorded and counted. For each resolution, after a vote has been taken, except where taken on a poll, the company should ensure that the following information is given at the meeting and made available as soon as reasonably practicable on a website which is maintained by or on behalf of the company:

- the number of shares in respect of which proxy appointments have been validly made;

- the number of votes for the resolution;

- the number of votes against the resolution; and

- the number of shares in respect of which the vote was directed to be withheld.

D.2.3 The chairman should arrange for the chairmen of the audit, remuneration and nomination committees to be available to answer questions at the AGM and for all directors to attend.

D.2.4 The company should arrange for the Notice of the AGM and related papers to be sent to shareholders at least 20 working days before the meeting.

SECTION 2   INSTITUTIONAL SHAREHOLDERS

E.   Institutional Shareholders[16]

E.1   Dialogue with companies

Main Principle

Institutional shareholders should enter into a dialogue with companies based on the mutual understanding of objectives.

Supporting Principles

Institutional shareholders should apply the principles set out in the Institutional Shareholders' Committee's 'The Responsibilities of Institutional Shareholders and Agents – Statement of Principles',[17] which should be reflected in fund manager contracts.

---

[16]   Agents such as investment managers, or voting services, are frequently appointed by institutional shareholders to act on their behalf and these principles should accordingly be read as applying where appropriate to the agents of institutional shareholders

[17]   Available at www.investmentuk.org/news/research/2005/topic/corporate_governance/isc0905.pdf

E.2   Evaluation of Governance Disclosures

Main Principle

When evaluating companies' governance arrangements, particularly those relating to board structure and composition, institutional shareholders should give due weight to all relevant factors drawn to their attention.

Supporting Principle

Institutional shareholders should consider carefully explanations given for departure from this Code and make reasoned judgements in each case. They should give an explanation to the company, in writing where appropriate, and be prepared to enter a dialogue if they do not accept the company's position. They should avoid a box-ticking approach to assessing a company's corporate governance. They should bear in mind in particular the size and complexity of the company and the nature of the risks and challenges it faces.

E.3   Shareholder Voting

Main Principle

Institutional shareholders have a responsibility to make considered use of their votes.

Supporting Principles

Institutional shareholders should take steps to ensure their voting intentions are being translated into practice.

Institutional shareholders should, on request, make available to their clients information on the proportion of resolutions on which votes were cast and non-discretionary proxies lodged.

Major shareholders should attend AGMs where appropriate and practicable. Companies and registrars should facilitate this.

Schedule A: Provisions on the design of performance-related remuneration

1.   The remuneration committee should consider whether the directors should be eligible for annual bonuses. If so, performance conditions should be relevant, stretching, and designed to enhance shareholder value. Upper limits should be set and disclosed. There may be a case for part payment in shares to be held for a significant period.

2.   The remuneration committee should consider whether the directors should be eligible for benefits under long-term incentive schemes. Traditional share-option schemes should be weighed against other kinds of long-term incentive scheme. In normal circumstances, shares granted or other forms of deferred remuneration should not vest, and options should not be exercisable, in less than three years. Directors should be encouraged to hold their shares for a further period after vesting or exercise, subject to the need to finance any costs of acquisition and associated tax liabilities.

3.   Any new long-term incentive schemes which are proposed should be approved by shareholders and should preferably replace any existing schemes or at least form part of a well-considered overall plan, incorporating existing schemes. The total rewards potentially available should not be excessive.

4.   Payouts or grants under all incentive schemes, including new grants under existing share option schemes, should be subject to challenging performance criteria reflecting the company's objectives. Consideration should be given to criteria which reflect the company's performance relative to a group of comparator companies in some key variables such as total shareholder return.

5.   Grants under executive share option and other long-term incentive schemes should normally be phased rather than awarded in one large block.

6.   In general, only basic salary should be pensionable.

7. The remuneration committee should consider the pension consequences and associated costs to the company of basic salary increases and any other changes in pensionable remuneration, especially for directors close to retirement.

Schedule B: Guidance on liability of non-executive directors: care, skill, and diligence

1. Although non-executive directors and executive directors have as board members the same legal duties and objectives, the time devoted to the company's affairs is likely to be significantly less for a non-executive director than for an executive director and the detailed knowledge and experience of a company's affairs that could reasonably be expected of a non-executive director will generally be less than for an executive director. These matters may be relevant in assessing the knowledge, skill, and experience which may reasonably be expected of a non-executive director and therefore the care, skill, and diligence that a non-executive director may be expected to exercise.

2. In this context, the following elements of the Code may also be particularly relevant.

    (i) In order to enable directors to fulfil their duties, the Code states that:

    -   the letter of appointment of the director should set out the expected time commitment (Code provision A.4.4); and

    -   the board should be supplied in a timely manner with information in a form and of a quality appropriate to enable it to discharge its duties. The chairman is responsible for ensuring that the directors are provided by management with accurate, timely, and clear information. (Code principle A.5).

(ii)   Non-executive directors should themselves:

- undertake appropriate induction and regularly update and refresh their skills, knowledge, and familiarity with the company (Code principle A.5 and provision A.5.1);

- seek appropriate clarification or amplification of information and, where necessary, take and follow appropriate professional advice (Code principle A.5 and provision A.5.2);

- where they have concerns about the running of the company or a proposed action, ensure that these are addressed by the board and, to the extent that they are not resolved, ensure that they are recorded in the board minutes (Code provision A.1.4);

- give a statement to the board if they have such unresolved concerns on resignation (Code provision A.1.4).

3.   It is up to each non-executive director to reach a view as to what is necessary in particular circumstances to comply with the duty of care, skill, and diligence they owe as a director to the company. In considering whether or not a person is in breach of that duty, a court would take into account all relevant circumstances. These may include having regard to the above where relevant to the issue of liability of a non-executive director.

Schedule C: **Disclosure of corporate governance arrangements**

Paragraph 9.8.6 of the Listing Rules states that in the case of a listed company incorporated in the United Kingdom, the following items must be included in its annual report and accounts:

- a statement of how the listed company has applied the principles set out in Section 1 of the Combined Code, in a manner that would enable shareholders to evaluate how the principles have been applied;[18]

- a statement as to whether the listed company has

  - complied throughout the accounting period with all relevant provisions set out in Section 1 of the Combined Code; or

  - not complied throughout the accounting period with all relevant provisions set out in Section 1 of the Combined Code and if so, setting out:

    (i)   those provisions, if any, it has not complied with;

    (ii) in the case of provisions whose requirements are of a continuing nature, the period within which, if any, it did not comply with some or all of those provisions; and

    (iii) the company's reasons for non-compliance.

In addition the Code includes specific requirements for disclosure which are set out below:

---

[18]   As noted in the Preamble, the form and content of this part of the statement are not prescribed, the intention being that companies should have a free hand to explain their governance policies in the light of the principles, including any special circumstances applying to them which have led to a particular approach.

The annual report should record:

- a statement of how the board operates, including a high-level statement of which types of decision are to be taken by the board and which are to be delegated to management (A.1.1);

- the names of the chairman, the deputy chairman (where there is one), the chief executive, the senior independent director, and the chairmen and members of the nomination, audit, and remuneration committees (A.1.2);

- the number of meetings of the board and those committees and individual attendance by directors (A.1.2);

- the names of the non-executive directors whom the board determines to be independent, with reasons where necessary (A.3.1);

- the other significant commitments of the chairman and any changes to them during the year (A.4.3);

- how performance evaluation of the board, its committees, and its directors has been conducted (A.6.1);

- the steps the board has taken to ensure that members of the board, and in particular the non-executive directors, develop an understanding of the views of major shareholders about their company (D.1.2).

The report should also include:

- a separate section describing the work of the nomination committee, including the process it has used in relation to board appointments and an explanation if neither external search consultancy nor open advertising has been used in the appointment of a chairman or a non-executive director (A.4.6);

- a description of the work of the remuneration

committee as required under the Directors'
Remuneration Report Regulations 2002, and
including, where an executive director serves as a
non-executive director elsewhere, whether or not the
director will retain such earnings and, if so, what the
remuneration is (B.1.4);

- an explanation from the directors of their responsibility
  for preparing the accounts and a statement by the
  auditors about their reporting responsibilities (C.1.1);

- a statement from the directors that the business is a
  going concern, with supporting assumptions or
  qualifications as necessary (C.1.2);

- a report that the board has conducted a review of the
  effectiveness of the group's system of internal
  controls (C.2.1);

- a separate section describing the work of the audit
  committee in discharging its responsibilities (C.3.3);

- where there is no internal audit function, the reasons
  for the absence of such a function (C.3.5);

- where the board does not accept the audit
  committee's recommendation on the appointment,
  reappointment, or removal of an external auditor, a
  statement from the audit committee explaining the
  recommendation and the reasons why the board has
  taken a different position (C.3.6); and

- an explanation of how, if the auditor provides
  non-audit services, auditor objectivity and
  independence is safeguarded (C.3.7).

**The following information should be made available (which
may be met by placing the information on a website that is
maintained by or on behalf of the company):**

- the terms of reference of the nomination,
  remuneration, and audit committees, explaining their

role and the authority delegated to them by the board (A.4.1, B.2.1, and C.3.3);

- the terms and conditions of appointment of non-executive directors (A.4.4) (see footnote 6 . . .); and

- where remuneration consultants are appointed, a statement of whether they have any other connection with the company (B.2.1).

The board should set out to shareholders in the papers accompanying a resolution to elect or re-elect directors:

- sufficient biographical details to enable shareholders to take an informed decision on their election or re-election (A.7.1);

- why they believe an individual should be elected to a non-executive role (A.7.2); and

- on re-election of a non-executive director, confirmation from the chairman that, following formal performance evaluation, the individual's performance continues to be effective and to demonstrate commitment to the role, including commitment of time for board and committee meetings and any other duties (A.7.2).

The board should set out to shareholders in the papers recommending appointment or reappointment of an external auditor:

- if the board does not accept the audit committee's recommendation, a statement from the audit committee explaining the recommendation and from the board setting out reasons why they have taken a different position (C.3.6).

■ INDEX

A

accounts 1
  Brazil 257
  European Union 55
  Germany 166–7
  social responsibility and 108–9
  see also audit
agency theory 12–14
Agnelli, Giovanni 73
Agnelli, Umberto 73
Agora SA 213
Amnesty International 107
Andersen 2
annual reports 1
Association of British Insurers
  (ABI) 27, 84, 88, 105, 145,
  146
audit
  board of directors'
      sub-committee 128–9
  Brazil 257, 258
  Denmark 171
  France 174
  Germany 166–7
  India 253
  Italy 176, 180
  Korea 227
  Malaysia 230
  Poland 201
  South Africa 250
  United States 38–9, 40–1
Australia
  corporate governance
    in 236–41
  directors and board
      structure 237, 239–40
  disclosure 239, 240
  institutional investors in 83–4,
    90
  risk management 239
  shareholders 239
  social responsibility in 106
  stakeholders 240
Austria, directors and board
    structure 121–2

B

Balino, T.J.T. 225

banks 160
  as institutional investors 163,
    220
Barings Bank 1–2, 4, 131
Basle Committee 35–6
Bebchuk, L. 143
Becht, M. 160
Begley, L.M. 70
Belgium, social responsibility
  in 106
Belikov, I. 207
Berg, Olena 90
Berglof, E. 190
Berle, A.A. 13–14, 80
Bianchi, M. 176
Black, Conrad 155
Blair, M. 13
board of directors *see* directors
Boeri, T. 189–90, 191
Bolkenstein, Frits 35
Bosch, H. 83
Bosch Report (1991–5) 90,
  237
Bouton Report (2002) 173–6
Boyd, D.P. 70
BP 137
Brazil
  accounts 257
  audit 257–8
  corporate governance in 254–9
    example 260
  directors and board
      structure 256, 258
  economy 254
  shareholders 255–6
Business in the Community
  (BITC) 108

C

Cadbury, Adrian 5, 24, 68, 69,
  108, 124, 127
Cadbury, John 72
Cadbury Report (1992) 22, 23–4,
  29–31, 69, 70, 82, 87, 123,
  132–3, 134, 266
Cadbury Schweppes 72
CalPERS 94
  Global Proxy Voting Principles
    (2001/5) 106

Carroll, A.B. 108
Caux Roundtable Principles 107
Centre for European Policy
  Studies (CEPS) 84, 89
Chakrabarti, R. 254
Charkham, J. 58, 71, 162, 167,
  221, 224–5, 269
Chen Jiulin 4
China
  codes of corporate
    governance 33, 232–5
  corporate governance in
    231–5
  directors and board
    structure 233–4
  disclosure 235
  economy 231
  shareholders 232–3
  stakeholders 234–5
China Aviation Oil 4, 5
civil law systems 13–14, 66, 159,
  198, 267
Claessens, S. 191, 219–20
Clarke, T. 12
Coalition for Environmentally
  Responsible Economies
  (CERES) 106, 107
Coase, R.H. 15
codes of corporate
  governance 21–44
  Australia 236–41
  Brazil 255–9
  China 33, 232–5
  Czech Republic 190–7
  Denmark 167–71
  France 172–6
  Germany 162–7
  growth of 21
  Hungary 207–12
  India 251–4
  influential 29
  international 22, 31–6
  Italy 177–8
  Japan 221–5
  Korea 225–8
  Malaysia 228–30
  Poland 198–201
  Russia 202–7
  South Africa 248–51
  UK 22–31

codes of corporate governance
(*cont.*)
  Cadbury Report (1992) 22,
    23–4, 29–31, 69, 70, 82,
    87, 123, 132–3, 134
  Combined Code (1998) 22,
    25
  Combined Code
    (2003) 22–3, 25, 27, 29,
    86, 168
  Combined Code (2006) 22,
    27, 29, 31, 69, 83,
    123–30, 132–5, 145
  US 22, 36–42
co-determination 162, 167
Coffee, J.C. 189, 190–1, 198
Collier, P. 69, 70
Commission on Public Trust and
  Private Enterprise 2003
  (USA) 39–42, 149
common law systems 13–14, 66,
  267
Commonwealth Association for
  Corporate Governance
  (CACG) 34
communities, as stakeholders
  52
company law, review of 28, 35
Company Law Reform
  Bill/Companies Bill, UK
  (2005) 28, 55–7, 88,
  125–6
confidentiality, Italy 179
conglomerates 15
convergence 18, 181
Conyon, M.J. 143
Cordero di Montezemolo,
  Luca 73
corporate collapses 1–5
corporate governance
  crises of 1–5
  definitions 5
  importance of 5–6
  see also individual topics
Cromme report 163–7
crony capitalism 220
customers, as stakeholders 52
Czech Republic
  audit 197
  codes of corporate
    governance 190–7
  directors and board
    structure 192–3, 195,
    196–7
  disclosure 194–5, 196–7
  institutional investors 195

privatization 190–1
shareholders 193–4, 195–6
stakeholders 196, 197

D

Daily, C.M. 93
Dalton, D.R. 93
Davis, J.H. 16–17
Delaware corporate law 37
Deminor 91
Denmark
  audit 171
  corporate governance
    in 167–71
  directors and board
    structure 122, 170–1,
    161–2
  disclosure 161
  institutional investors 167
  risk assessment 171
  shareholders 169
  stakeholders 169
Deutsche Bank 94, 183
developing countries 247–8
Dignam, A.J. 236
directors
  appointment 129–31
  Australia 237, 239–40
  board structure 121–36
    European countries 161–2
    role of board 124–6
    sub-committees 128–31,
      144–5
    unitary *vs.* dual
      board 121–2, 153–4,
      172, 196
  Brazil 256, 258
  China 233–4
  Commission on Public Trust
    and Private Enterprise
    2003 (USA) and 39–40
  corporate governance codes
    and 29–31, 123–6
  Czech Republic 192–3, 195,
    196–7
  Denmark 122, 161–2, 170–1
  evaluation of 134–5
  family firms 67–9, 70–1
  France 161, 172, 173–6
  Germany 121–2, 163–6
  Hungary 208–10
  India 252–3
  Italy 161, 176–80,
  Japan 221–2, 224
  Korea 226–7

Malaysia 229–30
non-executive *see*
  non-executive directors
  (NED)
Poland 199–200
remuneration *see* remuneration
  of directors
Russia 202, 204–6
South Africa 249
United Kingdom 121–36
  remuneration 142–3, 149
United States
  remuneration 142–3, 149
disclosure
  Australia 239, 240
  China 235
  Czech Republic 194–5
  Denmark 161
  France 176
  Germany 166, 167
  Hungary 209, 211
  Italy 183
  Japan 223, 224
  Poland 200–1
  remuneration of
    directors 147–8
  Russia 206
Disney 182
divergence *see* convergence
dividends, Russia 206
Donaldson, L. 16–17
Dow Jones Sustainability Indices
  (DJSI) 107–8
Draghi, Mario 176

E

Earle, J.S. 211–12
Ellstrand, A.E. 93
Employee Retrement Income
  Security Act (ERISA; USA) 37,
  90
employees, as stakeholders 51
Enron 2–3, 4, 266, 267
environmental groups, as
  stakeholders 52–3
Epstein, M.J. 125, 136
ethical investment *see* social
  responsibility
EuroDisney 182
European Union (EU)
  Accounts Modernization
    Directive (2005) 55, 160
  Action Plan (2003) 35, 160–1,
    168

Contribution to Sustainable
Development (CSR)
(2002) 107
corporate governance and 29,
35, 160–1
convergence/divergence 181
directors and board structure
in 121–2
institutional investors
in 89–90
Shareholders' Rights Directive
(2006) 67, 89–90
social responsibility in 106
see also individual countries
Ezzamel, M. 132

F

Fama, E.F. 12, 70
family firms 65–77
governance and 67–9
UK smaller quoted
companies 69–71
Fan, J.P.H. 219–20
Farrar, J. 236
Fiat 73–4
financial crisis, Asia 219–20
Financial Reporting Council
(FRC) 28–9
Financial Services Authority
(FSA) 28
focus lists 91
France
audit 174
corporate governance in 172–6
directors and board
structure 161, 172, 173–6,
disclosure 176
institutional investors in 89
legal system 66
role of shareholders and
stakeholders 57–8
social responsibility in 106,
175–6
Franks, J. 160
Fried, J. 143
Friends Provident 104
Frydmann, R. 202
FTSE4Good index 107

G

Galanis, M. 236
Germany
audit 166–7

code of corporate
governance 163–7
corporate governance in 162–7
directors and board
structure 122–3, 161–2,
163–6
disclosure 166, 167
institutional investors in 89
role of shareholders and
stakeholders 57–8
shareholders 164
social responsibility in 106
Gitsham, M. 103
GlaxoSmithKline 150–1
Global Corporate Governance
Forum (GCGF) 33
Global Reporting Initiative (GRI)
Sustainability
Guidelines 107
Global Sullivan Principles 106,
107
Gompers, P.A. 93
Governance Metrics International
(GMI) 91
government, as stakeholder 53,
172
Gray, R.H. 108
Greece, codes of corporate
governance 33
Greenbury Report (1995) 22, 24,
82, 147
Gregory, H.J. 161
Gribben, C. 103

H

Hampel Report (1998) 22, 24–5,
54, 58, 70, 82, 134–5
Hart, O. 15
Hermes [Corporate Governance]
Principles (2002/6) 28, 55,
83, 104–5, 126, 127
Hermes Pensions
Management 94, 104–5
Higgs Report (2003) 23, 26, 128,
134
HIH 3–4
Hirschman, A.O. 82
Hollinger International 155
Hungary
codes of corporate
governance 207–12
directors and board
structure 208–10
disclosure 209, 211
privatization 189–90, 207, 208

shareholders 211–12
stakeholders 211
Hutchison Whampoa 211

I

ICI 151–2
India
audit 253
corporate governance in 251–4
directors and board
structure 252–3
economy 251
shareholders 253–4
insider systems 160
Institute of Directors (IoD) 130
institutional investors 27–8,
80–96, 267–8
Australia 83–4, 90
corporate governance rating
systems 91–2
Czech Republic 195
Denmark 167
focus lists 91
France 89
Germany 89
growth of institutional share
ownership 81
influence of 80, 82–6
Italy 176
relationship with investee
companies 86
social responsibility
and 102–3, 104–5,
116–17
tools of corporate
governance 86–92
United Kingdom 81, 83, 84
voting by 87–9
United States 81, 83, 84, 90
voting rights 87–91
Institutional Shareholders'
Committee (ISC) 84–6
insurance companies 81
International Accounting
Standards Board (IASB) 148
international codes of corporate
governance 31–6, 266–7
International Corporate
Governance Network
(ICGN) 34, 55, 148–9,
266–7
International Monetary Fund
(IMF) 33
Italy
audit 176, 180

Italy (*cont.*)
    code of corporate
        governance 177–80
    confidentiality 179
    corporate governance
        in 176–80
    directors and board
        structure 161, 176–80
    institutional investors in 176
    shareholders 89, 180

J
Jang, H. 225
Japan
    corporate governance in 221–5
        example 243
    directors and board
        structure 221–2, 224
    disclosure 223, 224
    economy 220–1
    recession 219
    shareholders 222–4
    social responsibility in 106,
        107
Jensen, M. 12, 16, 70
Johnson, H.L. 93

K
Kaplan, R.S. 136
Kar, P. 251
Kim, J. 225
King Report (2002) 57, 248–51
Kingfisher plc 95
Klapper, L.F. 247
Kookmin Bank 242
Korea
    audit 227
    corporate governance in 225–8
        example 242
    directors and board
        structure 226–7
    financial crisis 219, 225
    shareholders 226
    stakeholders 227
Kostikov, I. 207
KPMG 135
Kreander, N. 109–10
Kucsera, C. 211–12
Kumar Mangarlam Birla Report
    (2000) 252–4

L
La Porta, R. 14, 65–6, 159

Lank, A.G. 68
Lantian Co Ltd 231–2
Lee, P. 142–3
Leeson, Nick 1–2, 4
legal system, ownership/control
    structure and 13–14, 66–7,
    159, 267
lenders, as stakeholders 51
Levrau, A.P.D. 135
Lewis, A. 109
Love, I. 247
Luther, R.G. 109

M
MacAvoy, P.W. 93
MacBride Principles 106
Mackenzie, C. 108
Malaysia
    audit 230
    corporate governance
        in 228–30
    directors and board
        structure 229–30
    economy 228
    shareholders 230
Mallin, C.A. 69, 70, 109, 143
Marchionne, Sergio 73
market systems 160
Marks and Spencer 138
Matatko, J. 109
Mayer, C. 160
McGreevy, Charlie 160
McKinsey & Co. 93, 135
Means, G.C. 13–14, 80
Meckling, W. 12
meetings, institutional investors
    and 86–7
Millstein, I.M. 93
Monks, R.A.G. 14, 83
Morck, R. 67
Morley Fund Management 111
Morrison, Ken 137
Morrison (Wm) Supermarkets 137
Murphy, K.J. 143
Myners, Paul 88, 138
Myners Report (2003) 22, 26, 84,
    146

N
National Association of Pension
    Funds (NAPF) 27, 84, 88,
    104, 145
Neoh, A. 235
Nesbitt, S.L. 92–3, 94

Netherlands
    directors and board structure
        in 121–2
    social responsibility in 106
Neubauer, F. 68
non-executive directors
    (NED) 70, 132–4
    contribution 134
    independence 132–3
    Italy 178
    remuneration 147
Nørby Report (2001) 167–71
Norton, D.P. 136
Novo Nordisk 111

O
Okumura, H. 221
On Kit Tam 231
Organization for Economic
    Co-operation and
    Development (OECD) 5
    guidance on sharehold-
        ers'/stakeholders'
        interests 53–4
    Guidelines for Multinational
        Enterpises 107
    Principles of Corporate
        Governance 22, 31–3, 34,
        53–4, 196, 203, 232, 266
    social responsibility and 102
outsider systems 160
Ow-Yong, K. 69, 70
ownership 65–7
    family firms 65, 67–9
    insider/outsider systems of 160
    separation from control 13–14

P
Pajuste, A. 190
Parmalat 3, 4, 266
Patterson, D.J. 93
Pearson, Terry 88
pension funds 37, 268
    as institutional investors 81,
        84, 90, 102–3
Perasso, G. 189–90, 191
performance
    corporate governance
        and 92–4
    directors and 145–7, 234, 239
Petrobras 260
Pistor, K. 202, 207
Poland
    audit 201

code of corporate
    governance 198–201
directors and board
    structure 199–200
disclosure 200–1
privatization 189, 190,
    198–201
    example 213
shareholders 199–200
Preda report 177–80
Premier Farnell 96
Prigge, S. 163
privatization 212
    Czech Republic 190–1
    Hungary 189–90, 207, 208
    implications 189–90
    Poland 189, 190, 198–201
        example 213
    Russia 189–90, 202–7
        example 213–14
    transition from socialism
        and 188–9
Public Company Accounting
    Oversight Board (USA) 38

Q

Quoted Companies Alliance
    (QCA) 69

R

Rapaczynski, A. 202
rating systems (for corporate
    governance) 91–2
religion, social responsibility
    and 101–2
remuneration of directors 142–50
    Australia 241
    board sub-committee on 129,
        144–5
    Czech Republic 197
    debate on 142–3
    Denmark 171
    disclosure of 147–8
    elements of 143–4
    examples 95, 150–2
    France 174–5
    Germany 165
    India 253
    international guidance
        on 148–9
    Italy 179
    Malaysia 230
    non-executive directors 147

performance measures 145–7
risk assessment/management 4, 6
    Australia 239
    board of directors and 131
    Denmark 171
    South Africa 250
Roy, M.J. 125, 136
Royal Ahold 3, 4, 266
Royal Society of Arts (RSA),
    Tommorrow's Company
    report 54
Rozlucki, W. 201
Russia
    code of corporate
        governance 202–7
    directors and board
        structure 202, 204–6
    disclosure 206
    dividends 206
    privatization 189–90, 202–7
        example 213–14
    shareholders 204, 206–7
    transition from socialism 188

S

SABMiller 260–1
Sarbanes-Oxley Act (USA) 23, 29,
    37–9, 41, 168, 267
Shareholder Voting Working
    Group 88
shareholders
    Australia 239
    Brazil 255–6
    China 232–3
    Commission on Public Trust
        and Private Enterprise
        2003 (USA) and 40
    Czech Republic 193–4, 195–6
    defined 49–50
    Denmark 169
    EU Directive on Rights
        (2006) 67, 89–90
    Germany 164
    guidance on interests of 53–7
    Hungary 211–12
    India 253–4
    institutional see institutional
        investors
    Italy 89, 180
    Japan 222–4
    Korea 226
    Malaysia 230
    Poland 199–200
    role 57–8
    Russia 204, 206–7

separation of ownership and
    control 13–14
South Africa 251
stakeholders and 16, 49
United States 40
shares, directors' remuneration
    and 144, 147
Shleifer, A. 5
Simmelkjaer, R.T. 161
Simpson, A. 58, 71
Smith, Adam 13
Smith, Stephen 90
Smith Report (2003) 23, 26–7,
    128
social responsibility 101–17
    accounting and 108–9
    corporate governance
        and 102–3, 268–9
    Ethical Investment Reserach
        Service (EIRIS) 103
    France 106, 175–6
    impact on shareholder
        value 109–10
    institutional investors
        and 102–3, 104–5,
        116–17
    international guidance 106–7
    South Africa 250
    stock market indices of 107–8
    strategies for 103–4
    United Kingdom 102, 104–6
socialism, transition from 188
    privatization and 188–90
South Africa
    audit 250
    corporate governance
        in 248–51
        example 260–1
    directors and board
        structure 249
    risk managament 250
    shareholders 251
    social responsibility 250
Soviet Union see Russia
special purpose entities (SPEs) 2
Spira, L. 129
Sprenger, C. 202
stakeholders 49–50
    Australia 240
    China 234–5
    Czech Republic 196, 197
    Denmark 169
    groups 50–3
    guidance in interests of 53–7
    Hungary 211
    Korea 227

stakeholders (*cont.*)
   role 57–8
   shareholders and 16, 49–50
   stakeholder theory 16, 49
Standard & Poor's 91
stewardship theory 16–17
Stiles, P. 15, 131
stock market indices, social
      responsibility and 107–8
suppliers, as stakeholders 51–2
Sykes, A. 145, 146

T

Tampoe, M. 131
Tanzi, Calisto 3
Taylor, B. 15, 131
Telecom Italia 183
Telegdy, A. 211–12
theoretical aspects of corporate
      governance 11–19
   agency theory 12–14
   convergence 18
   stakeholder theory 16
   stewardship theory 16–17
   theories in context 18–19
   transaction cost
         economics 14–15
Tokyo Electron 243
transaction cost
      economics 14–15
Turkewitz, J. 202, 207
Turnbull Report (1999) 22, 25,
      27, 147

U

Ubide, A. 225

UK Social Investment Forum
      (UKSIF) 106
Unilever plc 144
United Kingdom
   codes of corporate
         governance 22–31
      Cadbury Report (1992) 22,
         23–4, 29–31, 69, 70,
         87, 123, 132–3, 134,
         266
      Combined Code (1998) 22,
         25
      Combined Code (2003) 25,
         27, 29, 86, 168
      Combined Code (2006) 22,
         27, 29, 31, 69–70,
         83, 123–30, 132–5,
         145
   directors and board
         structure 121–36
   remuneration 129, 142–3,
         144–5, 149
   institutional investors 81, 83,
         84
   voting by 87–9
   role of shareholders and
         stakeholders 57
   smaller quoted
         companies 69–71
   social responsibility in 102,
         104–6
United Nations Global
      Compact 107
United States
   codes of corporate
         governance 22,
         36–42
   directors and board
         structure 122

   remuneration 142–3, 149
   institutional investors in 81,
         83, 84, 90
   pension funds 37
   role of shareholders and
         stakeholders 57
   social responsibility in 102,
         106
Useem, M. 14, 83

V

van den Berghe, L.A.A. 135
Viénot Reports 172
VimpelCom 213–14
Vishny, R. 5
Vodafone 112
voting rights, institutional
      investors and 87–91

W

Watson, R. 132
Wessel, D. 13–14
Williamson, O.E. 14–15
Winter Report (2002) 35, 89
works councils 160, 162
World Bank 33
World Trade Organization 231
Wymersch, E. 162–3, 172

X

Xerox Corporation 95–6

Y

Yeung, B. 67